OUR CONFEDERATE ANCESTORS

Our Confederate Ancestors

Buried in Cumberland, Putnam, Van Buren, and White Counties, Tennessee

Captain Sally Tompkins #2123
United Daughters of the Confederacy
Cookeville, Tennessee

Including,

Several Confederate burials in Overton, Jackson, and Warren Counties, Tennessee;

A list of Captain Sally Tompkins #2123 UDC Members' Ancestors
buried in these counties as well as in other locations; and,

A list of the Immortal 600 with ties to Tennessee

Chapter Cemetery Committee
Gladys Boyd Anderson, Martha Sue Bell Broyles, Donna Randolph Hamilton,
Barbara Buchanan Parsons, Carolyn Barnes Rankhorn, and Pamela Mikulski Wood

Copyright © 2007
Barbara Jean Buchanan Parsons (Mrs. Eugene H.)
and Pamela Marie Mikulski Wood (Mrs. Richard D.)
All rights reserved.

First Printing

Published by
Southern Lion Books
Historical Publications
1280 Westminster Way
Madison, Georgia 30650
www.southernlionbooks.com

Production and Layout by Burt & Burt Studio
www.burtandburt.com

Manufactured in the United States of America.

Library of Congress Control Number 2007932199

ISBN 978-0-9794203-1-3

The paper in this book meets the guidelines for permanence
and durability of the Committee on Production Guidelines
for Book Longevity of the Council on Library Resources.

No part of this book may be reproduced in any form without written permission
from the copyright holders, Barbara B. Parsons or Pamela M. Wood,
P. O. Box 1001, Crossville, Tennessee 38557-1001.

Photo of Rober E. Lee courtesy of the Library of Congress

The Southern Cross of Honor

The Southern Cross of Honor was a military decoration given to all Confederate veterans, to honor the officers, non-commissioned officers, and privates for their valor in the armed forces of the Confederate States of America during the War Between the States. It was formally approved by the Congress of the Confederate States on October 13, 1862.

The design for the face of the medal consists of a cross with a Confederate battle flag surrounded by a laurel wreath, with the inscription "The Southern Cross of Honor." On the back of the medal is the motto of the Confederate States of America, "Deo Vindice" (God Our Vindicator), the dates 1861 1865, and the inscription, "From the UDC to the UCV." UDC stands for the United Daughters of the Confederacy; UCV stands for the United Confederate Veterans.

During the war there were shortages of metals and many medals were not minted or awarded. However, the names of the soldiers were recorded in an Honor Roll and preserved in the Adjutant Inspector General's records.

While attending a reunion of Confederate veterans in Atlanta in 1898, members of the UDC decided to produce the original medals.

Contents

DEDICATION	VIII
ACKNOWLEDGEMENTS	IX
DISCLAIMER	X
INTRODUCTION	XI
PEOPLE INVOLVED	XIII
OUR FIELDWORK	XIV
Cumberland County	1
Putnam County	21
Van Buren County	89
White County	125
Overton County	247
Jackson County	257
Warren County	263
UDC Members' Ancestors	273
The Immortal 600	295
REFERENCES	327
INDEX	329

THIS BOOK IS DEDICATED TO
GENERAL ROBERT EDWARD LEE (1807–2007)
ON THE CELEBRATION OF HIS 200TH BIRTHDAY.

Death in its silent, sure march is fast gathering those whom I have longest loved, so that when He shall knock at my door I will more willingly follow.
—GENERAL ROBERT E. LEE

BY THE CAPTAIN SALLY TOMPKINS #2123
UNITED DAUGHTERS OF THE CONFEDERACY, COOKEVILLE, TENNESSEE
CHAPTER MOTTO: "CONTINUING TO HONOR"

Acknowledgements

Anderson, Gladys	Gwinn, David	Rose, Charlie
Anderson, Walter	Haas, Ann	Ruder, Paula A.
Beasley, Rasalie Ann	Hall, Alene	Ryan, Mike T.
Beauchamp, Louise	Hamilton, Donna	Schubert, Hope Parsons
Bentley, Jim	Hamilton, Matt	Shaw, Mary Ann
Boyd, Frances	Harris, Evelyn	Sickel, Marilyn
Briddell, Rebecca S.	Hill, Josephine	Simmons, Mary Ruth
Broyles, Kenneth	Hodge, Regina	Simmons, R. Hugh
Broyles, Martha Sue	Joslyn, Mauriel	Spencer, Trish
Campbell, Gilbert	Knuth, Vickie	Tays, Bob
Clower, Charlene	Lee, Dora Kate	Thompson, Shirley R.
Coley, Lila	McPeak, Karen Emerson	TSLA Staff
Cook, David	Miller, Mary Cooper	Vincent, Pat
Cook, Hoyte	Moore, Billie Beth	Volts, D. C.
Cooper, Joyce B. A.	Oxencis, Joyce Cordell	Waggoner, John, Jr.
Crutcher, Nelma	Parsons, Barbara B.	Ward-Smalley, Leigh Ann
Drake, Jim	Parsons, Eugene	Welch, Dale
Drake, Judy	Paschall, Sandra L.	West, Mary
England, Manuel	Pollard, Geraldine Elrod	Wilson, Harvey
Finnell, JoAnn	Rankhorn, Bill	Wood, Cathy Gordon
Flynn, J. Opal	Rankhorn, Carolyn	Wood, Pamela
Gilbert, Barbara	Rineheart, Dr. Margaret	Wood, Rick

If you have given assistance in the production of this book and your name has been omitted from this list due to our error, please forgive us and realize that your help was greatly appreciated. We have been compiling these records for four years and have been assisted from New Jersey to California, and all across Tennessee, so we may have misplaced the paper where your name was carefully recorded. Again, to everyone who had a part in this work, "Thank You!"

*Thanks be to God for His protection
as we completed this work.
All glory to God.
Amen.*

Disclaimer

Although every effort was made to ensure the accuracy of this publication, errors may exist. Since we were not around during the War Between the States, we must rely on documentation left behind, for which accuracy cannot be guaranteed. This publication should be used as a tool to further the research of your own ancestors in the Upper Cumberland region of Tennessee. The authors welcome corrections or additions to file for future use, should another volume be printed.

Regarding units of service. Remember you must put yourself back into 1861–1865 when using this book. Many Confederate units were so decimated by disease and combat fatalities that a soldier could be in several different units in the course of the War. Few men went into service in a unit and stayed with that same unit name and number until the end of the War, though the same men might have been together. There were many "consolidated" units, thus you must research all units for a total service record. For the most part the units listed in our book are the last unit of service.

Regarding Confederate or Union. We found tombstones that listed the soldier as being a Confederate, but the unit was clearly a well-known Union command. We did not list this soldier as we could not be sure of service. We found two men of the same name in the same county, one serving the CSA, the other the Union. Only one of the men had a grave marker. We did not list this soldier as we could not be sure if he was the Confederate or the one who was in "Tinker" Dave Beatty's infamous Union raiders.

Regarding Confederate soldier's photos. Photos of Confederate soldiers were given to us for publication in this book. Some of them are the only known photos of these soldiers. We identified the soldiers as we were told they were named when the photos were given. If there are mistakes, we apologize in advance.

If this publication helps even one person find their Confederate heritage then we have accomplished our purpose. Love and honor your Southern ancestors. These men suffered for you.

Introduction

Who cares? This may be your first question regarding the photographing and documenting of Confederate soldiers buried in the Upper Cumberland region of Tennessee.

The experiences of Tennesseans during the war and the reconstruction period were especially harsh due to the division in the State. After Union victory, our courageous Confederate ancestors found their way back to a ruined native land. In many cases, they were robbed and murdered as they returned home. Returning Confederates worked diligently to rebuild their beloved Southland along with their lives. They did this despite the fact they were deprived of their right to vote; though the burden of taxation was not alleviated. These men are indeed relics of the past. Noble men who stood for what they believed in, a rare quality in today's society. We honor valor, even if it lies in a long forgotten graveyard.

As Southern women, we feel it is our duty to study and know the history of our brave ancestors who were willing to give everything—home, family, and their very lives—in pursuit of their Constitutional freedom. We were spurred into action, not only by the prevailing winds of "political correctness," which has saturated the very fabric of modern thinking, but also the rapid disappearance of our old family cemeteries giving way to urban sprawl.

In 2003, our Chapter Registrar, Pamela M. Wood, suggested we, as a chapter, should endeavor to locate the gravesites of those men in our respective counties who served the Confederate States of America. For the last four years we have researched, documented, located, and photographed the burial places of known Confederate soldiers in Cumberland, Putnam, Van Buren, and White Counties in Tennessee. This was a huge undertaking! Research was done in the comfort of a library or at one's home, but the fieldwork was something else! Several of those working on this project became fast friends with barbed wire fences, dogs, and local cattle. Chiggers, ticks, and briars were dreaded enemies, and on occasion, there were snakes that came out to see who was treading on their territory.

The largest task was White County. Chapter member Pamela Wood and her husband Rick, member Martha Sue Broyles, member Donna Hamilton and her son, Matt, along with Jim and Judy Drake all worked hard to gather the over 500 photographs needed. Chapter member Gladys Anderson and her husband Walter photographed almost 300 burial sites in Putnam County. Mr. Dale Welch of *Hilltop Express* aided them in finding graves. Donna Hamilton filled in and assisted, also. Members Martha Sue Broyles and

Pamela Wood did the fieldwork for Van Buren County. They could not have located all the graves without the invaluable assistance of Dr. Margaret Rhinehart and Mr. David Cook.

In Cumberland County, Barbara and Gene Parsons, Hope Parsons Schubert, Regina Hodge and Bob Tays did Cumberland County's fieldwork. Having a great number of unmarked graves where only a fieldstone was used as a marker, (the print was long lost to time) hampered the work in this county. The 50/50 split between Union and Confederate service in the county added to the difficulty of locating gravesites with soldiers from both sides sometimes sharing the same names and many leaving the county after the War. Carolyn & Billy Rankhorn recorded the graves in Warren County with ties to our chapter. A very few of the more interesting burials in Overton County were included. Due to the size of the book, we could not venture into other Upper Cumberland Counties such as Overton and Jackson with our serious efforts of locating all Confederate graves in their counties at this time. We feel there will be at least another 1,000 Confederate soldiers buried in these two counties alone. This could possibly be a project for a later date.

One of our chapter members is a great granddaughter of Samuel J. Johnson, who was one of the Immortal 600. We felt it was important to include a section on those members of the Immortal 600 with ties to Tennessee. Information was found in the book, *Biographical Roster of the Immortal 600* by Mauriel Joslyn and from the *Confederate Veterans Magazine*. Assistance in obtaining the photographs of the gravesites for these men came from Texas, Arkansas, Missouri, Fort Delaware, New Jersey, UDC chapters, and helpful individuals all across Tennessee.

This has been a labor of love for our beloved Southland and for the service given by our ancestors. We are proud of the Southern heritage we were born with and will continue to preserve its history. We hope you will find this book a useful tool in the research of your own Confederate ancestors. Perhaps you will consider joining either the United Daughters of the Confederacy or the Sons of Confederate Veterans to remember the sacrifices of the past and the rich heritage of the Confederate soldier's descendants who, since 1865, have served and are serving today in our United States Armed Forces. God bless the South and God bless you, too.

—*Barbara Buchanan Parsons (Mrs. E. H.), President,*
and Pamela Mikulski Wood (Mrs. Richard D.), Registrar
Captain Sally Tompkins #2123 United Daughters of the Confederacy

Chapter Motto: "Continuing to Honor"

IN THE LITTLE TIME LEFT BEFORE WE REPORT TO OUR GREAT COMMANDER,
LET US ACQUIT OURSELVES LIKE MEN. WHEN THE PALE SERGEANT COMES
WE SHALL LISTEN TO VOICES IN THE UPPER AIR SAYING,
"WELCOME COMRADE! DO THEY LOVE US STILL IN DIXIE?"

General Stephen Dill Lee, C.S.A.

People Involved

Members and prospective members of the Captain Sally Tompkins #2123 United Daughters of the Confederacy, Cookeville, Tennessee. (Left to right) Front row: Carolyn Rankhorn, Anna Barnes, Norma Hay, Fran Benedict, Dot Brodhag. Second row: Martha Sue Broyles, Donna Hamilton, Ruth Traughber, Faye Monk, Gladys Anderson, Sarah Dodson, Margaret Markum, Pamela Wood. Back row: Judy Drake, Carolyn Carr, Bettye Parrish, Dee Watson Smith, Betty Jo Bryant, Barbara Parsons. Members not pictured: Margaret Cordell, Cynthia Diminovich, Ada Jewell Fox, Elizabeth Gentry, Rickie Harris, Susan Raye Harris, Sherrie Beth McCulley, Kimberly Parker, Ruby Pruett, Janet Randolph, Hope Parsons Schubert, Deborah Spriggs, Kristie Welch, Martha Willis, Janet Trubee, Deborah Powell Ward, Rhetta Wilkins, Mary West, Rebecca West, Annette England, Carol Baker, and Ramona Baker.

Captain Sally Tompkins #2123 UDC Cemetery Committee. (Top row, left to right) Gladys Boyd Anderson, Martha Sue Broyles, Donna Randolph Hamilton,

(Bottom row, left to right) Barbara Buchanan Parsons, Carolyn Barnes Rankhorn, Pamela Mikulski Wood.

Our Confederate Ancestors · xiii

Our Field Work

Even the cows were interested in our work.

Registrar, Pamela Mikulski Wood, works on grave markers hidden by fallen trees and in the briars of rural White County, Tennessee.

This entire book project was the idea of Pamela Mikulski Wood. We owe a huge debt of gratitude to her for encouraging us to finish. She did the lion's share of the work for this book. She and her husband, Rick, and Martha Sue Broyles made a dynamite team in White and Van Buren counties, bird-dogging-out long, lost Confederate graves.

Martha Sue Broyles (right), our master photographer, exhausted herself and her bank account making photos of the Confederate graves and copies of soldiers' photos. Husband, Kenneth Ray, went with her to some of the cemeteries.

(Top left and middle photos) Gladys and Walter Anderson "continue to honor" by their work and support for Confederate reenactments and memorial programs.

(Middle right) Donna Randolph Hamilton, along with her son, Matt, helped document the graves in Putnam County after Gladys Anderson had an accident that stopped her work.

(Left) Jim and Judy Drake assisted with the work in White County.

Our Confederate Ancestors • XV

Gene and Barbara Parsons. Are you having fun yet? Going to some places where no humans have been for a long time, lookin' up those Confederate graves!

Carolyn and Billy Ross Rankhorn documented graves in Warren County with ties to our chapter. They support and attend many memorial and historical programs on our Confederate history.

Two of our helpers, Rick Wood and Kenneth Ray Broyles, set the Confederate marker for Henry Henderson, recipient of a Tennessee Colored Confederate Pension, in Old Union Cemetery, White County, Tennessee.

(Left) Brian Wood helps haul a two hundred forty pound cemetery marker up the side of the mountains of Cocke County, Tennessee. (Below) Brian and Rick Wood place the Confederate marker.

xvi · Our Confederate Ancestors

CUMBERLAND COUNTY

Confederate Soldiers listed for the Crossville, Tennessee Monument

Monument located on Main Street in Crossville, Tennessee, honors the soldiers from Cumberland County who served on both sides during the War Between the States.

Alvin N. Andrews
Drury H. Bagwell
John Bazell
James A. Beam
Thomas Bibee
A. C. Blevins
John V. Bolin
Samuel H. Brady
George L. Brewer
George G. Bristow
William H. Brown
William Brown
Franklin Brown
O. G. M. Broyles
William Butram
David C. Crook
John DeRossett
Elijah J. DeRossett
Zachariah Dickson
Alford Elmore
Daniel Elmore
White Frost
John F. Ford
Christopher A. Ford
Thomas W. Ford
Dr. John Ford
Elijah J. Ford
Elbert H. Ford

Calvin G. Gibson
James C. Gibson
Joseph H. Gibson
Jerry P. Godsey
John F. Graham
Jessee W. S. Graham
Elijah W. Greer
Henry Clay Greer
Wothingston S. Greer
Andrew J. Hale
Albert Newton Hamby
Gilbert N. Hamby
Reuben M. Hamby
William A. Hamby
Benjamin Harris
Benjamin Harris, Jr.
Lorenzo D. Harris
William Harris
William L. Harris
Hugh L. Hedgecoth
John Hedgecoth
William J. Hedgecoth
James J. Henry
Arthur L. Hill
Thomas Hill
Thomas H. Hinch
George W. Jeffers
Claiborne Jeffers
John Jervis

Daniel C. Knox
Francis M. Lively
Rufus R. Lively
Benjamin Loden
Pleasant Loden
William Loden
Reuben Loden
James Loden
John F. Loden
Stephen H. Mathis
Malchi Monday
John Monday
James Moore
William H. Moore
Alexander Morrow
Thomas S. Morrow
Isham E. Morrow
William J. Morton
John C. Myatt
George W. Oakes
Lewis S. Oakes
John A. Patton
Robert Patton
James M. Rains
William Ray
Andrew J. Reed
George Renfro
James T. Revis
William J. Rices

William B. Rush
James Scott
Samuel S. Sherrill
Thomas Sherrill
William F. Smith
George W. Smith
Monroe Stephens
John Stephens
Richardson Taylor
Ervin C. Taylor
John Taylor
Alexander Taylor
John Tabor
James A. "Jack" Thompson
William H. Thompson
John Thompson
William W. Tollett
James K. "Jack" Turner
David C. Turner
George A. Vandever
James C. Vandever
Eli N. Vandever
James S. Walker
John M. B. Walker
James C. Webb
Alexander Woody
Harrison Woody

Baker's Chapel Cemetery
Hillbilly Hollow Road, Dorton Community

Oakes, Lewis S.

LOCATION: Baker's Chapel Cemetery **RANK:** Private
COMPANY: B **REGIMENT:** 2nd (Ashley's) Tennessee Cavalry / Consolidated 16th Battalion (Neal's) Cavalry, D Company
BIRTH: 28 May 1838, Tennessee **DEATH:** 20 April 1914

~

Smith, Alexander

LOCATION: Baker's Chapel Cemetery **RANK:** Private
COMPANY: A **REGIMENT:** 16th (Neal's) Cavalry
BIRTH: 26 November 1834, Tennessee **DEATH:** 23 December 1913 **MARRIED:** Martha J. (b. 17 December 1837 – d. 05 January 1914) **PENSION:** #S13844

Big Lick Cemetery
Calvary Presbyterian Church, Biglick Road

Brown, Willie (William)

LOCATION: Big Lick Cemetery **RANK:** Sergeant
COMPANY: E **REGIMENT:** 28th Tennessee Infantry
BIRTH: 28 June 1823 **DEATH:** 12 June 1925

Brady Cemetery
Private Property, Brady Lane, Grassy Cove

Brady, Samuel Houston

LOCATION: Brady Cemetery **RANK:** Private
COMPANY: D **REGIMENT:** 1st (Carter's) Cavalry
BIRTH: 22 December 1837, Grassy Cove
DEATH: 11 December 1909 **MARRIED:** (1) Mary Frances Majors (b. 28 June 1840 – d. 16 December 1894); (2) Ellen Gist (b. 24 November 1860) **PENSION:** #W4129 (Widow's pension application was rejected because they married after 1890)

Browntown Cemetery
Deck Road

Manier, Allen Howes
LOCATION: Browntown Cemetery
RANK: Private **COMPANY:** K
REGIMENT: 17th Infantry
BIRTH: 27 February 1839
DEATH: 10 February 1922

Clifty Cemetery
Clifty Community, Cumberland County, Tennessee

John Franklin Cooley

Cooley, John Franklin
LOCATION: Clifty Cemetery
RANK: Private / Sergeant
COMPANY: C **REGIMENT:** 5th Tennessee Cavalry (McKenzie's)
BIRTH: 19 March 1832, Meigs County, Tennessee **DEATH:** 29 May 1924 **OTHER:** In line of battle at Franklin, Tennessee; suffered shell shocked but received only a bruise. Worked for $1 per day in blacksmith shop after war; Married 5 times; had 24 children, ages 47 to 18 months per his pension application; Application further states he was a "good citizen" and a good soldier; He was the grandson of a Revolutionary War soldier, Private James Cooley, Franklin County, Virginia, who served in the Virginia Line 6th Regiment, 10th Regiment, 1780-1783.

~

Ragan, D. R. (Duke Riah)
LOCATION: Clifty Cemetery **RANK:** Private
COMPANY: I **REGIMENT:** 26th Tennessee Infantry (3rd East Tennessee Volunteers) **BIRTH:** 09 November 1838
DEATH: 21 March 1923 **PENSION:** #S918

Creston Cemetery
West Creston Road

Baker, Matthew (Mathew)

LOCATION: Creston Cemetery **RANK:** Private **COMPANY:** I **REGIMENT:** 10th Infantry **BIRTH:** 11 August 1828, North Carolina **DEATH:** 03 February 1865

~

Linder, George W.

LOCATION: Creston Cemetery **RANK:** Not listed
COMPANY: Not listed **REGIMENT:** 4th Cavalry
BIRTH: 07 September 1834 **DEATH:** 26 September 1911
MARRIED: Mary L. (12 December 1858–18 October 1929)
PENSIONS: #S2861 and #W5956

~

Morrow, Alexander
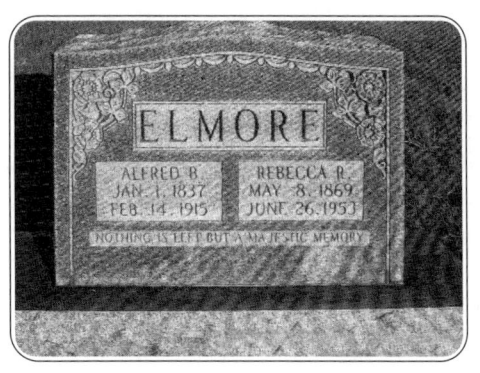
LOCATION: Creston Cemetery **RANK:** 3rd Corporal
COMPANY: A **REGIMENT:** 28th Infantry (2nd Regiment Tennessee Volunteers) **BIRTH:** 1805, Kentucky
DEATH: 03 February 1865 **MARRIED:** Elizabeth Tabor

Crossville City Cemetery
E. 1st Street, Crossville

Elmore, Alfred B.
LOCATION: Crossville City Cemetery **RANK:** Sergeant
COMPANY: A **REGIMENT:** 28th Tennessee Infantry
BIRTH: 01 January 1837, Tennessee **DEATH:** 14 February 1915
MARRIED: Rebecca R. (b. 08 May 1869 – d. 26 June 1953)
PENSION: #S13310

Hamby, William Anderson
LOCATION: Crossville City Cemetery RANK: Sergeant
COMPANY: A REGIMENT: 28th Infantry BIRTH: 10 May 1833
DEATH: 05 June 1919 MARRIED: Nancy Frances Tollett
(b.21 August 1850 – d. 10 January 1921)
PENSIONS: #S12074 and #W7221

~

Pollard, James
LOCATION: Crossville City Cemetery RANK: Not listed
COMPANY: Not listed REGIMENT: Not listed
BIRTH: c. 1839, Virginia DEATH: Unknown
OTHER: Crossville Newspaper dated 29 May 1895: "Memorial Day was observed by the John R. Swan Post, GAR, last Thursday with the usual ceremonies…The flower committee & friends decorated the graves of Two Federals, N. J. Vandever & Walter Dickson; one Confederate, James Pollard & one Revolutionary soldier, John Narramore. (All except Pollard have a marker.)"

Unmarked Grave

Dogwood Cemetery
Dogwood Community

Gibson, Calvin G.
LOCATION: Dogwood Cemetery RANK: Corporal
COMPANY: H REGIMENT: 8th (Smith's) Cavalry
BIRTH: 01 May 1824 DEATH: 02 April 1907
MARRIED: Rachel (b. 12 October 1831–d. 20 February 1907)

Fredonia Cemetery
Fredonia Road

Cox, David
LOCATION: Fredonia Cemetery RANK: Private COMPANY: C
REGIMENT: 45th Virginia Infantry BIRTH: 10 June 1838, Grayson County, Virginia DEATH: 28 April 1927
MARRIED: Mary Ann (b. 14 June 1853–d. 01 June 1929)
PENSIONS: #S13365 and #W8627 OTHER: Captured at Piedmont; Sent to Camp Morton, Indiana Union Prison.

Frost Cemetery
Frost Road, Crossville

Bandy, Thomas E.
LOCATION: Frost Cemetery **RANK:** Sergeant **COMPANY:** B / D
REGIMENT: 1st Infantry (Colm's) **BIRTH:** 11 December 1831
DEATH: 10 November 1895 **MARRIED:** Margaret
PENSION: #W2465

~

Frost, White
LOCATION: Frost Cemetery **RANK:** 1st Lieutenant
COMPANY: A **REGIMENT:** 28th Consolidated Infantry
BIRTH: 13 June 1837 **DEATH:** 22 January 1908
PARENTS: Son of Elijah and Emelia Frost

Graham Cemetery
Pomona, Howard Springs

Graham, Christopher Columbus
LOCATION: Graham Cemetery **RANK:** Private
COMPANY: E **REGIMENT:** 40th Alabama Infantry
BIRTH: 17 January 1838 **DEATH:** 28 July 1913
MARRIED: Henrietta Josephine (1845–1933)
PENSIONS: #S12040 and #W5119

Grassy Cove Baptist Cemetery
Grassy Cove

DeRossett, Elias (Elijah)
LOCATION: Grassy Cove Baptist Cemetery
RANK: Private **COMPANY:** A **REGIMENT:** 28th Infantry
BIRTH: 23 January 1832, Tennessee **DEATH:** 03 August 1913
OTHER: Name under "Derassett"

Gist, John

LOCATION: Grassy Cove Baptist Cemetery **RANK:** Private
COMPANY: A **REGIMENT:** (Carter's) 1st Tennessee Cavalry
BIRTH: c. 1809, Kentucky **DEATH:** 1863 **MARRIED:** Nancy Cox (b. 1836–d. 04 June 1913) **PENSION:** #W1944 **OTHER:** Soldier was bushwacked by unknown person (murdered) while home on leave; Parents buried, unmarked, near son's marker **SON:** John T. Gist (b. 10 December 1862–d. 16 May 1942)

Unmarked Grave

Knox, S. A. (Arch)

LOCATION: Grassy Cove Baptist Cemetery **RANK:** Private
COMPANY: I **REGIMENT:** 8th (Dibrell's) Cavalry
BIRTH: 02 November 1846, Rhea County, Tennessee
DEATH: 17 June 1920 Married: Nancy J. Lively (24 July 1852–21 March 1892) **PENSION** #S9651

Grassy Cove Methodist Cemetery
Grassy Cove, Tennessee

Cox, Hardy (Hardie)

LOCATION: Grassy Cove Methodist Cemetery
RANK: Private **COMPANY:** D **REGIMENT:** 16th Battalion (Neal's) Cavalry **BIRTH:** 07 January 1835 **DEATH:** 17 December 1915
PENSION: #S9910

Christopher Archibald Ford

Ford, Christopher Archibald

LOCATION: Grassy Cove Methodist Cemetery **RANK:** Private **COMPANY:** F **REGIMENT:** 4th Battalion (Branner's) Tennessee Cavalry / 2nd (Ashby's) Tennessee Cavalry **BIRTH:** 05 November 1833, Grassy Cove, Tennessee **DEATH:** 22 June 1904 **DAUGHTERS:** Maggie married an Evans; Lilly Ann married Curtis Hinch. **OTHER:** Before the War, Christopher Ford was married to Elizabeth Swan. The Swan family were all Unionists. Chris and Elizabeth divorced. Custody of the girls first went to Elizabeth. Chris counter-filed and got custody. The girls were left with their grandparents, Dr. John and Elizabeth Loden Ford in Grassy Cove when Chris went to serve in the Confederate Army. On 07 October 1863, Elizabeth with her father and two brothers rode into Grassy Cove, and while Elizabeth held the horses outside, her father and brothers burst into the home of Dr. John Ford, murdered him by bringing a huge knife down over his head, grabbed the two little girls, and sped off for the North. Chris was located and brought home from the Army to find a desperate situation. After his father was buried Chris tried to return to the Army but no record of further service can be found for him. His last CSA service record shows him as "deserted" so his service cannot be used to join UDC unless later proof of service is located. More details of this incident can be found in "Tales of the Civil War" by Stella Mowbray Harvey, or "Confederate Orphans" by Barbara Buchanan Parsons.

Unmarked Grave

Ford, Elbert Henley

LOCATION: Not listed **RANK:** Private **COMPANY:** A **REGIMENT:** 1st (Carter's) Tennessee Cavalry **BIRTH:** c. 1830, Grassy Cove, Tennessee **DEATH:** c. 1870–1880 **OTHER:** Children were in the household of their Uncle's in 1880.

Unmarked Grave

Ford, Elijah Jehu

LOCATION: Unknown **RANK:** Private **COMPANY:** A **REGIMENT:** 1st (Carter's) Tennessee Cavalry **BIRTH:** c. 1838, Grassy Cove, Tennessee **DEATH:** 1864 **OTHER:** Last CSA record, 08 December 1864, shows him as a prisoner in a Union hospital, Nashville, Tennessee, where he died. There were several mass burial pits around the foot of the Capital building and he may be there. None of the pits were marked and they are now covered with buildings.

Dr. John Ford

Ford, Dr. John
LOCATION: Grassy Cove Methodist Cemetery **RANK:** Not listed **COMPANY:** Not listed
REGIMENT: Not listed
BIRTH: 25 December 1796, Fluvanna County, Virginia
DEATH: 07 October 1863, murdered by his son's ex-inlaws
MARRIED: Mary Nancy Loden
OTHER: Non-combatant doctor who took care of Confederate soldiers; David C. Knox stated in his Confederate Pension Application that he came home from the War due to getting Smallpox and that Dr. John (Jack) Ford attended him when he got home in Jan/Feb 1863.

Ford, John Fletcher
LOCATION: Grassy Cove Methodist Cemetery
RANK: Private **COMPANY:** A **REGIMENT:** 1st (Carter's) Tennessee Cavalry **BIRTH:** 18 March 1825, Grassy Cove, Tennessee **DEATH:** 04 February 1905. Grassy Cove
OTHER: Never married

John Fletcher Ford

Thomas Wesley Ford

Ford, Thomas Wesley
LOCATION: Grassy Cove Methodist Cemetery
RANK: Private **COMPANY:** A
REGIMENT: 1st (Carter's) Tennessee Cavalry, 3rd Battalion Tennessee Cavalry Volunteers
BIRTH: 21 May 1821, Grassy Cove, Tennessee
DEATH: 07 June 1885, Grassy Cove, Tennessee **MARRIED:** (1) Haney Barger, burial unknown; (2) Letitia Tollett; (3) Elizabeth Brown **UDC MEMBER RELATIVES:** Mrs. Rickie Harris, Mrs. Thelma Ford Parsons, Ms. Hope Parsons Schubert

Matthews, James W. (Soup)

LOCATION: Grassy Cove Methodist Church **RANK:** Private
COMPANY: A **REGIMENT:** 1st (Carter's) Tennessee Cavalry
BIRTH: 02 November 1827, Grassy Cove, Tennessee **DEATH:** 11 November 1911 **PENSION:** #S2129 **OTHER:** County Coroner; Marker says, "Civil War Soldier."

~

Rush William B. (Parson)

LOCATION: Grassy Cove Methodist Cemetery **RANK:** Private
COMPANY: D **REGIMENT:** 1st (Carter's) Tennessee Cavalry
BIRTH: 12 August 1812, Tennessee **DEATH:** 27 September 1895
MARRIED: Catherine E. (31 March 1821–5 April 1885)

Haley's Grove Cemetery
Crab Orchard

Holloway, S. (Samuel) H., Jr.

LOCATION: Haley's Grove Cemetery **RANK:** Private
COMPANY: E **REGIMENT:** 8th (Dibrell's) Cavalry / 13th (Gore's) Cavalry **BIRTH:** 17 April 1840 **DEATH:** 26 December 1906
MARRIED: Margaret A. (27 October 1842–6 March 1904)
PENSION: #S1662

~

Steelmon, John M.

LOCATION: Haley's Grove Cemetery **RANK:** Not listed
COMPANY: Not listed **REGIMENT:** 2nd North Carolina Home Guards **BIRTH:** 25 April 1845 **DEATH:** 27 December 1927
MARRIED: Mary S. (24 July 1845–12 September 1912)
PENSION: #S3853

Harris Cemetery
Alloway

Knox, David C.
LOCATION: Harris Cemetery RANK: Private
COMPANY: A REGIMENT: 1st (Carter's) Tennessee Cavalry
BIRTH: 08 April 1839 DEATH: 12 December 1919
MARRIED: Rachel (b. 02 April 1833– d. 16 May 1913)
PENSION: #S12510 OTHER: In his deposition taken in Grassy Cove by Hon. T. E. Wilson, David Knox states that he is a resident of the Verdie Community of Cumberland County, Tennessee, and that he served in Company A, 1st Tennessee Cavalry. He was in the battles of Perryville, Kentucky and Murfreesboro, Tennessee. He contracted small pox in January/ February 1863, and never recovered. When asked, "Did you ever take the oath of allegiance?" His reply, "No". Q: "Why didn't you take it?" Reply: "I told the federal authorities who had me a prisoner that I would die before I took it."; A Southern Cross of Honor is at his gravesite.

Hinch Mountain Cemetery
Jewett Road

Harris, Lorenzo Dow
LOCATION: Hinch Mountain Cemetery, South of marker for daughter, Susan, wife of John Hinch, and left of marker for daughter, Ida. RANK: Private COMPANY: D REGIMENT: 1st (Carter's) Tennessee Cavalry BIRTH: c. 1817, North Carolina
DEATH: 23 February 1902, at 85 MARRIED: Lucinda Monday
OTHER: Cemetery vandalized; No marker for L. D. Harris

Unmarked Grave

Sherrill, Andrew (Andy)
LOCATION: Hinch Mountain Cemetery
RANK: Private COMPANY: F
REGIMENT: (Ashby's) 2nd Tennessee Cavalry
BIRTH: 27 March 1838 DEATH: 11 July 1903
MARRIED Nancy (b. 16 May 1854 – d. 01 November 1936)
PENSION: #S2103, #W3272

Linary Cemetery
Linary

Renfro, John A.
LOCATION: Linary Cemetery **RANK:** Private
COMPANY: G **REGIMENT:** 1st (Carter's) Tennessee Cavalry
BIRTH: 11 October 1835, Tennessee **DEATH:** 02 August 1906
MARRIED: Mary E. (13 January 1841–23 August 1908)

Mill Creek Cemetery
Mill Creek, off Potato Farm Road

Myatt, John C.
LOCATION: Mill Creek Cemetery **RANK:** Private **COMPANY:** A
REGIMENT: 28th Tennessee Infantry / 2nd Mountain Regiment Tennessee Volunteers **BIRTH:** c. 1830, Tennessee
DEATH: Unknown **MARRIED:** Elizabeth (07 January 1829–01 November 1884) **PENSIONS:** #S1099 and #W1346

Miller Stand or Hinch Cemetery
Private property of Hobert Orme

Sherrell, Adam
LOCATION: Miller Stand or Hinch Cemetery **RANK:** Not listed
COMPANY: F **REGIMENT:** 2nd (Ashby's) Tennessee Cavalry
BIRTH: 18 December 1833 **DEATH:** 19 November 1912
PENSION: #S2102 **OTHER:** Grave is not marked.

Mount Zion
East of Alloway

Loden, James
LOCATION: Mount Zion Cemetery **RANK:** Private
COMPANY: D **REGIMENT:** 16th (Neal's) Battalion Tennessee Cavalry **BIRTH:** 20 August 1839 **DEATH:** 09 June 1912
MARRIED: H. J. (b. 31 July 1837 – d. 15 February 1902)
PENSION: #S10107

Loden, W. M.

LOCATION: Mount Zion Cemetery **RANK:** Private
COMPANY: E **REGIMENT:** 26th Tennessee Infantry / 3rd East Tennessee Volunteers **BIRTH:** 26 January 1827
DEATH: 07 November 1912 **MARRIED:** Sarah A. (b. 15 February 1839 – d. 23 December 1921)

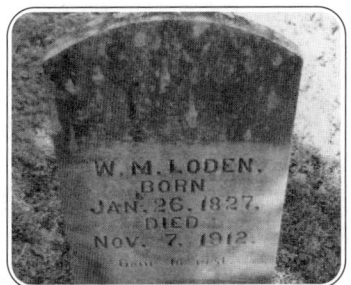

~

Smith, George W.

LOCATION: Mount Zion Cemetery **RANK:** Private
COMPANY: C **REGIMENT:** 28th / 2nd Mountain Regiment Tennessee Volunteers **BIRTH:** 27 March 1841, Tennessee
DEATH: 27 January 1912 **MARRIED:** Susanna (b. 22 September 1837 – d. 06 March 1901)

Pleasant Hill Cemetery
Pleasant Hill

Brown, Jackson Van Buren, Rev.

LOCATION: Pleasant Hill Cemetery
RANK: Brevet 2nd Lieutenant
COMPANY: H **REGIMENT:** 16th Tennessee Infantry
BIRTH: 19 July 1840 **DEATH:** 07 November 1910
MARRIED: Abbie (b. 06 April 1856 – d. 27 April 1934)
PENSION: #W4175

~

Eldridge, John F.

LOCATION: Pleasant Hill Cemetery **RANK:** Corporal
COMPANY: E **REGIMENT:** 8th (Dibrell's) Tennessee Cavalry / 13th (Gore's) Tennessee Cavalry **BIRTH:** 22 February 1842
DEATH: 20 September 1912 **MARRIED:** Frances Finley (b. 02 May 1846; date of death unknown) **PENSION:** #W4622

Rains Cemetery
Claysville, Baker's Road

Rains, James Mat
LOCATION: Rains Cemetery **RANK:** 3rd Lieutenant **COMPANY:** A **REGIMENT:** 28th Tennessee Infantry / 2nd Moutain Regiment, Tennessee Volunteers **BIRTH:** 24 February 1831, Kentucky **DEATH:** 01 April 1917 **MARRIED:** Mary Ann (b. 03 June 1849 – d. 28 July 1925) **PENSION:** Pension #W8112 **OTHER:** Pension was rejected. Wife owned a lot of real estate.

Rock Island Prison Cemetery
Rock Island, Illinois

Myatt, Eldridge
LOCATION: Rock Island Prison Cemetery, #442 **RANK:** Captain **COMPANY:** Not listed **REGIMENT:** Not listed **BIRTH:** c. 1799, North Carolina **DEATH:** 10 March 1864 **MARRIED:** Nancy Kingten (b. 12 July 1812 – d. 10 November 1862) **OTHER:** Like so many widows of the War, Nancy Kingten Myatt is buried in the Mill Creek Cemetery of Cumberland County, Tennessee, and her husband, Eldridge Myatt, is buried at the Rock Island Union Prison in Illinois. Eldridge Myatt introduced the bill to form the county of Cumberland in Tennessee. He was an early road commissioner, helping lay out the roads across the Plateau, and served in the Tennessee Militia. He was captured at the Battle Above the Clouds, Lookout Mountain, Tennessee, and was taken to Rock Island Prison where many of the early prisoners froze to death. He died 10 March 1864 and was buried in grave #442 (Photo of grave by Jim Bently).

Smith Chapel Church Cemetery
Smith Chapel

Jarvis, James Alexander
LOCATION: Smith Chapel Church Cemetery **RANK:** Private **COMPANY:** D **REGIMENT:** 13th (Gore's) Tennessee Cavalry **BIRTH:** 26 January 1837, North Carolina **DEATH:** 11 November 1906

Wallace, William C.
LOCATION: Smith Chapel Cemetery   RANK: Sergeant
COMPANY: G   REGIMENT: 4th Arkansas Cavalry
BIRTH: 04 July 1835
DEATH: 17 August 1910

Tabor Cemetery
Family Farm in Creston

Tabor, John
LOCATION: Tabor Cemetery
RANK: Private   COMPANY: A
REGIMENT: 28th Tennessee Infantry
BIRTH: 1825, Tennessee
DEATH: 1897   MARRIED: Martha (1832–1882)

Marker Photo
Not Available

Turner Cemetery #4
Off Peavine Road

Hamby, Albert N.
LOCATION: Turner Cemetery #4   RANK: Unknown
COMPANY: Unknown   REGIMENT: 16th (Neal's) Battalion,
Tennessee Cavalry   BIRTH: 01 October 1846
DEATH: 07 August 1894   MARRIED: Kate   PENSION: #W8753

Hyder, Jasper Sevier
LOCATION: Turner Cemetery #4   RANK: Private   COMPANY: D
REGIMENT: 16th (Neal's) Battalion, Tennessee Cavalry
BIRTH: 1840, Tennessee   DEATH: 1905
MARRIED: Martha Turner (b. 1853 – d. 1936)
PENSIONS: #S2573 and #W4151

Unknown Grave Locations

Harris, W. H. H.
LOCATION: Not listed **RANK:** Not listed **COMPANY:** I **REGIMENT:** 8th Tennessee Cavalry / 1st (Carter's) Cavalry **BIRTH:** Unknown **DEATH:** Unknown **PENSION:** #S8991 **OTHER:** Gave notary statement for Arch Knox pension application. Said he joined same unit for 2 months and went to his command. Full name is probably William Henry Harrison.

~

Loden, Benjamin
LOCATION: Not listed **RANK:** Private **COMPANY:** E **REGIMENT:** 26th Tennessee Infantry / 3 East Tennessee Volunteers **BIRTH:** c. 1808, Virginia **DEATH:** 14 March 1862, Camp Morton Union Prison

~

Loden, N. H.
LOCATION: Not listed **RANK:** Private **COMPANY:** E **REGIMENT:** 26th Tennessee Infantry / 3 East Tennessee Volunteers **BIRTH:** c. 1842, Tennessee **DEATH:** Unknown **OTHER:** Captured at Fort Donelson. POW at Camp Morton, Indiana; He was at Camp Morton in June and August, 1862; Last note read, "Left sick in hospital in Jackson, Mississippi September 1862".

Loden, Reuben
LOCATION: Unknown **RANK:** Private **COMPANY:** E **REGIMENT:** 26th Tennessee Infantry / 3 East Tennessee Volunteers **BIRTH:** c. 1832, Grassy Cove, Tennessee **DEATH:** Unknown **OTHER:** Listed as deserted 28 April 1863; however, shown on Muster Roll as being in Dalton, Georgia on 26 January 1864. This proof of service is accepted for UDC membership.

Loden, Pleasant
LOCATION: Unknown **RANK:** Private **COMPANY:** E **REGIMENT:** 26th Tennessee Infantry / 3 East Tennessee Volunteers **BIRTH:** c. 1821, Tennessee **DEATH:** 15 December 1861, Bowling Green, Kentucky

~

UNKNOWN GRAVE LOCATIONS FOR SOLDIERS WHOSE PENSIONS WERE FILED IN CUMBERLAND COUNTY, TENNESSEE

Adams, R. Thomas

Agee, I. N.

Baker, Samuel

Brown, L. B.

Chastain, John
2nd Georgia Infantry

Copeland, Soloman Addison
25th Tennessee Infantry

Dixon, Daniel H.
4th (Murray's) Cavalry

Glass, Alexander
22nd North Carolina Infantry

Graham, William
40th Alabama Infantry

Harris, W. H. H.
1st (Carter's) Cavalry

Hennessee, Scott Patrick

Horn, Sherard
28th Tennessee Infantry

Huges, J. B.
12th Battalion, Tennessee Infantry

Jones, B. F. M.
28th Tennessee Infantry

Parson, W. F.
37th North Carolina Infantry

Sparks, Nicholaz
25th Tennessee Infantry

Turner, D. C.
28th Tennessee Infantry

Wallace, Simon Doyle

Woody, Preston Alexander
16th Battalion, Tennessee Cavalry

Woody, Harrison
28th Tennessee Infantry

Petrified Confederate Soldier
Locations: (1) Grassy Cove Methodist Church Cemetery; (2) Unknown

Though it is folklore, we treat the Petrified Confederate Soldier as if it was a true story because our "old folks" weren't bad to tell tales!—A few years after the War a guide and some boys went into the Grassy Cove Saltpeter Cave. On a natural shelf inside they found a Confederate soldier in full dress uniform. They sent for the County coroner, James Matthews, himself a Confederate soldier. Matthews brought the body to the entrance of the cave. The body had petrified while inside the cave and the coroner could not fold back the clothing to look for wounds or other signs of foul play. When no one could identify the body the soldier was buried in the third grave space to the left of the vault of the Floyd children. This is the only raised vault in the Grassy Cove Methodist Church cemetery. The children began stories of the soldier haunting the church/school, so a pact was made by some men in the cove. The soldier was dug up and moved to a new grave, never to be divulged, and they all died with the secret location untold.

Floyd children's vault

PUTNAM COUNTY

Sons of Confederate Veterans Confederate Memorial Monument, located at Cookeville City Cemetery, Putnam County, Tennessee

The Sixteenth Regiment, Tennessee Infantry, CSA, known as "The Highlanders," was organized in May 1861, in Putnam County, Tennessee, as Company K with H. H. Dillard, Captain. This photo was taken May 19, 1904, at the unveiling of the monument to the Battle of Perryville, Kentucky (October 8, 1862). W. H. White was Color Bearer. John McConnell, J. C. Biles, H. L. Moffit, and Jasper Roberts were Color Guards of the Sixteenth Regiment, all of whom were wounded. Mr. Roberts was mortally wounded.

Putnnam County · Our Confederate Ancestors · 23

Algood Cemetery
Brotherton Mt. Rd., Algood City, Tennessee

Ford, Andrew J.
LOCATION: Algood Cemetery **RANK:** Not listed
COMPANY: Not listed **REGIMENT:** Not listed
BIRTH: 22 January 1828 **DEATH:** 29 January 1908
PENSION: #S5096

~

Reace, John A.
LOCATION: Algood Cemetery **RANK:** Private
COMPANY: E **REGIMENT:** 15th Tennessee Cavalry
BIRTH: 02 August 1843 **DEATH:** 09 November 1909
MARRIED: Rana (Roann) Webb **PENSION:** #W9000

~

Williamson, Amos K.
LOCATION: Algood Cemetery **RANK:** Private
COMPANY: K **REGIMENT:** 17th Tennessee Infantry
BIRTH: 28 April, 1842 **DEATH:** 08 April, 1939
MARRIED: (1) Julia E. Goodall; (2) Sarah J. Bilbrey
PENSION: #S9416 **PARENTS:** Joseph H. Williamson and Elizabeth Emily (Kirkpatrick) Williamson

Allison Cemetery
Boxtown Rd., between Burgess Falls Rd and Cookeville Boat Dock Rd, south of Cookeville, Tennessee

Sliger, Samuel
LOCATION: Allison Cemetery
RANK: Private **COMPANY:** A
REGIMENT: 26th Tennessee Infantry
BIRTH: 1832 **DEATH:** 1890

Ammonett-Medley Cemetery

Buffalo Valley, Tennessee

Amonett, Francis Marion

LOCATION: Ammonett-Medley Cemetery **RANK:** Captain
COMPANY: F **REGIMENT:** 16th Tennessee Infantry
BIRTH: 22 May 1839 **DEATH:** 13 August 1901
MARRIED: Virginia Taylor Maddux
PARENTS: John H. Amonett and Matilda (Dedman) Amonett

Bartlett Cemetery

Bartlett Dr., Cookeville, Tennessee

Bartlett, Joseph D.

LOCATION: Bartlett Cemetery **RANK:** Private / 2nd Lieutenant
COMPANY: A / H / F **REGIMENT:** 28th (Consolidated) Tennessee Infantry / 13th Tennessee Cavalry / 84th Tennessee Infantry
BIRTH: September 1834 **DEATH:** August 1891

Bear Creek Baptist Church Cemetery

Bear Creek Road, Algood, Tennessee

Judd, Ben

LOCATION: Bear Creek Baptist Church Cemetery
RANK: Unknown **COMPANY:** Not listed
REGIMENT: Not listed **BIRTH:** Unknown
DEATH: Unknown **MARRIED:** Patsy

Beasley Cemetery

Macedonia Community, Poplar Grove Road, Putnam County, Tennessee

Beasley, Hiriam H.

LOCATION: Beasley Cemetery **RANK:** Private **COMPANY:** C
REGIMENT: 13th Tennessee Cavalry **BIRTH:** 22 June 1828
DEATH: 22 June 1902 **MARRIED:** Mary Malissa Wassom
PENSION: #W8195 **PARENTS:** Jesse and Rebecca Beasley

Unmarked Grave

Bloomington Cemetery
Cookeville, Tennessee

Dyer, James P.
LOCATION: Bloomington Cemetery **RANK:** Private
COMPANY: D / K **REGIMENT:** 17th Tennessee Infantry
BIRTH: 18 October 1841 **DEATH:** 20 November 1917
MARRIED: (1) Sally Jane Pippin; (2) Elizabeth Smith
PENSIONS: #S13874 and #W10074
PARENTS: William Riley Dyer and Mahala Carr Dyer

~

Proffitt, George C.
LOCATION: Bloomington Cemetery **RANK:** 1st Lieutenant
COMPANY: B **REGIMENT:** 84th Tennessee Infantry
BIRTH: 11 December 1835 **DEATH:** 26 May 1901
MARRIED: Martha Jane Slagle **PENSION:** #W3187

Campbell Bohanon Cemetery
Poplar Grove Community on Rocky Point Road

Bohanon, John
LOCATION: Campbell Bohannon Cemetery **RANK:** Private
COMPANY: H **REGIMENT:** 13th Tennessee Cavalry
BIRTH: 18 August 1835, White County (now Putnam County)
DEATH: 15 November 1904 **MARRIED:** Cynthia Henry, 25 November 1860, White County, Tennessee
PARENTS: Campbell Bohannon and Mary Agnes Buck

James Bohanon Cemetery
Poplar Grove Road, Cookeville, Tennessee

Barnes, William H.
LOCATION: James Bohanon Cemetery **RANK:** Private
COMPANY: H **REGIMENT:** 13th Tennessee Cavalry
BIRTH: 19 June 1826, White County, Tennessee (now Putnam County, Tennessee) **DEATH:** 08 April 1869
MARRIED: Nancy J. Saylors **PARENTS:** John Adams Barnes and Margaret Welch Barnes

Bohannon, James E.
LOCATION: James Bohanon Cemetery **RANK:** Private
COMPANY: B. **REGIMENT:** 84th Tennessee Infantry
BIRTH: 1833 **DEATH:** 1918

~

Bohannon, Thomas
LOCATION: James Bohanon Cemetery
RANK: Private **COMPANY:** B / D
REGIMENT: 16th / 22nd Infanatry Battalion, Tennessee
BIRTH: 14 September 1839 **DEATH:** 18 February 1925
MARRIED: Margaret **PENSION:** #S7774
PARENTS: James Bohannon and Sarah Barnes Bohannon

~

Bohannon, William
LOCATION: James Bohanon Cemetery
RANK: Private **COMPANY:** H
REGIMENT: 28th (Consolidated) Tennessee Infantry
BIRTH: 09 November 1838 **DEATH:** 03 June 1900
MARRIED: Jane **OTHER:** Scottish crest on marker

~

Walker, William H.
LOCATION: James Bohanon Cemetery **RANK:** Private
COMPANY: H **REGIMENT:** 8th / 13th Tennessee Cavalry
BIRTH: 28 March 1845 **DEATH:** 17 December 1913
MARRIED: Sallie Bohannon **PENSIONS:** #S11459 and #W5541

Boiling Springs Cemetery
Hwy 135 South, Cookeville, Tennessee

Pistole, James H.
LOCATION: Boiling Springs Cemetery **RANK:** Corporal
COMPANY: E **REGIMENT:** 25th Tennessee Infantry
BIRTH: 30 November 1848 **DEATH:** 28 April 1925
MARRIED: Margaret **OTHER:** a Mason

James A. Boyd Cemetery

1st Ave. North, Baxter, Tennessee

Boyd, James Alexander

LOCATION: James A. Boyd Cemetery **RANK:** Lieutenant
COMPANY: K **REGIMENT:** 16th Tennessee Infantry
BIRTH: 04 December 1843 **DEATH:** 07 October 1927
MARRIED: Rhoda Nichols **PENSION** #S1208
PARENTS: John C. Boyd and Martha Holladay Boyd

Bradford Cemetery

Old Kentucky Road, Cookeville, Tennesse

Bradford, Charlie

LOCATION: Bradford Cemetery **RANK:** Corporal **COMPANY:** F
REGIMENT: 25th Tennessee Infantry **BIRTH:** 15 January 1844
DEATH: 07 August 1918 **MARRIED:** Mary Ann Pullen
PENSIONS: #S10796 and #W7046 **PARENTS:** William and Elizabeth (Huddleston) Bradford

Denton, Holland

LOCATION: Bradford Cemetery
RANK: 2nd Lieutenant
COMPANY: K **REGIMENT:** 16th Tennessee Infantry
BIRTH: 06 November 1818
DEATH: 10 December 1896
MARRIED: (1) Cynthia B. Dejoyrnatt; died 04 March 1852, (2) Lucinda Barnes Whitson; 1st husband, John Walter Whitson
PROFESSION: Attorney; served in the State Senate

Holland Denton

Brassel Cemetery

Baxter, Tennessee

Cox, Nathan M.

LOCATION: Brassel Cemetery **RANK:** Not listed
COMPANY: Not listed **REGIMENT:** 4th Tennessee Cavalry
BIRTH: 1845 **DEATH:** 21 September 1919 **MARRIED:** Amanda
PENSION: #S2132 **PROFESSION:** Lawyer **OTHER:** Marker broken

Brewington Cemetery

Buffalo Valley Road, Cookeville, Tennessee

Brown, Stephen W.

LOCATION: Brewington Cemetery **RANK:** Private
COMPANY: Not listed **REGIMENT:** 8th (Smith's) Tennessee Cavalry **BIRTH:** 05 March 1852 **DEATH:** 02 November 1937 **MARRIED:** Mary Frances Jared **PENSION:** #S9608

Brotherton Cemetery

Brotherton Road, Cookeville, Tennessee

Cooper, Gabreil M.

LOCATION: Brotherton Cemetery
RANK: Private **COMPANY:** C
REGIMENT: 8th (13) Tennessee Cavalry
BIRTH: 04 February 1838
DEATH: 02 December 1906
MARRIED: Martha Ann Barnes
PENSIONS: #S5373 and #W1961 **PARENTS:** Thomas Cooper and Catherine Rogers

Gabreil M. Cooper

Rector, William J.

LOCATION: Brotherton Cemetery
RANK: Private **COMPANY:** K
REGIMENT: 28th Tennessee Infantry
BIRTH: 22 May 1817 **DEATH:** 21 February 1888 **MARRIED:** Elizabeth Parham
PARENTS: Bennett Rector and Sarah Bryant Rector

William J. Rector

Rector, William J., Jr.

LOCATION: Brotherton Cemetery **RANK:** Private **COMPANY:** C
REGIMENT: 13th (Gore's) Tennessee Cavalry
BIRTH: 1841 **DEATH:** 1864, died as a POW

Tabor, Wheeler Reece
LOCATION: Brotherton Cemetery **RANK:** Private
COMPANY: Not listed **REGIMENT:** 26th Tennessee Infantry
BIRTH: Unknown **DEATH:** 03 August 1926

Brown's Mill Cemetery
Brown's Mill Road

Brown, Hiram A.
LOCATION: Brown's Mill Cemetery
RANK: Private **COMPANY:** H
REGIMENT: 13th Tennessee Cavalry
BIRTH: 10 November 1834
DEATH: 22 October 1889
MARRIED Elizabeth Bartlett
PENSION: #W925
PARENTS: Hyram Brown and Mary Allison Brown

Hiram A. Brown

~

Phifer, Joseph
LOCATION: Brown's Mill Cemetery **RANK:** Private
COMPANY: K **REGIMENT:** 25th Tennessee Infantry
BIRTH: 22 June 1844 **DEATH:** 14 February 1913
MARRIED: Martha **PENSIONS:** #S2391 and #W5761

~

Phifer, William H.
LOCATION: Browns' Mill Cemetery **RANK:** 1st Sergeant
COMPANY: K **REGIMENT:** 25th Tennessee Infantry
BIRTH: 13 March 1843 **DEATH:** 20 January 1924
MARRIED: Susan **PENSIONS:** #S6790 and #W8012

Bryant Cemetery
Bryant Ridge Road, Baxter, Tennessee

Elrod, Giles
LOCATION: Bryant Cemetery **RANK:** Private **COMPANY:** B
REGIMENT: 1st Battalion (Colm's), Tennessee Infantry
BIRTH: 1838 **DEATH:** 1904

Gipson, Joseph
LOCATION: Bryant Cemetery **RANK:** Private **COMPANY:** K
REGIMENT: 4th Tennessee Cavalry **BIRTH:** 25 December 1833
DEATH: 22 September 1918 **MARRIED:** Elizabeth
PENSION: #W7075

Buck Cemetery
Dry Valley Road, Cookeville, Tennessee

Buck, Enoch J.
LOCATION: Buck Cemetery
RANK: Private **COMPANY:** H / D
REGIMENT: 28th / 84th Tennessee Infantry **BIRTH:** 12 April 1827
DEATH: 10 November 1904
MARRIED: Catharine Quarles on 16 April 1846

Enoch J. Buck

Buck Family Cemetery
Buck Mountain Road, near Buck Lake, Cookeville, Tennessee

Webb, Isaac N.
LOCATION: Buck Family Cemetery **RANK:** Private
COMPANY: B **REGIMENT:** 5th Tennessee Cavalry
BIRTH: 13 October 1835 **DEATH:** 18 October 1896

Unmarked Grave

Bullington Cemetery
Knight's Chapel Road, Cookeville, Tennessee

Kinnaird, Alexander
LOCATION: Bullington Cemetery **RANK:** Private **COMPANY:** K
REGIMENT: 13th Tennessee Cavalry **BIRTH:** 01 January 1838
DEATH: 05 July 1905 **MARRIED:** Virginia Bullington Kinnaird

Qualls, Francis R.
LOCATION: Bullington Cemetery **RANK:** Corporal **COMPANY:** F
REGIMENT: 8th Tennessee Infantry **BIRTH:** 18 February 1837
DEATH: 25 March 1897 **MARRIED:** Parthena
PENSION: #W690

Putnam County · Our Confederate Ancestors · 31

Burton Cemetery
Old Walton Road, Cookeville, Tennessee

Burton, Frank
LOCATION: Burton Cemetery **RANK:** Private
COMPANY: A **REGIMENT:** 7th Tennessee Cavalry
BIRTH: 12 August 1836 **DEATH:** 23 December 1900
MARRIED: Ann

~

McClain, Lemuel Rux
LOCATION: Burton Cemetery **RANK:** Not listed
COMPANY: Not listed **REGIMENT:** 8th Tennessee Cavalry
BIRTH: 29 December 1844 **DEATH:** 29 April 1936
MARRIED: Emily Burton **PARENTS:** William Alexander and Mary Crane Bransford McClain **PROFESSION:** Physician

A. F. Byers Cemetery
Clemons Road, Cookeville, Tennessee

Rector, Isaac E.
LOCATION: A. F. Byers Cemetery **RANK:** Private **COMPANY:** C
REGIMENT: 13th / 8th (Dibrell's) Tennessee Cavalry
BIRTH: February 1835 **DEATH:** December 1910
MARRIED: (1) Nancy Reynolds; (2) Mary Flatt
PENSION: #S10302 **PARENTS:** James and Manerva Bennett Rector

Campbell Cemetery
Highway 70, Baxter, Tennessee

Campbell, Isaac S.
LOCATION: Campbell Cemetery **RANK:** Private **COMPANY:** D
REGIMENT: 8th (Smith's) Tennessee Cavalry
BIRTH: 09 January 1827 **DEATH:** 08 September 1864

Clouse Cemetery
Board Valley Road, Cookeville, Tennessee

Clouse, Thomas J.
LOCATION: Clouse Cemetery
RANK: Private **COMPANY:** D
REGIMENT: 22nd Battalion Tennessee Infantry
BIRTH: 01 January 1837
DEATH: 11 December 1895
MARRIED: Unetta/Eunetta Bumbalough Clouse **PROFESSION:** Baptist preacher at Board Valley

Thomas J. Clouse

~

Hill, Isaac A.
LOCATION: Clouse Cemetery **RANK:** Private **COMPANY:** B
REGIMENT: 1st Battalion (Colm's) Tennessee Invantry
BIRTH: 23 September 1825 **DEATH:** 18 June 1912
MARRIED: Rhoda

~

Scarbrough, James
LOCATION: Clouse Cemetery
RANK: Private **COMPANY:** K
REGIMENT: 25th Tennessee Infantry
BIRTH: 10 October 1820
DEATH: 09 December 1908
MARRIED: Phoebe Sparks
PENSION: #S5031

James Scarbrough

Cookeville City Cemetery
Spring Street, Cookeville, Tennessee

Bryant, A. B.
LOCATION: Cookeville City Cemetery **RANK:** Sergeant
COMPANY: K **REGIMENT:** 17th Tennessee Infantry
BIRTH: 10 March 1842 **DEATH:** 18 March 1914
MARRIED: Mary Caroline **PENSION:** #W6057

Unmarked Grave

Unmarked Grave

Carr, Elijah W.
LOCATION: Cookeville City Cemetery
RANK: Corporal **COMPANY:** A
REGIMENT: 25th Tennessee Infantry
BIRTH: 13 October 1838 **DEATH:** 15 October 1903
MARRIED: Elizabeth F. Harrison on 13 November 1862
PENSION: #W19

~

Chapin, Hiram Foster
LOCATION: Cookeville City Cemetery **RANK:** Private
COMPANY: I **REGIMENT:** 25th Tennessee Infantry
BIRTH: 13 October 1838 **DEATH:** 15 October 1903
MARRIED: (1) Milly Judd; (2) Margaret Elizabeth

~

Chapin, William P.
LOCATION: Cookeville City Cemetery
RANK: Major **COMPANY:** E
REGIMENT: 13th Tennessee Cavalry
BIRTH: 14 December 1838 **DEATH:** 27 February 1909
MARRIED: Sibba Daughtery **PENSION:** #W5218

~

Copeland, James E.
LOCATION: Cookeville City Cemetery **RANK:** Private
COMPANY: F **REGIMENT:** 28th (Consolidated) Tennessee
Infantry **BIRTH:** 17 May 1823 **DEATH:** 22 March 1903
PENSION: #S4400

~

Crutcher, Joseph W.
LOCATION: Cookeville City Cemetery **RANK:** Not listed
COMPANY: Not listed **REGIMENT:** Not listed
BIRTH: 27 December 1827 **DEATH:** 14 August 1878
MARRIED: Mary

Curtis, James H.
LOCATION: Cookeville City Cemetery **RANK:** Captain
COMPANY: I **REGIMENT:** 25th Tennessee Infantry
BIRTH: January 1842 **DEATH:** 1907

~

Davis, Henry Polk
LOCATION: Cookeville City Cemetery **RANK:** Private
COMPANY: C **REGIMENT:** 13th (Dibrell's) Tennessee Cavalry
BIRTH: 14 November 1844
DEATH: 22 March 1903
MARRIED: Lydia Ann Solomon
PENSION: #W2467
OTHER: Elected County Court Clerk in 1870

Henry Polk Davis

~

Ditty, Alexander H.
LOCATION: Cookeville City Cemetery **RANK:** Private
COMPANY: K **REGIMENT:** 13th Tennessee Cavalry
BIRTH: 26 October 1834 **DEATH:** 17 October 1908
MARRIED: Margaret Jane Apple
PARENTS: Abraham and Jincy Fergus Ditty

~

Early, Robert
LOCATION: Cookeville City Cemetery **RANK:** Private
COMPANY: D **REGIMENT:** 12th Tennessee Cavalry
BIRTH: 14 February 1829 **DEATH:** 19 January 1897
MARRIED: Sarah Moore **DAUGHTER:** Nina Douglas
OTHER: Wife and daughter charter members of Cookeville #608 UDC

~

Elrod, John E.
LOCATION: Cookeville City Cemetery **RANK:** Sergeant
COMPANY: A **REGIMENT:** 28th (Consolidated) Tennessee Infantry
BIRTH: 25 September 1838 **DEATH:** 11 June 1916
MARRIED: Betty Warren

Freeze, Joseph C.
LOCATION: Cookeville City Cemetery **RANK:** Major / Quartermaster **COMPANY:** AQM **REGIMENT:** 25th Tennessee Infantry **BIRTH:** 13 July 1826 **DEATH:** 26 August 1896 **MARRIED:** Margaret S. Bounds **OTHER:** Record under the name "Freese"

~

Gabbert, Joel C.
LOCATION: Cookeville City Cemetery **RANK:** 3rd Corporal **COMPANY:** F **REGIMENT:** 16th Tennessee Infantry **BIRTH:** July 1845 **DEATH:** 04 August 1910 **MARRIED:** Nancy Jane (Saylors) Barnes **PARENTS:** Dr. Benjamin and Diana Gabbert **PROFESSION:** Attorney

~

Henry, Jacob
LOCATION: Cookeville City Cemetery **RANK:** Lieutenant **COMPANY:** Not listed **REGIMENT:** 25th Tennessee Infantry **BIRTH:** 26 August 1830 **DEATH:** 28 June 1893 **MARRIED:** Martha L. Miller on 1 May 1870 **PARENTS:** George Washington and Lucy Lowery Henry

~

Jared, William J.
LOCATION: Cookeville City Cemetery **RANK:** 2nd Lieutenant **COMPANY:** K **REGIMENT:** 28th Tennessee Infantry **BIRTH:** 27 June 1841 **DEATH:** 27 April 1919 **MARRIED:** Elizabeth Huddleston Jared **PENSION:** #W7188 **PARENTS:** Samuel Rawlston Jared and Mary Safroni Scruggs Jared **OTHER:** William J. Jared was shot in the shoulder at Shiloh and in the hip at Egypt Station, Mississippi. He was paroled 20 May 1865, at Greensboro, North Carolina.

William J. Jared

~

Lee, Zebulon P.
LOCATION: Cookeville City Cemetery **RANK:** Private
COMPANY: C **REGIMENT:** 23rd Tennessee Infantry
BIRTH: 29 March 1843 **DEATH:** Unknown
MARRIED: Virginia F. Atwell

~

Lewis, Martin V.
LOCATION: Cookeville Cemetery **RANK:** Private
COMPANY: I **REGIMENT:** 25th Tennessee Infantry
BIRTH: 27 July 1834 **DEATH:** 04 May 1920
MARRIED: Susan Farmer

~

Lowe, Leonard John
LOCATION: Cookeville Cemetery **RANK:** Major
COMPANY: E **REGIMENT:** 18th Tennessee Infantry
BIRTH: 02 April 1826 **DEATH:** 27 March 1909
MARRIED: Nancy Jane Quarles
GRANDCHILDREN: Mary Lowe Jared

~

McKinley, James Donald
LOCATION: Cookeville Cemetery **RANK:** 3rd Lieutenant
COMPANY: K **REGIMENT:** 17th Tennessee Infantry
BIRTH: 21 July 1831 **DEATH:** 5 August 1919
MARRIED: Sarah Frances Maddux **PENSION:** #S7246

~

Moore, William
LOCATION: Cookeville Cemetery **RANK:** Private
COMPANY: D **REGIMENT:** 8th Tennessee Infantry
BIRTH: Unknown **DEATH:** 01 September 1861, at Huntersville, Virginia

Morgan, George H.
LOCATION: Cookeville Cemetery **RANK:** Not listed
COMPANY: Not listed **REGIMENT:** Dibrell's Staff
BIRTH: 05 September 1841, Jackson County, Tennessee
DEATH: 20 August 1900 **MARRIED:** Mary Ann Butler, Mary Trogden **PARENTS:** Daniel and Susannah Smith Morgan
PROFESSION: Judge; Attorney; Tennessee Attorney General, 1870–78; Elected to State Senate 1880.

~

Morgan, William C.
LOCATION: Cookeville Cemetery **RANK:** Private **COMPANY:** Not listed **REGIMENT:** Hamilton J. Shaw's Battalion, organized in Jackson County, Tennessee **BIRTH:** 03 February 1845 **DEATH:** 08 January 1926 **MARRIED:** Marina Pharris **PENSION:** #S8701 **PARENTS:** Austin Hawkins and Barbara Johnson Morgan

~

Neese, H. H.
LOCATION: Cookeville Cemetery **RANK:** Corporal
COMPANY: A **REGIMENT:** 41st Tennessee Infantry
BIRTH: Unknown **DEATH:** Unknown
MARRIED: Laura A. **PENSION:** #W7735

~

Parkins, Levi J.
LOCATION: Cookeville Cemetery **RANK:** Not listed
COMPANY: Not listed **REGIMENT:** Not listed **BIRTH:** 25 January 1830 **DEATH:** 04 June 1908 **MARRIED:** Amanda M.

~

Parkison, Richard F.
LOCATION: Cookeville Cemetery **RANK:** Private **COMPANY:** C
REGIMENT: 13th Tennessee Cavalry **BIRTH:** 08 November 1831
DEATH: 04 December 1912 **MARRIED:** Sarah C.
PENSIONS: #S8555 and #W4639

Pieland, R. H.
LOCATION: Cookeville Cemetery **RANK:** Private **COMPANY:** E
REGIMENT: 19th and 20th (Consolidated) Tennessee Cavalry
BIRTH: Unknown **DEATH:** Unknown

Quarles, John S.
LOCATION: Cookeville Cemetery **RANK:** Captain **COMPANY:** G
REGIMENT: 8th Tennessee Infantry **BIRTH:** 03 January 1838
DEATH: 18 June 1924 **MARRIED:** (1) in 1875 to Emily Frances Dewitt - 3 children; (2) Sarah Thompson **PENSION:** #S15428
OTHER: Wounded 20 times during the War.

Ragland, William H.
LOCATION: Cookeville Cemetery **RANK:** Private
COMPANY: D **REGIMENT:** 4th (McLemore's) Cavalry
BIRTH: 22 September 1842, Smith County, Tennessee
DEATH: 06 April 1927
MARRIED: (1) Ann Burton on 14 January 1865; (2) Elizabeth Butler **CHILDREN:** with Elizabeth Butler— Mattie, Mary, C.B., John, Edward, Ernest, Nan, Grace **PENSION:** #S16001 **PARENTS:** Dr. William and Martha Biggers Hughes Ragland **PROFESSION:** Physician

William H. Ragland

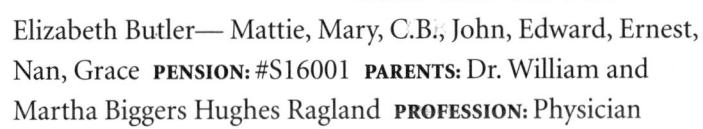

Rash, William A.
LOCATION: Cookeville Cemetery **RANK:** Private
COMPANY: A **REGIMENT:** 4th Tennessee Cavalry
BIRTH: Not listed **DEATH:** Not listed
MARRIED: Martha Elizabeth
PENSION: #W1302

Reagan, Alvin Alexander
LOCATION: Cookeville Cemetery **RANK:** 2nd Lieutenant
COMPANY: C **REGIMENT:** 13th Tennessee Cavalry
BIRTH: 25 October 1842 **DEATH:** 31 December 1917
MARRIED: Farmetta Horn **CHILDREN:** Daisy, Mamie
GRANDCHILDREN: Rebecca **PENSIONS:** #S10008 and #W6929
PARENTS: Charles and Anna Denton Reagan

~

Reagan, Isaac D.
LOCATION: Cookeville Cemetery **RANK:** Not listed
COMPANY: Not listed **REGIMENT:** Not listed
BIRTH: 26 October 1829 **DEATH:** 16 November 1872
MARRIED: Louisa Woolsey
CHILDREN: Mary Ann Reagan Staley

~

Shaw, Joseph
LOCATION: Cookeville Cemetery **RANK:** Captain
COMPANY: F **REGIMENT:** 25th Tennessee Infantry
BIRTH: c. 1829-1839 **DEATH:** 1864, killed in Georgia
MARRIED: Margaret Apple **PARENTS:** Thomas Jefferson and Mahala Wiley Shaw

Unmarked Grave

~

Slaughter, Samuel G.
LOCATION: Cookeville Cemetery **RANK:** Captain
COMPANY: I **REGIMENT:** 28th (Consolidated) Tennessee Infantry **BIRTH:** 02 February 1820 **DEATH:** 22 April 1903
MARRIED: (1) Aletha Evalina Young; (2) Dulcinea Dottobozo Young

~

Smith, Thomas G.
LOCATION: Cookeville Cemetery **RANK:** Private
COMPANY: H **REGIMENT:** 25th Tennessee Infantry
BIRTH: 14 February 1842 **DEATH:** 29 April 1917
MARRIED: (1) Lucinda C. Minor, 11 October 1869; (2) Alta Cora Terry, 10 June 1894 **PARENTS:** Jesse Benton and Susannah Smith

Speakman, William

LOCATION: Cookeville Cemetery **RANK:** Private
COMPANY: Hamilton's **REGIMENT:** Battallion (Shaw's)
Tennessee Cavalry **BIRTH:** 24 November 1822
DEATH: 21 June 1907 **MARRIED:** Frances A.
CHILDREN: Nina Embrey

~

Staley, Elmore Douglass

LOCATION: Cookeville Cemetery **RANK:** Sergeant
COMPANY: B / A **REGIMENT:** 50th Tennessee Infantry / 1st
Tennessee Infantry **BIRTH:** 29 November 1843 **DEATH:** 09
December 1913 **MARRIED:** Mary Ann Reagan Staley

~

Stamps, James J.

LOCATION: Cookeville Cemetery **RANK:** Private
COMPANY: B **REGIMENT:** 28th Tennessee Infantry
BIRTH: 02 September 1834 **DEATH:** 26 December 1905
MARRIED: Nancy **PENSION:** #S1040
PARENTS: John and Polly Stamps

~

Taylor, Henry C.

LOCATION: Cookeville Cemetery **RANK:** Private **COMPANY:** A
REGIMENT: 25th Tennessee Infantry **BIRTH:** 25 March 1833
DEATH: 29 March 1923 **MARRIED:** Emily Frances Cameron
PENSION: #S7695 **PARENTS:** Silas and Mary A. Smith Walker
Taylor **OTHER:** Captured at Rogersville, Tennessee, and
paroled on 25 March 1865.

~

Watson, J. R.

LOCATION: Cookeville Cemetery **RANK:** Not listed
COMPANY: Not listed **REGIMENT:** 8th Tennessee Cavalry
BIRTH: 09 May 1840 **DEATH:** 12 June 1927
MARRIED (1) Rebecca Officer; (2) Rozie Holford
GRANDCHILDREN: Mamie Hunter Carlen, Elizabeth Rice
PENSION: #S12087 **PARENTS:** Thomas Townsend and Sabra
Bennett Watson

Williams, John H.
LOCATION: Cookeville Cemetery
RANK: Sergeant COMPANY: C
REGIMENT: 1st Arkansas Mounted Rifles
BIRTH: 19 February 1836
DEATH: 13 November 1908

Cooper Cemetery
Brotherton (past Brotherton Cemetery, on right of road)

Cooper, Nathan C.
LOCATION: Cooper Cemetery
RANK: Private COMPANY: H
REGIMENT: (8th) 13th Tennessee Cavalry
BIRTH: January 1843
DEATH: Unknown
MARRIED: Martha Rector
PENSION: #W4704, S#2542
PARENTS: Thomas and Catherine Rogers Cooper

Nathan C. Cooper

Cooper, William Kennedy
LOCATION: Cooper Cemetery RANK: Private
COMPANY: C / F REGIMENT: (8th) 13th Tennessee Cavalry
BIRTH: 22 December 1831 DEATH: 22 March 1914
MARRIED: Caroline PENSION: #S5325 PARENTS: Thomas and Catherine Rogers Cooper

Davis Cemetery
Spring Creek near Bethel Baptist Church

Davis, A. G.
LOCATION: Davis Cemetery RANK: Private
COMPANY: I REGIMENT: 5th Tennessee Cavalry
BIRTH: 25 November 1842
DEATH: 26 March 1910

Unmarked Grave

Dodson Branch

Highway 135, Dodson Branch Road, North of Cookeville, Tennessee

Gentry, Martin B.
LOCATION: Dodson Branch Cemetery **RANK:** Private
COMPANY: I **REGIMENT:** 25th Tennessee Infantry
BIRTH: 12 December 1818 **DEATH:** June 1904
MARRIED Mary Peek **PENSION:** #S706

~

Hamilton, Hiram H.
LOCATION: Dodson Branch Cemetery **RANK:** Private
COMPANY: K **REGIMENT:** 4th Tennessee Infantry
BIRTH: 1834 **DEATH:** 1863 **MARRIED:** Rebecca Nelson
CHILDREN: Hiram W. **GRANDCHILDREN:** Rebecca Hamilton Anderson

~

Martin, Hiram L.
LOCATION: Dodson Branch Cemetery **RANK:** Private
COMPANY: I **REGIMENT:** 25th Tennessee Infantry
BIRTH: 08 April 1839 **DEATH:** 21 May 1936
MARRIED: Almeda **PENSIONS:** #S13595 and #S15506
CHILDREN: Joe, Eliza, Rebecca, Ezra, Terry, Susie, Alec, and James **OTHER:** He served for three years and 90 days. He was wounded in the battle of Murfreesboro, Tennessee

~

Loftis, Bailey P.
LOCATION: Dodson Branch Cemetery **RANK:** Private
COMPANY: K **REGIMENT:** 8th / 13th Tennessee Cavalry
BIRTH: 07 October 1844 **DEATH:** 13 February 1925

Double Springs
Highway 70 West, Cookeville, Tennessee

Barnes, Jesse
LOCATION: Double Springs Cemetery **RANK:** Corporal **COMPANY:** H **REGIMENT:** 8th / 13th (Dibrell's) Tennessee Cavalry **BIRTH:** 24 November 1827 **DEATH:** 16 March 1903 **MARRIED** Cindiarillia Pippin **PARENTS:** Thomas Barnes and Mary Strain

Jesse Barnes

~

Palk, Adam Littleton
LOCATION: Double Springs Cemetery **RANK:** Private **COMPANY:** A **REGIMENT:** 28th (Consolidated) Tennessee Infantry **BIRTH:** 02 January 1829 **DEATH:** 10 November 1914 **MARRIED** (1) Malissa Manier; (2) Nancy P. Byers Rector; (3) Sarah Frances Moore Netherton

~

Pippin, Richard F.
LOCATION: Double Springs Cemetery **RANK:** Corporal **COMPANY:** K **REGIMENT:** 28th (Consolidated) Tennessee Infantry **BIRTH:** 01 March 1837 **DEATH:** 20 June 1913 **MARRIED:** (1) Celia Emeline Laycock; (2) Amanda Jane Huddleston; (3) Sarah M. Bohannon

~

Rayburn, John M.
LOCATION: Double Springs Cemetery **RANK:** Not listed **COMPANY:** Not listed **REGIMENT:** 16th Tennessee Infantry **BIRTH:** 1832 **DEATH:** 1932 **MARRIED:** (1) Nancy Ann Chism; (2) Mrs. Alice Freeman Kirby **OTHER:** John M. Rayburn was the driver of a mail stagecoach when the last robbery in Putnam County occurred. He was wounded in foot and lost a leg at Battle of Chickamauga, Georgia.

Roberts, Nathan A.
LOCATION: Double Springs Cemetery **RANK:** Corporal
COMPANY: K **REGIMENT:** 17th Tennessee Infantry
BIRTH: 09 July 1844 **DEATH:** 09 July 1920
MARRIED: (1) Lella Spurlock; (2) Margaret J. Denson
PENSION: #W7446 **PARENTS:** Caleb and Sarah Roberts

~

Scarlett, Thomas N.
LOCATION: Double Springs Cemetery **RANK:** Private
COMPANY: K **REGIMENT:** 28th Tennessee Infantry
BIRTH: 15 May 1830 **DEATH:** 06 September 1901
MARRIED: Mahalia Bullington **PENSION:** #W2053
PARENTS: John and Deliah Scarlett

~

West, Granville F.
LOCATION: Double Springs Cemetery **RANK:** Private
COMPANY: H **REGIMENT:** 8th Tennessee Cavalry
BIRTH: 10 September 1842 **DEATH:** 15 March 1867
MARRIED: Elizabeth Ray **PENSION:** #W687
PARENTS: John and Mary Brown West

Dry Valley
Highway 70 North, Cookeville, Tennessee

Bullock, Frank M.
LOCATION: Dry Valley Cemetery **RANK:** Private
COMPANY: B **REGIMENT:** 10th Tennessee Infantry
BIRTH: 23 January 1843
DEATH: 08 March 1917
MARRIED: Frances Bartlett Dowell **PENSION:** #W10040
PARENTS: Thomas R. and Naomi Brown Bullock

Watson, Henry Thomas
LOCATION: Dry Valley Cemetery
RANK: Private COMPANY: K REGIMENT: 25th Tennessee Infantry BIRTH: 06 June 1836 DEATH: 02 November 1902
MARRIED: (1) Louise Williams; (2) Elizabeth Salina Orgie Miller PARENTS: Thomas Townsend and Sabra Bennett Watson

Henry Thomas Watson

Elrod Cemetery
On Little Indian Creek in Elrod Hollow, northeast of Gentry

Sherrel, John J.
LOCATION: Elrod Cemetery RANK: Sergeant COMPANY: I REGIMENT: 5th Tennessee Infantry BIRTH: Unknown DEATH: Unknown MARRIED: (1) Nancy B. Howell; (2) Elizabeth Martin PARENTS: Elam and Elizabeth Saylors Sherrell

Unmarked Grave

Evans Winchester Cemetery
Rock Springs in Buffalo Valley on old Jared place

Evans, John D.
LOCATION: Evans Winchester Cemetery RANK: Private COMPANY: E REGIMENT: 28th (Consolidated) Tennessee Infantry BIRTH: Unknown DEATH: Unknown

Unmarked Grave

Farley/Scott Cemetery
Ditty Road, Cookeville, Tennessee

Farley, Jesse
LOCATION: Farley/Scott Cemetery
RANK: Major COMPANY: A
REGIMENT: 22nd Battalion, Tennessee Infantry BIRTH: 15 January 1825
DEATH: 04 August 1895
MARRIED: Elizabeth Allison
PARENTS: Pleasant C. and Nancy Farley

Jesse Farley

Fletcher Family Cemetery

on Guy Boyd Farm

Fletcher, J. C.

LOCATION: Fletcher Family Cemetery **RANK:** Private
COMPANY: K **REGIMENT:** 13th Tennessee Cavalry
BIRTH: 25 May 1829 **DEATH:** 05 October 1896

Unmarked Grave

Halfacre Cemetery

Baxter, Tennessee

Halfacre, Andrew

LOCATION: Halfacre Cemetery
RANK: Private **COMPANY:** E
REGIMENT: 28th Tennessee Infantry **BIRTH:** 1831
DEATH: 1909

Andrew Halfacre

Hill Cemetery

Stone Seminary Road, Cookeville, Tennessee

Hill, John

LOCATION: Hill Cemetery **RANK:** Private / Major **COMPANY:** I
REGIMENT: 28th (Consolidated) Tennessee Infantry
BIRTH: 17 June 1828 **DEATH:** 12 January 1901
MARRIED: Maniza Holmes in 1853; They had 10 children.
PARENTS: William and Lucinda Chisom Hill

Holly-Palmer Cemetery

Near Boma

Maxwell, C. W.

LOCATION: Holly-Palmer Cemetery
RANK: Private **COMPANY:** A
REGIMENT: 8th (Smith's) Tennessee Cavalry
BIRTH: 30 July 1845 **DEATH:** 08 July 1925

Unmarked Grave

Howard Cemetery
Burgess Mills Road, Cookeville, Tennessee

Bray, William R.
LOCATION: Howard Cemetery **RANK:** Private **COMPANY:** E / C
REGIMENT: 25th Tennessee Infantry / 1st Tennessee Cavalry
BIRTH: 04 January 1839 **DEATH:** 23 June 1916
MARRIED: Letha **PENSION:** #S8359
PARENTS: Joseph and Syntha Ann Mills Bray

~

Burgess, Charles L.
LOCATION: Howard Cemetery **RANK:** Private **COMPANY:** E
REGIMENT: 25th Tennessee Infantry **BIRTH:** 27 September 1843 **DEATH:** 17 May 1915 **MARRIED:** America / Margaret

~

Howard, Allen
LOCATION: Howard Cemetery **RANK:** Private **COMPANY:** A
REGIMENT: 22nd Battalion, Tennessee Infantry
BIRTH: 02 November 1837 **DEATH:** 14 January 1897
MARRIED: Margaret

Hughes Cemetery
Highway 70 West, Baxter, Tennessee

Hughes, H. I.
LOCATION: Hughes Cemetery **RANK:** Corporal **COMPANY:** K
REGIMENT: 16th Tennessee Infantry **BIRTH:** 15 March 1840
DEATH: 07 March 1885

~

Jared, Brice B.
LOCATION: Hughes Cemetery
RANK: Private **COMPANY:** G
REGIMENT: 84th Tennessee Infantry
BIRTH: 07 June 1830 **DEATH:** 14 June 1887 **MARRIED:** Amanda Jane "Mitty" Carr Jared **PARENTS:** Joseph and Dorcas Byrne Jared

Brice B. Jared

Old Hyder Family Cemetery

Poplar Grove, Rocky Point Road, Cookeville, Tennessee

Hyder, Jesse (Elkannah / Elkanah)
LOCATION: Old Hyder Family Cemetery **RANK:** Private
COMPANY: D **REGIMENT:** 22nd Battalion, Tennessee Infantry
BIRTH: 21 April 1840 **DEATH:** 02 December 1914
MARRIED: Margaret Madewell **PARENTS:** Joseph Denton and Jemima Whitaker Hyder

~

Hyder, Joseph Nelson
LOCATION: Old Hyder Family Cemetery **RANK:** Private
COMPANY: H **REGIMENT:** 13th (8th) Tennessee Cavalry
BIRTH: 08 August 1842 **DEATH:** 26 August 1932
MARRIED: Elizabeth Ann Madewell **PENSION:** #S9012
PARENTS: Joseph Denton and Jemima Whitaker Hyder

~

Hyder, Jacob Simon (J. S., or Jac Sim)
LOCATION: Old Hyder Family Cemetery **RANK:** Private
COMPANY: D **REGIMENT:** 84th Tennessee Infantry
BIRTH: 28 April 1838 **DEATH:** 25 March 1902
MARRIED: Frances **PARENTS:** Joseph Denton and Jemima Whitaker Hyder

~

Hyder, Pleasant Milton
LOCATION: Old Hyder Family Cemetery **RANK:** Private **COMPANY:** H **REGIMENT:** 28th (Consolidated) Tennessee Infantry **BIRTH:** 09 November 1828 **DEATH:** 18 November 1898 **MARRIED:** Rachel Green, 17 March 1850. They had 9 children **PARENTS:** Joseph Denton and Jemima Whitaker Hyder **OTHER:** Prisoner of War; Captured at Tullahoma, Tennessee, 01 July 1863.

Pleasant Milton Hyder

Putnam County · Our Confederate Ancestors · 49

Jared-Huddleston Cemetery

Stanton Ridge Road, Baxter, Tennessee

Huddleston, Byrum F.
LOCATION: Jared-Huddleston Cemetery **RANK:** Private
COMPANY: K **REGIMENT:** 13th Tennessee Cavalry
BIRTH: 21 June 1843 **DEATH:** 13 April 1912
MARRIED: Ruth Jared **PARENTS:** Isaac A. and Judith Nicholas Wallace Huddleston

~

Huddleston, William Jasper
LOCATION: Jared-Huddleston Cemetery **RANK:** 1ST Sergeant
COMPANY: G **REGIMENT:** 84th Tennessee Infantry
BIRTH: 26 April 1831 **DEATH:** 08 February 1906
MARRIED: Amanda Jane Jared

~

Jared, Archibald S.
LOCATION: Jared-Huddleston Cemetery **RANK:** Private
COMPANY: K **REGIMENT:** 28th (Consolidated) Tennessee Infantry **BIRTH:** 08 May 1837 **DEATH:** 06 October 1864
PARENTS: Samuel Raulston Jared and Mary S. Scruggs Jared
OTHER: Buried at Rose Hill Cemetery near Macon, Georgia; Reinterred 20 October 1990; Full military honors

~

Jared, John
LOCATION: Jared-Huddleston Cemetery **RANK:** 2nd Lieutenant
COMPANY: G **REGIMENT:** 84th Tennessee Infantry
BIRTH: 22 February 1836
DEATH: 07 May 1911
MARRIED: Amanda Huddleston
PARENTS: Samuel Raulston and Mary S. Scruggs Jared

John Jared

W. C. Jared Cemetery

1 mile south of Gentry on Stanton Ridge

Jared, William Cleveland
LOCATION: W. C. Jared Cemetery **RANK:** Private
COMPANY: B **REGIMENT:** 7th Tennessee Infantry
BIRTH: 25 February 1836 **DEATH:** 25 December 1922
MARRIED: Matilda Hughes Baker **PENSION:** #S13231
PARENTS: William Alton and Elizabeth Elrod Jared

Unmarked Grave

Johnson Cemetery

Johnson Baptist Church, Highway 84, Cookeville/Monterey Tennessee

Henry, Jasper
LOCATION: Johnson Cemetery **RANK:** Private
COMPANY: H / D **REGIMENT:** 28th (Consolidated) Tennessee Infantry / 84th Tennessee Infantry **BIRTH:** 23 May 1832
DEATH: 10 September 1924 **MARRIED:** Mary Jane Finley
PENSION: #S15014 **PARENTS:** George W. and Lucy Lowery Henry

~

Horn, J. R.
LOCATION: Johnson Cemetery **RANK:** Corporal
COMPANY: H **REGIMENT:** 28th (Consolidated) Tennessee Infantry **BIRTH:** 16 September 1844
DEATH: 14 December 1907 **MARRIED:** Leah

~

Johnson, Samuel J.
LOCATION: Johnson Cemetery **RANK:** Captain
COMPANY: K **REGIMENT:** 25th Tennessee Infantry
BIRTH: 09 June 1843 **DEATH:** 12 January 1900
MARRIED: Frances Marchbanks Officer
OTHER: One of Immortal 600 Confederate Officers used as human shields in the seige of Charleston, South Carolina
BROTHER: Solomon Johnson, Company K, 25th Tennessee Infantry; Killed at Stones River, 31 December 1862
UDC MEMBER: Maragret H. Cordell

Officer, John H.
LOCATION: Johnson Cemetery RANK: Private COMPANY: F
REGIMENT: 13th Tennessee Cavalry BIRTH: 25 January 1818
DEATH: 06 June 1894 MARRIED: Zillah Elms

~

Suttles, Jesse
LOCATION: Johnson Cemetery RANK: Private COMPANY: I
REGIMENT: 4th (Consolidated) Tennessee Infantry
BIRTH: 15 December 1824 DEATH: Unknown

~

Smith, Abner C.
LOCATION: Johnson Cemetery RANK: Private COMPANY: E / I
REGIMENT: 1st (Colms) Battalion Tennessee Infantry /1st Louisiana Cavalry BIRTH: 30 December 1823 DEATH: 08 May 1907 MARRIED: Martha Ann Burden PENSION: #S3026

Jones Cemetery
Across from Silver Point Church

Williams, William W.
LOCATION: Jones Cemetery RANK: Private COMPANY: K
REGIMENT: 25th Tennessee Infantry
BIRTH: 27 January 1824 DEATH: 26 December 1876
MARRIED: Mary PENSION: #W5619

Joseph Jared Cemetery
Highway 70 West, Baxter, Tennessee

Ensor, William A.
LOCATION: Joseph Jared Cemetery RANK: Captain COMPANY: G
REGIMENT: 84th Tennessee Infantry BIRTH: 14 March 1825
DEATH: 12 March 1901 MARRIED: Naomi Florilla Huddleston
PARENTS: Jonathan L. and Ruth Jared Ensor
UDC MEMBERS: Frances Benedict, Maureen Patton

Unmarked Grave

Unmarked Grave

Jared, Charles Brasford
LOCATION: Joseph Jared Cemetery RANK: Private COMPANY: K
REGIMENT: 8th Tennessee Cavalry / 13th Tennessee Cavalry
BIRTH: 15 January 1834 DEATH: 07 May 1911
MARRIED: Mariah Benson PENSIONS: #S12029 and #W3978
PARENTS: Charles and Lucy Matthews Jared

~

Jared, Josiah
LOCATION: Joseph Jared Cemetery RANK: Private
COMPANY: G REGIMENT: 84th Tennessee Infantry
BIRTH: 14 September 1843 DEATH: 05 February 1880
FATHER: Joseph Jared

Judd Cemetery

Holliday Road, Cookeville, Tennesee

Elrod, William
LOCATION: Judd Cemetery
RANK: 2nd Lieutenant COMPANY: B
REGIMENT: 28th (Consolidated) Tennessee Infantry

Unmarked Grave

~

Judd, George W.
LOCATION: Judd Cemetery RANK: Sergeant COMPANY: C
REGIMENT: 8th Tennesee Cavalry / 13th Tennesee Cavalry
BIRTH: 10 January 1846, Adair County, Kentucky
DEATH: 07 April 1936 MARRIED: (1) Mollie Brown; (2) Celia Ann Pendergrass PENSION: #S7428 PARENTS: Robert and Malinda Breeding Judd

~

Judd, John
LOCATION: Judd Cemetery RANK: Private COMPANY: D
REGIMENT: 84th Tennesee Infantry BIRTH: May 1836
DEATH: August 1916 PARENTS: Nathan Jackson Judd and Rebecca Nancy Grime

Putnam County · Our Confederate Ancestors · 53

Phrasier, John A.
LOCATION: Judd Cemetery **RANK:** Private **COMPANY:** K
REGIMENT: 25th Tennessee Infantry **BIRTH:** 10 January 1846
DEATH: 02 August 1915 **MARRIED:** Harriet **PENSION:** #S785

Kemp-Allison Cemetery
On Cookeville Boat Dock Road

Allison, John H.
LOCATION: Kemp-Allison Cemetery
RANK: Captain **COMPANY:** A
REGIMENT: Allison's Squadron, Tennessee Cavalry

Allison, Robert Donald
LOCATION: Kemp-Allison Cemetery **RANK:** Colonel
COMPANY: Not listed **REGIMENT:** (Allison's Squadron) Tennessee Cavalry **BIRTH:** 25 September 1810, North Carolina **DEATH:** 15 December 1900 **MARRIED:** (1) Martha Ann Tucker; (2) Louisa D. Goodner Dowell
PARENTS: Joseph and Elizabeth Maddin Allison

Kuykendall Cemetery
Putnam County, Tennesee

Kuykendall, Newton C.
LOCATION: Kuykendall Cemetery **RANK:** Private **COMPANY:** B
REGIMENT: 28th Tennessee Infantry (2 Mountain Regiment Tennessee Volunteers) **BIRTH:** 26 March 1837
DEATH: 30 April 1911 **MARRIED:** Tappath Caruth
SON: William B. **UDC MEMBER:** Martha Willis

Draper, Ridley
LOCATION: Kuykendall Cemetery **RANK:** 1st Lieutenant
COMPANY: B **REGIMENT:** 28th (Consolidated) Tennessee Infantry **BIRTH:** 30 December 1825 **DEATH:** 10 June 1873
MARRIED: Rebecca Kuykendall **UDC MEMBER:** Martha Willis

Lane-Moody-Greenwood Cemetery
Near Waterloo on Spring Creek Bluff on Mayberry Farm

Moody, Robert F.
LOCATION: Lane-Moody-Greenwood Cemetery
RANK: Private **COMPANY:** H **REGIMENT:** 5th Tennessee Infantry
BIRTH: 24 May 1840 **DEATH:** 15 August 1933
MARRIED: Nancy Jane Gentry **PENSION:** #S707

Lee Cemetery
Shaw Branch Road, Baxter, Tennessee

Lee, James P.
LOCATION: Lee Cemetery **RANK:** Private
COMPANY: Not listed **REGIMENT:** 10th Tennessee Cavalry
BIRTH: 11 December 1829 **DEATH:** 24 March 1862

~

Lee, John M.
LOCATION: Lee Cemetery **RANK:** 2nd Sergeant
COMPANY: A **REGIMENT:** 13th Tennesee Cavalry
BIRTH: 03 February 1844 **DEATH:** 25 February 1891
MARRIED: Martha Montgomery

James H. Lee Cemetery
On Highway 70 west of Baxter Crossroads

Lee, James H.
LOCATION: James H. Lee Cemetery **RANK:** Corporal
COMPANY: K **REGIMENT:** 62nd Tennessee Mounted Infantry / (Rowan's Regiment) 80th Tennessee Infantry
BIRTH: 23 August 1845 **DEATH:** 13 May 1904

Unmarked Grave

Unmarked Grave

Putnam County • Our Confederate Ancestors • 55

Leftwich Cemetery

Leftwich Ridge Road, Baxter, Tennesee

Carlen, William B.

LOCATION: Leftwich Cemetery **RANK:** Captain **COMPANY:** A
REGIMENT: 4th (Hamilton's) Battalion Tennessee Cavalry
BIRTH: 07 May 1824 **DEATH:** 08 August 1901 **MARRIED:** Sarah
PENSION: #S2299

Lewis Family Cemetery

Highway to Cookeville, Tennesee

Lewis, William P.

LOCATION: Lewis Family Cemetery **RANK:** Captain
COMPANY: D **REGIMENT:** 53rd Tennessee Infantry
BIRTH: 18 March 1834 **DEATH:** 11 March 1884
MARRIED: Elizabeth Fox **OTHER:** Marker is in the Lewis Family Cemetery; William P. Lewis is buried in the Rob Draper Cemetery in Gainesboro, Tennessee.

Lovelady Cemetery

Lovelady Road, Cookeville, Tennessee

Farris, John

LOCATION: Lovelady Cemetery **RANK:** Private **COMPANY:** H
REGIMENT: 8th (Dibrell's) Tennessee Cavalry / 13th Tennessee Cavalry **BIRTH:** 20 February 1828 **DEATH:** 14 April 1914
MARRIED: Mary **PENSIONS:** #S5009 and #W5420

Maxwell, David Mock

LOCATION: Lovelady Cemetery **RANK:** Private **COMPANY:** H
REGIMENT: 13th Tennessee Cavalry **BIRTH:** c. 1828
DEATH: Unknown **MARRIED:** Nancy **PENSION:** #W685

Nickles, James M.

LOCATION: Lovelady Cemetery **RANK:** Private
COMPANY: H **REGIMENT:** 8th (Dibrell's) Tennessee Cavary
BIRTH: 29 June 1838 **DEATH:** 26 December 1925
MARRIED: Synthia **PENSION:** #S7650

Unmarked Grave

Maddux Cemetery

East of Buffalo Valley on W. Shanks Farm

Maddux, William C.

LOCATION: Maddux Cemetery **RANK:** Private **COMPANY:** F
REGIMENT: 25th Tennessee Infantry **BIRTH:** 1846 **DEATH:** 1865
PARENTS: Snowden Horton and Lucy Ann Leftwich Maddux

Unmarked Grave

Marlow Cemetery

McBroom Branch Road, Baxter, Tennessee

Alcorn, Richard A.

LOCATION: Marlow Cemetery **RANK:** Private
COMPANY: K **REGIMENT:** 17th Tennessee Infantry
BIRTH: 14 September 1836 **DEATH:** 21 August 1914
MARRIED Nancy R. Lewis **PENSION:** #S1069
PARENTS: Richard and Mary Blackburn Alcorn

Marlow, James

LOCATION: Marlow Cemetery **RANK:** Private
COMPANY: E / K **REGIMENT:** 8th Tennessee Infantry / 17th Tennessee Infantry **BIRTH:** 1834 **DEATH:** 27 January 1875
MARRIED Sarah / Sally McGhee Williams, 1828–1915
PENSION: #W970 **FATHER:** Thomas Marlow

Maxwell Cemetery

Baxter, Tennessee

Maxwell, David W.

LOCATION: Maxwell Cemetery **RANK:** Private
COMPANY: K **REGIMENT:** 16th Tennessee Infantry
BIRTH: 05 March 1822 **DEATH:** 24 August 1869
MARRIED: Mary Elizabeth Shanks **PARENTS:** Samuel and Martha Patton Maxwell

Minton, William Carroll
LOCATION: Maxwell Cemetery **RANK:** Private **COMPANY:** G
REGIMENT: 22nd (Barteau's) Tennessee Cavalry
BIRTH: 15 March 1832 **DEATH:** 09 October 1920
MARRIED: (1) Mary Elizaberth House; (2) Mary Frances Pritchard **PENSIONS:** #S13132 and #W7627

McBroom Cemetery
Cookeville, Tennessee (near Bloomington Springs)

Bowen, Henry Porter
LOCATION: McBroom Cemetery **RANK:** Private
COMPANY: D **REGIMENT:** 2nd Tennessee Infantry
BIRTH: 1846 **DEATH:** 21 March 1937
MARRIED: (1) Susan Cox; (2) Mary Margaret Julian

~

Bowington, John B.
LOCATION: McBroom Cemetery **RANK:** Private **COMPANY:** H
REGIMENT: 2nd Tennessee Infantry **BIRTH:** 04 July 1817
DEATH: 17 June 1912 **MARRIED:** Margaret

~

Cowen, George W.
LOCATION: McBroom Cemetery **RANK:** Corporal **COMPANY:** E
REGIMENT: 28th (Consolidated) Tennessee Infantry
BIRTH: 16 November 1843 **DEATH:** 01 March 1915
MARRIED: Martha, b. 1844 **PENSION:** #W5810

Andrew McDonald Cemetery
On Little Indian Creek on Oval Herron Farm

McDonald, Andrew
LOCATION: Andrew McDonald Cemetery **RANK:** Not listed
COMPANY: Not listed **REGIMENT:** Hamilton's Battalion Cavalry **BIRTH:** 04 December 1834 **DEATH:** 09 March 1928
MARRIED: Mary Jane Shaw **PENSION:** #S16364
PARENTS: James Porter and Susan Edelman McDonald

Unmarked Grave

Messenger Cemetery
Putnam County

Messenger, Samuel M.
LOCATION: Messenger Cemetery **RANK:** Private **COMPANY:** A **REGIMENT:** 22nd Tennessee Infantry **BIRTH:** 25 March 1831, Patrick County, Virginia **DEATH:** 04 November 1904 **MARRIED:** (1) Pelina Turner; (2) Caroline M. Carter; (3) Canzada Breeding **PENSION:** #S5565 **PARENTS:** Daniel and Martha Varner Messenger

Mills Wiggins Cemetery
In woods off Burgess Falls Road, Cookeville, Tennessee

Wiggins, Tillman
LOCATION: Mills WigginsCemetery **RANK:** Private **COMPANY:** E **REGIMENT:** 25th Tennessee Infantry **BIRTH:** 20 October 1844 **DEATH:** 23 November 1899

Morgan Pippin Cemetery
Old Gainsboro Grade, Cookeville, Tennessee

Montgomery, Robert
LOCATION: Morgan Pippin Cemetery **RANK:** Private **COMPANY:** E **REGIMENT:** 28th Tennessee Infantry **BIRTH:** 18 May 1833 **DEATH:** 23 May 1889

~

Pippin, Andrew
LOCATION: Morgan Pippin Cemetery **RANK:** Private **COMPANY:** B **REGIMENT:** 28th Tennessee Infantry **BIRTH:** 01 March 1825 **DEATH:** 09 January 1913

~

Pippin, Simeon
LOCATION: Morgan Pippin Cemetery **RANK:** 1st Sergeant **COMPANY:** K **REGIMENT:** 28th (Consolidated) Tennessee Infantry **BIRTH:** 02 May 1832 **DEATH:** 05 February 1915 **MARRIED** Nancy

Unmarked Grave

Nash Cemetery
Cookeville Boat Dock Road, Cookeville, Tennessee

Nash, Newton H.
LOCATION: Nash Cemetery **RANK:** Private **COMPANY:** A
REGIMENT: 8th Tennessee Infantry **BIRTH:** 03 December 1838
DEATH: 09 May 1916 **MARRIED:** America

New Home Baptist Church Cemetery
Boma/Baxter, Tennessee

Brown, W. A.
LOCATION: New Home Baptist Church Cemetery
RANK: Corporal **COMPANY:** F **REGIMENT:** 8th (Smith's)
Tennessee Cavalry **BIRTH:** 21 April 1846
DEATH: 05 August 1928

~

Coleman, B. F.
LOCATION: New Home Baptist Church Cemetery
RANK: Private **COMPANY:** B **REGIMENT:** 13th Tennessee Infantry
BIRTH: 15 September 1818 **DEATH:** 29 December 1928
MARRIED: Mary Jane

Norris Cemetery
Paran Road, Cookeville, Tennessee

Norris, David M.
LOCATION: Norris Cemetery **RANK:** Private **COMPANY:** E
REGIMENT: 13th / 8th (Dibrell's) Cavalry **BIRTH:** 03 November
1841 **DEATH:** 05 April 1917 **PENSION:** #S14831

Oddfellow Cemetery
Baxter, Tennessee

Smotherman, James H.
LOCATION: Oldfellow Cemetery **RANK:** Private **COMPANY:** G
REGIMENT: 44th Tennessee Infantry **BIRTH:** May 1844 **DEATH:**
Unknown **MARRIED:** Malinda O. Maxwell **PENSION:** #S12188

Unmarked Grave

Old Flatt Creek Cemetery

Swift, Harvey L.
LOCATION: Old Flatt Creek Cemetery **RANK:** Private
COMPANY: G **REGIMENT:** 13th Tennessee Cavalry

Unmarked Grave

Old Zion Cemetery
Silver Point, Old Zion Church

Cass, James Milas
LOCATION: Old Zion Cemetery **RANK:** Not listed
COMPANY: Not listed **REGIMENT:** 25th Tennessee Infantry
BIRTH: 1845, North Carolina **DEATH:** 1936
MARRIED: Patricia M.

Unmarked Grave

Paran Cemetery
Paran Road, Algood, Tennessee

Caruthers, Benjamin F.
LOCATION: Paran Cemetery **RANK:** Private **COMPANY:** Not listed **REGIMENT:** 28th (Consolidated) Tennessee Infantry
BIRTH: 28 August 1834 **DEATH:** 30 September 1903
MARRIED: Margaret Ward **PENSION:** #S2356

Judd, Andrew J.
LOCATION: Paran Cemetery **RANK:** Private **COMPANY:** E
REGIMENT: 13th / 8th Tennessee Cavalry
BIRTH: 03 January 1839 **DEATH:** 09 June 1907
PENSION: #S6875

Pearson Cemetery
Putnam County

Thompson, William H.
LOCATION: Pearson Cemetery **RANK:** Private
COMPANY: C / K **REGIMENT:** 13th / 8th Tennessee Cavalry
BIRTH: 05 January 1838 **DEATH:** 24 March 1914
MARRIED: Frances Pearson **PENSION:** #S7891
PARENTS: Esquire Looney and Arena Sarah Davis Thompson
BROTHERS: Newton, Thomas C., James Franklin, E. L.; all the Thompson brothers werein the Confederate Army

Putnam County · Our Confederate Ancestors · 61

Phillips Cemetery
Phillips Cemetery Road, Algood, Tennessee

Sliger, William L.
LOCATION: Phillips Cemetery **RANK:** Sergeant **COMPANY:** E / H
REGIMENT: 25th Tennessee Infantry / 13th Tennessee Cavalry
BIRTH: 06 May 1846 **DEATH:** 05 December 1923
MARRIED: Pelina Carr **PENSION:** #S7210
PARENTS: John C. and Lucinda Wilhite Sliger

Quarles Cemetery
Old Walton Road, Cookeville, Tennessee

Quarles, Stephen D.
LOCATION: Quarles Cemetery **RANK:** Private **COMPANY:** H
REGIMENT: 13th Tennessee Cavalry **BIRTH:** 13 May 1843
DEATH: 10 March 1920 **MARRIED:** (1) Zerelda M. Jones; (2) Mary Ann King **PENSIONS:** #S6834 and #W8737, #W8045
PARENTS: William H. and Ruth Hyder Quarles

~

Quarles, William Braxton
LOCATION: Quarles Cemetery **RANK:** Private **COMPANY:** H
REGIMENT: 13th Tennessee Cavalry **BIRTH:** 31 July 1842
DEATH: 08 August 1916 **MARRIED:** Celia Ann White
PENSIONS: #S8696 and #W8750
PARENTS: John A. and Mary Hunter Quarles

Rhea Cemetery
Ditty Road, Cookeville, Tennessee

Mitchell, James H.
LOCATION: Rhea Cemetery **RANK:** Private **COMPANY:** D
REGIMENT: 17th Tennessee Infantry **BIRTH:** 13 November 1844
DEATH: 20 April 1916 **MARRIED:** Mary **PENSION:** #S8022

Roberson Cemetery
Cherry Creek Road, Cookeville, Tennessee

Clark, I. P.
LOCATION: Roberson Cemetery **RANK:** Sergeant
COMPANY: H **REGIMENT:** 9th Tennessee Infantry
BIRTH: 14 February 1825 **DEATH:** 24 July 1899
MARRIED: (1) Dicy; (2) Mary

~

Daniel, William N.
LOCATION: Roberson Cemetery **RANK:** Private **COMPANY:** H
REGIMENT: 8th Tennessee Cavalry / 13th Tennessee Cavalry
BIRTH: 28 December 1837 **DEATH:** 23 December 1897
MARRIED: Mary **PENSIONS:** #S630 and #W2139
PARENTS: William and Cassa Daniel

~

Isom, Elizirah
LOCATION: Roberson Cemetery **RANK:** Private
COMPANY: I **REGIMENT:** 8th Tennessee Infantry
BIRTH: 28 June 1825 **DEATH:** 16 June 1901

~

Long, William H.
LOCATION: Roberson Cemetery **RANK:** Private **COMPANY:** H
REGIMENT: 13th Tennessee Cavalry **BIRTH:** 25 January 1841
DEATH: 21 August 1883 **MARRIED:** Almira

~

Roberson, Pleasant Prior
LOCATION: Roberson Cemetery **RANK:** Sergeant
COMPANY: E / D **REGIMENT:** 84th Tennessee Infantry / 28th (Consolidated) Tennessee Infantry **BIRTH:** 1835
DEATH: 23 October 1888 **MARRIED:** Lucy A. Murphy
PENSION: #W1849 **PARENTS:** Thomas and Susannah Pryor Roberson

Rocky Point Cemetery

Rocky Point Road, Cookeville/Monterey, Tennessee

Claghorn, Wyatt

LOCATION: Rocky Point Cemetery **RANK:** Private **COMPANY:** I **REGIMENT:** 34th Tennessee Infantry / 4th Tennessee Cavalry **BIRTH:** 13 September 1827 **DEATH:** 12 February 1911

~

Wiser, James M.

LOCATION: Rocky Point Cemetery **RANK:** Private **COMPANY:** C **REGIMENT:** 13th Tennessee Cavalry / 8th Tennessee Cavalry **BIRTH:** 23 January 1842 **DEATH:** 18 July 1923 **MARRIED:** Elizabeth Rockhold

Rodgers Road Cemetery

Bryant Ridge Road, Baxter, Tennessee

Elrod, Andrew J.

LOCATION: Rodgers Road Cemetery **RANK:** Private **COMPANY:** B / I **REGIMENT:** 84th Tennessee Infantry / 28th (Consolidated) Tennessee Infantry **BIRTH:** 12 September 1836 **DEATH:** 04 April 1904 **MARRIED:** (1) Nancy; (2) Sabra Jane Richardson **PENSIONS:** #S1302, #W5010 **PARENTS:** William Elrod, Jr. and Mary E. Elrod **OTHER:** Brother John Elrod was killed in the War.

~

Rodgers, Benjamin F.

LOCATION: Rodgers Road Cemetery **RANK:** Private **COMPANY:** F **REGIMENT:** 28th (Consolidated) Tennessee Infantry **BIRTH:** 27 February 1832 **DEATH:** 20 April 1912 **MARRIED:** Mary Adeline Fuqua

Salem Cemetery
Salem Road, Cookeville, Tennessee

Buck, Isaac N.
LOCATION: Salem Cemetery **RANK:** Not listed
COMPANY: Not listed **REGIMENT:** Not listed
BIRTH: 28 July 1838 **DEATH:** 24 May 1917
MARRIED: (1) Eliza J. France; (2) Nancy Ann Wilmoth
PENSION: #W9418 **PARENTS:** Isaac and Mary Simmerly Buck

~

Buck, Jesse H.
LOCATION: Salem Cemetery **RANK:** Sergeant **COMPANY:** H
REGIMENT: 13th Tennessee Cavalry / 8th Tennessee Cavalry
BIRTH: 15 December 1837 **DEATH:** 23 February 1930
MARRIED: Samantha Pippin (b. 15 August 1840 – d. 3 March 1902) **PENSION:** #S11454 **PARENTS:** Jonathan, Sr. and Elizabeth Barnett Buck

~

Burgess, James M.
LOCATION: Salem Cemetery **RANK:** Sergeant
COMPANY: H **REGIMENT:** 13th Tennessee Cavalry / 8th Tennessee Cavalry **BIRTH:** 23 August 1839
DEATH: 09 February 1917 **MARRIED:** (1) Nancy W. Huddleston; (2) Rebecca Ann **PENSION:** #W6660
PARENTS: Joel and Rutha Allison Burgess

~

Gracey, Crockett D.
LOCATION: Salem Cemetery **RANK:** Private
COMPANY: D **REGIMENT:** 13th Tennessee Cavalry
BIRTH: 01 August 1836 **DEATH:** 20 January 1894
MARRIED: Alta Moore (b. 02 November 1858 – d. 14 January 1916) **PENSION:** #W3737 **PARENTS:** Hugh and Mary Jones Gracey

Huddleston, Alvin C.

LOCATION: Salem Cemetery **RANK:** Private **COMPANY:** C
REGIMENT: 8th Tennessee Cavalry / 13th Tennessee Cavalry
BIRTH: 05 March 1840 **DEATH:** 18 August 1906
MARRIED: Elizabeth Robinson **PENSION:** #S2012
PARENTS: Hugh Greene and Malissa Taylor Huddleston

~

Huddleston, David D.

LOCATION: Salem Cemetery **RANK:** Private **COMPANY:** C
REGIMENT: 8th Tennessee Cavalry / 13th Tennessee Cavalry
BIRTH: 22 December 1842 **DEATH:** 08 October 1906
MARRIED: Eunice Bennett **PENSIONS:** #S7485 and #W3706
PARENTS: John L. and Lucilla Taylor Huddleston

~

Huddleston, John P.

LOCATION: Salem Cemetery **RANK:** Private **COMPANY:** F
REGIMENT: 25th Tennessee Infantry **BIRTH:** 30 January 1838
DEATH: 03 January 1931 **MARRIED:** Sarah Caroline Hyder / Roena Huddleston **PENSIONS:** #S7979 and #W10049
PARENTS: John L. and Rebecca Moore Huddleston

~

Nicholas, Henry M.

LOCATION: Salem Cemetery **RANK:** Private **COMPANY:** H
REGIMENT: 8th Tennessee Cavalry / 13th Tennessee Cavalry
BIRTH: 26 March 1833 **DEATH:** 10 September 1913
MARRIED: Sarah Ann Peek **PENSIONS:** #S11457 and #W6158
PARENTS: Thomas T. and Susannah Travis Nicholas

~

Peek, Robert

LOCATION: Salem Cemetery **RANK:** Private **COMPANY:** I
REGIMENT: 25th Tennessee Infantry **BIRTH:** 28 March 1836
DEATH: 11 August 1919 **MARRIED:** (1) Nancy Jane Burgess; (2) Adaline Stafford **PENSIONS:** #S15011 and #W10364
PARENTS: Robert and Judith Fowler Peek

Unknown

LOCATION: Salem Cemetery **RANK:** Not listed
COMPANY: Not listed **REGIMENT:** Not listed
BIRTH: Unknown **DEATH:** 1863

~

Whitson, Jeremiah M.

LOCATION: Salem Cemetery **RANK:** Private **COMPANY:** H
REGIMENT: 13th Tennessee Cavalry **BIRTH:** 10 November 1834
DEATH: 27 October 1917 **MARRIED:** Sallie Barnes (b. 24 April 1837 – d. 14 November 1925)

Sand Springs

Highway 70 North, Monterey, Tennessee

Brogden, J. S.

LOCATION: Sand Springs Cemetery **RANK:** Private
COMPANY: I **REGIMENT:** 13th Tennessee Cavalry
BIRTH: 19 June 1835 **DEATH:** 27 January 1913
MARRIED: Catherine

~

Burnett, James

LOCATION: Sand Springs Cemetery **RANK:** Private
COMPANY: H **REGIMENT:** 28th (Consolidated) Tennessee Infantry **BIRTH:** 18 October 1836 **DEATH:** 23 September 1903
MARRIED: Luvsey (b. 25 March 1835 – 2d. 6 March 1903)

~

Farley, John

LOCATION: Sand Springs Cemetery **RANK:** Sergeant
COMPANY: H **REGIMENT:** 8th Tennessee Cavalry / 13th Tennessee Cavalry **BIRTH:** 03 May 1831
DEATH: 23 February 1904 **MARRIED:** Celia Dalton (13 April 1847–26 December 1935) **PENSION:** #S8197

Ford, Abraham
LOCATION: Sand Springs Cemetery **RANK:** Captain
COMPANY: K **REGIMENT:** 25th Tennessee Infantry
BIRTH: 03 January 1821 **DEATH:** 14 December 1890
MARRIED: Nancy **PROFESSION:** Baptist Minister
PARENT: John F. Ford

~

Ford, Thomas W.
LOCATION: Sand Springs Cemetery **RANK:** Private **COMPANY:** K
REGIMENT: 25th Tennessee Infantry **BIRTH:** 25 January 1844
DEATH: 12 January 1916 **MARRIED:** Martha Margaret Myatt
PARENTS: Abraham and Nancy Womack Ford

~

Henry, George W.
LOCATION: Sand Springs Cemetery **RANK:** Private
COMPANY: K **REGIMENT:** 25th Tennessee Infantry
BIRTH: 06 October 1841 **DEATH:** 08 November 1915
MARRIED: Rachel E. Williams, (b. 20 December 1843 – d. 01 August 1917) **PENSION:** #W6197 **PARENTS:** Lidgard F. and Nancy Thomas Henry

~

Howard W. S.
LOCATION: Sand Springs Cemetery **RANK:** Private
COMPANY: D / B **REGIMENT:** 25th Tennessee Infantry
BIRTH: 12 July 1822 **DEATH:** 06 April 1906 **MARRIED:** Nancy

~

Jackson, James
LOCATION: Sand Springs Cemetery **RANK:** Private
COMPANY: A / K **REGIMENT:** 28th (Consolidated) Infantry / 13th Tennessee Cavalry **BIRTH:** 06 March 1842
DEATH: 25 December 1895 **MARRIED:** Jane

Jackson, John W.

LOCATION: Sand Springs Cemetery **RANK:** Private **COMPANY:** H **REGIMENT:** 28th Tennessee Infantry **BIRTH:** 10 March 1832 **DEATH:** 01 August 1911 **MARRIED:** (1) Catherine (b. 05 April 1851 – d. 27 January 1902); (2) Mahala (b. 08 May 1834 – d. 10 November 1889) **PENSIONS:** #S521 and #S1319

~

Jackson, Levi

LOCATION: Sand Springs Cemetery **RANK:** Private **COMPANY:** K **REGIMENT:** (Nixon's) Tennessee Cavalry / 25th Tennessee Infantry **BIRTH:** 06 March 1840 **DEATH:** 17 June 1923 **MARRIED:** Luzany (19 June 1842–15 May 1899)

~

Neal, John

LOCATION: Sand Springs Cemetery **RANK:** Private **COMPANY:** K **REGIMENT:** 8th Tennessee Infantry **BIRTH:** 25 January 1817 **DEATH:** 12 January 1893 **MARRIED:** Theney Ray

~

Neal, W. R.

LOCATION: Sand Springs Cemetery **RANK:** Private **COMPANY:** G **REGIMENT:** 32nd Tennessee Infantry **BIRTH:** 16 December 1835 **DEATH:** 26 November 1898 **MARRIED:** Rebecca

~

Roberson, Charles

LOCATION: Sand Springs Cemetery **RANK:** Not listed **COMPANY:** K **REGIMENT:** 25th Tennessee Infantry **BIRTH:** 16 April 1862 **DEATH:** 21 November 1894 **MARRIED:** Sarah Roberson **CHILDREN:** George, Andrew, Noah, Chrissy, Rena, and Mary

Charles Roberson

Robinson, Preston
LOCATION: Sand Springs Cemetery **RANK:** Not listed
COMPANY: K **REGIMENT:** 25th Tennessee Infantry
BIRTH: 20 June 1829 **DEATH:** 14 February 1884
MARRIED: Jane

~

Sparks, Solomon
LOCATION: Sand Springs Cemetery **RANK:** Private
COMPANY: H **REGIMENT:** 28 Tennessee Infantry
BIRTH: September 1829 **DEATH:** December 1912
MARRIED: (1) Sarah; (2) Malidda Jackson; (3) Permelia Jackson **PENSION:** #S6595

~

Walker, Abraham Washington
LOCATION: Sand Springs Cemetery **RANK:** Sergeant
COMPANY: F **REGIMENT:** 28 Tennessee Infantry
BIRTH: 14 February 1836 **DEATH:** 03 August 1906
MARRIED: Martha Jane Myatt **PENSION:** #S7436, #W4220
PARENTS: William and Mary Conaster Walker

~

Welch, Alexander
LOCATION: Sand Springs Cemetery **RANK:** Sergeant
COMPANY: K **REGIMENT:** 25th Tennessee Infantry
BIRTH: 29 November 1842 **DEATH:** 30 June 1915
MARRIED: Catherine Lee **PENSION:** #S3759, #W5794

~

Welch, James Thomas
LOCATION: Sand Springs Cemetery **RANK:** Private **COMPANY:** F
REGIMENT: 25th Tennessee Infantry **BIRTH:** 25 February 1844
DEATH: 29 February 1920 **MARRIED:** Nancy

Whitaker, John H.

LOCATION: Sand Springs Cemetery **RANK:** Not listed
COMPANY: K **REGIMENT:** 4th Tennessee Infantry
BIRTH: 29 November 1840 **DEATH:** 15 March 1922
MARRIED: (1) Jane Catherine Miller; (2) Mary Elizabeth Roberson **PENSIONS:** #S13921, #W8508
PARENTS: James Madison and Nancy Henry Whitaker

Shady Grove Cemetery

Shady Grove Road, Monterey, Tennessee

Ray, George W.

LOCATION: Shady Grove Cemetery **RANK:** Private **COMPANY:** D
REGIMENT: 25th Tennessee Infantry **BIRTH:** June 1839
DEATH: 20 November 1911 **PENSION:** #S6835

Romines, Isaac

LOCATION: Shady Grove Cemetery **RANK:** Private
COMPANY: C **REGIMENT:** 13th Tennessee Cavalry
BIRTH: 09 June 1832 **DEATH:** 23 June 1915 **MARRIED:** Martha
OTHER: Captured at Rock Island, Tennessee

Tinch, A. G.

LOCATION: Shady Grove Cemetery **RANK:** Corporal
COMPANY: K and H **REGIMENT:** 25th Tennessee Infantry
BIRTH: 25 December 1822 **DEATH:** 15 July 1885

Whiteaker, James M.

LOCATION: Shady Grove Cemetery **RANK:** Private
COMPANY: D **REGIMENT:** 84th Tennessee Infantry / 25th Tennessee Infantry **BIRTH:** 04 April 1840
DEATH: 03 January 1920 **MARRIED:** Nancy Hunter
PENSION: #S15434 **PARENTS:** David and Nancy Rogers Whitaker

Putnam County · Our Confederate Ancestors · 71

Shipley Cemetery
Shipley Road, Cookeville, Tennessee

King, Joseph C.
LOCATION: Shipley Cemetery **RANK:** Private **COMPANY:** F
REGIMENT: 8th Tennessee Infantry **BIRTH:** 10 September 1825
DEATH: 03 January 1905 **MARRIED:** Fannie Rebecca Quarles
PENSIONS: #S2461, #W1274

Sliger Cemetery
South Maple, Cookeville, Tennessee

Sliger, Elias
LOCATION: Sliger Cemetery **RANK:** Not listed **COMPANY:** Not listed **REGIMENT:** Not listed **BIRTH:** 27 January 1834
DEATH: 10 October 1921 **MARRIED:** Mary Ann Welch
DAUGHTER: Inda Bell Sliger **GRANDDAUGHTER:** Delia Chaffin
GREAT-GRANDSON: Walter Anderson **PARENTS:** John C. and Lucinda Wilhite Sliger

~

Sliger, John W.
LOCATION: Sliger Cemetery **RANK:** Private **COMPANY:** E
REGIMENT: 25th Tennessee Infantry **BIRTH:** 14 February 1836
DEATH: 21 November 1912 **MARRIED:** Elizabeth Wassom
PENSION: #S7525 **PARENTS:** Charles and Mary M. Sliger

~

Sliger, Thomas L.
LOCATION: Sliger Cemetery **RANK:** Private
COMPANY: F **REGIMENT:** 28th (Consolidated) Tennessee Infantry **BIRTH:** 07 February 1841 **DEATH:** 26 December 1912
MARRIED: Sarah M. Mills **PARENTS:** John C. and Lucinda Wilhite Sliger

Smellage Cemetery
Near Boma, Baxter, Tennessee

Anderson, Riley W.
LOCATION: Smellage Cemetery **RANK:** Private **COMPANY:** F
REGIMENT: 25th Tennessee Infantry **BIRTH:** 19 December 1839
DEATH: 12 November 1885 **MARRIED:** Michael Elizabeth Alexander **PARENTS:** Garland and Sarah Jones Anderson

~

Butler, William L.
LOCATION: Smellage Cemetery **RANK:** Private **COMPANY:** I
REGIMENT: 25th Tennessee Infantry **BIRTH:** 27 July 1815
DEATH: November 1865, Ashley County, Kentucky
MARRIED: Elizabeth Mathas, 01 March 1842, Halifax County, Virginia **PENSION:** #W665

~

Carr, Zebidee C.
LOCATION: Smellage Cemetery **RANK:** Private **COMPANY:** C
REGIMENT: 8th (Smith's) Tennessee Cavalry
BIRTH: 24 April 1845 **DEATH:** 06 November 1908
MARRIED: Marry Eliza Kinnaird, d. 1915 **PENSION:** #S9420
PARENTS: Elijah and Elizabeth Lollar Carr

~

Fisher, James Harvey
LOCATION: Smellage Cemetery **RANK:** Private **COMPANY:** F
REGIMENT: 16th Tennessee Infantry **BIRTH:** 1834
DEATH: December 1861

~

Taylor, James W.
LOCATION: Smellage Cemetery **RANK:** Private **COMPANY:** C
REGIMENT: 14th Tennessee Cavalry **BIRTH:** 06 July 1839
DEATH: 20 August 1928 **MARRIED:** Martha

Unmarked Grave

Thompson, Esquire L.

LOCATION: Smellage Cemetery **RANK:** Private **COMPANY:** K
REGIMENT: 13th Tennessee Cavalry / 8th (Dibrell's) Tennessee Cavalry **BIRTH:** 26 May 1839 **DEATH:** 21 January 1926
MARRIED: Naomi B. Jared **PENSION:** #S6966
PARENTS: Esquire Looney and Arena Sarah Davis Thompson

Smith Chapel
Cookeville, Tennessee

Mabery, Joshua M.

LOCATION: Smith Chapel Cemetery **RANK:** Private
COMPANY: C **REGIMENT:** 13th Tennessee Cavalry
BIRTH: 23 November 1839 **DEATH:** 12 August 1901
MARRIED: Martha

~

McDaniel, Thomas F.

LOCATION: Smith Chapel Cemetery **RANK:** Private **COMPANY:** B
REGIMENT: 5th Tennessee Cavalry **BIRTH:** 1839 **DEATH:** 1903
MARRIED: Nancy Parilla Davis (b. 1848 – d. 1940)
PENSION: #W3510

~

Merritt, Larkin

LOCATION: Smith Chapel Cemetery **RANK:** Private **COMPANY:** I
REGIMENT: 25th Tennessee Infantry **BIRTH:** 1812 **DEATH:** 1897
MARRIED: Mary Ann Smith **PENSION:** #S885

~

Owen, Milton M.

LOCATION: Smith Chapel Cemetery **RANK:** Sergeant
COMPANY: F **REGIMENT:** 16th Tennessee Infantry
BIRTH: 07 September 1840 **DEATH:** 05 April 1922
MARRIED: (1) Margaret; (2) Henrietta Dowell
PENSION: #S10090 **PARENTS:** Wiley U. and Nancy Smith Owen

Smith, Matthew S.
LOCATION: Smith Chapel Cemetery **RANK:** 1st Sergeant
COMPANY: K **REGIMENT:** 16th Tennessee Infantry
BIRTH: 27 July 1821 **DEATH:** 28 July 1907
MARRIED: Mary Ann Matheney **PENSION:** #S717
PARENTS: John and Elizabeth Sims Smith

Smyrna Cemetery
Highway 135, Cookeville, Tennessee

Bartlett, Nathan
LOCATION: Smyrna Cemetery **RANK:** Corporal
COMPANY: K **REGIMENT:** 13th Tennessee Cavalry
BIRTH: 01 April 1831 **DEATH:** 07 July 1897
MARRIED: Mary A. (12 May 1833–18 May 1915)

~

Cole, William A.
LOCATION: Smyrna Cemetery **RANK:** Corporal **COMPANY:** D
REGIMENT: 29th Tennessee Infantry **BIRTH:** 05 February 1833
DEATH: 27 March 1904

~

Dowell, George R.
LOCATION: Smyrna Cemetery **RANK:** Private **COMPANY:** K
REGIMENT: 13th Tennessee Cavalry **BIRTH:** 07 March 1839
DEATH: 06 October 1894 **MARRIED:** Sarah Ann Bartlett
PENSION: #W4798 **PARENTS:** John M. and Nancy Elizabeth Terry Dowell

~

Dowell, Joseph L.
LOCATION: Smyrna Cemetery **RANK:** Private **COMPANY:** B
REGIMENT: 28th Tennessee Infantry **BIRTH:** 16 August 1834
DEATH: 29 May 1907 **MARRIED:** Frances

Dowell, Matisson N.
LOCATION: Smyrna Cemetery **RANK:** Private **COMPANY:** B
REGIMENT: 28th Tennessee Infantry
BIRTH: 01 September 1842 **DEATH:** Unknown

Unmarked Grave

Gilliam, W. S.
LOCATION: Smyrna Cemetery **RANK:** Private **COMPANY:** K
REGIMENT: 28th Tennessee Infantry **BIRTH:** Unknown
DEATH: Unknown

Terry, Elijah W.
LOCATION: Smyrna Cemetery **RANK:** Captain **COMPANY:** K
REGIMENT: 13th Tennessee Cavalry **BIRTH:** 07 April 1823
DEATH: 05 July 1901 **MARRIED:** (1) Lizzie Anderson; (2) Angelina Denton **DAUGHTER:** Elretta **PENSION:** W1350
PARENTS: Curtis and Elizabeth Kuykendall Terry

Terry, John
LOCATION: Smyrna Cemetery **RANK:** Private **COMPANY:** K / K
REGIMENT: 28th Tennessee Infantry / 13th Tennessee Cavalry
BIRTH: 19 June 1815 **DEATH:** 04 December 1885

Terry, Roland
LOCATION: Smyrna Cemetery **RANK:** Private **COMPANY:** K
REGIMENT: 13th Tennessee Cavalry **BIRTH:** 06 December 1831
DEATH: 10 April 1899 **MARRIED:** Sarah Ann

Terry, William A.
LOCATION: Smyrna Cemetery **RANK:** Private **COMPANY:** B
REGIMENT: 28th Tennessee Infantry **BIRTH:** 24 August 1832
DEATH: 07 January 1913 **MARRIED:** Martha

Terry, W. C.
LOCATION: Smyrna Cemetery **RANK:** Private
COMPANY: I **REGIMENT:** 25th Tennessee Infantry
BIRTH: 20 August 1842 **DEATH:** 17 September 1915

~

Terry, W. J.
LOCATION: Smyrna Cemetery **RANK:** Private **COMPANY:** I
REGIMENT: 25th Tennessee Infantry **BIRTH:** 20 October 1834
DEATH: 26 November 1914 **MARRIED:** Mary

~

Thompson, Newton J.
LOCATION: Smyrna Cemetery **RANK:** 1st Lieutenant
COMPANY: D **REGIMENT:** 1st (Colm's) Battalion, Tennessee Infantry **BIRTH:** 26 January 1834 **DEATH:** 30 November 1864, "Fell at Franklin, Tennessee" **PARENTS:** Squire Looney and Arena Davis Thompson

~

Thompson, Thomas C.
LOCATION: Smyrna Cemetery **RANK:** Private **COMPANY:** K
REGIMENT: 16th Tennessee Infantry **BIRTH:** 24 April 1835
DEATH: 08 October 1862 **MARRIED:** Martha Davis
PARENTS: Squire Looney and Arena Davis Thompson
OTHER: Killed at Perryville, Kentucky

~

Welch, James A.
LOCATION: Smyrna Cemetery **RANK:** Sergeant
COMPANY: F **REGIMENT:** 25th Tennessee Infantry
BIRTH: 21 November 1841 **DEATH:** 11 October 1918
MARRIED: Rebecca Thompson **CHILDREN:** Newton, Whitley, Lee, Frances, Sallie, Byram, Grover, Avery **PENSION:** #S6193
PARENTS: James Thomas and Sarah Conway Welch

Stamps Cemetery
Brotherton Road, Monterey, Tennessee

Neal, B. J.
LOCATION: Stamps Cemetery **RANK:** Private
COMPANY: K **REGIMENT:** 25th Tennessee Infantry
BIRTH: 13 September 1842 **DEATH:** 22 March 1904

Stewart Cemetery
Bennett Road, Cookeville, Tennessee

Grider, William
LOCATION: Stewart Cemetery
RANK: Private **COMPANY:** F
REGIMENT: 16th Tennessee Infantry **BIRTH:** 21 February 1836 **DEATH:** 05 March 1909
MARRIED: Nancy Scarlett
PENSION: #S1976 **PARENTS:** John and Plesile Grime Grider

William Grider

~

Head, Thomas Anthony
LOCATION: Stewart Cemetery
RANK: Private **COMPANY:** I
REGIMENT: 16th Tennessee Infantry **BIRTH:** 12 October 1838, Warren County, Tennessee **DEATH:** 30 June 1921
MARRIED: Martha Jane Grider
PENSION: #W7592, #W9451, and #S1721 **PROFESSION:** Attorney

Thomas Anthony Head

~

Holman, James Spencer
LOCATION: Stewart Cemetery **RANK:** Private
COMPANY: H **REGIMENT:** 28th Tennessee Infantry
BIRTH: 18 December 1842 **DEATH:** 30 October 1915
MARRIED: Hannah Frances Welch
PENSION: #S2045 **PARENTS:** Albert James and Mary Jane Spears Holman **UDC MEMBER:** Lola Belle Brown McCormick

Terry, Hugh R.
LOCATION: Stewart Cemetery **RANK:** Corporal
COMPANY: I **REGIMENT:** 8th Tennessee Cavalry / 25th Tennessee Infantry **BIRTH:** 05 January 1843
DEATH: 15 April 1916 **MARRIED:** Julia Ann Quarles Jackson
PENSION: #S8732 **PARENTS:** Eddin and Arrintha Tucker Terry

Terry Cemetery
Fairview Road, Cookeville, Tennessee

Matheny, Thomas R.
LOCATION: Terry Cemetery **RANK:** Private **COMPANY:** K
REGIMENT: 16th Tennessee Infantry
BIRTH: 17 December 1830
DEATH: 18 September 1861 **MARRIED:** Mary J.

A. B. Thompson
Thompson Ridge Road, Baxter, Tennessee

Parkinson, Odicia Denton
LOCATION: A. B. Thompson Cemetery **RANK:** Private
COMPANY: E **REGIMENT:** 28th (Brown's) Tennessee Infantry
BIRTH: 08 December 1837 **DEATH:** 18 October 1904
MARRIED: Rhonda Patton on 23 June 1864
PARENTS: William and Nancy Parkinson

Verble Cemetery
Highway 84, Calfkiller Road, Monterey/Cookeville, Tennessee

Stamps, Edmond
LOCATION: Verble Cemetery **RANK:** Private **COMPANY:** D
REGIMENT: 22nd Battalion, Tennessee Infantry
BIRTH: Unknown **DEATH:** Unknown

Unmarked Grave

Walker Cemetery
Near Putnam-Overton County line

West, Alexander Washington
LOCATION: Walker Cemetery **RANK:** Not listed **COMPANY:** Not listed **REGIMENT:** 3rd Confederate Engineer Corps **BIRTH:** 10 May 1840 **DEATH:** 06 August 1928 **MARRIED:** Esther Elvirey Walker
PARENTS: Anderson and Mary West

Wasson Cemetery
Cookeville, Tennessee

Knight, James C.
LOCATION: Wasson Cemetery **RANK:** Private **COMPANY:** K **REGIMENT:** 28th Tennessee Infantry **BIRTH:** 11 May 1835 **DEATH:** 07 March 1890 **MARRIED:** Mary

Wasson, Pleasant M.
LOCATION: Wasson Cemetery **RANK:** Private **COMPANY:** F **REGIMENT:** 16th Tennessee Infantry **BIRTH:** 05 April 1841 **DEATH:** 22 October 1914 **MARRIED:** Sarah Margaret Jaquess
PARENTS: Elijah Marvin and Cassa Garrison Wasson
OTHER: Wounded at Murfreesboro; Tennessee. Imprisoned at Camp Douglas, Illinois

Watson Cemetery
Watson Road, Cookeville, Tennessee

Watson Benjamin
LOCATION: Watson Family Cemetery **RANK:** Private **COMPANY:** K **REGIMENT:** 16th Infantry **BIRTH:** 1825, Pittsylvania, Virginia **DEATH:** 1900 **MARRIED:** Martha F., c. 1853, Putnam County, Tennessee

Watson, John Saul
LOCATION: Watson Cemetery **RANK:** Sergeant **COMPANY:** L
REGIMENT: 1st (Field's) and 27th (Consolidated) Tennessee
Infantry **BIRTH:** c. 1816 **DEATH:** c. 1900

John W. Watts Family Cemetery
Lower Putnam County near Smith County Line

Watts, John W.
LOCATION: John W. Watts Family Cemetery **RANK:** Private **COMPANY:** G
REGIMENT: 28th Tennessee Infantry / 2nd Mountain Reg. Volunteers **BIRTH:** 10 May 1838 **DEATH:** 28 May 1909
MARRIED: Elizabeth "Bettie" Young, 1858
PARENTS: Mason and Mary Clemons Watts

John W. Watts

Marker Photo Not Available

Daniel C. Webb Cemetery
Spring Creek off Fairview Road, Little Mill Creek

Ferguson, Benjamin T.
LOCATION: Daniel C. Webb Cemetery **RANK:** Private
COMPANY: F **REGIMENT:** 13th (8th) Tennessee Cavalry **BIRTH:** 03 March 1839 **DEATH:** 15 November 1909 **MARRIED:** Jessie Goodman **PENSION:** #S5326

Unmarked Grave

Tallent, Isel
LOCATION: Daniel C. Webb Cemetery **RANK:** Not listed
COMPANY: Not listed **REGIMENT:** 8th Kentucky Infantry
BIRTH: 11 February 1837 **DEATH:** 24 August 1908
MARRIED: (1) Louticia Eldridge; (2) Drucilla
PENSION: #S1051 and #W8009

Unmarked Grave

West Cemetery
West Cemetery Road, Cookeville, Tennessee

Davis, Columbus J.
LOCATION: West Cemetery **RANK:** 2nd Lieutenant
COMPANY: C **REGIMENT:** 13th Tennessee Cavalry / 8th Tennessee Cavalry **BIRTH:** 08 August 1840
DEATH: 07 February 1917 **MARRIED:** Almira Pendergrass
PENSION: #W6680 **PARENTS:** Henry and Susannah West Davis

~

Farris, Thomas
LOCATION: West Cemetery **RANK:** Private **COMPANY:** H
REGIMENT: 13th Tennessee Cavalry / 8th Tennessee Cavalry
BIRTH: 13 September 1842 **DEATH:** 30 June 1914
MARRIED: Emily **PENSIONS:** #S5563, #W5522

~

Gentry, George W.
LOCATION: West Cemetery **RANK:** Private **COMPANY:** G
REGIMENT: 13th Tennessee Cavalry **BIRTH:** 07 April 1848
DEATH: 03 June 1936

~

Peek, Martin
LOCATION: West Cemetery **RANK:** Private
COMPANY: K **REGIMENT:** 13th Tennessee Cavalry
BIRTH: 16 December 1844
DEATH: 23 April 1924

~

Randolph, Jesse V.
LOCATION: West Cemetery **RANK:** Sergeant **COMPANY:** H
REGIMENT: 28th (Consolidated) Tennessee Infantry
BIRTH: 24 September 1839 **DEATH:** 10 September 1916
MARRIED: Julia Ann Randolph **PENSION:** #S13567
PARENTS: Lancaster and Nancy Rice Randolph

Ray, William L.
LOCATION: West Cemetery **RANK:** Private **COMPANY:** H
REGIMENT: 13th Tennessee Cavalry / 8th (Dibrell's) Tennessee Cavalry **BIRTH:** 29 April 1837 **DEATH:** 05 January 1916
MARRIED: Celia Margaret West **PENSION:** #S9061
PARENTS: Samuel H. and Nancy J. McCaleb Ray

~

Thompson, James F.
LOCATION: West Cemetery **RANK:** Sergeant **COMPANY:** F
REGIMENT: 25th Tennessee Infantry **BIRTH:** 15 January 1842, Jackson County, Tennessee **DEATH:** 22 August 1920
MARRIED: Permelia Ann Carr **PENSION:** #S5048
PARENTS: Squire Looney and Arena Davis Thompson

~

West, Wilson
LOCATION: West Cemetery **RANK:** Private **COMPANY:** F / B
REGIMENT: 28th (Consolidated) Tennessee Infantry / 84th Tennessee Infantry **BIRTH:** 10 July 1835
DEATH: 21 September 1916 **MARRIED:** Nancy Jane Jones
PARENTS: Anderson and Polly West

Whittaker Cemetery
Monterey, Tennessee

Byrne, George D.
LOCATION: Whittaker Cemetery **RANK:** Private **COMPANY:** K
REGIMENT: 17th Tennessee Infantry **BIRTH:** 08 July 1844
DEATH: 24 March 1931 **MARRIED:** Mary Malinda Nichols
PENSION: #S12248 **PARENTS:** Lawrence and
Sarah Carlile Byrne

~

Deck, John V.
LOCATION: Whittaker Cemetery **RANK:** Private
COMPANY: D **REGIMENT:** 25th Tennessee Infantry
BIRTH: 14 October 1837
DEATH: 02 June 1918

Unmarked Grave

Hall, John T.
LOCATION: Whittaker Cemetery **RANK:** Private
COMPANY: I **REGIMENT:** 8th (Dibrell's) Tennessee Cavalry / 13th Tennessee Cavalry **BIRTH:** 28 February 1844
DEATH: July 1918 **MARRIED:** Paulina Goodwin
PENSIONS: #S5482, #W4197, and #W4256

~

Horn, Sherod
LOCATION: Whittaker Cemetery **RANK:** 2nd Lieutenant
COMPANY: K **REGIMENT:** 25th Tennessee Infantry
BIRTH: 14 March 1841 **DEATH:** 19 November 1924
MARRIED: Mary A. **PENSION:** #W8165 **BROTHER:** Samuel; served with 13th Tennessee Cavalry during War
PARENTS: Albert and Jane Johnson Horn

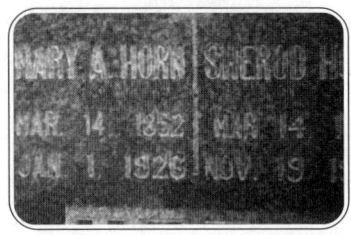

~

Matheny, M. S.
LOCATION: Whittaker Cemetery **RANK:** Private
COMPANY: I **REGIMENT:** 25th Tennessee Infantry
BIRTH: 26 December 1846
DEATH: 16 June 1924

~

Riddle, Joseph J.
LOCATION: Whittaker Cemetery **RANK:** 1st Lieutenant
COMPANY: F **REGIMENT:** 4th (Murray's) Tennessee Cavalry
BIRTH: 15 December 1824 **DEATH:** 04 March 1914
MARRIED: Nancy

~

Sehon, John F.
LOCATION: Whittaker Cemetery **RANK:** Not listed
COMPANY: Not listed **REGIMENT:** 5th (McKenzie's) Tennessee Cavalry **BIRTH:** 26 December 1845 **DEATH:** 11 October 1929
MARRIED: Sarah Copeland **PENSION:** #S11613

Swallows, I. J.
LOCATION: Whittaker Cemetery **RANK:** Private **COMPANY:** D
REGIMENT: 25th Tennessee Infantry **BIRTH:** 17 May 1848
DEATH: 31 August 1938

~

Whittaker, J. J.
LOCATION: Whittaker Cemetery **RANK:** Private **COMPANY:** K
REGIMENT: 3rd (Forrest's) Tennessee Cavalry
BIRTH: 16 March 1843 **DEATH:** 26 December 1922
MARRIED: Nancy

Leige Whiteaker Cemetery
Near Cole's Store

Whitaker, Ligard J.
LOCATION: Leige Whiteaker Cemetery **RANK:** Corporal
COMPANY: K **REGIMENT:** 25th Tennessee Infantry
BIRTH: 16 February 1843 **DEATH:** 10 January 1932
MARRIED: Fannie Byrne **PARENTS:** James Madison and Nancy Henry Whiteaker

Unmarked Grave

Whitehead-Taylor Cemetery
On David Crawford Farm near Boma

Whitehead, James Madison
LOCATION: Whitehead-Taylor Cemetery **RANK:** Private
COMPANY: C **REGIMENT:** 8th / 13th Tennessee Cavalry
BIRTH: 25 December 1838 **DEATH:** 14 February 1909
MARRIED: Louisa Jane Brown **PENSION:** #W2516
PARENTS: Moses and Mary Brown Whitehead

Unmarked Grave

Wm. "Plunk" Whitson Cemetery
Blackburn Fork Road, Cookeville, Tennessee

Pippin, A. C.
LOCATION: Wm. "Plunk" Whitson Cemetery **RANK:** Captain
COMPANY: K **REGIMENT:** 28th Tennessee Infantry
BIRTH: 31 March 1836 **DEATH:** 13 January 1864

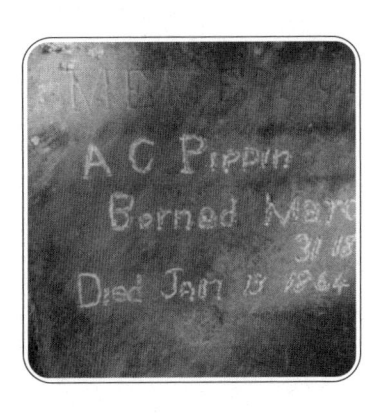

Tyree, Robert J.
LOCATION: Wm. "Plunk" Whitson Cemetery RANK: Private
COMPANY: C REGIMENT: 8th (Smith's) Tennessee Cavalry
BIRTH: 16 August 1834 DEATH: 25 April 1901
MARRIED: Mary Emerline PENSIONS: #S2578 and #W3829

Williams Cemetery
Cherry Creek Road, Cookeville, Tennessee

Farley, David
LOCATION: Williams Cemetery RANK: Private
COMPANY: H REGIMENT: 13th Tennessee Cavalry / 8th (Dibrell's) Tennessee Cavalry BIRTH: 16 October 1844
DEATH: 20 September 1913 MARRIED: Rachel
PENSION: #S6825

~

Hudgens, Joseph
LOCATION: Williams Cemetery RANK: Private COMPANY: D
REGIMENT: 8th Tennessee Cavalry / 13th Tennessee Cavalry
BIRTH: 25 April 1836 DEATH: 31 May 1917
MARRIED: (1) Caroline Williams; (2) Clarinda Williams
PENSION: #S7941 PARENTS: William and Mary Hudgens

~

Williams, Jesse
LOCATION: Williams Cemetery RANK: Private COMPANY: K
REGIMENT: 8th (Smith's) Tennessee Cavalry
BIRTH: 18 October 1846 DEATH: 17 January 1923

Woodcliff Cemetery
Woodcliff Road, Monterey, Tennessee

Howard, Sampson J.
LOCATION: Woodcliff Cemetery RANK: Private COMPANY: D
REGIMENT: 22nd Tennessee Infantry BIRTH: 1831
DEATH: 1919 MARRIED: Betty

Unknown and Unmarked Locations

Bush, Frances Asbury
LOCATION: Unknown **RANK:** Private **COMPANY:** E
REGIMENT: 3rd (Forrest's) Tennessee Cavalry
BIRTH: 1819 **DEATH:** 24 May 1865
MARRIED: Matilda Simpson
OTHER: Died of wounds received in War

Unmarked Grave

Daniel, George D.
LOCATION: Unknown **RANK:** Private **COMPANY:** E
REGIMENT: 8th Tennessee Infantry

Unmarked Grave

Dyer, Logan R.
LOCATION: Unknown **RANK:** Private **COMPANY:** K
REGIMENT: 28th (Consolidated) Tennessee Infantry
BIRTH: 30 September 1839 **DEATH:** 01 November 1920
MARRIED: Hannah Frances America Buck
PARENTS: James and Jane Finn Dyer

Unmarked Grave

Gillihan, Uriah R.
LOCATION: Buffalo Valley, Tennessee in the woods
RANK: Sergeant **COMPANY:** G **REGIMENT:** 28th Tennessee Infantry **BIRTH:** Unknown **DEATH:** May 1865
OTHER: Murdered by Home Guards in Willis Hollow as he and T. W. Phillips were returning home from Greensboro, North Carolina, to Giles County, Tennessee

Hughes, J. D.
LOCATION: Unknown **RANK:** Private **COMPANY:** E
REGIMENT: 22nd (Barteau's) Tennessee Cavalry
BIRTH: Unknown **DEATH:** Unknown

Unmarked Grave

Moore, George M.
LOCATION: Unknown RANK: Private COMPANY: C
REGIMENT: 13th Tennessee Cavalry BIRTH: August 1847
DEATH: Unknown MARRIED: Elizabeth F.

Phillips, T. W.
LOCATION: Buffalo Valley, Cookeville, Tennessee in the woods
RANK: Private COMPANY: K REGIMENT: 28th (Consolidated)
Infantry BIRTH: Unknown DEATH: May 1865
OTHER: Murdered by Home Guards in Willis Hollow as he and Uriah R. Gillihan were returning home from Greensboro, North Carolina, to Giles County, Tennessee

Smith, Walton W.
LOCATION: Unknown RANK: Captain OTHER: Attorney
BIRTH: Unknown DEATH: 1903 MARRIED: Marion Richardson Black PARENTS: Thomas Jefferson and Matilda Puckett Smith (daughter of John Puckett, Revolutionary War soldier)

Stanton, Sidney Smith
LOCATION: Calhoun, Georgia RANK: Colonel
COMPANY: Field and Staff REGIMENT: 28th Tennessee
BIRTH: c. 1830 DEATH: 14 May 1864, Resaca, Georgia
MARRIED: Mary Thackston Apple PARENTS: Champ and Sarah Lindsay Stanton OTHER: Attorney; Orator; At the Battle of Resaca, Georgia, "far in advance of his regiment, he was shot through the breast and fell dead upon the field, and was buried in the cemetery at Calhoun, Georgia." *Military Annals of Tennessee* by John Berrien Lindsley describes Colonel Stanton as, "A more brilliant intellect, a more captivating orator, a more warm-hearted and genial gentleman, a closer and more solid friend, a more gallant and chivalrous soldier sleeps not among the Confederate dead." His brother-in-law, Colonel Joseph Shaw, was also killed in battle near Savannah, Georgia.

VAN BUREN COUNTY

Van Buren County Courthouse, Spencer, Tennessee monument with names
of Confederate soldiers from Van Buren County

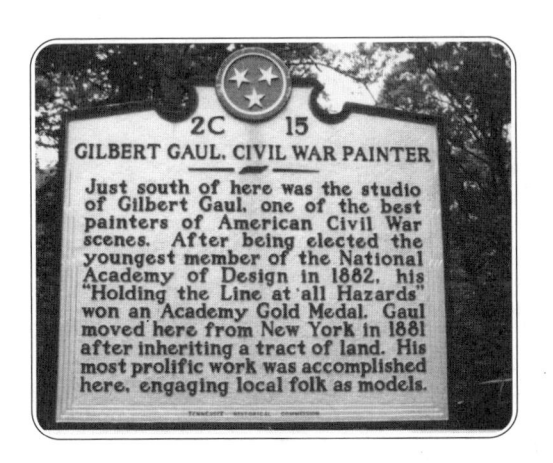

2C 15
GILBERT GAUL, CIVIL WAR PAINTER

Just south of here was the studio of Gilbert Gaul, one of the best painters of American Civil War scenes. After being elected the youngest member of the National Academy of Design in 1882, his "Holding the Line at 'all Hazards'" won an Academy Gold Medal. Gaul moved here from New York in 1881 after inheriting a tract of land. His most prolific work was accomplished here, engaging local folk as models.

2C 16
BRAGG'S MARCH TO KENTUCKY

In the late summer of 1862, Confederate General Braxton Bragg marched northward down this valley with an army of several thousand soldiers, supply wagons, and artillery pieces en route to invade Kentucky. They traveled and camped along the east side of nearby Cane Creek. After the October 8, 1862, Battle of Perryville, Kentucky, the campaign to invade Kentucky was abandoned. During the battle, twelve soldiers from Van Buren County were killed and several others wounded.

Tennessee historical commission markers placed in Van Buren County, numbers 2c-15,
at Fall Creek Falls State Park and 2C-16, located on Highway 285

Van Buren County • *Our Confederate Ancestors* • 91

Beech Cove Cemetery
Sparkman Town Road

Denny, Nathan Austin
LOCATION: Beech Cove Cemetery **RANK:** 1st Sergeant
COMPANY: C **REGIMENT:** 35th Tennessee Infantry
BIRTH: Unknown **DEATH:** 01 August 1886 **MARRIED:** Sarah Bryant, 12 October 1851, Van Buren County, Tennessee

Big Fork Cemetery

Cummings, Joseph D.
LOCATION: Big Fork Cemetery **RANK:** 1st Sergeant
COMPANY: C **REGIMENT:** 35 Tennessee Infantry **BIRTH:** 1802
DEATH: 1868 **MARRIED:** Ann Denny **PENSION:** #S12608
PARENTS: Joseph and Rosannah Collier Seibers Cummings

~

Haston, Montgomery Greenfield
LOCATION: Big Fork Cemetery **RANK:** Private **COMPANY:** C
REGIMENT: 35th Tennessee Infantry **BIRTH:** 16 August 1823
DEATH: 20 December 1869 **MARRIED:** Rachel Wheeler, 28 March 1847, Van Buren County, Tennessee

~

Madewell, Charles, Jr.
LOCATION: Big Fork Cemetery **RANK:** Private **COMPANY:** C
REGIMENT: 35th Tennessee Infantry **BIRTH:** 1827
DEATH: Unknown **MARRIED:** Nancy Phillips, 14 December 1847, Van Buren County, Tennessee

~

Shockley, William Burrell
LOCATION: Big Fork Cemetery **BIRTH:** 1819 **DEATH:** 1875
MARRIED: Emeline Denny **OTHER:** Provided "Material Aid" to the Confederacy; Procured salt under contract
PARENTS: Samuel and Darcus (Hoodenpyle) Shockley

92 · Our Confederate Ancestors · Van Buren County

Whitley, John H.
LOCATION: Big Fork Cemetery RANK: Private COMPANY: B
REGIMENT: 24th Tennessee Infantry BIRTH: 20 October 1831
DEATH: 01 May 1872 MARRIED: Sarah C. Cummings, 29 June 1867, Van Buren County, Tennessee

Blankenship Cemetery
Blankenship Cemetery Road

Blankenship, Gilford G.
LOCATION: Blakenship Cemetery RANK: Corporal COMPANY: E
REGIMENT: 25th Tennessee Infantry BIRTH: 13 April 1840
DEATH: 20 October 1926 MARRIED: (1) Nancy Martin; (2) Mary "Polly" Miller; (3) Mary "Sally" Poore
PARENTS: Bennett and Catharine (Huddleston) Blankenship

~

Martin, Absolam
LOCATION: Blakenship Cemetery RANK: Private
COMPANY: A REGIMENT: 25th Tennessee Infantry
BIRTH: 1820 DEATH: 23 April 1883
MARRIED: Bettie Milam

Boyd Cemetery

Martin, James I.
LOCATION: Boyd Cemetery RANK: Corporal COMPANY: I
REGIMENT: 16th Tennessee Infantry BIRTH: 23 May 1844
DEATH: 08 November 1920 MARRIED: (1) Betty Rutledge; (2) Ellen Wiseman Whiteacre, 22 March 1891, Van Buren County, Tennessee; (3) Violet Grissom PARENTS: William Carroll and Mary (Grissom) Martin

Phronie Boyd Cemetery
Rocky River Road

Boyd, William M.
LOCATION: Phronie Boyd Cemetery **RANK:** Private
COMPANY: A **REGIMENT:** 25th Tennessee Infantry
BIRTH: 18 January 1831 **DEATH:** 17 November 1891
MARRIED: Eliza Hillis, 28 December 1850, Van Buren County, Tennessee **PARENTS:** William, Jr. and ---- (Lucas) Boyd

~

Hillis, James H.
LOCATION: Phronie Boyd Cemetery **RANK:** Private
COMPANY: E **REGIMENT:** 22nd (Murray's) Battalion Tennessee Infantry **BIRTH:** 1843 **DEATH:** 1905 **MARRIED:** (1) Josephine Johnson, 30 November 1861, Van Buren County, Tennessee; (2) Martha McCaskey **PARENTS:** Dickson and Mahala (Hale) Hillis

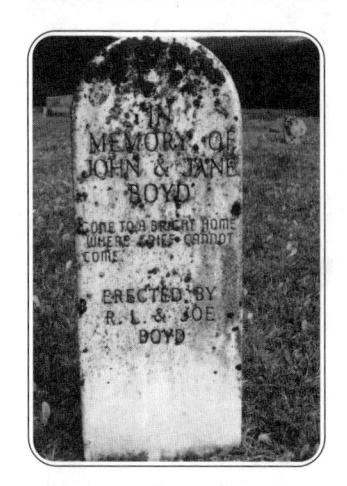

Crain Hill Cemetery
Rocky River Road

Boyd, John
LOCATION: Crain Hill Cemetery **RANK:** 1st Lieutenent
COMPANY: I **REGIMENT:** 16th Tennessee Infantry **BIRTH:** 1831
DEATH: 11 November 1897 **MARRIED:** (1) Margaret Mitchell, 17 January 1850, Van Buren County, Tennessee; (2) Jane Hutchison McCaskey, 06 August 1869, Van Buren County, Tennessee **PARENTS:** William, Jr. and ---- (Lucas) Boyd

~

Crain, Oliver Cleveland
LOCATION: Crain Hill Cemetery **RANK:** Captain
COMPANY: District #8 **REGIMENT:** Van Buren County Home Guard **BIRTH:** 25 November 1824 **DEATH:** 03 October 1877
MARRIED: Fannie York Ballard, 22 February 1844, Van Buren County, Tennessee **PARENTS:** Abijah and Emily (Sparks) Crain

Hillis, Lawson H.
LOCATION: Crain Hill Cemetery **RANK:** Sergeant **COMPANY:** E
REGIMENT: 22nd (Murray's) Battalion Tennessee Infantry
BIRTH: 27 February 1841 **DEATH:** 24 November 1921
MARRIED: (1) Amanda Sparkman, 10 December 1867, Van Buren County, Tennessee; (2) Cora Jarrett Jones
PENSION: #S7356 **PARENTS:** Isaac and Jane Logue Boyd Hillis

~

Jones, Robert (Robin)
LOCATION: Crain Hill Cemetery **RANK:** Private
COMPANY: A / D **REGIMENT:** 35th Tennessee Infantry
BIRTH: 17 February 1820 **DEATH:** 15 September 1901
MARRIED: Nancy Walker **PARENTS:** Abraham and Ceallie Jones

~

McBride, Danal
LOCATION: Crain Hill Cemetery **RANK:** Private
COMPANY: A **REGIMENT:** 13th (Gore's) Tennessee Cavalry
BIRTH: 29 December 1812 **DEATH:** 08 February 1887
MARRIED: Rebecca Davis

~

McBride, Nathan Mathew
LOCATION: Crain Hill Cemetery **RANK:** Private **COMPANY:** I
REGIMENT: 16th Tennessee Infantry **BIRTH:** 1840
DEATH: 10 May 1918 **MARRIED:** Jane Talley, 02 June 1866, Van Buren County, Tennessee **PARENTS:** Daniel and Rebecca (Davis) McBride

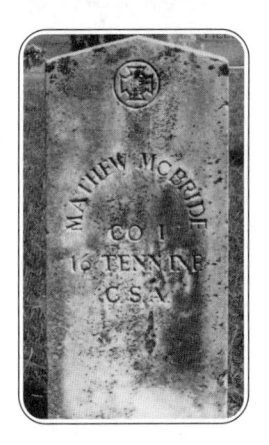

~

Payne, William R.
LOCATION: Crain Hill Cemetery **RANK:** Private
COMPANY: C **REGIMENT:** 28th Tennessee Infantry
BIRTH: 18 May 1837 **DEATH:** 11 October 1921
MARRIED: (1) Sophronia Mitchell;
(2) Nancy McDaniel Hutchings, 28 May 1881, Van Buren County, Tennessee **PENSION:** #S5294
PARENTS: Charles and Martha (Medley) Payne

William R. Payne

Unmarked Grave

Roberts, F. M.
LOCATION: Crain Hill Cemetery **RANK:** Private
COMPANY: I **REGIMENT:** 16th Tennessee Infantry
BIRTH: c. 1834 **DEATH:** 03 October 1914

Robirds, John Wesley
LOCATION: Crain Hill Cemetery **RANK:** Corporal
COMPANY: H **REGIMENT:** 47th Tennessee Infantry
BIRTH: 02 June 1833 **DEATH:** 29 March 1917
MARRIED: (1) Eady Earls; (2) Bettie Stoner Williams
PARENTS: William Bennett and Sarah (Martin) Roberts

Rutledge, James M.
LOCATION: Crain Hill Cemetery **RANK:** Private **COMPANY:** C
REGIMENT: 25th Tennessee Infantry **BIRTH:** 27 February 1844
DEATH: 04 May 1915 **MARRIED:** Nancy Keener, 26 February 1868, Van Buren County, Tennessee **PENSION:** #S5978

York, Uriah
LOCATION: Crain Hill Cemetery **RANK:** Private
COMPANY: District #8 **REGIMENT:** Van Buren County Home Guard **BIRTH:** 17 May 1784, North Carolina **DEATH:** 27 October 1865 **MARRIED:** Fannie Ray **PARENT:** Seymour York

Cummingsville Cemetery
Cummingsville United Methodist Church

Brock, Allen
LOCATION: Cummingsville Cemetery **RANK:** Not Listed
COMPANY: Not Listed **REGIMENT:** 4th (Murray's) Tennessee Cavalry **BIRTH:** 08 April 1826 **DEATH:** 22 September 1901
MARRIED: (1) Sarah Trogden, 18 October 1851, Van Buren County, Tennessee; (2) Luisa Mayer Riddles Mitchell, 22 December 1858, Van Buren County, Tennessee; (3) Elizabeth Haston Coots White, 21 November 1879, Van Buren County, Tennessee **PARENT:** Nancy Brock

Unmarked Grave

Cummings, Gabriel Marion
LOCATION: Cummingsville Cemetery
RANK: Captain **COMPANY:** C
REGIMENT: 35th Tennessee Infantry
BIRTH: 10 January 1834
DEATH: 25 November 1903
MARRIED: Martha L. Morgan, 19 May 1860, Van Buren County, Tennessee
PARENTS: William Burrell and Martha A. (Denny) Cummings

Gabriel Marion Cummings

~

Cummings, Joseph Denney
LOCATION: Cummingsville Cemetery
RANK: 1st Sergeant **COMPANY:** C
REGIMENT: 35th Tennessee Infantry
BIRTH: 01 January 1841 **DEATH:** 18 March 1914 **MARRIED:** Jennie Frasier
PARENTS: William Burrell and Martha A. (Denny) Cummings

Joseph Denney Cummings

~

Cummings, William Burrell
LOCATION: Cummingsville Cemetery **RANK:** Captain
COMPANY: C **REGIMENT:** 35th Tennessee Infantry
BIRTH: 10 May 1810 **DEATH:** 23 October 1884
MARRIED: Martha A. Denney **PARENTS:** Joseph and Rosannah Collier Seibers Cummings **UDC MEMBERS:** Martha Sue Bell Broyles, Susan Broyles Harris, Sherrie Beth Broyles McCulley, Josephine Bell McDonald, Deborah McDonald Spriggs

~

Morgan, Isaac Clinton
LOCATION: Cummingsville Cemetery **RANK:** Private
COMPANY: C **REGIMENT:** 35th Tennessee Infantry
BIRTH: 08 January 1837, Polk County, Georgia
DEATH: 21 December 1920 **MARRIED:** (1) Lucinda E. Cummings; (2) Virginia Brady, 24 January 1885, Van Buren County, Tennessee **PENSION:** #S11220 and #W7550
PARENTS: Joseph D. and Martha Ann (Payne) Morgan

Stipes, Alf C.
LOCATION: Cummingsville Cemetery RANK: Drummer
COMPANY: I REGIMENT: 16th Tennessee Infantry
BIRTH: 1832 DEATH: 1908 PENSION: #S1177
PARENTS: George and Elizabeth Stipes

Drake Cemetery
Highway 30 and Rasco Road

Groves, George W.
LOCATION: Drake Cemetery RANK: Private COMPANY: I
REGIMENT: 16th Tennessee Infantry BIRTH: 01 July 1838
DEATH: 30 April 1930 MARRIED: (1) Pariet Drake, 24 October 1868, Van Buren County, Tennessee; (2) Elvira Talley, 24 March 1888, Van Buren County, Tennessee PENSION: #S5594
PARENTS: Hiram and Mary Ann Groves

Gillentine Cemetery
Fall Creek Fals Area

Gillentine, Harrison C
LOCATION: Gillentine Cemetery RANK: Private
COMPANY: District #10 REGIMENT: Van Buren County Home Guard BIRTH: 1841 DEATH: 1901 MARRIED: Sallie Mooney
PARENTS: John and Margret (Parker) Gillentine

~

Gillentine, John
LOCATION: Gillentine Cemetery RANK: Private
COMPANY: District #10 REGIMENT: Van Buren County Home Guard BIRTH: 16 November 1797 DEATH: 02 July 1870
MARRIED: (1) Polly Martin; (2) Margaret Parker
PARENTS: Nicholas and Jane (Terry) Gillentine

Gully, Alfred J.
LOCATION: Gillentine Cemetery
RANK: Private **COMPANY:** I
REGIMENT: 62nd Tennessee Mounted Infantry
BIRTH: 16 September 1819 **DEATH:** 01 March 1898
MARRIED: Elizabeth Mooney
PARENT: Lewis Gully

Gravel Hill Cemetery
Cummingsville, Cane Creek Road

Simmons, Benjamin Lewis
LOCATION: Gravel Hill Cemetery **RANK:** Not Listed
COMPANY: H **REGIMENT:** 7th Tennessee Cavalry
BIRTH: 05 October 1817 **DEATH:** 16 September 1902
MARRIED: (1) Nancy Caroline Beaty; (2) M. Catherine Sparkman **PARENTS:** Joseph and Mary (Lewis) Simmons

~

Walker, Joseph
LOCATION: Gravel Hill Cemetery **RANK:** Private **COMPANY:** I
REGIMENT: 16th Tennessee Infantry **BIRTH:** 1807
DEATH: 22 June 1882 **MARRIED:** (1) Mamie Elizabeth Simmons Baker, 18 July 1855, Van Buren County, Tennessee; (2) Nancy Haston, 09 May 1861, Van Buren County, Tennessee; (3) Catherine Johnson, 11 June 1870, Van Buren County, Tennessee

Unmarked Grave

Graveyard Ridge Cemetery

Dodson, Simpson
LOCATION: Graveyard Ridge Cemetery **RANK:** Private
COMPANY: C / District #9 **REGIMENT:** 84th Tennessee Infantry / Van Buren County Home Guard **BIRTH:** Unknown **DEATH:** Unknown **MARRIED:** Elizabeth Prater **PARENTS:** Jesse and Sarah (Yates) Dodson

Unmarked Grave

Haston Cemetery
Tandy Lane off of Cane Creek Road

Haston, Isaac T.
LOCATION: Haston Cemetery **RANK:** Private
COMPANY: District #3 **REGIMENT:** Van Buren County Home Guard **BIRTH:** 28 March 1827 **DEATH:** 19 September 1875
MARRIED: Elizabeth Sparkman, 30 January 1846, Van Buren County, Tennessee **PARENTS:** David and Margaret (Roddy) Haston

~

Haston, William C.
LOCATION: Haston Cemetery **RANK:** Private **COMPANY:** E
REGIMENT: 1st (Colm's) Battalion Tennessee Infantry
BIRTH: 18 January 1848 **DEATH:** 10 January 1922
MARRIED: (1) Aminda Shockley, 16 February 1866, Van Buren County, Tennessee; (2) Julia Ann Felton Haston
PARENTS: Isaac T. and Elizabeth (Sparkman) Haston

Head Cemetery

Head, John A.
LOCATION: Head Cemetery **RANK:** Private **COMPANY:** A
REGIMENT: 47th Tennessee Infantry **BIRTH:** 1831 **DEATH:** 1889
MARRIED: Margret Fleming, 1858 Van Buren County, Tennessee **PARENTS:** Anthony and Fanny (Payne) Head

Unmarked Grave

Archibald Hillis Cemetery
Rocky River Road, off Highway 30

Hillis, Archibald M.
LOCATION: Archibald Hillis Cemetery **RANK:** Private
COMPANY: District #8 **REGIMENT:** Van Buren County Home Guard **BIRTH:** 1818 **DEATH:** 1872 **MARRIED:** Elizabeth Logue, 17 August 1844, Van Buren County, Tennessee
PARENTS: James and Mary (Boyd) Hillis

Hillis, Robert Oliver
LOCATION: Archibald Hillis Cemetery **RANK:** Private
COMPANY: I / District #8 **REGIMENT:** 16th Tennessee Infantry / Van Buren County Home Guard **BIRTH:** 07 December 1844
DEATH: 03 December 1930 **MARRIED:** Elizabeth Clark, 07 November 1866, Van Buren County, Tennessee
PARENTS: Dixon Naylor and Lydia (Logue) Hillis

Blackstone Hills Cemetery
Norton Springs Road

Hillis, Esquire
LOCATION: Blackstone Hills Cemetery **RANK:** Private
COMPANY: E **REGIMENT:** 22nd (Murray's) Battalion Tennessee Infantry **BIRTH:** 24 March 1832 **DEATH:** 21 June 1907
MARRIED: (1) Elizabeth Ann Barnes, 31 August 1854, Van Buren County, Tennessee; (2) Mattie Dudley
PARENTS: Isaac and Rebecca (Naylor) Hillis

John Hillis Cemetery
Baker Mountain Road (top of mountain)

Baker, Jordan Jabes
LOCATION: John Hillis Cemetery **RANK:** Private
COMPANY: District #6 **REGIMENT:** Van Buren County Home Guard **BIRTH:** 1825 **DEATH:** c. 1890 **MARRIED:** (1) Stacy Simmons, 21 January 1847, Van Buren County, Tennessee; (2) Elizabeth Howard, 30 March 1852, Van Buren County, Tennessee

Unmarked Grave

Grissom, Elisha
LOCATION: John Hillis Cemetery **RANK:** Private **COMPANY:** E **REGIMENT:** 22nd (Murray's) Battalion Tennessee Infantry
BIRTH: 10 March 1847 **DEATH:** 19 May 1919 **MARRIED:** (1) Mary Ann "Polly" Talley; (2) Martha Scott Moffitt
PARENTS: Robert Thomas and Sarah (Bouldin) Grissom

Unmarked Grave

Hillis, Robert
LOCATION: John Hillis Cemetery **RANK:** Private **COMPANY:** District #8 **REGIMENT:** Van Buren County Home Guard **BIRTH:** 1830 **DEATH:** c. 1885 **MARRIED:** Frances Scott Overturf, 07 August 1857, Van Buren County, Tennessee **PARENTS:** James and Mary (Boyd) Hillis

Hodges Cemetery
Cummingsville

Hodges, Jasper
LOCATION: Hodges Cemetery **RANK:** Private **COMPANY:** Distrct #3 **REGIMENT:** Van Buren County Home Guard **BIRTH:** 12 December 1838 **DEATH:** 09 May 1881 **MARRIED:** Lucinda Earls **PARENTS:** William and Mary (McBride) Hodges

~

Hollingsworth, John
LOCATION: Hodges Cemetery **RANK:** 4th Sergeant **COMPANY:** C **REGIMENT:** 35th Tennessee Infantry **BIRTH:** 1843 **DEATH:** 1879 **MARRIED:** Martha Jane Hodges **PARENTS:** William "Buck" and Mary (Sparkman) Hollingsworth

~

Sparkman, W. B.
LOCATION: Hodges Cemetery **RANK:** Private **COMPANY:** District #2 **REGIMENT:** Van Buren County Home Guard **BIRTH:** 26 October 1843 **DEATH:** 23 June 1896 **MARRIED:** Lydia M. Hodges **PARENTS:** Jim and Judy (McBride) Sparkman

Laurel Creek Cemetery
Laurel Creek Baptist Church

Grissom, Elijah
LOCATION: Laurel Creek Cemetery
RANK: Private **COMPANY:** E
REGIMENT: 22nd (Murray's) Tennessee Infantry **BIRTH:** 10 March 1836, Van Buren County, Tennessee
DEATH: 07 March 1911
MARRIED: (1) Nancy Cathleen Johnson; (2) Phronia Johnson; (3) Darthulia Shockley
PARENTS: Robert Thomas and Sarah (Bouldin) Grissom **UDC MEMBERS:** Martha Sue Bell Broyles, Susan Broyles Harris, Sherrie Beth Broyles McCulley, Josephine Bell McDonald, Deborah McDonald Spriggs

Elijah Grissom

~

Johnson, Francis Marion
LOCATION: Laurel Creek Cemetery
RANK: Private **COMPANY:** E
REGIMENT: 22nd (Murray's) Battalion Tennessee Infantry
BIRTH: 02 June 1842 **DEATH:** 29 August 1902 **MARRIED:** (1) Winnie Evaline Sparkman, 19 December 1860, Van Buren County, Tennessee; (2) Rachel **PARENTS:** Squire and Lavina (Hill) Johnson
UDC MEMBERS: Martha Sue Bell Broyles, Susan Broyles Harris, Sherrie Beth Broyles McCulley, Josephine Bell McDonald, Deborah McDonald Spriggs

Francis Marion Johnson

Johnson, Greenberry

LOCATION: Laurel Creek Cemetery
RANK: 1st Lieutenent
COMPANY: I / E **REGIMENT:** 16th Tennessee Infantry / 22nd (Murray's) Battalion Tennessee Infantry
BIRTH: 18 September 1832 **DEATH:** 28 September 1903 **MARRIED:** (1) Angeline Russell, 08 February 1865, Van Buren County, Tennessee; (2) Mary C. Denton Dyer
PARENTS: Squire and Lavina (Hill) Johnson **UDC MEMBERS:** Martha Sue Bell Broyles, Susan Broyles Harris, Sherrie Beth Broyles McCulley, Josephine Bell McDonald, Deborah McDonald Spriggs

Greenberry Johnson

~

Johnson, Squire

LOCATION: Laurel Creek Cemetery
RANK: Private **COMPANY:** District #5
REGIMENT: Van Buren County Home Guard **BIRTH:** 22 February 1811
DEATH: 06 September 1872 **MARRIED:** Lavina Hill **PARENTS:** Allen and Nancy (Whitely) Johnson **UDC MEMBERS:** Martha Sue Bell Broyles, Susan Broyles Harris, Sherrie Beth Broyles McCulley, Josephine Bell McDonald, Deborah McDonald Spriggs

Squire Johnson

~

Johnson, William Rye

LOCATION: Laurel Creek Cemetery
RANK: Private **COMPANY:** E
REGIMENT: 22nd (Murray's) Battalion Tennessee Infantry **BIRTH:** 1835
DEATH: 1921 **MARRIED:** Nancy Bouldin, 29 March 1859, Van Buren County, Tennessee **PARENTS:** Squire and Lavina (Hill) Johnson

William Rye Johnson

Kell, George Easterly
LOCATION: Laurel Creek Cemetery **RANK:** Private
COMPANY: L **REGIMENT:** 11th (Holman's) Tennessee Cavalry
BIRTH: 17 August 1830 **DEATH:** 10 March 1906
MARRIED: Amanda Thomas, 20 September 1855, Van Buren County, Tennessee **PARENTS:** Thomas and Lydia (Lakey) Kell

~

McCoy, John L.
LOCATION: Laurel Creek Cemetery **RANK:** Private
COMPANY: C **REGIMENT:** 25th Tennessee Infantry
BIRTH: 20 February 1840 **DEATH:** 10 August 1918
MARRIED: Zerra Ware Gibson **PENSION:** #S13552
PARENTS: John and Nancy (Hatfield) McCoy

~

Moore, Reverand William Patrick
LOCATION: Laurel Creek Cemetery **RANK:** Private
COMPANY: District #6 **REGIMENT:** Van Buren County Home Guard **BIRTH:** 17 October 1825 **DEATH:** 07 January 1899
MARRIED (1) Elizabeth Jane Neal, 03 December 1845, Van Buren County, Tennessee; (2) Nancy Cunningham
PARENTS: Thomas and Rebecca (Stepp) Moore

~

Page, Dr. Titus
LOCATION: Laurel Creek Cemetery **RANK:** Private
COMPANY: I **REGIMENT:** 8th (Smith's) Tennessee Cavalry
BIRTH: 22 February 1842 **DEATH:** 10 May 1911
MARRIED: (1) Mary Jane Johnson, 01 July 1870, Van Buren County, Tennessee; (2) Clearinda Stipe, 07 February 1899, Van Buren County, Tennessee **PARENTS:** John S. and Louisa Page

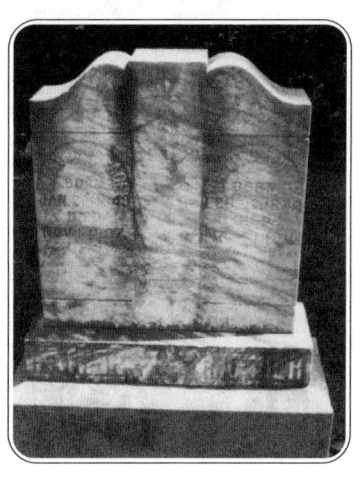

Simons, George Washington
LOCATION: Laurel Creek Cemetery **RANK:** Corporal
COMPANY: B **REGIMENT:** 35th Tennessee Infantry
BIRTH: 11 November 1836 **DEATH:** 08 January 1909
MARRIED: Eva Russell, 24 September 1866, Van Buren County, Tennessee **PENSION:** #S7889 **PARENTS:** Archibald and Christina (Moore) Simons

~

Russell, Thomas
LOCATION: Laurel Creek Cemetery **RANK:** Private
COMPANY: District #5
REGIMENT: Van Buren County Home Guard
BIRTH: 15 November 1822
DEATH: 18 July 1906
MARRIED: (1) Frances Dyer; (2) Eleanor M. Hammonds
PARENT: Myra Russell Tosh

Thomas Russell

~

Tosh, Daniel Alexander
LOCATION: Laurel Creek Cemetery **RANK:** Private
COMPANY: B **REGIMENT:** 35th Tennessee Infantry
BIRTH: 10 December 1826 **DEATH:** 27 January 1923
MARRIED: Nancy Jane Chambers
PARENTS: Tasker and Myra (Russell) Tosh

Lewis Cemetery
Near small church, next to Old John Baker Place, on Cane Creek

McCormick, Samuel
LOCATION: Lewis Cemetery **RANK:** Private
COMPANY: District #4 **REGIMENT:** Van Buren County Home Guard **BIRTH:** 1833 **DEATH:** c. 1885 **MARRIED** Loumisa Walker, 18 November 1853, Van Buren County, Tennessee
PARENTS: Clayton and Elizabeth McCormick

Unmarked Grave

Long Cemetery

Six miles from Spencer Courthouse on Highway 30 North

Bouldin, Nathan

LOCATION: Long Cemetery **RANK:** Private **COMPANY:** C **REGIMENT:** 35th Tennessee Infantry **BIRTH:** 28 December 1836 **DEATH:** 10 April 1898 **MARRIED:** Ann Safley **PENSION:** #W5739 **PARENTS:** Elisha and Elizabeth (Southerland) Bouldin **UDC MEMBERS:** Martha Sue Bell Broyles, Susan Broyles Harris, Sherrie Beth Broyles McCulley, Josephine Bell McDonald, Deborah McDonald Spriggs

~

Clenny, James T.

LOCATION: Long Cemetery **RANK:** Private **COMPANY:** D **REGIMENT:** 1st (Colm's) Battalion Tennessee Infantry **BIRTH:** 16 January 1814 **DEATH:** 26 June 1877 **MARRIED:** Malinda Rowland **PARENTS:** Jonathan and Rebecca Jane (Hewitt) Clenny

~

Grissom, Alexander

LOCATION: Long Cemetery **RANK:** 2nd Lieutenant **COMPANY:** C **REGIMENT:** 35th Tennessee Infantry **BIRTH:** 08 August 1816 **DEATH:** 29 May 1897 **MARRIED:** Rutha Shockley **PARENTS:** Charles and Margaret Grissom **UDC MEMBERS:** Martha Sue Bell Broyles, Susan Broyles Harris, Sherrie Beth Broyles McCulley, Josephine Bell McDonald, Deborah McDonald Spriggs

~

Grissom, Esau

LOCATION: Long Cemetery **RANK:** Private **COMPANY:** D **REGIMENT:** 35th Tennessee Infantry **BIRTH:** 05 March 1843 **DEATH:** 01 April 1878 **MARRIED:** Permelie Johnson **PENSION:** #W6227 **PARENTS:** Robert Thomas and Sarah (Bouldin) Grissom **UDC MEMBERS:** Martha Sue Bell Broyles, Susan Broyles Harris, Sherrie Beth Broyles McCulley, Josephine Bell McDonald, Deborah McDonald Spriggs

Grissom, James C.
LOCATION: Long Cemetery **RANK:** Private **COMPANY:** E
REGIMENT: 22nd (Murray's) Battalion Tennessee Infantry
BIRTH: 08 December 1829 **DEATH:** 08 June 1906
MARRIED: Ann Boyd, 25 March 1852, Van Buren County,
Tennessee **PENSION:** #S1239 and #W1054
PARENTS: William and Evey (Rhodes) Grissom

Grissom, John R.
LOCATION: Long Cemetery **RANK:** Sergeant
COMPANY: I **REGIMENT:** 16th Tennessee Infantry
BIRTH: 05 November 1847 **DEATH:** 19 June 1914
MARRIED: Louisa McCoy **PARENTS:** Toliver and Isabelle
(Shockley) Grissom

Grissom, Samuel Burton
LOCATION: Long Cemetery
RANK: Private **COMPANY:** A
REGIMENT: 13th (Gore's)
Tennessee Cavalry
BIRTH: 14 November 1847
DEATH: 01 November 1908
MARRIED (1) Harriet Bouldin;
(2) Elizabeth Irene Gribble
PENSION #S9571
PARENTS: Alexander and Rutha
(Shockley) Grissom **UDC MEMBERS:** Martha Sue Bell Broyles,
Susan Broyles Harris, Sherrie Beth Broyles McCulley,
Josephine Bell McDonald, Deborah McDonald Spriggs

Samuel Burton Grissom

Grissom, Toliver
LOCATION: Long Cemetery **RANK:** Private
COMPANY: District #6 **REGIMENT:** Van Buren County Home
Guard **BIRTH:** 12 April 1821 **DEATH:** 25 November 1888
MARRIED Isabelle Shockley, 18 January 1843, Van Buren
County, Tennessee **PARENTS:** William and Evey
(Rhodes) Grissom

Grissom, William Buck

LOCATION: Long Cemetery **RANK:** 2nd Lieutenent **COMPANY:** E **REGIMENT:** 22nd (Murray's) Battalion Tennessee Infantry **BIRTH:** 06 July 1834 **DEATH:** 31 March 1909 **MARRIED:** Permelia D. Passons **PARENTS:** William and Evey (Rhodes) Grissom

~

Hale, James

LOCATION: Long Cemetery **RANK:** Private **COMPANY:** E **REGIMENT:** 35th Tennessee Infantry **BIRTH:** 16 July 1848 **DEATH:** 23 May 1924 **MARRIED:** (1) Margaret Ann Gross, 12 October 1867, Van Buren County, Tennessee; (2) Polly Hillis **PARENTS:** William Taylor and Adaline (Elsey) Hale

~

Haston, E. Cyrus

LOCATION: Long Cemetery **RANK:** 1st Lieutenent **COMPANY:** A **REGIMENT:** 3rd (Consolidated) Tennessee Infantry **BIRTH:** 17 June 1841 **DEATH:** 17 March 1898 **MARRIED:** Caroline Grissom, 18 June 1860, Van Buren County, Tennessee; **OTHER:** E. C. Haston's name was E. Cyrus Moore, but he took the name of his foster parents: David and Margaret (Roddy) Haston.

~

Haston, Richmond T.

LOCATION: Long Cemetery **RANK:** Not Listed **COMPANY:** A **REGIMENT:** 4th (Murray's) Tennessee Cavalry **BIRTH:** 1838 **DEATH:** 1882

~

Hillis, James K.

LOCATION: Long Cemetery **RANK:** Private **COMPANY:** E **REGIMENT:** 22nd (Murray's) Battalion Tennessee Infantry **BIRTH:** 28 April 1835 **DEATH:** 25 March 1877 **MARRIED:** Margaret Worthington, 06 November, 1865, Van Buren County, Tennessee **PARENTS:** Isaac and Elizabeth (Drake) Hillis

Hitchcock, John
LOCATION: Long Cemetery **RANK:** Sergeant
COMPANY: C **REGIMENT:** 35th Tennessee Infantry
BIRTH: 23 September 1838 **DEATH:** 04 February 1921
MARRIED: Margaret York, 09 January 1867, Van Buren County, Tennessee **PENSION:** #S1240
PARENTS: James and Charlotte (Fleming) Hitchcock

~

Martin, William Carroll
LOCATION: Long Cemetery **RANK:** 2nd Lieutenent
COMPANY: C **REGIMENT:** 35th Tennessee Infantry
BIRTH: 28 October 1820 **DEATH:** 23 August 1894
MARRIED: Mary Grissom, 22 March 1842, Van Buren County, Tennessee **PARENTS:** David and Nancy (Cole) Martin

~

McCormick, James M. "Mack"
LOCATION: Long Cemetery **RANK:** Sergeant **COMPANY:** C
REGIMENT: 35th Tennessee Infantry **MARRIED:** Jane E. Graham, 10 August 1843, Van Buren County, Tennessee

~

Parker, Reverand Arthur L.
LOCATION: Long Cemetery **RANK:** 1st Lieutenent
COMPANY: District #6 **REGIMENT:** Van Buren County Home Guard **BIRTH:** 26 December 1825 **DEATH:** 01 September 1901
MARRIED: Lodemia Worthington, 19 December 1849, Van Buren County, Tennessee **PARENTS:** Arthur and Eleanor (Ballard) Parker

~

Parker, William B.
LOCATION: Long Cemetery **RANK:** 2nd Lieutenent
COMPANY: C **REGIMENT:** 25th Tennessee Infantry
BIRTH: 06 May 1834 **DEATH:** 21 January 1863 **MARRIED:** Mary A. Worthington, 15 August 1854, Van Buren County, Tennessee **PARENTS:** Arthur and Eleanor (Ballard) Parker

~

Passons, Andrew Jackson
LOCATION: Long Cemetery
RANK: Private **COMPANY:** I
REGIMENT: 16th Tennessee Infantry **BIRTH:** 27 December 1843 **DEATH:** 20 November 1888 **MARRIED:** Margaret E. Cotton **PARENTS:** Major and Anna (Anderson) Passons

Andrew Jackson Passons

Unmarked Grave

Passons, Edward Thockmorton
LOCATION: Long Cemetery **RANK:** Private **COMPANY:** I
REGIMENT: 16th Tennessee Infantry **BIRTH:** 25 July 1836
DEATH: 28 November 1919 **MARRIED:** Evaline York
PARENTS: Major and Anna (Anderson) Passons

Passons, James
LOCATION: Long Cemetery **RANK:** 1st Lieutenent
COMPANY: District #10 **REGIMENT:** Van Buren County Home Guard **BIRTH:** November 1841 **DEATH:** c. 1872
MARRIED: Nancy Rachel Talley **PARENTS:** Tilford A. and Sarah M. (Hutson) Passons

Unmarked Grave

Passons, Tilford A.
LOCATION: Long Cemetery **RANK:** Private **COMPANY:** C
REGIMENT: 35th Tennessee Infantry **BIRTH:** 26 August 1818
DEATH: 26 November 1861 **MARRIED:** Sarah Moore Hutson
PARENTS: Major and Anna (Anderson) Passons

Unmarked Grave

Shockley, Louis D.

LOCATION: Long Cemetery
RANK: Private **COMPANY:** C
REGIMENT: 35th Tennessee
Infantry **BIRTH:** 10 June 1828
DEATH: 06 October 1919
MARRIED: Rachel Stipe, 14
August 1853, Van Buren County,
Tennessee **PENSION:** #S3018 and
#W7303 **PARENTS:** William and
Mary (Crawley) Shockley

Louis D. Shockley

~

Shockley, Phillip

LOCATION: Long Cemetery **RANK:** 1st Sergeant **COMPANY:** I
REGIMENT: 16th Tennessee Infantry **BIRTH:** 1824, White
County, Tennessee **DEATH:** 1865 **MARRIED:** Elizabeth Rhodes
PARENTS: Samuel and Arminda Dorcas (Hoodenpyle) Shockley
UDC MEMBERS: Martha Sue Bell Broyles, Susan Broyles Harris,
Sherrie Beth Broyles McCulley, Josephine Bell McDonald,
Deborah McDonald Spriggs

~

Walker, Jefferson J.

LOCATION: Long Cemetery **RANK:** Private
COMPANY: District #4 **REGIMENT:** Van Buren County Home
Guard **BIRTH:** 16 December 1826 **DEATH:** 09 November 1906
MARRIED: (1) Cynthia Shockley; (2) Margaret Lewis
PARENTS: David and Polly Ann (Stultz) Walker

~

Worthington, James

LOCATION: Long Cemetery **RANK:** 1st Lieutenent
COMPANY: I **REGIMENT:** 16th Tennessee Infantry
BIRTH: 05 November 1833 **DEATH:** 16 March 1908
MARRIED: Emily I. Clenney Brown, 01 January 1865, Van Buren
County, Tennessee **PARENTS:** William and Elizabeth
(Worthington) Worthington

112 · Our Confederate Ancestors · Van Buren County

Worthington, Samuel

LOCATION: Long Cemetery **RANK:** 2nd Sergeant **COMPANY:** I
REGIMENT: 16th Tennessee Infantry **BIRTH:** 17 April 1839
DEATH: 19 April 1928 **MARRIED:** Sarah Jane Neal, 17 August 1865, Van Buren County, Tennessee **PENSION:** #S14895
PARENTS: William and Elizabeth (Worthington) Worthington

~

Worthingon, William

LOCATION: Long Cemetery **RANK:** Private
COMPANY: I / District #7 **REGIMENT:** 16th Tennessee Infantry / Van Buren County Home Guard **BIRTH:** 02 December 1801
DEATH: 15 April 1875 **MARRIED:** Elizabeth Worthington
PARENTS: James and Lettis (Tunnel) Worthington

~

York, Harmon

LOCATION: Long Cemetery **RANK:** Captain **COMPANY:** I
REGIMENT: 16th Tennessee Infantry **BIRTH:** 06 June 1810
DEATH: 30 March 1901 **MARRIED:** (1) Nancy Talley; (2) Lousia Talley, 20 April 1880, Van Buren County, Tennessee
PARENT: Mary "Polly" York

McElroy Cemetery

Church of Christ at McElroy, McElroy Cemetery Road

Carter, Peter

LOCATION: McElroy Cemetery **RANK:** Private
COMPANY: District #1 **REGIMENT:** Van Buren County Home Guard **BIRTH:** 22 November 1814 **DEATH:** 17 November 1871
MARRIED: (1) Sarah; (2) Olevy Dillon **PARENTS:** Peter and Sarah Carter

~

Dillon, Carter

LOCATION: McElroy Cemetery **RANK:** Private / Captain
COMPANY: A / District #1 **REGIMENT:** 13th (Gore's) Tennessee Cavalry / Van Buren County Home Guard **BIRTH:** 1824
DEATH: 15 August 1883 **MARRIED:** Caroline Sparkman, 27 December 1846, Van Buren County, Tennessee

Head, W. H.
LOCATION: McElroy Cemetery **RANK:** Private
COMPANY: I **REGIMENT:** 16th Tennessee Infantry
BIRTH: 1841 **DEATH:** 1918 **PENSION** #S1966
PARENTS: Anthony and Fanny (Payne) Head

~

Hillis, Woodson P.
LOCATION: McElroy Cemetery **RANK:** Private
COMPANY: E **REGIMENT:** 22nd (Murray's) Tennessee Infantry
BIRTH: 27 August 1844 **DEATH:** 01 January 1916
MARRIED: Randa Sparkman **PENSION:** #S14187
PARENTS: Isaac and Nancy Jane Logue Boyd Hillis

~

Kirby, Laban
LOCATION: McElroy Cemetery
RANK: Private **COMPANY:** D **REGIMENT:** 13th (Gore's) Tennessee Cavalry **BIRTH:** 11 October 1835
DEATH: 18 November 1928
PENSION #S1098

~

McElroy, Andrew J.
LOCATION: McElroy Cemetery
RANK: General Commander
COMPANY: District #1
REGIMENT: Van Buren County Home Guard
BIRTH: 1791 **DEATH:** June 1864
MARRIED: (1) Martha Shropshire

~

Slatton, William Edward
LOCATION: McElroy Cemetery **RANK:** Private **COMPANY:** C
REGIMENT: 35th Tennessee Infantry **BIRTH:** 04 October 1810
DEATH: 19 January 1897 **MARRIED:** Mary Mitchell

114 · Our Confederate Ancestors · Van Buren County

Sparkman, James
LOCATION: McElroy Cemetery **RANK:** Private
COMPANY: District #1 **REGIMENT:** Van Buren County Home Guard **BIRTH:** 16 June 1819 **DEATH:** 07 September 1889
MARRIED: Eliza McElroy, 26 May 1840, Van Buren County, Tennessee **PARENTS:** James and Frances (Hughes) Sparkman

~

Sparkman, Solomon Clay
LOCATION: McElroy Cemetery **RANK:** Private
COMPANY: I **REGIMENT:** 13th (Gore's) Tennessee Cavalry
BIRTH: 14 April 1844 **DEATH:** 05 December 1920
MARRIED: (1) Ellen Gribble; (2) Mary Ellen Parker Johnson Troglin **PENSION:** #S15332 and #S10604 **PARENTS:** John and Lavina (McElroy) Sparkman

~

Steakley, William L.
LOCATION: McElroy Cemetery **RANK:** Sergeant
COMPANY: E **REGIMENT:** 1st (Colm's) Battalion Tennessee Infantry **BIRTH:** 08 March 1832 **DEATH:** 17 February 1891
MARRIED: Sarah Wheeler, 16 August 1851, Van Buren County, Tennessee **PARENTS:** Wiley and Priscilla (Lewis) Steakley

~

Wood, Errage "Er"
LOCATION: McElroy Cemetery **RANK:** Private
COMPANY: District #1 **REGIMENT:** Van Buren County Home Guard **BIRTH:** 22 July 1821 **DEATH:** 18 October 1905
MARRIED: Nancy Hash **PARENTS:** George and Elisabeth (Irwin) Wood

Molloy Cemetery
West of Spencer

Brock, John
LOCATION: Molloy Cemetery **RANK:** Private **COMPANY:** E
REGIMENT: 35th Tennessee Infantry **BIRTH:** 1824 **DEATH:** 1864
MARRIED: Susie Shockley, 25 December 1844, Van Buren County, Tennessee **OTHER:** Marker is a memorial

Denny, James Preston
LOCATION: Molloy Cemetery
RANK: Sergeant COMPANY: C
REGIMENT: 35th Tennessee
Infantry BIRTH: 13 February
1826 DEATH: December 1886
MARRIED: (1) Hannah Shockley,
21 May 1851, Van Buren
County, Tennessee; (2) Sarah
E. Grissom PARENTS: William
and Patsy (Burnett) Denny

James Preston Denny

Medley, Alen
LOCATION: Molloy Cemetery RANK: Private
COMPANY: District #5 REGIMENT: Van Buren County Home
Guard BIRTH: 06 May 1834 DEATH: 21 August 1900
MARRIED: (1) Sarah Howard, 28 April 1851, Van Buren
County, Tennessee; (2) Ruthie Shockley, 21 October 1855,
Van Buren County, Tennessee; (3) Bernice Sullivan, 18 June
1897, Van Buren County, Tennessee
PARENT: Morning Medley

Reagor, Samuel
LOCATION: Molloy Cemetery RANK: Captain
COMPANY: A REGIMENT: 37th Tennessee Infantry
BIRTH: 26 March 1831 DEATH: 14 February 1876
MARRIED: Retie

Mooneyham Cemetery
Highway 30 toward Pikeville

Dodson, Noah, Jr.
LOCATION: Mooneyham Cemetery RANK: Not Listed
COMPANY: A REGIMENT: 4th (Murray's) Tennessee Cavalry
BIRTH: 1827 DEATH: 1894 MARRIED: Virginia Hale PENSION:
#S345 PARENTS: Noah and Nancy Dodson

Neal Cemetery

Located in pasture at 190 Earl Lane

Johnson, John Manus

LOCATION: Neal Cemetery **RANK:** Corporal **COMPANY:** C
REGIMENT: 35th Tennessee Infantry **BIRTH:** 17 January 1844
DEATH: 17 January 1907 **MARRIED:** (1) Tennessee Martin, 08 October 1867, Van Buren County, Tennessee; (2) Betty Martin, 09 June 1903, Van Buren County, Tennessee
PENSION: #S5595 **PARENTS:** James Calvin and Sarah (Neal) Johnson

Old Drake Cemetery

Behind house in pasture at 8973 Highway 30 (Earl McCoy home)

Drake, Eligha

LOCATION: Old Drake Cemetery **RANK:** Private **COMPANY:** H
REGIMENT: 11th (Holman's) Tennessee Cavalry **BIRTH:** 12 February 1818 **DEATH:** 15 September 1888 **MARRIED:** Sarah Carter, 12 December 1842, Van Buren County, Tennessee
PARENTS: Elijah and Phoebe (Ray) Drake

Head, Richard J.

LOCATION: Old Drake Cemetery **RANK:** 2nd Lieutenent
COMPANY: District #7 **REGIMENT:** Van Buren County Home Guard **BIRTH:** 07 November 1824 **DEATH:** 04 March 1894
MARRIED: Jane **PARENTS:** Anthony and Fanny (Payne) Head

Old Laurel Creek Cemetery

Shockley, Hickman

LOCATION: Old Laurel Creek Cemetery **RANK:** Private
COMPANY: I **REGIMENT:** 16th Tennessee Infantry **BIRTH:** 1845
DEATH: 1882 **MARRIED:** Mary Slatton **PARENTS:** William Burrell and Emeline (Denny) Shockley

Unmarked Grave

Old Rocky Cemetery
Located in pasture at 2671 Goodbar Road

Hillis, William Robisson
LOCATION: Old Rocky Cemetery **RANK:** Private **COMPANY:** I **REGIMENT:** 16th Tennessee Infantry **BIRTH:** 19 February 1837 **DEATH:** 25 July 1861 **MARRIED:** Sarah Elizabeth Barnes, 02 September 1854, Van Buren County, Tennessee **PARENTS:** Dixon Naylor and Lydia (Logue) Hillis

Pleasant Hill Cemetery
Fall Creek Falls area

Clark, Byrd
LOCATION: Pleasant Hill Cemetery **RANK:** Private **COMPANY:** D **REGIMENT:** 4th (Murray's) Tennessee Cavalry **BIRTH:** 01 October 1832 **DEATH:** 22 February 1907 **MARRIED:** Sarah Elizabeth Williams, 29 May 1858, Van Buren County, Tennessee **PARENTS:** Charles and Hannah (Denton) Clark

Byrd Clark

Savage Family Cemetery
Corner of Van Buren County which adjoins Warren and Sequatchie Counties

Savage, Starling John
LOCATION: Savage Family Cemetery **RANK:** Private **COMPANY:** Not listed **REGIMENT:** 35th Tennessee Infantry **BIRTH:** 18 September 1841 **DEATH:** 18 April 1896 **MARRIED:** Nancy Elliott, Warren County, Tennessee **PARENT:** Sterling Savage

Starling Savage Lynched

On last Saturday morning, April 18th, a little after 2 o'clock, a mob of masked men appeared at the residence of Mr. Dread Roberts, on the Irving College Road, 7 miles southeast of McMinnville, and told Roberts they wanted Sterling Savage, who was spending the night there. Savage was ordered to come out of his room, which he refused to do. The mob then broke down the door with a fence rail and covered Savage with guns and pistols. His hands and feet were tied and he was dragged from the house. Roberts being given orders by the mob not to leave the house until after daylight. When Roberts went out after daylight he found the body of Savage hanging in the limb of a tree near the main road from McMinnville to Irving College, about one hundred yards from his house. A coroner's jury was impaneled by Esq. J. J. Meadows and an inquest held over the body, but no facts were developed in the direction of identifying any of the lynchers. Several weeks ago Savage was arrested at Bon Air by Revenue officers while selling wildcat liquor, his wagon and team of mules were seized and they were sold here by the Revenue officials the day Savage was hanged. Since the arrest of Savage, a number of other arrests and seizures have been made, and it is supposed Savage gave the Revenue officers the information which led to the arrests. He was regarded as a spy and spotter for the Revenue officers, and doubtless for this reason was lynched. Savage was 55 or 60 years of age, and lived near Doyle, White County, where he had a wife and several children.

preemptory —1896 newspaper article

Seitz Cemetery
Near Fall Creek Falls, off Highway 111

Seitz, Logan
LOCATION: Seitz Cemetery **RANK:** Private **COMPANY:** District #9 **REGIMENT:** Van Buren County Home Guard **BIRTH:** 12 February 1823 **DEATH:** 18 February 1900 **MARRIED:** (1) Matilda Walling, 09 December 1847, Van Buren County, Tennessee; (2) Nellie Hayes McGregor Deering **PARENTS:** Thomas and Margaret Hoyles (Rudisill) Seitz

Marker Photo Not Available

Sparkman Cemetery
Sparkman Road

Billingsley, Cyrus
LOCATION: Sparkman Cemetery **RANK:** Private **COMPANY:** I **REGIMENT:** 16th Tennessee Infantry **BIRTH:** 13 January 1839 **DEATH:** 21 April 1867 **MARRIED:** Elizabeth Plumlee, 22 December 1858, Van Buren County, Tennessee **PARENTS:** John M. and Melie (Metcalf) Billingsley

Plumlee, Finis E.
LOCATION: Sparkman Cemetery RANK: Private
COMPANY: District #3 REGIMENT: Van Buren County Home
Guard BIRTH: 05 June 1820 DEATH: 05 February 1864
MARRIED: Lucinda Sparkman, 30 December 1841, Van Buren
County, Tennessee

~

Sparkman, George W.
LOCATION: Sparkman Cemetery RANK: Private COMPANY: C
REGIMENT: 35th Tennessee Infantry BIRTH: 1843 DEATH: 1862
MARRIED: Armindy Shockley, 13 August 1859, Van Buren
County, Tennessee OTHER: George Sparkman was killed in
battle. Marker is a memorial.

~

Sparkman, John B.
LOCATION: Sparkman Cemetery RANK: Private
COMPANY: District #2 REGIMENT: Van Buren County Home
Guard BIRTH: 06 April 1837 DEATH: 12 September 1910
MARRIED: Sarah Moore PARENTS: George and Berthina
(Goddard) Sparkman

~

Stipes, George W.
LOCATION: Sparkman Cemetery RANK: Private
COMPANY: District #3 REGIMENT: Van Buren County Home
Guard BIRTH: Unknown DEATH: Unknown MARRIED: Susan
Ann Sparkman, 07 August 1859, Van Buren County,
Tennessee

Unmarked Grave

John R. Sparkman Cemetery
Sparkman Road past Stoney Point Cemetery Road

Sparkman, John R.
LOCATION: John R. Sparkman Cemetery RANK: Private
COMPANY: I REGIMENT: 13th (Gore's) Tennessee Cavalry
BIRTH: 25 October 1815 DEATH: 03 March 1906
MARRIED: Cynthia Jane Sanderson, 12 December 1867, Van
Buren County, Tennessee PARENTS: William and Louisa
(Howard) Sparkman

Spencer Town Cemetery
One-quarter mile from courthouse in Spencer

Acuff, Jasper Sylvester
LOCATION: Spencer Town Cemetery **RANK:** Private **COMPANY:** F **REGIMENT:** 4th (Branner's) Battalion Tennessee Infantry **BIRTH:** 19 August 1841 **DEATH:** 13 October 1893 **MARRIED:** Nancy Jane Billingsly **PARENTS:** John H. and Matilda Emily (Billingsly) Acuff

~

Clark, Carroll Henderson
LOCATION: Spencer Town Cemetery **RANK:** 2nd Lieutenent **COMPANY:** I **REGIMENT:** 16th Tennessee Infantry **BIRTH:** 26 February 1842 **DEATH:** 26 April 1931 **MARRIED:** (1) Keziah Mooneyham, 16 October 1867, Van Buren County, Tennessee; (2) Harriet Sutton; (3) Joan Wilson **PENSION:** #S3771 **PARENTS:** James and Rebecca (Sanders) Clark

Carroll Henderson Clark

~

Clark, John E.
LOCATION: Spencer Town Cemetery **RANK:** Private **COMPANY:** F **REGIMENT:** 11th (Gordon's) Battalion Tennessee Infantry **BIRTH:** 18 April 1819 **DEATH:** 11 August 1885 **MARRIED:** (1) Jane Parker, 27 November 1841, Van Buren County, Tennessee; (2) Caroline Moore, 26 July 1855, Van Buren County, Tennessee **PARENTS:** Martha Clark

~

Davis, Henry "Tinker"
LOCATION: Spencer Town Cemetery **RANK:** Private **COMPANY:** E **REGIMENT:** 50th (Consolidated) Tennessee Infantry **BIRTH:** 07 January 1828, Ireland **DEATH:** 16 February 1907 **MARRIED:** Meribeth Hines

Freiley, J. M.
LOCATION: Spencer Town Cemetery
RANK: Captain **COMPANY:** C
REGIMENT: 22nd (Murray's) Battalion Tennessee Infantry
BIRTH: 28 May 1824 **DEATH:** 07 April 1901
MARRIED: Nancy A. Billingsly

~

Haston, John Taylor
LOCATION: Spencer Town Cemetery **RANK:** Not Listed
COMPANY: D / District #3 **REGIMENT:** 1st Tennessee Cavalry / Van Buren County Home Guard **BIRTH:** 25 April 1844
DEATH: 02 January 1923 **MARRIED:** Nancy Ford, 08 January 1871, Van Buren County, Tennessee **PENSION:** #S3539
PARENTS: James Alfred and Louvina Fidelia (King) Haston

~

Haston, Wiley B.
LOCATION: Spencer Town Cemetery **RANK:** Private
COMPANY: H **REGIMENT:** 16th Tennessee Infantry
BIRTH: 12 April 1836 **DEATH:** 09 October 1862
PARENTS: James Alfred and Louvina Fidelia (King) Haston

~

Jones, David
LOCATION: Spencer Town Cemetery
RANK: Private **COMPANY:** District #2
REGIMENT: Van Buren County Home Guard
BIRTH: 26 October 1811 **DEATH:** 03 August 1879
MARRIED: Beersheba

~

Walker, Joseph Hardy
LOCATION: Spencer Town Cemetery **RANK:** Private
COMPANY: I **REGIMENT:** 16th Tennessee Infantry
BIRTH: 04 December 1839 **DEATH:** 26 Octobter 1931
MARRIED: Nancy Jane Haston, 09 May 1861, Van Buren County, Tennessee **PENSION:** #S14783
PARENTS: David and Polly Ann (Stultz) Walker

Wheeler, Burdin
LOCATION: Spencer Town Cemetery **RANK:** 1st Lieutenent
COMPANY: A **REGIMENT:** 4th (Murray's) Tennessee Cavalry
BIRTH: 1804 **DEATH:** 1887 **MARRIED:** (1) Lathy Steakley;
(2) Charlotte Harriet Southern **OTHER:** Marker identifies service in Cherokee War.

Walling Cemetery
Entrance to Fall Creek Falls from Highway 30, second road on the left

Whittenburg, Issac
LOCATION: Walling Cemetery **RANK:** Captain
COMPANY: District #10 **REGIMENT:** Van Buren County Home Guard **BIRTH:** April 1815 **DEATH:** c. 1910 **MARRIED:** Marilla Walling, 24 June 1841, Van Buren County, Tennessee

Unmarked Grave

White Hill Cemetery

Hillis, Isaac Jr.
LOCATION: White Hill Cemetery **RANK:** Private
COMPANY: District #8 **REGIMENT:** Van Buren County Home Guard **BIRTH:** 19 December 1810 **DEATH:** 04 December 1878
MARRIED: (1) Hannah Johnson, 02 November 1852, Van Buren County, Tennessee; (2) Nancy McBride, 11 March 1867, Van Buren County, Tennessee **PARENTS:** Isaac and Rebecca (Naylor) Hillis

Hillis, James
LOCATION: White Hill Cemetery **RANK:** Sergeant
COMPANY: I **REGIMENT:** 16th Tennessee Infantry
BIRTH: 28 August 1823 **DEATH:** 28 February 1901
MARRIED: Jane Tosh, 28 February 1852, Van Buren County, Tennessee **PARENTS:** Isaac and Rebecca (Naylor) Hillis

Hillis, Roswell

LOCATION: White Hill Cemetery
RANK: Private **COMPANY:** E
REGIMENT: 22nd (Murray's) Battalion Tennessee Infantry
BIRTH: 15 March 1825 **DEATH:** 21 August 1898
MARRIED: (1) Elizabeth Grissom, 02 August 1849, Van Buren County, Tennessee; (2) Nancy Caroline Mitchell Caulder
PARENTS: Isaac and Rebecca (Naylor) Hillis

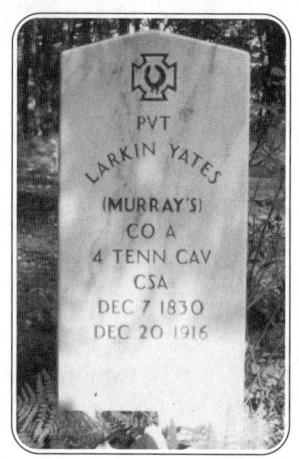

Yates Mountain Cemetery

Yates, Larkin

LOCATION: Yates Mountain Cemetery **RANK:** Private
COMPANY: A **REGIMENT:** 4th (Murray's) Tennessee Cavalry
BIRTH: 07 December 1830 **DEATH:** 20 December 1916
MARRIED: (1) Eleanor Sparkman, 07 September 1854, Van Buren County, Tennessee; (2) Milly Crain, 23 August 1908, Van Buren County, Tennessee **PENSION:** #S3769

WHITE COUNTY

White County, Tennessee Confederate Reunion, c. 1921–1925

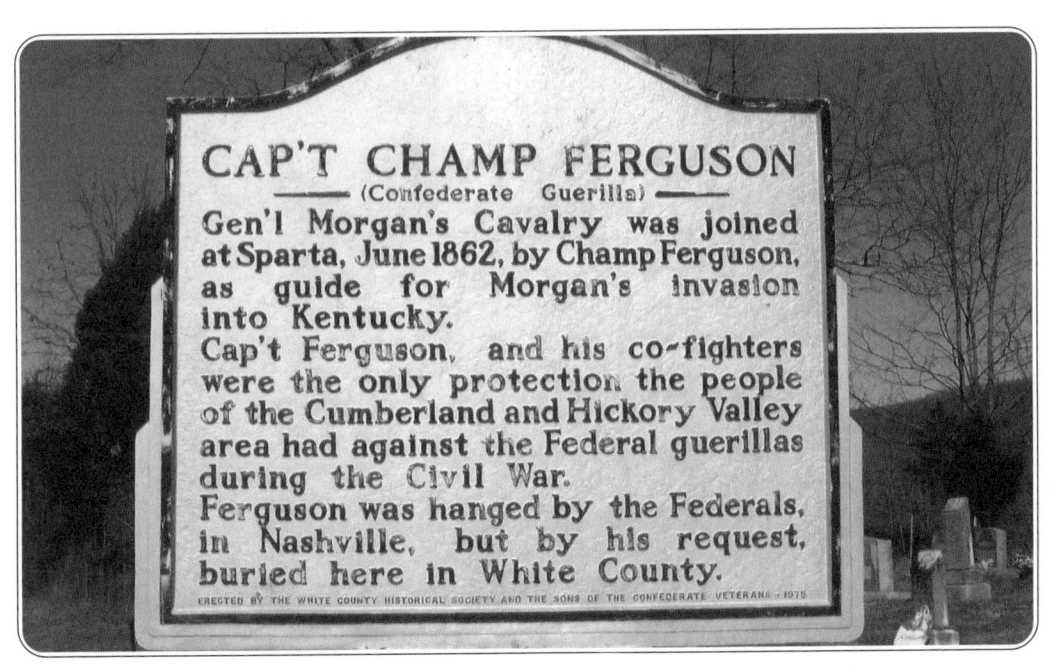

CAP'T CHAMP FERGUSON
——— (Confederate Guerilla) ———
Gen'l Morgan's Cavalry was joined at Sparta, June 1862, by Champ Ferguson, as guide for Morgan's invasion into Kentucky.
Cap't Ferguson, and his co-fighters were the only protection the people of the Cumberland and Hickory Valley area had against the Federal guerillas during the Civil War.
Ferguson was hanged by the Federals, in Nashville, but by his request, buried here in White County.
ERECTED BY THE WHITE COUNTY HISTORICAL SOCIETY AND THE SONS OF THE CONFEDERATE VETERANS - 1975

Monterey Highway (SR84), France Cemetery, White County, Tennessee

2D 17
GEORGE GIBBS DIBRELL
April 12, 1822 - May 9, 1888

Born in a house which stood here. A leading citizen, he was elected a Union delegate to the proposed secession convention of 1861, but enlisted for the Confederacy at Tennessee's withdrawal; recruited and commanded brigades under Forrest and Wheeler; on the flight from Richmond was guardian of Confederate archives. Member of Congress, 1874-84; prominent in railroad and coal mining activities in this area. He is buried in Sparta.

Gaines Street, Sparta, White County, Tennessee

2D 19
BRAGG INVADES KENTUCKY
Sept.-Oct., 1862

The Army of Mississippi passed here. Forrest's Cavalry Brigade, reporting Sept. 3, moved out to screen the left flank. Here, Sept. 5, Bragg advised his army of Kirby Smith's victory at Richmond, Ky., Aug. 30. At Milledgeville, 10 mi. N., Bragg, with Polk's Right Wing, turned west to pass through Carthage; Hardee's Left Wing, screened by Wheeler's Cavalry Brigade, moved north through Gainesboro. The columns reunited at Tompinsville, Ky.

Bockman Way, Sparta, White County, Tennessee

1920 Reunion of the 8th Tennessee Cavalry (photo courtesy of Sons of Confederate Veterans)

General George Gibbs Dibrell's Reunion Brigade, 1885. Left to right: Col. J. H. Snodgrass, Surgeon; Major W. M. Dingess, Chaplain; "Col." Eliphelet Jarvis (not a soldier, but a reunion brigade member); William Fleming; Waman Leftwich Dibrell, aide de camp; Col. Sam V. McManus, Chief of Staff; Gen. W. Gooch Smith (Information courtesy of Charlie Leonard, Photo courtesy of Sons of Confederate Veterans)

1917 Reunion. Four men on front row, from left to right: W. L. Dibrell, Soloman Sparkman, Nelson Hyder, and Wiley Steakley. Due to General G. G. Dibrell's position during and after the war, many active Confederate reunions were held in White County (photo courtesy of Sons of Confederate Veterans)

Stories and Documents of White County

A story relayed by General Dibrell in his final report

Many soldiers returning with General Dibrell told the same story to family and friends after the war.

"Leaving Cleveland late in the evening, we marched through rain and mud to Chattanooga next day, and reported in person first to Lieut. Sargent, Provost-marshal, who informed us his instructions were to dismount all the private soldiers. We then reported in person to General Judah, commanding the post, whom we found playing a game of whist with Judge Rousseau, of Kentucky, a brother of the General. Gen. Judah received us kindly, but declined to interfere. We stated to Lieut. Sargent and Gen. Judah that all of our horses were private property, and by terms of Gen. Johnston's surrender all soldiers were allowed to retain their horses; and that, in addition to this, before we surrendered to Capt. Abrahams, who paroled us, we had telegraphed from Augusta, Ga., to Gen.

Wilson, at Macon, and he had instructed Capt. Abrahams to allow us to keep our horses. But all this failed. This bigoted Provost-marshal (Lieut. Sargent) insisted that he had orders from Gen. Thomas to take the horses—which proved to be false, as he had no such orders—and Gen. Judah was too much engaged in his game of cards to give us any attention; hence we were compelled to submit to seeing the horses taken from all the private soldiers, which was downright robbery. Lieut. Sargent was told that if we had our arms back he would get the horses and arms together after we were overpowered, and not before. After the horses were taken we marched for our homes, this same Provost-marshal with a guard taking his stand on the bridge and inspecting every parole. We were greatly humiliated at the bad treatment we had received after reaching our own State, both at Cleveland and Chattanooga. As soon as we could we sent an application to Gen. Thomas, at Nashville, to have the horses returned, which order he promptly granted, and we sent a detachment back to Chattanooga for the horses. The Quartermaster in charge had put them in dry lots, without food or water, and several had died, while many were so poor they could scarcely walk, and several of the best were seen in the possession of United States officers, branded "U.S." and they of course refused to deliver them up. So the Eighth Tennessee lost one hundred and eight horses, this wrongfully taken from our destitute soldiers, who were returning to their desolated homes after three and a half years hard service. The gallant boys of the Eighth bore these insults and indignities like heroes, and struck out across Cumberland Mountain and Walden's Ridge for their homes on foot. Many of them were cheerful, and would give the cavalry commands as they tramped overland. As they neared their homes they were met by anxious friends, who received them with loads of provisions and many congratulations for their safe return."

"Be it said to their credit that nearly every soldier of the Eight Tennessee Cavalry who served to the close of the war has made a good and prosperous citizen. They suffered immense hardships, were driven from pillar to post under many regimental commanders, with many local troubles to encounter; but when the bugle sounded the call to arms they never faltered, and always did their duty. They were always loud in their praises of the treatment they received at the hands of citizens of the vicinity when camped at Rains's lot, who gave them provisions, clothing, blankets, etc."

—*from Military Annals of Tennessee and Regimental Histories and Memorial Rolls.*

The Battle of Dug Hill

Of all the skirmishes that occurred in White County during the War Between the States, the fight at Dug Hill was the most ferocious and fatal. Union troops occupied White County at the time. The Federals belonged to Colonel Stokes' Cavalry and a large number of them were killed in the battle. It has been said, about one-third of the Federals survived.

This battle was known locally as the "Battle of the Calfkiller." In the winter of 1864, Colonel Stokes and six companies of soldiers were stationed in Sparta. At other times, Colonel Garrett's Federals, according to Confederate General Dibrell, were harassing the local people. A number of Southern men, some of them belonging to regular Confederate commands were cut off from their units and retaliated bitterly against the harassment. Some of the Confederate guerillas were George Carter, who was a captain of Company A, Eighth Tennessee Cavalry; John M. Hughes, a colonel in S. S. Stanton's old regiment, the Twenty-fifth Tennessee Infantry, W. S. Bledsoe, a captain in Stanton's regiment and Champ Ferguson. The small force of guerillas, under the direct leadership of each of these men, with a few Texas Rangers, was about forty.

Stokes, it is said, had raised the black flag as far as these men were concerned and sent word that he would give no quarter. Their reply to the threat was that his proclamation just suited them, and they would not give any of his regiment quarter. So this was understood.

A crowd had assembled in Sparta on February 22nd to listen to a speech being delivered by Colonel Stokes. He had sent out about eighty men to scour the countryside for guerillas. They were to take the Old Kentucky or Cookeville road to Cookeville, and return through Dry Valley, near the Calf Killer River. Captain E. W. Bass of Liberty commanded the Union force.

Ferguson and his friends had been informed of the movement and gathered in the hills sloping down to Dry Valley. The plan of the guerrillas was to form an ambush and send forward two men to decoy the Federals on their return. They selected the steep borders of the Dug Hill road. This road leads out of Dry Valley into the mountains. On either side were immense boulders and scrub cedars and laurel. This was an ideal place for concealment. They waited patiently beside this desolate road.

By afternoon, the Federals filed into the valley, reaching the Dug Hill road. They were suddenly startled by a shot and discovered two men riding rapidly up the hill. It was natural for them to start in pursuit, not dreaming of an ambush. When nearly all the Federals reached the valley, the roadsides blazed. There was a deafening volley and men in blue began tumbling headlong from their saddles. A wild race for safety on the part of the survivors began. One of them, Russell Gan, had been knocked from his horse. There was a hollow log near by and into this he crawled. He made his escape after darkness. Captain Bass fled to Sparta bareheaded, which he reached the following forenoon.

Union soldiers fled everywhere and anywhere. Along with the cries of the wounded and dying, the sharp cracks of pistols multiplied the resounding echoes from mountain to valley, blended with the metallic clanging of the hoofs of scampering and riderless horses. This was a memory never forgotten by those who survived. Many turned back, while a few dashed up the mountain. The guerillas had hitched their horses some distance off and the pursuit was on foot. John Gatewood intercepted five of the Yankees with an army pistol in each hand and he called on them to surrender. Not thinking him alone, they did so. But after seeing that he was by himself, two broke away after the surrender. Fearing the remaining three would follow their example; Gatewood was in the act of shooting them when Captain George Carter appeared on the scene.

"Hold on John," he called as he gathered up one or two stones. "Don't waste your ammunition, as we have to fight for all we get."

The next day when Stokes sent out wagons for his dead soldiers, forty-one were found. They were laid side by side in an old store in Sparta. The exact number of men killed that day was never known. After all the dead could be found, they were taken away and buried. Later, others were found along the road, and skeletons were found scattered in the woods the next winter.

~

The Battle of Dug Hill is an example of guerilla warfare not normally used in our country at that time. Without understanding the circumstances of the War, to some it seems cruel that rocks were used instead of bullets to kill men. In many cases, the Confederate soldiers had to pay for their own bullets, thus the comment in the story, "Don't waste your ammunition, as we have to fight for all we get." This is a fact not mentioned in most history books. It has always amazed me that Union General Stokes left the bodies of his men out in the fields until the next day. Obviously his speech was more important to him than his men were. In this skirmish at Dug Hill, guerilla warfare made for very effective tactics. If the South had chosen to continue the War, guerilla warfare would have been seen on a much larger scale. This is what makes the admonition of General Robert E. Lee so important when he dismissed his army. He told the men of the South to go home and become good citizens. Only thirty years later the Spanish-American War began and the men of the South would answer the call to war. They have never failed to do so since 1865. Consider where we would be if all the troops from the South came home from Iraq and Afghanistan today.

—*Barbara Parsons*

~

Home Guard of White County, Tennessee, 3 June 1861
White County, Tennessee Minute Book 1858–Oct. 1865, pages 370-371

Ordered by Court that Thomas Snodgrass and Thomas B. Eastland be appointed a committee to wait upon the Physicians of White County and get the names of such as willing to lend their services when called on free of charge for the families of the gallant soldiers that have volunteered and gone to fight in defense of their homes and property and report so the next time of this court.

Ordered by Court that Thomas B. Eastland be appointed to confer with Isham G. Harris, Govenor of the State of Tennessee and try to procure the use of the muskitts belonging to the State that is now in White County or such of them as can be found for the use of the Home Guards of White County and report to the next time of this Court.

This day the following named persons was appointed by this Court to serve for three months as a Home Guard of Minute Men according to Act of Assembly of the State, passed at the extra session of the General Assembly of said State passed on the 6th of May 1861-Whose duty it shall be to procure a warrant from some Justice of the Peace and arrest all suspected persons and bring them before the court authorities for trial. To see that all slaves are disarmed: To prevent the assemblages of slaves in unusual numbers. To keep the slave population in proper subjection and to see that peace and order is observed. The Home Guard shall assemble in their respective Districts to take free action or measures, at least once in each week at the call of the Commanding Officer and shall be momentarily ready for service at his call. Passions enjoyed in this branch of duty shall upon failure to obey the call to duty by the Commander, forfeit not less than one dollar nor more than five dollars each offense to be collected in the name of the Chairman of the County Court before any Justice of the Peace to be applied by the County Court defraying the expenses of this branch of public service unless such failure was the result of sickness or other good course. A General Commander shall be appointed for each County by the several County Courts whose duty it shall be when necessary to take charge of all the Home Guards Minute Men in this County and direct their operations. The Home Guard are as follows:

District 1: Leftwich Herd, Benjamin Smith, Waman Clark, John M. Carrick, Charles Lowery, Dudley Hudgins, James Scott, Francis Arnold, William Simpson, PW Wallen.

District 2: William Wilson, N.G. Austin, John Wallace, William R. Tucker, H. J. Camp, William L. Mitchell, William Wallace, Colbird S. Arnold, W. G. Lewis, James M. Lewis.

District 3: H. P. Smith, J. M. Sanderson, William Scoggins, James M. Phifer, William C. Warren, Vance Gist, Joshua Cope, R. T. Downy, Larking Howard, John M. Doyle.

District 4: J. A. Teeters, Mat Hutson, Forrester Phifer, Overton Chissom, J. D. Anderson, J. M. Anderson, John R. Rascoe, J. D. Holder, James Fisher, L. L. Hutson

District 5: William Crane, T. E. Hutson, P. A. Glen, Greenville Templeton, J. W. Knowles, A. Crane, F. A. Badger, Jeremiah Knowles, B. B. Humphreys, Hiram Little.

District 6: C. S. Crowder, William M. Cope, Sol Overton, Goodwin Baker, James Bryant, Berry Slatten, E. D. Simerell, Bony Arnold, John Olliver, Wiseman Alexander.

District 7: Giles Elrod, Martin Taylor, William L. Hitchcock, E. J. Russell, Harrold Williams, A. L. Holms, John M. Dow, Lewis Howell, Alexander Payne, A. F. McConnell.

District 8: Davis S. England, H. J. Lida, James Nowlin, A. M. Goodwin, Isaac T. Irwin, William H. Boyd, Edward Austin, Sylvester Jarvis, Rizi Walker, A. Olliver.

District 9: D. M. Southard, C. B. Crook, Samuel Brown, Edington James, Simpson Farly, W. A. Dorin, J. M. Southard, David Farley, William Willhite, Peter Goodwin.

District 11: G. W. Barger, G. W. Cannon, J. L. Quarles, Charley Anderson, Alexander Officer, R. W. Glen, A. A. Bradley, Preston Conley, Hance Carmichael, James Stone.

District 12: Dempsy Stewart, John Williams, T. G. Little, J. W. Meredith, M. J. Brooks, Lawson Brown, John M. Lance, S. J. Bradley, Luin Miller.

District 13: John Davis, Robert Davis, Cumberland Eastland, William Acred, Thomas J. McKinny, George Eastland, Mark Ray, W. W. Scarborough, L. Saterfield, Charles Eastland.

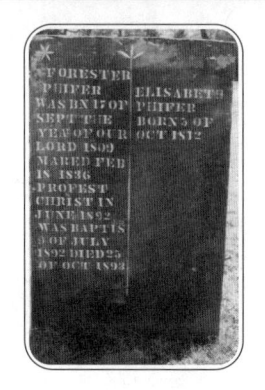

Anderson Cemetery #2

About 3 miles south of Doyle and 1 mile east of Hwy 70 on Anderson Cemetery Road.

Black, George W.
LOCATION: Anderson Cemetery #2 **RANK:** Private **COMPANY:** K **REGIMENT:** 28th Tennessee Infantry **BIRTH:** 04 January 1831 **DEATH:** 03 February 1924 **MARRIED:** (1) Jane Kirby, 30 January 1865, White County, Tennessee (2) Alice Tallent, 19 September 1878, White County, Tennessee **PENSION:** #S5390 **PARENTS:** Isaac and Margaret Mary (Tallent) Black

~

Cole, Walter Wilkins
LOCATION: Anderson Cemetery #2 **RANK:** Private **COMPANY:** A **REGIMENT:** 16th Tennessee Infantry **BIRTH:** 23 November 1826 **DEATH:** 27 January 1901 **MARRIED:** Elizabeth Crage **PENSIONS:** #S222 and #W1485

~

Goddard, James C.
LOCATION: Anderson Cemetery #2 **RANK:** Private **COMPANY:** C **REGIMENT:** 25th Tennessee Infantry **BIRTH:** 21 July 1835 **DEATH:** 10 February 1908 **MARRIED:** Phebe Hollingsworth, 20 February 1868, White County, Tennessee **PARENTS:** Edmund and Martha (Anderson) Goddard

~

Goddard, Robert A.
LOCATION: Anderson Cemetery #2 **RANK:** Private **COMPANY:** E **REGIMENT:** 84th Tennessee Infantry **BIRTH:** 25 March 1824, Tennesssee **DEATH:** 26 April 1893 **MARRIED:** Susannah Teaters, 12 September 1844, White County, Tennessee

~

Phifer, Forrester
LOCATION: Anderson Cemetery #2 **RANK:** Private **COMPANY:** District #4 **REGIMENT:** White County Home Guard of Minute Men **BIRTH:** 17 September 1809, Virginia **DEATH:** 25 October 1893 **MARRIED:** Elizabeth Dodson, 20 January 1876, White County, Tennessee

Phifer, J. W.
LOCATION: Anderson Cemetery #2 **RANK:** Private **COMPANY:** I
REGIMENT: 25th Tenneessee Infantry **BIRTH:** 14 February 1826
DEATH: 10 January 1904 **MARRIED:** Mary Underwood, 27 July 1871, White County

~

Phifer, James M.
LOCATION: Anderson Cemetery #2 **RANK:** Private
COMPANY: District #3 **REGIMENT:** White County Home Guard of Minute Men **BIRTH:** 06 December 1823
DEATH: 14 March 1862

~

Price, Elijah W.
LOCATION: Anderson Cemetery #2 **RANK:** Private
COMPANY: D **REGIMENT:** 4th Tennessee Infantry
BIRTH: 04 July 1839, Tennessee **DEATH:** 17 April 1884
MARRIED: Martha M. Goddard, 22 January 1874, White County, Tennessee

~

Price, George W.
LOCATION: Anderson Cemetery #2 **RANK:** Private
COMPANY: K **REGIMENT:** 22nd (Murray's) Battalion Tenneesse Infantry **BIRTH:** 17 April 1837 **DEATH:** 17 August 1906
MARRIED: Martha C. Stewart, 05 February 1859, Hawkins County, Tennessee

~

Stewart, Thomas W.
LOCATION: Anderson Cemetery #2 **RANK:** Private
COMPANY: I **REGIMENT:** 13th (Gore's) Tennessee Cavalry
BIRTH: 1843, Tennessee **DEATH:** 1926 **MARRIED:** Martha Miranda Anderson, 31 October 1866, White County, Tennessee **PARENTS:** William and Rebecca (Cody) Stewart

Anderson-Felton-Little, Anderson Cemetery #1

Shady Grove

Anderson, Thomas J.
LOCATION: Anderson Cemetery #1 **RANK:** Private **COMPANY:** B
REGIMENT: 1st (Colm's) Battalion Tennessee Infantry
BIRTH: 12 March 1836 **DEATH:** 07 May 1896
MARRIED: Charlotte Little, 11 December 1856, White County, Tennessee **PARENTS:** Zachariah and Rebecca (England) Anderson

~

England, Wesley
LOCATION: Anderson Cemetery #1 **RANK:** Private **COMPANY:** K
REGIMENT: 25th Tennessee Infantry **BIRTH:** 14 February 1822
DEATH: 29 April 1864 **MARRIED:** Ann Elizabeth Little, 02 November 1848, White County, Tennessee **PARENTS:** Elijah and Alcy (Scott) England

Anderson Graveyard #4 (Brook Mead)

Austin, John Jr.
LOCATION: Anderson Graveyard #4 **RANK:** Private **COMPANY:** K
REGIMENT: 16th Tennessee Infantry **BIRTH:** 08 November 1818 **DEATH:** 16 August 1903 **MARRIED:** Rebecca England, 27 June 1841, White County, Tennessee **PENSION:** #S1952
PARENTS: John and Rachel (Denny) Austin

Arnold Cemetery

Southeast side of Pollard Road at junction Oak Grove Road, 0.4 miles west of junction Will Thompson Road.

Arnold, Bonaparte
LOCATION: Arnold Cemetery **RANK:** 2nd Lieutenant
COMPANY: K / District #6 **REGIMENT:** 28th Tennessee Infantry / White County Home Guard of Minute Men
BIRTH: 21 September 1835, Tennessee **DEATH:** 30 March 1918
MARRIED: (1) Martha Ann Denton, 05 June 1881, White County, Tennessee (2) Malissa Camilla Thweatt
OTHER: Immortal 600 member **PARENTS:** Samuel D. and Elizabeth (Glenn) Arnold

Austin-Anderson Cemetery
Lost Creek

Anderson, Thomas M.
LOCATION: Austin-Anderson Cemetery **RANK:** Private
COMPANY: A **REGIMENT:** 25th Tennessee Infantry
BIRTH: 28 February 1810, Tennessee **DEATH:** 03 March 1872

~

Anderson, William Pleasant
LOCATION: Austin-Anderson Cemetery **RANK:** Corporal
COMPANY: E **REGIMENT:** 1st (Colm's) Battalion Tennessee Infantry, Army of Tenneesse Bugler **BIRTH:** 15 August 1843
DEATH: 26 February 1889
MARRIED: Mary Elizabeth Austin, 24 December 1863, White County, Tennessee
PARENTS: Matthias and Marion Anderson

William Pleasant Anderson

Baker Cemetery
Across field 200 feet southeast of Swamp Road, 1 mile southwest of Burgess Falls Road, Black Oak

Farmer, Thomas
LOCATION: Baker Cemetery **RANK:** Private **COMPANY:** K
REGIMENT: 16th Tennessee Infantry **BIRTH:** c. 1828, Tennessee
DEATH: 14 April 1902 **MARRIED:** Elizabeth

~

King, Hiram Houston
LOCATION: Baker Cemetery **RANK:** Private **COMPANY:** C
REGIMENT: 16th Tennessee Infantry **BIRTH:** 06 May 1847
DEATH: 25 May 1892 **MARRIED:** Amanda Baker

Billy Baker Cemetery

End of Baker Cemetery Road (gravel), 3 miles west of Fanchers Mill Road, .5 miles north of junction Hutchings College Road

Baker, Goodwin

LOCATION: Billy Baker Cemetery **RANK:** Captain **COMPANY:** H **REGIMENT:** 50th (Consolidated) Tennessee Infantry **BIRTH:** 15 November 1838 **DEATH:** 21 November 1895 **MARRIED:** Harriet Gracey, 29 February 1880, White County, Tennessee **PARENTS:** Richard T. and Jane E. Baker

Bethlehem Cemetery

North side of East Bethlehem Road, 0.7 miles southwest of junction with County House Road, or 0.9 miles east of junction with US 70S behind Bethlehem Church of Christ

Bruce, O. P.

LOCATION: Bethlehem Cemetery **RANK:** 2nd Lieutenant **COMPANY:** K **REGIMENT:** 3rd (Clack's) Tennessee Infantry **BIRTH:** 1832 **DEATH:** 1907 **MARRIED:** Alice R.

~

Camp, Miles Newton

LOCATION: Bethlehem Cemetery **RANK:** 1st Lieutenant **COMPANY:** C **REGIMENT:** 25th Tennessee Infantry **BIRTH:** 1836 **DEATH:** 1909 **MARRIED:** Elizabeth C.

~

Dibrell, Wayman Leftwich

LOCATION: Bethlehem Cemetery **RANK:** 2nd Lieutenant **REGIMENT:** 8th (Dibrell's) Tennessee Cavalry **BIRTH:** 03 December 1842, White County, Tennessee **DEATH:** 16 March 1932 **MARRIED:** Evaline Morgan, 15 January 1863, White County, Tennessee **PENSIONS:** #S14758, #W10502 **PARENTS:** George Gibbs and Mary Elizabeth (Leftwich) Dibrell **UDC MEMBER:** Carolyn Rollins Carr

Wayman Leftwich Dibrell

Green, A. J.
LOCATION: Bethlehem Cemetery **RANK:** Private
COMPANY: I **REGIMENT:** 17th Tennessee Infantry
BIRTH: 1844 **DEATH:** 1925 **MARRIED:** Ella B.
PARENTS: Avery and Mary Green

~

Green, Harrison T.
LOCATION: Bethlehem Cemetery **RANK:** Private
COMPANY: A **REGIMENT:** 22nd (Murray's) Battalion Tennessee Infantry **BIRTH:** 18 January 1823 **DEATH:** 06 June 1890

~

Green, William E.
LOCATION: Bethlehem Cemetery **RANK:** Private
COMPANY: A **REGIMENT:** 22nd (Murray's) Battalion Tennessee Infantry **BIRTH:** 25 October 1846 **DEATH:** 29 September 1929

~

Haston, J. W., Sr.
LOCATION: Bethlehem Cemetery **RANK:** Corporal
COMPANY: A **REGIMENT:** 4th (Murray's) Tennessee Cavalry
BIRTH: 25 April 1845 **DEATH:** 3 February 1926
MARRIED: Cela J.

~

Hayes, W. C., Dr.
LOCATION: Bethlehem Cemetery **RANK:** Corporal
COMPANY: C **REGIMENT:** 12th Cavalry Battalion
BIRTH: 26 September 1834 **DEATH:** 10 May 1902
MARRIED: Minerva J.

Hill, James Anderson

LOCATION: Bethlehem Cemetery **RANK:** Private **COMPANY:** D **REGIMENT:** 13th (Gore's) Tennessee Cavalry **BIRTH:** 10 November 1824 **DEATH:** 01 March 1892 **MARRIED:** (1) Huldy Greer; (2) Mary Lowrey

~

Hill, William Ransom

LOCATION: Bethlehem Cemetery **RANK:** Captain **REGIMENT:** 8th (Dibrell's) Tennessee Cavalry **BIRTH:** 08 November 1842 **DEATH:** 04 June 1901 **MARRIED:** Amanda (Meredith) Evans, 16 December 1879, White County, Tennessee **PARENTS:** Joab and Elizabeth (Pinner) Hill

~

Lowery, Simpson

LOCATION: Bethlehem Cemetery **RANK:** Private **COMPANY:** A **REGIMENT:** 25th Tennessee Infantry **BIRTH:** 09 January 1833 **DEATH:** 22 August 1912 **MARRIED:** Stacy Elizabeth Kerby, 04 August 1861, White County, Tennessee **PENSION:** #S3002

Simpson Lowery

~

Moore, James M.

LOCATION: Bethlehem Cemetery **RANK:** Private **COMPANY:** A **REGIMENT:** 13th (Gore's) Tennessee Cavalry / 8th (Dibrell's) Tennessee Cavalry **BIRTH:** 13 November 1842 **DEATH:** 06 September 1920 **MARRIED:** Martha E. **PENSIONS:** #S1163, #S14526

~

Morgan, Algernon Sidney

LOCATION: Bethlehem Cemetery **RANK:** 1st Lieutenant **COMPANY:** A **REGIMENT:** 25th Tennessee Infantry **BIRTH:** 27 December 1834 **DEATH:** 03 April 1902 **MARRIED:** Vina **PENSION:** #W2501 **OTHER:** Member of the Immortal 600

Richards, D. R.

LOCATION: Bethlehem Cemetery **RANK:** Private
COMPANY: I **REGIMENT:** 13th (Gore's) Tennessee Cavalry
BIRTH: 25 June 1832 **DEATH:** 22 May 1901 **MARRIED:** Mary Jane Taylor, 03 April 1855, White County, Tennessee
PARENTS: Daniel and Elizabeth Richards

~

Simpson, William Martin

LOCATION: Bethlehem Cemetery **RANK:** Private
COMPANY: I **REGIMENT:** 8th (Dibrell's) Tennessee Cavalry
BIRTH: 27 November 1832 **DEATH:** 07 October 1875
MARRIED: (1) Lee Ann Wallace, 01 December 1852; (2) Lou Carrick, 29 December 1870

~

Smith, Henry P.

LOCATION: Bethlehem Cemetery **RANK:** Private
COMPANY: A / District #3 **REGIMENT:** 28th (Consolidated) Tennessee Infantry / White County Home Guard of Minute Men **BIRTH:** 10 February 1827 **DEATH:** 01 October 1886
MARRIED: Cinthia C. Hill, 14 March 1858, White County, Tennessee

~

Stroud, Rezi Jarvis

LOCATION: Bethlehem Cemetery **RANK:** Captain
COMPANY: District #7 **REGIMENT:** Van Buren County Home Guard **BIRTH:** 1828 **DEATH:** 1906 **MARRIED:** Nancy Walling

~

Swindell, John Rasco

LOCATION: Bethlehem Cemetery **RANK:** Private **COMPANY:** G **REGIMENT:** 16th Tennessee Infantry **BIRTH:** 05 December 1843 **DEATH:** 28 July 1915 **MARRIED:** Mary Elizabeth Pennington, 27 April 1867, White County, Tennessee **PARENTS:** John and Elizabeth (Roberts) Swindell

Taylor, Hosea
LOCATION: Bethlehem Cemetery **RANK:** Private **COMPANY:** A
REGIMENT: 25th Tennessee Infantry **BIRTH:** 01 November 1841
DEATH: 29 May 1904 **MARRIED:** Martilia J. Webb
PENSION: #W2548 **PARENTS:** Creed A. and Sarah Taylor

Yates, Samuel
LOCATION: Bethlehem Cemetery **RANK:** Private
COMPANY: K **REGIMENT:** 28th Tennessee Infantry
BIRTH: 10 October 1842 **DEATH:** 06 November 1880

Young, D. H.
LOCATION: Bethlehem Cemetery **RANK:** Private
COMPANY: I **REGIMENT:** 13th (Gore's) Tennessee Cavalry
BIRTH: 25 September 1843 **DEATH:** 13 September 1908
MARRIED: Mary Lowery, 18 June 1866, White County, Tennessee
PARENTS: Austin C. and Lucetta (Clark) Young

Young, James S.
LOCATION: Bethlehem Cemetery **RANK:** Corporal
COMPANY: F **REGIMENT:** 13th (Gore's) Tennessee Cavalry
BIRTH: 20 February 1841 **DEATH:** Unknown **MARRIED:** Rutha Worley, 20 March 1873, White County, Tennessee

Big Springs Cemetery
East side of Mack Floyd Road, 0.1 miles south of Junction SR84, Monterey Highway

Bradley, Charles H.
LOCATION: Big Springs Cemetery
RANK: Sergeant **COMPANY:** H
REGIMENT: 28th (Consolidated) Tennessee Infantry **BIRTH:** 12 February 1828 **DEATH:** 20 November 1891 **MARRIED:** Mary Ann "Polly" Geer, 17 October 1852, White County, Tennessee
PARENTS: Thomas Walton and Elizabeth (Williams) Bradley

Charles H. Bradley

Mitchell, Martin
LOCATION: Big Springs Cemetery **RANK:** Private **COMPANY:** I
REGIMENT: 16th Tennesssee Infantry **BIRTH:** August 1830
DEATH: May 1912 **PENSION:** #S4424

~

Swack, Andrew Jackson
LOCATION: Big Springs Cemetery **RANK:** Corporal
COMPANY: D **REGIMENT:** 1st (Colm's) Battalion Tennessee Infantry **BIRTH:** 23 December 1830 **DEATH:** 17 May 1908
MARRIED: Sarah Angeline Weaver, 11 June 1858, White County, Tennessee
PENSIONS: #S2241 and #S7288

Andrew Jackson Swack

~

Walker, James M.
LOCATION: Big Springs Cemetery **RANK:** Captain **COMPANY:** A
REGIMENT: 28th Tennessee Infantry **BIRTH:** 01 August 1820
DEATH: 1865

~

Weaver, William J.
LOCATION: Big Springs Cemetery **RANK:** Private **COMPANY:** H
REGIMENT: 28th (Consolidated) Tennessee Infantry
BIRTH: 07 January 1834 **DEATH:** 05 January 1910
MARRIED: Martha Miller, 28 November 1876, White County, Tennessee

Black Oak Cemetery
Both sides of Burgess Falls Road, 0.7 miles west of Old Cookeville Highway

Grayham, John T.
LOCATION: Black Oak Cemetery **RANK:** Private **COMPANY:** I
REGIMENT: 16th Tennessee Infantry **BIRTH:** 26 June 1846
DEATH: After 1879 **MARRIED:** Margaret Lucinda Taylor, 13 January 1879, White County, Tennessee

Green, Joseph A.
LOCATION: Black Oak Cemetery **RANK:** Private
COMPANY: I **REGIMENT:** 35th Tennessee Infantry
BIRTH: 1843 **DEATH:** 1929 **MARRIED:** Martha A.

~

Osborn, Henry
LOCATION: Black Oak Cemetery **RANK:** Private
COMPANY: A **REGIMENT:** 8th (Dibrell's) Tennessee Cavalry / 13th (Gore's) Tennessee Cavalry **BIRTH:** 10 November 1833
DEATH: 05 May 1925 **MARRIED:** Armilda (pension says, Permelia) **PENSION:** #W8639

~

Willhite, Haliard
LOCATION: Black Oak Cemetery **RANK:** Private
COMPANY: A **REGIMENT:** 22nd (Murray's) Battalion Tennessee Infantry **BIRTH:** 21 January 1838 **DEATH:** 28 February 1925
MARRIED: Amanda E. French, 15 December 1859
PENSION: #S5192

~

Wilhite, R. H.
LOCATION: Black Oak Cemetery **RANK:** Private **COMPANY:** D
REGIMENT: 13th (Gore's) Tennessee Cavalry **BIRTH:** 05 September 1825 **DEATH:** 13 January 1907 **MARRIED:** Polly Ann

Board Valley Cemetery
Board Valley Freewill Baptist Church

Daniels, Emery
LOCATION: Board Valley Cemetery **RANK:** Private **COMPANY:** F
REGIMENT: 28th Tennessee Infantry **BIRTH:** 04 January 1836
DEATH: 10 December 1922 **MARRIED:** Elizabeth S.
PENSION: #S1185

Hale, John H.
LOCATION: Board Valley Cemetery **RANK:** Private **COMPANY:** C **REGIMENT:** 25th Tennessee Infantry **BIRTH:** 25 August 1844 **DEATH:** 04 January 1917 **PENSION:** #S2278

~

Robinson, John H.
LOCATION: Board Valley Cemetery **RANK:** Private **COMPANY:** D **REGIMENT:** 8th (Dibrell's) Tennessee Cavalry / 13th (Gore's) Tennessee Cavalry **BIRTH:** 14 January 1826 **DEATH:** 04 November 1907 **PENSION:** #S2270

~

Selby, James
LOCATION: Board Valley Cemetery **RANK:** Private **COMPANY:** I **REGIMENT:** 25th Tennessee Infantry **BIRTH:** 19 September 1847 **DEATH:** 19 May 1921 **MARRIED:** Rachel

~

Weaver, Benjamin
LOCATION: Board Valley Cemetery **RANK:** Private **COMPANY:** A **REGIMENT:** 25th Tennessee Infantry **BIRTH:** 12 October 1824 **DEATH:** 15 October 1905 **MARRIED:** Rhoda Jane Bumbalough, 14 September 1851 **PARENTS:** Samuel D. P. and Annie (Hickman) Weaver

~

Weaver, William
LOCATION: Board Valley Cemetery **RANK:** Private **COMPANY:** E **REGIMENT:** 17th Tennessee Infantry **BIRTH:** 13 September 1832 **DEATH:** 20 January 1905

Williams, Henry
LOCATION: Board Valley Cemetery RANK: Private
COMPANY: E REGIMENT: 28th (Consolidated) Tennessee
Infantry BIRTH: 16 January 1834 DEATH: 15 August 1893
MARRIED: Sarah

Bradley Family Cemetery
Taylors

Bradley, Thomas D.
LOCATION: Bradley Family Cemetery RANK: Private
COMPANY: D REGIMENT: 13th (Gore's) Tennessee Cavalry
BIRTH: 18 January 1832 DEATH: 01 March 1866
PARENTS: Richard and Arminta "Minty" (Bradley) Bradley Jr.

Broyles Cemetery
Rural White County, Tennessee

Broyles, George G.
LOCATION: Broyles Cemetery BIRTH: 19 February 1797, White County, Tennessee DEATH: 04 April 1886, White County, Tennessee OTHER: Provided material aid to the South
MARRIED: Margaret Johnson, c. 1830 (Tennessee)
UDC MEMBERS: Sherrie Beth Broyles McCulley, Susan Broyles Harris

Cameron-Floyd Cemetery
Taylors

Floyd, William T.
LOCATION: Cameron-Floyd Cemetery RANK: Private
COMPANY: A REGIMENT: 7th Tennessee Infantry BIRTH: 24 August 1837 DEATH: 18 October 1912 PENSION: #S12679

Cash-Farley Cemetery
Mt. Herman

Cash, William M. Simpson
LOCATION: Cash-Farley Cemetery **RANK:** Private **COMPANY:** K **REGIMENT:** 25th Tennessee Infantry **BIRTH:** 18 March 1831 **DEATH:** 15 January 1900 **MARRIED:** Mary Cartwright **PARENTS:** Simpson and Edith (Flannigan) Cash

~

Farley, Simpson M.
LOCATION: Cash-Farley Cemetery **RANK:** Private **COMPANY:** K / District #9 **REGIMENT:** 16th Tennessee Infantry / White County Home Guard of Minute Men **BIRTH:** 09 March 1823 **DEATH:** 22 May 1879 **MARRIED:** Elizabeth Isom, 01 April 1841, White County, Tennessee **PARENT:** Malinda Farley of Virginia

Cherry Creek (Lower) Cemetery
Cherry Creek Church of Christ

Cooper, Levi P.
LOCATION: Cherry Creek (Lower) Cemetery **RANK:** Private **COMPANY:** D **REGIMENT:** 84th Tennessee Infantry **BIRTH:** 21 February 1842 **DEATH:** 18 May 1903 **MARRIED:** Mary T. Stanley, 14 January 1881, White County, Tennessee

~

Stewart, Dempsy
LOCATION: Cherry Creek (Lower) Cemetery **RANK:** Private **COMPANY:** District #12 **REGIMENT:** White County Home Guard of Minute Men **BIRTH:** c. 1798, North Carolina **DEATH:** After 1870

~

Stewart, James "Jim" Daniel
LOCATION: Cherry Creek (Lower) Cemetery **RANK:** Private **COMPANY:** K **REGIMENT:** 13th (Gore's) Tennessee Cavalry **BIRTH:** 14 February 1829 **DEATH:** 07 June 1899

White County · Our Confederate Ancestors · 149

Stewart, Samuel Levi
LOCATION: Cherry Creek (Lower) Cemetery **RANK:** Private **COMPANY:** K **REGIMENT:** 8th (Dibrell's) Tennessee Cavalry **BIRTH:** 12 August 1837, South Carolina **DEATH:** 03 November 1913 **MARRIED:** Michal Louiza Cooper, 11 September 1956, White County, Tennessee **PARENTS:** Dempsey and Sarah Stewart

~

Treadway, Henry H.
LOCATION: Cherry Creek (Lower) Cemetery **RANK:** Private **COMPANY:** K **REGIMENT:** 37th North Carolina Infantry **BIRTH:** 16 December 1845, North Carolina **DEATH:** 28 February 1914 **PARENT:** John Treadway

~

Treadway, John
LOCATION: Cherry Creek (Lower) Cemetery **RANK:** Private **COMPANY:** K **REGIMENT:** 37th North Carolina Infantry **BIRTH:** 1814, North Carolina **DEATH:** 1905

~

Vandever, James C.
LOCATION: Cherry Creek (Lower) Cemetery **RANK:** Private **COMPANY:** A **REGIMENT:** 28th Tennessee Infantry **BIRTH:** 18 March 1812 **DEATH:** 23 April 1889

~

Walker, John W.
LOCATION: Cherry Creek (Lower) Cemetery **RANK:** Not listed **COMPANY:** A **REGIMENT:** 10th Kentucky Regiment **BIRTH:** Unknown **DEATH:** Unknown **PENSION:** #S6385

Cherry Creek (Upper) Cemetery
Cherry Creek Presbyterian / Baptist Church

Burgess, James C.
LOCATION: Cherry Creek (Upper) Cemetery **RANK:** Sergeant **COMPANY:** H **REGIMENT:** 13th (Gore's) Tennessee Cavalry **BIRTH:** 27 July 1832 **DEATH:** 02 February 1877 **MARRIED:** Caroline

Burgess, William S.
LOCATION: Cherry Creek (Upper) Cemetery **RANK:** Sergeant
COMPANY: H **REGIMENT:** 13th (Gore's) Tennessee Cavalry
BIRTH: 24 August 1830 **DEATH:** 30 July 1905

~

Coatney, Samuel Frank
LOCATION: Cherry Creek (Upper) Cemetery **RANK:** Sergeant
COMPANY: D / H **REGIMENT:** 84th Tennessee Infantry / 28th (Consolidated) Tennessee Infantry **BIRTH:** 23 January 1833
DEATH: 17 May 1918 **MARRIED:** Clementine Henry, 13 September 1855, White County, Tennessee **OTHER:** During the war, Frank Coatney came home on furlough to see his family. Bushwackers heard he was on leave and went looking for him for the sole purpose of killing him. Frank saw them coming and ran out the back door. The bushwackers saw him leave and were certain he was making a desperate attempt to reach the creek as a means of escape and they ran after him. In the meantime, Frank, in his flight, passed the wash place and seeing an old-fashioned washtub hewn from a log, turned the trough over and slipped under it. The bushwackers searched the surrounding country for nearly an hour. Trees were searched, both banks of the creek were closely watched and bullets were fired into the bushes along the bank in case he should be hiding there. Frank, who lay under the trough, could hear the horses' hooves strike the top of his hiding place as they jumped over the log. The murderers left cursing because they thought they had let him escape. Frank survived that day and lived to be an old man of eighty-five.

~

Coffman, David B.
LOCATION: Cherry Creek (Upper) Cemetery **RANK:** Private
COMPANY: E **REGIMENT:** 1st (Carter's) Tennessee Cavalry
BIRTH: 06 May 1832 **DEATH:** 22 January 1892

~

Mason, Elyhu (Eli)
LOCATION: Cherry Creek (Upper) Cemetery **RANK:** Private
COMPANY: D / H **REGIMENT:** 84th Tennessee Infantry / 28th (Consolidated) Tennessee Infantry **BIRTH:** 02 January 1834
DEATH: 13 November 1904 **PARENTS:** William and Ann Mason

McDowell, Lucien Lafayette

LOCATION: Cherry Creek (Upper) Cemetery **RANK:** 1st Sergeant / Adjutant **COMPANY:** F / Field and Staff **REGIMENT:** 25th Tennessee Infantry **BIRTH:** 1843 **DEATH:** 1883 **MARRIED:** Mary Frances Cantrell, 04 June 1866, White County, Tennessee **OTHER:** Lucien Lafayette McDowell was the brother of Amanda McDowell who kept a diary during the war. One brother fought for the Union and Lucien fought for the Confederacy. **PARENTS:** Curtis and Margaret (Jadwin) McDowell

~

Morris, William R.

LOCATION: Cherry Creek (Upper) Cemetery **RANK:** Corporal **COMPANY:** A **REGIMENT:** 25th Tennessee Infantry **BIRTH:** 10 January 1843 **DEATH:** 30 January 1926 **MARRIED:** (1) Catherine Anderson, 06 January 1867, White County, Tennessee; (2) Louraney Clark, 29 January 1885, White County, Tennessee **PENSION:** #S8230 **PARENTS:** George W. and Elizabeth Morris

~

Weaver, Jephthath

LOCATION: Cherry Creek (Upper) Cemetery **RANK:** Private **COMPANY:** D / H **REGIMENT:** 84th / 28th (Consolidated) Tennessee Infantry **BIRTH:** 10 December 1831 **DEATH:** 02 June 1917 **MARRIED:** Nancy Jane Deering, 24 November 1857 **PARENTS:** Samuel D. P. and Annie (Hickman) Weaver

~

Willhite, Steven

LOCATION: Cherry Creek (Upper) Cemetery **RANK:** Private **COMPANY:** E **REGIMENT:** 11th Battalion Tennessee Cavalry **BIRTH:** 22 March 1835 **DEATH:** 03 January 1908

~

Williams, James T.

LOCATION: Cherry Creek (Upper) Cemetery **RANK:** Private **COMPANY:** H **REGIMENT:** 8th (Dibrell's) Tennessee Cavalry **BIRTH:** 09 May 1844 **DEATH:** 23 February 1917 **MARRIED:** Margaret **PENSION:** #8187

Chism Cemetery #1

Walling

Chisam, Overton Deweese

LOCATION: Chism Cemetery **RANK:** Private **COMPANY:** District #4 **REGIMENT:** White County Home Guard of Minute Men **BIRTH:** 18 February 1811 **DEATH:** 05 December 1891 **MARRIED:** Celia Hash

Chisam-Walker Cemetery

Yankeetown, in edge of woods by pasture, 1200 feet bearing 250 degrees from house at 4687 Monteray Hwy (SR84)

Walker, John A.

LOCATION: Chisam Walker Cemetery **RANK:** Private **COMPANY:** I **REGIMENT:** 13th (Gore's) Tennessee Cavalry **BIRTH:** 07 May 1821 **DEATH:** 05 February 1880

William Chisam Cemetery

Southwest side of Webb's Camp Road, 1.2 miles west of Junction to Old Kentucky Road

Chisam, William M.

LOCATION: William Chisam Cemetery **RANK:** Private **COMPANY:** A **REGIMENT:** 22nd (Murray's) Battalion Tennessee Infantry **BIRTH:** 07 December 1822 **DEATH:** 04 December 1905 **MARRIED:** Mary Lodema Cotton **PENSION:** #W807 **PARENTS:** John and Mary Chisam

~

Tallent, Samuel

LOCATION: William Chisam Cemetery **RANK:** Private **COMPANY:** C **REGIMENT:** 28th (Consolidated) Tennessee Infantry **BIRTH:** 1820 **DEATH:** After 1880 **MARRIED:** Nancy A. Black

Civil War Soldiers Graveyard
Brock Cove

Unknowns
LOCATION: At one time there were six tent-style graves at this site. The graveyard is in the front yard of an old abandoned house. Tent-style graves would indicate "Confederate" burials.

Cooley Cemetery
Cooley Ridge Road

Webster, John C.
LOCATION: Cooley Cemetery **RANK:** Private
COMPANY: H **REGIMENT:** 28th (Consolidated) Tennessee Infantry **BIRTH:** c. 1814, Tennessee **DEATH:** After 1910
MARRIED: (1) Lucy Weatherford, 15 August 1862, White County, Tennessee; (2) Louisa Puss Kirby Cody, 17 August 1894, White County, Tennessee **PARENTS:** Joseph and Elizabeth Webster

Cope Cemetery #1
South side of Cedar Creek Road, 0.2 miles west of Toy Slatten Road, or 1.2 miles west of junction to Oak Grove Road, which is 0.4 miles west of Pollard Road.

Mabe, David
LOCATION: Cope Cemetery #1
RANK: Private **COMPANY:** K
REGIMENT: 28th Tennessee Infantry **BIRTH:** 07 June 1824
DEATH: 17 December 1909
PENSION: #S1998 **MARRIED:** (1) Mary Milan; (2) Serilda Cates

David Mabe

Unmarked Grave

Martin, Daniel
LOCATION: Cope Cemetery #1 RANK: Private COMPANY: K
REGIMENT: 16th Tennessee Infantry BIRTH: 04 June 1845
DEATH: 15 October 1869

Cope-Turner Cemetery
O'Conner

Turner, William
LOCATION: Cope-Turner Cemetery RANK: Captain COMPANY: E
REGIMENT: 25th Tennessee Infantry BIRTH: 13 March 1839
DEATH: 28 November 1896 MARRIED: Sarah Ann Cope, 26
March 1872 PARENTS: James and Ann (Lyda) Turner

Corinth Church of Christ Cemetery
Northwest corner of Old Smithfield Highway and Corinth Road, 0.3 miles west of Old Kentucky Road.

Kirby, Thomas J.
LOCATION: Corinth Church of Christ Cemetery RANK: Private
COMPANY: I REGIMENT: 13th (Gore's) Tennessee Cavalry
BIRTH: 20 July 1832 DEATH: 02 June 1893 MARRIED: Matilda

~

Lewis, John P.
LOCATION: Corinth Church of Christ Cemetery
RANK: Corporal COMPANY: C REGIMENT: 25th Tennessee
Infantry BIRTH: 02 December 1838 DEATH: 09 December
1916 MARRIED: Catharine Cope, 16 November 1858
PARENT: Jane C. Lewis

~

Ramsey, William Jason
LOCATION: Corinth Church of Christ Cemetery
RANK: Private COMPANY: H REGIMENT: 25th Tennessee
Infantry BIRTH: 1838 DEATH: 1903 PENSION: #S1950

Rector, Jackson Burnett
LOCATION: Corinth Church of Christ Cemetery RANK: Private
COMPANY: C REGIMENT: 13th (Gore's) Tennessee Cavalry
BIRTH: 04 July 1842 DEATH: 03 August 1914
MARRIED: Mary Lou PENSION: #W9526

Crowder-Lisk Cemetery

In hayfield 200 feet west of House at 10874 Old Kentucky Road, 2.0 miles south of junction, Smithville Hwy (US70).

Crowder, John A.
LOCATION: Crowder-Lisk Cemetery RANK: Private
COMPANY: E REGIMENT: 1st (Colm's) Battalion Tennessee Infantry BIRTH: 21 November 1819 DEATH: 29 July 1896
MARRIED: Mary Rust Faulkner

~

Hawkins, John D.
LOCATION: Crowder-Lisk Cemetery RANK: Private COMPANY: I
REGIMENT: 25th Tennessee Infantry BIRTH: 07 March 1844
DEATH: 06 February 1864

Cunningham Family Cemetery (Cunningham-Huddleston Cemetery)

On gravel lane 0.15 miles south of Cunningham Road, 0.45 miles west of junction, Post Oak Bridge Road, 1.0 miles north of P. O. B. Road and Walnut Grove Road.

Cunningham, Lane
LOCATION: Cunningham-Huddleston Cemetery RANK: Private
COMPANY: G REGIMENT: 28th (Consolidated) Tennessee Infantry BIRTH: 15 June 1829 DEATH: 02 January 1915
MARRIED: (1) Catherine Wilhite; (2) Lucy Eller
PARENTS: Edmund and Nancy (Anderson) Cunningham

B. Davis Cemetery

Behind Pleasant Hill Baptist Church

Davis, Tillmon
LOCATION: B. Davis Cemetery **RANK:** Private **COMPANY:** C
REGIMENT: 25th Tennessee Infantry **BIRTH:** 31 August 1842
DEATH: 23 September 1920 **MARRIED:** Elutha

Davis Cemetery

Taft Community

Davis, Nelson Clay
LOCATION: Davis Cemetery **RANK:** 1st Lieutenant
COMPANY: D / D **REGIMENT:** 8th (Dibrell's) Tennessee Cavalry / 4th (McLemore's) Tennessee Cavalry **BIRTH:** 23 September 1836 **DEATH:** 07 November 1904 **MARRIED:** Parrasetta Lay, 06 August 1864, White County, Tennessee **PENSION:** #W273
PARENTS: Jonathan Clay and Winnie (Brown) Davis

~

Lay, Zaccharyer A.
LOCATION: Davis Cemetery **RANK:** Private **COMPANY:** K
REGIMENT: 16th Tennessee Infantry **BIRTH:** 15 May 1822
DEATH: 14 March 1864 **MARRIED:** Dosea E. Hooper

Davis Cemetery

Scott's Gulf (4 wheel drive required!)

Davis, Absolom
LOCATION: Davis Cemetery **RANK:** Private **COMPANY:** E
REGIMENT: 25th Tennessee Infantry **BIRTH:** 29 May 1833
DEATH: 09 February 1920 **MARRIED:** (1) Mary Elizabeth Scarbrough, 06 June 1858, White County, Tennessee; (2) Helen S. Dodson, 01 June 1893, White County, Tennessee
PARENTS: Ephriam and Catharine (Nichols) Davis

Marker Photo Not Available

Davis, James

LOCATION: Davis Cemetery
RANK: Private **COMPANY:** E
REGIMENT: 25th Tennessee Infantry **BIRTH:** 10 February 1831 **DEATH:** 06 March 1917
MARRIED: (1) Louisa Brown, 26 July 1855, White County, Tennessee; (2) Bettie Grissom, 10 December 1888, White County, Tennessee; (3) Mary Elizabeth Austin Anderson, 4 October 1901, White County, Tennessee **PARENTS:** Ephriam and Catharine (Nichols) Davis

James Davis

~

Davis, Robert

LOCATION: Davis Cemetery **RANK:** Private **COMPANY:** District #13 **REGIMENT:** White County, Tennessee Home Guard of Minute Men **BIRTH:** 28 May 1825 **DEATH:** 08 April 1887 **MARRIED:** Susan Scarbrough, 25 June 1867, White County, Tennessee **PARENTS:** Ephriam and Catharine (Nichols) Davis

~

Wilson, Hartwell G.

LOCATION: Davis Cemetery **RANK:** Private **COMPANY:** C **REGIMENT:** 84th Tennessee Infantry **BIRTH:** 1827 **DEATH:** About 1910 **MARRIED:** Martha Evans, 31 March 1859, White County, Tennessee **PARENTS:** Littleberry and Jane (Frasier) Wilson

Darius Davis Cemetery

North side of Pates Ford Road, 1.2 miles west of junction, Pollard Road.

Davis, Darius

LOCATION: Darius Davis Cemetery **RANK:** Private **COMPANY:** B / F **REGIMENT:** 84th Tennessee Infantry / 28th (Consolidated) Tennessee Infantry **BIRTH:** 06 July 1839 **DEATH:** September 1899 **MARRIED:** Dorthula Arzella Hunter

Dyer-Cash Cemetery

Top of hill 200 feet north of Dyer Cove Road, 0.2 miles east of Junction, Cherry Creek Road, 6.2 miles from Monteray Hwy. (SR84)

Dyer, William L.
LOCATION: Dyer-Cash Cemetery **RANK:** Private **COMPANY:** H **REGIMENT:** 13th (Gore's) Tennessee Cavalry **BIRTH:** 05 November 1834 **DEATH:** 11 July 1917 **MARRIED:** Margaretta **PARENTS:** Samuel and Margaret (Robinson) Dyer

~

Farley, Howard
LOCATION: Dyer-Cash Cemetery **RANK:** Private **COMPANY:** H **REGIMENT:** 13th (Gore's) Tennessee Cavalry **BIRTH:** 26 November 1834 **DEATH:** 01 June 1916 **MARRIED:** Caroline Dyer, 18 October 1866, White County, Tennessee **PARENTS:** John and Malinda (Cash) Farley

~

Gooch, Talamachus C.
LOCATION: Dyer-Cash Cemetery **RANK:** Private **COMPANY:** H **REGIMENT:** 13th (Gore's) Tennessee Cavalry **BIRTH:** 29 May 1829 **DEATH:** 16 November 1909 **MARRIED:** Catherine Farley, 07 April 1862, White County, Tennessee **PARENTS:** John and Elizabeth Gooch

~

Gooch, William Alexander
LOCATION: Dyer-Cash Cemetery **RANK:** Private **COMPANY:** D / H **REGIMENT:** 84th Tennessee Infantry / 28th Tennessee Infantry **BIRTH:** 04 April 1823 **DEATH:** 08 January 1908 **MARRIED:** Alvira Dyer, 24 March 1854, White County, Tennessee

~

Robinson, John Jacob
LOCATION: Dyer-Cash Cemetery **RANK:** Corporal **COMPANY:** E **REGIMENT:** 25th Tennessee Infantry **BIRTH:** 01 March 1842 **DEATH:** 05 May 1937 **MARRIED:** Elsie Jane Johnson, 21 November 1867, White County, Tennessee **PENSION:** #S15785 **PARENTS:** Immanuel and Lucinda (Cash) Robinson **UDC MEMBER:** Sarah Looney Dodson

Eastland Cemetery

South side Eastland Cemetery Road, 0.7 miles from junction Eastland Road, 0.3 miles southwest of Railroad Grade Road

Scott, Elijah

LOCATION: Eastland Cemetery **RANK:** Private **COMPANY:** C **REGIMENT:** 61st Tennessee Mounted Infantry **BIRTH:** 18 September 1846 **DEATH:** 07 February 1928 **MARRIED:** Mary J. Swillings **PARENTS:** J. H. and Jane Scott

Eldridge Cemetery

End of Eldridge Cemetery Road, 0.2 miles west of junction Browntown Road, 1.2 miles southwest of junction Austin Road, or 1.1 miles north of junction Fancher's Mill Road

Eldridge, John David

LOCATION: Eldridge Cemetery **RANK:** 1st Sergeant **COMPANY:** B **REGIMENT:** 1st (Colm's) Battalion Tennessee Infantry **BIRTH:** 1835 **DEATH:** 1877 **MARRIED:** Elizabeth Taylor, 14 July 1858, White County, Tennessee

Anthony Elrod Cemetery

Old Bethel

Elrod, Anthony J.

LOCATION: Anthony Elrod Cemetery **RANK:** Private **COMPANY:** B / I **REGIMENT:** 84th Tennessee Infantry / 28th (Consolidated) Tennessee Infantry **BIRTH:** 12 October 1833 **DEATH:** 13 April 1909 **MARRIED:** Mary Ward **PARENTS:** James and Elizabeth (McDowell) Elrod

Elrod Cemetery

End of Elrod Cemetery Road 0.1 miles east of Burgess Falls Road, 2.5 miles northwest of Junction, Old Kentucky Road (SR136) Baker's Crossroads

Elrod, Giles

LOCATION: Elrod Cemetery **RANK:** Private **COMPANY:** B **REGIMENT:** 1st (Colm's) Battalion Tennessee Infantry **BIRTH:** 23 April 1823 **DEATH:** 28 January 1903 **MARRIED:** Senith Howell, 04 March 1847, White County, Tennessee **PENSIONS:** #S1953 and #W1000 **PARENTS:** Giles and Elizabeth (Thomas) Elrod

Howell, John
LOCATION: Elrod Cemetery **RANK:** 1st Sergeant **COMPANY:** C **REGIMENT:** 21st and 22nd (Consolidated) Tennessee Cavalry **BIRTH:** 1792 **DEATH:** 07 July 1861 **MARRIED:** Nancy Brewer

England Cemetery #2
Brock Cove in pasture beyond pond 400 feet northeast of abandoned frame farmhouse, northeast side of Bill Carter Mountain Road, 0.7 miles east of Roberts Matthews Highway

England, Aaron W.
LOCATION: England Cemetery #2 **RANK:** Private **COMPANY:** D **REGIMENT:** 1st (Colm's) Battalion Tennessee Infantry **BIRTH:** 01 January 1823 **DEATH:** 07 July 1886 **MARRIED:** (1) Mary Elizabeth Walker, 02 December 1850, White County, Tennessee; (2) Mary Ann "Polly" Conley, 09 May 1870, White County **PARENTS:** John and Mary (Scott) England

Aaron W. England

~

England, Enos
LOCATION: England Cemetery #2 **RANK:** Corporal **COMPANY:** E **REGIMENT:** 25th Tennessee Infantry **BIRTH:** 03 April 1837 **DEATH:** 18 August 1861 **PARENTS:** John and Mary (Scott) England

Farris-Lance-Bohannon Cemetery
Wild Cat Cove

Brown, Wamon
LOCATION: Farris-Lance-Bohannon Cemetery **RANK:** Private **COMPANY:** H **REGIMENT:** 8th (Dibrell's) Tennessee Cavalry / 13th (Gore's) Tennessee Cavalry **BIRTH:** c. 1824, White County, Tennessee **DEATH:** Unknown

Unmarked Grave

White County · Our Confederate Ancestors · 161

Hunter, James W.
LOCATION: Farris-Lance-Bohannon Cemetery
RANK: Not listed REGIMENT: Unassigned
BIRTH: 12 January 1833 DEATH: 27 November 1907
MARRIED: (1) Mary E. Lance, 26 January 1854, White County, Tennessee; (2) Hannah Lance, 23 January 1862, White County, Tennessee PENSION: #S9224

~

Ogden, George W.
LOCATION: Farris-Lance-Bohannon Cemetery RANK: Private
COMPANY: D REGIMENT: 13th (Gore's) Tennessee Cavalry
BIRTH: 28 December 1836 DEATH: 06 August 1868
MARRIED: Sarah Lance, 17 November 1858, White County, Tennessee

Fisher Cemetery
Horseshoe Bend

Fisher, Alford T.
LOCATION: Fisher Cemetery RANK: Private COMPANY: A
REGIMENT: 13th (Gore's) Tennessee Cavalry / 8th (Dibrell's) Tennessee Cavalry BIRTH: 25 October 1825 DEATH: 07 December 1910 MARRIED: Sarah "Sallie" Hutson PENSION: #S11710 and #W3442 PARENTS: William and Nancy (Chisam) Fisher

~

Fisher, George Washington
LOCATION: Fisher Cemetery RANK: Private
COMPANY: D REGIMENT: 8th (Dibrell's) Tennessee Cavalry
BIRTH: 15 September 1830 DEATH: 07 October 1893
MARRIED: (1) Julia A. Hutson (2) Amanda J. Clark
PENSIONS: #W8425 and #W3774 PARENTS: William and Nancy (Chisam) Fisher

Fisk Cemetery
Wild Cat Cove

Fisk, Andrew Jackson
LOCATION: Fisk Cemetery **RANK:** Not listed **COMPANY:** Not listed **REGIMENT:** Not listed **BIRTH:** 23 October 1846 **DEATH:** 12 March 1864 **OTHER:** "Participated in Battle of Dug Hill" **PARENTS:** Barlow and Elizabeth (Lance) Fisk

Unmarked Grave

Fisk, Marion
LOCATION: Fisk Cemetery **RANK:** Private **COMPANY:** D **REGIMENT:** 1st (Colm's) Battalion Tennessee Infantry **BIRTH:** 18 November 1840 **DEATH:** 15 June 1879 **MARRIED:** Kitty Hudgens, 06 September 1868, White County, Tennessee **PARENTS:** Barlow and Elizabeth (Lance) Fisk

Unmarked Grave

France Cemetery
Monterey Highway (SR84)

Carmichael, Hance
LOCATION: France Cemetery **RANK:** Private **COMPANY:** H / District #11 **REGIMENT:** 28th (Consolidated) Tennessee Infantry / White County Home Guard of Minute Men **BIRTH:** 23 October 1823 **DEATH:** 25 June 1863

Carmichael, Solomon
LOCATION: France Cemetery **RANK:** 1st Sergeant **COMPANY:** K **REGIMENT:** 25th Tennessee Infantry **BIRTH:** 06 April 1828 **DEATH:** 20 November 1861

Carmichael, Thomas
LOCATION: France Cemetery **RANK:** Private **COMPANY:** K **REGIMENT:** 25th Tennessee Infantry **BIRTH:** 31 January 1822 **DEATH:** 31 December 1861

Carmichael, William L.

LOCATION: France Cemetery **RANK:** Private **COMPANY:** H **REGIMENT:** 8th (Dibrell's) Tennessee Cavalry **BIRTH:** 27 May 1838 **DEATH:** 08 December 1864

~

Cobb, William P.

LOCATION: France Cemetery **RANK:** Sergeant **COMPANY:** D **REGIMENT:** Thomas' Legion North Carolina, Walker's Battalion **BIRTH:** 1842 **DEATH:** Unknown **PENSION:** #S2456

~

Ferguson, Champ

LOCATION: France Cemetery **RANK:** Captain **COMPANY:** Not listed **REGIMENT:** General Morgan's Tennessee Cavalry **BIRTH:** 29 November 1821 **DEATH:** 20 October 1865 **MARRIED:** (1) Eliza Smith, 12 May 1844, Clinton County, Kentucky; (2) Martha Owens, 23 July 1848, Clinton County, Kentucky **OTHER:** One of only two men executed by the U.S. government for "war crimes" after the War between the States.

Champ Ferguson

Champ Ferguson was born November 29, 1821 on a branch of Spring Creek about one and a half miles from Elliott's Crossroads in Clinton County, Kentucky. He was named after his grandfather, Champion Ferguson, the pioneer Spring Creek settler. His father, William R. Ferguson, married Zilphia Huff and raised a family of ten children, of which Champ was the oldest.

On May 12, 1844, Champ married Eliza Smith, daughter of Jesse Bowen Smith, who bore him one child, a boy. Both his wife and child died about three years after the marriage. On July 23, 1848, he married Martha Owen, daughter of Samuel Owen. To this union, one child, a girl, Ann Elizabeth, was born.

Ferguson liked to hunt. Hunting not only enabled him to get out into the mountains that he loved, but it was also a means of putting food on the table for his family. He made long hunting trips through the Cumberlands, in the process gaining an intimate knowledge of the foothills and mountains—a knowledge that was to prove invaluable during the war years, enabling him to elude the Union Guerillas and Federal Soldiers who hunted him relentlessly. He was an expert shot. According to his own statement, the only thing he ever shot at and missed was "Tinker Dave" Beatty!

Champ Ferguson enlisted after the "Camp Meeting Fight" and just prior to the Battle of Mill Springs (exact date unknown) in 1861. Ferguson started raising an independent company in April of 1862 and by June of 1862, he and some of his men were attached to General John Hunt Morgan's Cavalry command as scouts. Ferguson was also attached at times to the commands of General John C. Breckenridge and General Joseph Wheeler in late 1864 and 1865. Most times, however, Champ Ferguson operated as an independent cavalry command.

Captain Champ Ferguson was a guerilla leader and the most hated man by the Union Army of Tennessee. He carried a price on his head throughout the war. After the war, Champ surrendered himself under "verbal promise" of parole on May 26, 1865. He was taken to Nashville, Tennessee for trial. Champ said, "If I had known this was a lie, I could have stayed hidden for five years and never left White County."

Denied the opportunity to mount an adequate defense on his behalf, Champ Ferguson was found guilty of "war crimes" by a 2/3 vote of the jurors on October 10, 1865 and sentenced to hanging. The judge ruled that he was an outlaw and was not protected under the acts of war. Ferguson made the following statement after the verdict: "I am yet and will die a Rebel…I killed a good many men, of course, but I never killed a man who I did not know was seeking my life…I repeat, that I die a Rebel out and out and my last request is that my body be removed to White County, Tennessee and be buried in good Rebel soil."

On October 20, 1865, Champ Ferguson was hung in Nashville, Tennessee. His wife, Martha Owen Ferguson buried Champ in the France Cemetery near their home, north of Sparta, as per his request. Ann Elizabeth Ferguson married George Metcalf in Sparta, White County, Tennessee on May 8, 1867. George, Ann Elizabeth and Martha left White County around 1872 and eventually settled near Independence, Kansas. Martha never remarried.

Note: For further reading: "Champ Ferguson; Confederate Guerilla" by Thurman Sensing

Robertson, R.
LOCATION: France Cemetery **RANK:** Captain **COMPANY:** H
REGIMENT: 28th (Consolidated) Tennessee Infantry
BIRTH: 20 September 1829 **DEATH:** 30 October 1909

Fraser's Chapel Cemetery
Frasier's Chapel United Methodist Church - Dodson

Davis, George W.
LOCATION: Fraser's Chapel Cemetery **RANK:** Private
COMPANY: D **REGIMENT:** 8th (Dibrell's) Tennessee Cavalry
BIRTH: 25 October 1820, White County, Tennessee
DEATH: 03 November 1903 **MARRIED:** Nancy
PENSION: #S12359

Goodwin Cemetery
Hampton's Crossroads

Goodwin, John W.
LOCATION: Goodwin Cemetery **RANK:** 2nd Lieutenant
COMPANY: E **REGIMENT:** 25th Tennessee Infantry
BIRTH: 16 March 1838 **DEATH:** 11 July 1922
MARRIED: Harriet

~

Goodwin, John W.
LOCATION: Goodwin Cemetery **RANK:** Not listed
COMPANY: D **REGIMENT:** 8th (Dibrell's) Tennessee Cavalry
BIRTH: 17 November 1844 **DEATH:** 29 December 1932
MARRIED: Nancy E.

Graham-Dalton Cemetery
Fountain Head

Dalton, James Isom
LOCATION: Graham-Dalton Cemetery **RANK:** Sergeant
COMPANY: E **REGIMENT:** 25th Tennessee Infantry
BIRTH: 25 February 1840 **DEATH:** Unknown

Greene Cemetery
Lost Creek

Green, Henry G.
LOCATION: Greene Cemetery **RANK:** Private
COMPANY: I **REGIMENT:** 13th (Gore's) Tennessee Cavalry
BIRTH: 10 November 1845 **DEATH:** 23 January 1876
MARRIED: Eliza Rogers, 15 September 1864, White County, Tennessee **PARENTS:** William and Mary (Fryer) Green

Greenwood Cemetery

Greenwood Southern Baptist Church - Doyle; Across Hodges Bridge Road from GSBC at junction East Gooseneck Road, 0.4 miles east of junction Gooseneck Road and US 70 S.

Austin, William H.
LOCATION: Greenwood Cemetery **RANK:** Sergeant **COMPANY:** C **REGIMENT:** 25th Tennessee Infantry **BIRTH:** 25 June 1840 **DEATH:** 15 January 1914 **PENSION:** #S10724 **PARENTS:** James M. and Mary (Anderson) Austin

~

Clenny, William H.
LOCATION: Greenwood Cemetery **RANK:** Private **COMPANY:** C **REGIMENT:** 25th Tennessee Infantry **BIRTH:** 13 July 1826 **DEATH:** 18 November 1897 **MARRIED:** Susan Hollingsworth (Susan is buried in Hollingsworth Cemetery in Van Buren County, Tennessee) **PARENTS:** Jonathan and Rebecca Jane (Hewitt) Clenny

~

Franks, Spencer Holder
LOCATION: Greenwood Cemetery **RANK:** Private **COMPANY:** D **REGIMENT:** 13th (Gore's) Tennessee Cavalry / 8th (Dibrell's) Tennessee Cavalry **BIRTH:** 23 August 1846 **DEATH:** 25 November 1935 **MARRIED:** Altamira "Altie Myer" Dillion, 14 January 1869, White County, Tennessee **PENSION:** #S10201 **PARENTS:** John W. and Martha (Holder) Franks

~

Hollingsworth, William M.
LOCATION: Greenwood Cemetery **RANK:** Private **COMPANY:** G **REGIMENT:** 12th Cavalry Battalion **BIRTH:** 19 July 1847 **DEATH:** 29 November 1934 **MARRIED:** Catherine Stipe, 30 December 1867, White County, Tennessee **PENSION:** #S9203 **PARENTS:** Thomas and Catherine (Kuhn) Hollingsworth

~

Horton, Newton M.
LOCATION: Greenwood Cemetery **RANK:** Private **COMPANY:** D **REGIMENT:** 13th (Gore's) Tennessee Cavalry **BIRTH:** 04 February 1836 **DEATH:** 08 May 1862 **MARRIED:** Sarah A. Hannah, 15 November 1858, Franklin County, Tennessee. (Sarah is buried in Shady Grove Cemetery, Lincoln County, Tennessee.)

Johnson, Stokely D.

LOCATION: Greenwood Cemetery **RANK:** Private
COMPANY: District #7 **REGIMENT:** Van Buren County Home Guard **BIRTH:** 22 April, 1832 **DEATH:** 29 January 1891
MARRIED: Melcena Cope, 22 September 1853, White County, Tennessee **PARENTS:** Allen and Nancy (Whitely) Johnson
UDC MEMBERS: Martha Sue Bell Broyles, Susan Broyles Harris, Sherrie Beth Broyles McCulley, Josephine Bell McDonald, Deborah McDonald Spriggs

~

Lansden, Dr. Hugh H.

LOCATION: Greenwood Cemetery **RANK:** Captain
COMPANY: F **REGIMENT:** 28th (Consolidated) Tennessee Infantry **BIRTH:** 28 February 1837 **DEATH:** 26 June 1902
MARRIED: Lee Ann McGee

~

McBride, William B.

LOCATION: Greenwood Cemetery **RANK:** 2nd Corporal
COMPANY: C **REGIMENT:** 25th Tennessee Infantry
BIRTH: March 1835 **DEATH:** 25 February 1912

~

Odell, James L.

LOCATION: Greenwood Cemetery **RANK:** Private **COMPANY:** Not listed **REGIMENT:** 16th Tennessee Infantry **BIRTH:** 01 February 1834 **DEATH:** 01 February 1907 **MARRIED:** Narcissa (Earls) Underwood, 09 September 1865, White County, Tennessee **PARENTS:** John F. and Abigale Odell

~

Sanderson, James M.

LOCATION: Greenwood Cemetery **RANK:** 1st Sergeant
COMPANY: C **REGIMENT:** 25th Tennessee Infantry
BIRTH: 01 November 1823 **DEATH:** 13 April 1895
MARRIED: Elizabeth A. Hill

Scoggins, William M.
LOCATION: Greenwood Cemetery **RANK:** 2nd Lieutenant
COMPANY: C **REGIMENT:** 25th Tennessee Infantry
BIRTH: 04 January 1820 **DEATH:** 05 October 1900
MARRIED: Susan "Sookey" Mason, 03 April 1840, White County, Tennessee

~

Simmons, Andrew Jackson
LOCATION: Greenwood Cemetery **RANK:** Private **COMPANY:** E
REGIMENT: 18th Tennessee Infantry **BIRTH:** 25 December 1843
DEATH: 21 December 1906 **MARRIED:** Canzada Stipe, 31 July 1864, White County, Tennessee **PARENTS:** Joseph N. and Mary Elizabeth (Lewis) Simmons

~

Sparkman, Thomas Bryant
LOCATION: Greenwood Cemetery **RANK:** Private **COMPANY:** C
REGIMENT: 35th Tennessee Infantry **BIRTH:** 10 October 1842
DEATH: 18 March 1923 **MARRIED:** Sarah E. Dodson, 25 March 1860, Van Buren County, Tennessee **PENSION:** #S11221
PARENTS: George W. and Malissa (Hill) Sparkman

~

Steakley, Wiley Jr.
LOCATION: Greenwood Cemetery
RANK: Private **COMPANY:** A
REGIMENT: 4th (Murray's) Tennessee Cavalry / 8th (Dibrell's) Tennessee Cavalry **BIRTH:** 23 February 1844 **DEATH:** 21 June 1941 **MARRIED:** Vina Elizabeth Sparkman **PARENTS:** Wiley and Priscilla (Lewis) Steakley
PENSION: #S16505 **OTHER:** First served as a Scout; In 1862 when the company was surrounded and captured, Wiley escaped and worked his way through Federal lines to join the 8th Tennessee Cavalry; After the war, he was a steamboat watchman, postmaster, and bought lumber for Singer Sewing Machine Company, fashioning the lumber into a raft and sending it down the river at Rock Island; Wiley Steakley outlived every other Confederate soldier in White County.

Wiley Steakley, Jr.

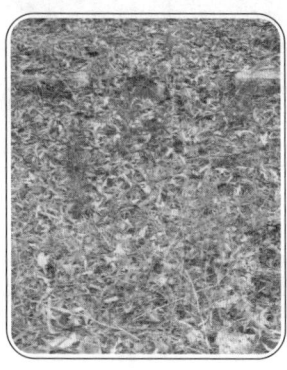

Taylor, Martin Kittsworth
LOCATION: Greenwood Cemetery **RANK:** Private **COMPANY:** A
REGIMENT: 22nd (Murray's) Battalion Tennessee Infantry
BIRTH: 1833 **DEATH:** 1903 **MARRIED:** Lucy Jane Williams, 27 September 1862, White County, Tennessee **PENSION:** #S3755
PARENTS: James and Easter Taylor

~

Ward, Henry B.
LOCATION: Greenwood Cemetery **RANK:** Private **COMPANY:** D
REGIMENT: 1st (Colm's) Battalion Tennessee Infantry
BIRTH: 26 April 1842, Milan, Ohio **DEATH:** 21 August 1918
MARRIED: Sallie E. Anderson

~

Webster, Daniel Stewart
LOCATION: Greenwood Cemetery **RANK:** Private **COMPANY:** C / G **REGIMENT:** 84th Tennessee Infantry / 28th (Consolidated) Tennessee Infantry **BIRTH:** 01 March 1830 **DEATH:** 07 June 1933 **MARRIED:** Arra Jane Oakes, 31 September 1867
PENSION: #S1807 **PARENTS:** Joseph and Elizabeth Webster

~

Womack, James Knowles P.
LOCATION: Greenwood Cemetery **RANK:** Private **COMPANY:** A
REGIMENT: 18th Tennessee Infantry **BIRTH:** 19 June 1828
DEATH: 27 January 1912 **MARRIED:** (1) Nancy Jane Craine, Wilson County, Tennessee (2) Sarah Lodema Crain, 23 February 1864, White County, Tennessee

Herd-Lowery-Smith Cemetery
East Foot Gum Spring Mountain

Smith, Benjamin David
LOCATION: Herd-Lowery-Smith Cemetery, inside a curbed lot. Names are on curb (destroyed). B. D. Smith lies inside the curb where it is notched because he was so tall.
RANK: Private **COMPANY:** District #1 **REGIMENT:** White County Home Guard of Minute Men **BIRTH:** 17 September 1836
DEATH: 27 April 1905 **PARENTS:** Charles and Synthia Smith

Hickey Cemetery

Plainview

Hickey, Cornelius

LOCATION: Hickey Cemetery **RANK:** Private **COMPANY:** C
REGIMENT: 154th Senior Regiment Tennessee Infantry
BIRTH: 01 January 1822 **DEATH:** 26 September 1900
MARRIED: Eliza J. Brown, 01 September 1842,
White County, Tennessee

Hickory Valley Cemetery

Hickory Valley Road

Lewis, Byrd A.

LOCATION: Hickory Valley Cemetery **RANK:** Private
COMPANY: G **REGIMENT:** 16th Tennessee Infantry **BIRTH:** 23
November 1846 **DEATH:** 02 April 1937 **MARRIED:** Sarah C.

~

Wallace, John Calvin

LOCATION: Hickory Valley Cemetery **RANK:** Private
COMPANY: I **REGIMENT:** 13th (Gore's) Tennessee Cavalry / 8th
(Dibrell's) Tennessee Cavalry **BIRTH:** 28 August 1844
DEATH: 26 December 1923 **MARRIED:** Sallie Burden
PENSIONS: #S14735 and #W7984

Highland Cemetery

East Sparta

Anderson, William T.

LOCATION: Highland Cemetery **RANK:** Private **COMPANY:** D / K
REGIMENT: 1st (Colm's) Battalion Tennessee Infantry / 50th
(Consolidated) Tennessee Infantry **BIRTH:** 13 July 1846
DEATH: 16 November 1928

~

Baker, Richard D.

LOCATION: Highland Cemetery **RANK:** Sergeant **COMPANY:** K
REGIMENT: 16th Tennessee Infantry **BIRTH:** 24 November
1841 **DEATH:** 24 November 1914 **MARRIED:** Harriet
PENSION: #S731

Bronson, Robert L.
LOCATION: Highland Cemetery **RANK:** Private **COMPANY:** K
REGIMENT: 16th Tennessee Infantry **BIRTH:** 24 February 1836
DEATH: 25 November 1888 **MARRIED:** Mary A. Rogers

~

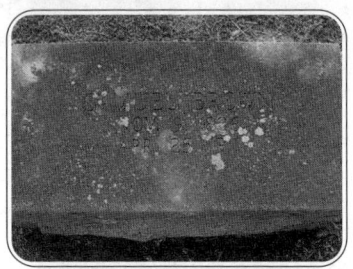

Brown, Samuel
LOCATION: Highland Cemetery **RANK:** 1st Sergeant
COMPANY: F / District #9 **REGIMENT:** 13th (Gore's) Tennessee
Cavalry / White County Home Guard of Minute Men
BIRTH: 09 November 1826 **DEATH:** 25 April 1911
MARRIED: Rebecca Henry, 08 September 1853

~

Broyles, Onslow G.
LOCATION: Highland Cemetery **RANK:** 1st Sergeant **COMPANY:**
D **REGIMENT:** 13th (Gore's) Tennessee Cavalry **BIRTH:** 01
January 1828 **DEATH:** 08 December 1902 **PENSION:** #S3301

~

England, George Dallas
LOCATION: Highland Cemetery **RANK:** Private **COMPANY:** H
REGIMENT: 13th (Gore's) Tennessee Cavalry **BIRTH:** 31 January
1845 **DEATH:** 29 January 1916 **MARRIED:** Mary Carmichael

~

Gamble, William S.
LOCATION: Highland Cemetery **RANK:** Private **COMPANY:** I
REGIMENT: 17th Tennessee Infantry **BIRTH:** 31 March 1845
DEATH: 05 March 1931 **MARRIED:** Mary B. Paul, 05 August
1869, White County, Tennessee

~

Harris, Thomas F.
LOCATION: Highland Cemetery **RANK:** 1st Sergeant **COMPANY:** I
REGIMENT: 8th (Dibrell's) Tennessee Cavalry **BIRTH:** 1848
DEATH: 1921

Hill, Richard

LOCATION: Highland Cemetery **RANK:** 2nd Lieutenant **COMPANY:** D **REGIMENT:** 13th (Gore's) Tennessee Cavalry **BIRTH:** 24 February 1839 **DEATH:** 18 November 1921 **MARRIED:** Martha J. Officer, 03 June 1869, White County, Tennessee **PARENTS:** William and Isabella (Brown) Hill

Richard Hill

~

Little, Harmon

LOCATION: Highland Cemetery **RANK:** 1st Lieutenant **COMPANY:** District #1 **REGIMENT:** Van Buren County Home Guard **BIRTH:** 14 February 1847 **DEATH:** 08 February 1925 **MARRIED:** Mary Catherine Bussel, 06 October 1867 **PARENTS:** Freeland Simpson and Rebecca (England) Little

~

Matlock, William H.

LOCATION: Highland Cemetery **RANK:** Private **COMPANY:** A **REGIMENT:** 25th Tennessee Infantry **BIRTH:** 12 February 1844 **DEATH:** 29 March 1922

~

McManus, Samuel V.

LOCATION: Highland Cemetery **RANK:** 2nd Lieutenant **COMPANY:** E **REGIMENT:** 1st (Colm's) Battalion Tennessee Infantry **BIRTH:** 29 January 1830 **DEATH:** 19 February 1915 **MARRIED:** Mary J.

~

Quarles, Joseph L.

LOCATION: Highland Cemetery **RANK:** Private **COMPANY:** H **REGIMENT:** 13th (Gore's) Tennessee Cavalry **BIRTH:** 1843 **DEATH:** 1934 **MARRIED:** Sarah J.

Joseph L. Quarles

Richardson, R.

LOCATION: Highland Cemetery **RANK:** Private
COMPANY: A **REGIMENT:** 16th Tennessee Infantry
BIRTH: 22 December 1839 **DEATH:** 17 July 1911
MARRIED: Maggie

~

Sims, Henry W.

LOCATION: Highland Cemetery **RANK:** Private
COMPANY: D **REGIMENT:** 13th (Gore's) Tennessee Cavalry / 8th (Dibrell's) Tennessee Cavalry **BIRTH:** 1844 **DEATH:** 1925
MARRIED: Monie Leftwich **PENSION:** #S12360

~

Sims, William Glenn

LOCATION: Highland Cemetery **RANK:** Brevet 2nd Lieutenant
COMPANY: K **REGIMENT:** 16th Tennessee Infantry
BIRTH: 04 January 1841 **DEATH:** 18 May 1912
MARRIED: Emma Cummings, 04 January 1872
PENSIONS: #S12180 and #W4488 **PARENTS:** William Glen, Sr. and Lucinda M. Sims

~

Smith, William Gooch

LOCATION: Highland Cemetery **RANK:** Lieutenant Colonel
COMPANY: Field and Staff **REGIMENT:** 84th / 28th (Consolidated) Tennessee Infantry **BIRTH:** 1828, Granville, North Carolina **DEATH:** 1908 **MARRIED:** Amanda B. Templeton, 10 May 1857, White County, Tennessee
PARENTS: George C. and Martha (Gooch) Smith
OTHER: Lawyer

~

Young, Charles Coker

LOCATION: Highland Cemetery **RANK:** Private **COMPANY:** K
REGIMENT: 16th Tennessee Infantry **BIRTH:** 25 February 1845
DEATH: 23 December 1913 **MARRIED:** Annette Catherine
PENSIONS: #S13767 and #W5245

Hill Cemetery
Fountain Head

Cash, Carroll
LOCATION: Hill Cemetery **RANK:** Private **COMPANY:** K
REGIMENT: 16th Tennessee Infantry **BIRTH:** 02 January 1840
DEATH: 26 January 1905 **MARRIED:** Eliza Ann Sliger, 06 June 1866, White County, Tennessee

~

Hatfield, William G.
LOCATION: Hill Cemetery **RANK:** Private
COMPANY: E **REGIMENT:** 25th Tennessee Infantry
BIRTH: 13 September 1839 **DEATH:** 25 April 1926
MARRIED: Nancy E. **PENSION:** #S5933

~

Howard, James
LOCATION: Hill Cemetery **RANK:** Private **COMPANY:** C
REGIMENT: 35th Tennessee Infantry **BIRTH:** 23 August 1818
DEATH: 01 September 1877 **MARRIED:** Julia A. Broyles, 14 June 1855, White County, Tennessee **PARENT:** James Howard, Sr.

~

Jared, John Madison
LOCATION: Hill Cemetery **RANK:** 2nd Lieutenant
COMPANY: G **REGIMENT:** 84th Tennessee Infantry
BIRTH: 03 September 1845 **DEATH:** 30 May 1926
MARRIED: Mary C. Shugart, 06 January 1874, White County, Tennessee **PARENTS:** William and Martha P. (Jett) Jared

~

Parker, Rev. C. A.
LOCATION: Hill Cemetery **RANK:** Private **COMPANY:** I
REGIMENT: 13th (Gore's) Tennessee Cavalry **BIRTH:** c. 1842
DEATH: Before 1900 **MARRIED:** Mary Emma Hudgens, 09 December 1869, White County, Tennessee **PENSION:** #W2424

Unmarked Grave

Shugart, Thomas Coats
LOCATION: Hill Cemetery RANK: Corporal COMPANY: E
REGIMENT: 25th Tennessee Infantry BIRTH: 06 April 1843
DEATH: 02 July 1926 MARRIED: Amanda Robinson, 07 January
1869 PARENTS: William Harden and Mary (Coats) Shugart

~

Stone, James
LOCATION: Hill Cemetery RANK: Private
COMPANY: A / District #11 REGIMENT: 22nd (Murray's)
Battalion Tennessee Infantry / White County Home Guard
of Minute Men BIRTH: 1816 DEATH: 1889

Holder Cemetery
Quebeck

Holder, John D.
LOCATION: Holder Cemetery RANK: Private
COMPANY: District #4 REGIMENT: White County Home Guard
of Minute Men BIRTH: 03 December 1838
DEATH: 17 February 1901

Howard Cemetery
Hampton's Crossroads

Carroll, S. L.
LOCATION: Howard Cemetery RANK: Private
COMPANY: A REGIMENT: 22nd (Murray's) Battalion Tennessee
Infantry BIRTH: 11 July 1833 DEATH: 28 December 1917
MARRIED: Mary J.

~

Cumby, Jimmie
LOCATION: Howard Cemetery RANK: Corporal COMPANY: E
REGIMENT: 25th Tennessee Infantry BIRTH: 24 October 1841
DEATH: 08 December 1893 MARRIED: Fannie PENSION: #W285

Howell Cemetery
Pistole

Howell, Rev. Lewis
LOCATION: Howell Cemetery **RANK:** Private **COMPANY:** Dist #7
REGIMENT: White County Home Guard of Minute Men
BIRTH: 11 May 1824 **DEATH:** 06 October 1907
MARRIED: Gerusha Duncan

Hudgens-Swift Cemetery
Bear Cove

Hudgens, James
LOCATION: Hudgens-Swift Cemetery **RANK:** Private
COMPANY: D **REGIMENT:** 13th (Gore's) Tennessee Cavalry / 8th (Dibrell's) Tennessee Cavalry **BIRTH:** 11 September 1836
DEATH: 11 September 1868 **MARRIED:** Ann Carrick, 03 July 1859, White County, Tennessee **PENSION:** #W1001

Hurd-Rogers Cemetery
Herd Cemetery Road

Herd, James Vance
LOCATION: Hurd-Rogers Cemetery **RANK:** Sergeant
COMPANY: I **REGIMENT:** 13th (Gore's) Tennessee Cavalry
BIRTH: 04 January 1834 **DEATH:** 01 November 1892
MARRIED: Sarah E. Herd, 05 February 1856 **PENSION:** #W125
PARENTS: James, Sr. and Rutha (Felton) Herd

~

Rogers, James W.
LOCATION: Hurd-Rogers Cemetery **RANK:** Not listed
COMPANY: C **REGIMENT:** 84th Tennessee Infantry / 28th (Consolidated) Tennessee Infantry **BIRTH:** 18 April 1839
DEATH: 09 April 1924 **MARRIED:** Mary Jane Herd, 12 September 1861 **PENSION:** #S4056 **PARENTS:** Isham and Malinda Rogers

Abel Hutson Cemetery
Mt. Pisgah

Hutchings, Francis Marion
LOCATION: Abel Hutson Cemetery **RANK:** Sergeant **COMPANY:** C **REGIMENT:** 28th (Consolidated) Tennessee Infantry **BIRTH:** 1836 **DEATH:** Before 1870 **MARRIED:** Arminda C. Moore, 15 July 1858, White County, Tennessee **PARENTS:** Benjamin and Ann Margaret Hutchings

Hutson Cemetery #3
Mt. Pisgah

Carter, Meredith "Bud"
LOCATION: Hutson Cemetery #3 **RANK:** 1st Sergeant **COMPANY:** A **REGIMENT:** 4th (Murray's) Tennessee Cavalry **BIRTH:** 10 August 1842 **DEATH:** 26 August 1869 **MARRIED:** Sarah E. Cathcart, 19 November 1863, White County, Tennessee **PARENTS:** Meredith and Elizabeth Carter

~

Clark, James P.
LOCATION: Hutson Cemetery #3 **RANK:** Private **COMPANY:** Not listed **REGIMENT:** 8th (Dibrell's) Tennessee Cavalry **BIRTH:** 16 March 1843 **DEATH:** 13 January 1906 **PENSION:** #S2269 **PARENTS:** Darius and Sarah Elizabeth (Hutson) Clark

~

Fisher, Ambrose "Ambers" Thomas
LOCATION: Hutson Cemetery #3 **RANK:** Private **COMPANY:** D **REGIMENT:** 13th (Gore's) Tennessee Cavalry **BIRTH:** 23 March 1823 **DEATH:** 20 December 1906 **MARRIED:** Cynthia Clark, 13 December 1851, White County, Tennessee **PARENTS:** William and Nancy (Chisam) Fisher

~

Hutson, Isaiah Asbury
LOCATION: Hutson Cemetery #3 **RANK:** Private **COMPANY:** D **REGIMENT:** 13th (Gore's) Tennessee Cavalry **BIRTH:** 30 June 1825 **DEATH:** 26 May 1880 **MARRIED:** Sarah H. Hutchings, 05 May 1850, White County, Tennessee **PARENTS:** Isaiah and Eleanor (Knowles) Hutson

Indian Mound Cemetery

Dekalb County, just over the White County line

Atnip, John

LOCATION: Indian Mound Cemetery **RANK:** Private
COMPANY: A **REGIMENT:** 16th Tennessee Infantry
BIRTH: 25 November 1844
DEATH: 31 August 1921
MARRIED: Oma Rigsby, 01 February 1900, Dekalb County, Tennessee

John Atnip

~

Cope, James Madison

LOCATION: Indian Mound Cemetery **RANK:** Private
COMPANY: K **REGIMENT:** 16th Tennessee Infantry **BIRTH:** 1837
DEATH: 1904 **MARRIED:** Nancy Jane Harris **PENSION:** #W3605

~

Hutchens, Lawson H.

LOCATION: Indian Mound Cemetery **RANK:** Private
COMPANY: Not listed **REGIMENT:** 50th (Consolidated) Tennessee Infantry **BIRTH:** 16 June 1839
DEATH: 31 March 1913 **MARRIED:** Sarah Jain Pinegar, 27 July 1866, Dekalb County, Tennessee

~

Lack, Benjamin

LOCATION: Indian Mound Cemetery **RANK:** Sergeant
COMPANY: K **REGIMENT:** 16th Tennessee Infantry
BIRTH: 13 September 1829 **DEATH:** 20 August 1905
MARRIED: (1) Eliza Quillen, 05 April 1854, White County, Tennessee; (2) Lucy Quillen, 09 February 1857, White County, Tennessee

Quillen, Elijah
LOCATION: Indian Mound Cemetery RANK: Private
COMPANY: C REGIMENT: 16th Tennessee Infantry
BIRTH: 18 January 1831 DEATH: 28 May 1928
MARRIED: (1) Elizabeth Cantrell, 21 November 1868, White County, Tennessee; (2) Harriett Crowder, July 1881

~

Slatten, Samuel D.
LOCATION: Indian Mound Cemetery RANK: Private
COMPANY: C REGIMENT: 1st (Colm's) Battalion Tennessee Infantry BIRTH: 04 March 1828, Hawkins County, Tennessee
DEATH: 03 January 1895 MARRIED: Loucrecy Hutchings, 25 March 1844, White County, Tennessee

Isom (Isom-Sliger) Cemetery
Mt. Herman

Sliger, Adam, Sr.
LOCATION: Isom (Isom-Sliger) Cemetery RANK: 2nd Lieutenant COMPANY: Captain John B. McLin's
REGIMENT: Local Defense Troops BIRTH: 14 October 1817
DEATH: 04 October 1896 MARRIED: Elizabeth E. Miller, 31 August 1844, Washington County, Tennessee

~

Sliger, Christopher III
LOCATION: Isom (Isom-Sliger) Cemetery RANK: Private
COMPANY: D REGIMENT: Ragsdale's Battalion Texas Cavalry
BIRTH: 08 May 1833 DEATH: 31 March 1912 MARRIED: (3) Amanda Isham 23, October 1895 PENSION: #S8478
PARENTS: Christopher, II, and Elizabeth Sliger

Jericho Cemetery
Jericho Church of Christ, Quebeck

Chisam, James R.
LOCATION: Jericho Cemetery RANK: Private COMPANY: I
REGIMENT: 13th (Gore's) Tennessee Cavalry BIRTH: 23 January 1842 DEATH: 14 August 1918 MARRIED: Sarah Anderson, 02 April 1864, White County, Tennessee PARENTS: Overton and Celia (Hash) Chisam

Denton, Elijah W.

LOCATION: Jericho Cemetery **RANK:** Private **COMPANY:** C
REGIMENT: 25th Tennessee Infantry **BIRTH:** 15 March 1815
DEATH: 22 March 1889 **MARRIED:** Malvina Halterman
PARENTS: Elijah and Sarah (Heuff) Denton

~

Denton, Erasmus R.

LOCATION: Jericho Cemetery **RANK:** Private **COMPANY:** C
REGIMENT: 84th Tennessee Infantry **BIRTH:** 14 April 1843
DEATH: 07 July 1903 **MARRIED:** Sarah Knowles, 01 October 1871, White County, Tennessee. (Sarah is buried in Mt. Pisgah Cemetery, White County, Tennessee.) **PARENTS:** Sterling and Judea (Province) Denton

~

Eanes, Joseph Cloud

LOCATION: Jericho Cemetery **RANK:** Private **COMPANY:** I
REGIMENT: 4th (McLemore's) Tennessee Cavalry
BIRTH: 17 July 1836 **DEATH:** 25 February 1912
MARRIED: Mattie Clark, Van Buren County, Tennessee
PENSION: #S12901

~

Galloway, James S.

LOCATION: Jericho Cemetery **RANK:** Private **COMPANY:** I
REGIMENT: 8th (Dibrell's) Tennessee Cavalry / 13th (Gore's) Tennessee Cavalry **BIRTH:** 16 November 1840 **DEATH:** 20 July 1905 **MARRIED:** Mary Ann Walker, 24 August 1964, Van Buren County, Tennessee **PENSION:** #S5896 **PARENTS:** Samuel and Lucinda (Evans) Galloway

~

Halteman, John S.

LOCATION: Jericho Cemetery **RANK:** Private **COMPANY:** C
REGIMENT: 25th Tennessee Infantry **BIRTH:** 06 November 1819 **DEATH:** 04 June 1890 **MARRIED:** Mary Holder, 23 July 1840, White County, Tennessee **PARENTS:** John and Mary Ann (Sevier) Halteman

Holder, John Simpson

LOCATION: Jericho Cemetery **RANK:** Private
COMPANY: B **REGIMENT:** 1st (Carter's) Tennessee Cavalry
BIRTH: 05 January 1844 **DEATH:** 02 January 1929
MARRIED: Mary M. (Underwood) Anderson, 15 August 1867, White County, Tennessee **PENSIONS:** #S11121 and #W9329
PARENTS: Spencer and Elizabeth (Nichols) Holder

~

Moore, George W.

LOCATION: Jericho Cemetery **RANK:** Not listed
COMPANY: Not listed **REGIMENT:** 16th Tennessee Infantry
BIRTH: 1841 **DEATH:** 1923 **MARRIED:** Darthula Templeton, 26 December 1867, White County, Tennessee **PENSION:** #W8364
PARENTS: Samuel Ottison and Malissa (Fisher) Moore

~

Moores, W. T.

LOCATION: Jericho Cemetery **RANK:** Private **COMPANY:** E
REGIMENT: 16th Tennessee Infantry **BIRTH:** 05 December 1838
DEATH: 23 June 1892 **MARRIED:** Florence E. Montgomery, 14 November 1878, Warren County, Tennessee

~

Richardson, William Crockett

LOCATION: Jericho Cemetery **RANK:** Private **COMPANY:** B
REGIMENT: 25th Tennessee Infantry **BIRTH:** 19 March 1846
DEATH: 08 November 1919 **MARRIED:** Sarah E. Jane Knowles, 27 February 1870, White County, Tennessee

~

Rives, Thomas M.

LOCATION: Jericho Cemetery **RANK:** Private
COMPANY: C **REGIMENT:** 16th Tennessee Infantry
BIRTH: 25 January 1836 **DEATH:** 18 January 1900
MARRIED: Sarah "Sallie" Hancock, 14 September 1868, Coffee County, Tennessee **PENSION:** #W1178

Slatten, Martin Van Buren
LOCATION: Jericho Cemetery
RANK: Private COMPANY: C
REGIMENT: 25th Tennessee Infantry BIRTH: 09 November 1842 DEATH: 25 May 1901
MARRIED: Mary P. Anderson, 21 January 1866, White County, Tennessee
PENSION: #W2492 PARENTS: William Hellon and Elizabeth (Williams) Slatten

Martin Van Buren Slatten

Knowles Cemetery
Shady Grove

Humphrey, Benjamin B.
LOCATION: Knowles Cemetery RANK: Private COMPANY: B
REGIMENT: 1st (Colm's) Battalion Tennessee Infantry
BIRTH: 05 November 1833 DEATH: 19 November 1915
MARRIED: Rachel Knowles, 09 October 1856, White County, Tennessee PENSION: #S6754 PARENTS: John B. and Christianna (Mayes) Humphrey

~

Knowles, John Monroe
LOCATION: Knowles Cemetery RANK: Sergeant
COMPANY: B REGIMENT: 1st (Colm's) Battalion Tennessee Infantry BIRTH: 26 October 1838 DEATH: 20 November 1911
MARRIED: Martha Jane Cope, 22 May 1870, White County, Tennessee

Lewis Cemetery
Hickory Valley

Lewis, William I.
LOCATION: Lewis Cemetery RANK: Not listed
COMPANY: Not listed REGIMENT: 1st (Colm's) Battalion Tennessee Infantry BIRTH: 21 March 1841
DEATH: 08 July 1915

Liberty Baptist Cemetery
Liberty Southern Baptist Church

Cope, Harrison H.
LOCATION: Liberty Baptist Cemetery **RANK:** Private
COMPANY: K **REGIMENT:** 16th Tennessee Infantry
BIRTH: 15 January 1841 **DEATH:** 16 January 1922
MARRIED: Arrena McGarr, 26 September 1861, White County, Tennessee **PENSION:** #W8908 **PARENTS:** William and Margaret "Peggy" (Baker) Cope

Little Cemetery
Blue Spring

Gilliland, Robert
LOCATION: Little Cemetery **RANK:** Private **COMPANY:** A
REGIMENT: 32nd Tennessee Infantry **BIRTH:** 18 October 1828, Cocke County, Tennessee **DEATH:** 28 January 1898
MARRIED: Sara Caroline Rose

Lost Creek Cemetery
Lost Creek United Methodist Church and Lost Creek Church of Christ

Broom, Joel
LOCATION: Lost Creek Cemetery **RANK:** Private **COMPANY:** C
REGIMENT: 10th Battalion North Carolina Heavy Artillery
BIRTH: 13 June 1830 **DEATH:** 10 June 1890 **MARRIED:** Martha J. Gay **PARENTS:** Andrew and Susanna (Presley) Broom

~

Johnson, Wesley J.
LOCATION: Lost Creek Cemetery **RANK:** Private
COMPANY: F **REGIMENT:** 22nd (Murray's) Battalion Tennessee Infantry **BIRTH:** 01 January 1848 **DEATH:** 18 March 1923
MARRIED: Margrett Jane "Janie" Parks, 14 August 1869, White County, Tennessee **PENSION:** #W10978 **PARENTS:** Thomas B. and Mary H. Johnson

Martin Cemetery
Old Zion

Martin, Jesse
LOCATION: Martin Cemetery **RANK:** Private
COMPANY: Not listed **REGIMENT:** 28th (Consolidated) Tennessee Infantry **BIRTH:** 02 April 1830
DEATH: 26 February 1879 **MARRIED:** Jane Grissom
PARENTS: John and Margaret "Peggy" (Cope) Martin

McCoy Cemetery
Black Oak

Green, Lewis L.
LOCATION: McCoy Cemetery **RANK:** Private
COMPANY: B **REGIMENT:** 13th (Gore's) Tennessee Cavalry / 8th (Dibrell's) Tennessee Cavalry **BIRTH:** c. 1827, Kentucky
DEATH: After 1880 **MARRIED:** Mary A.

McKinney Family Cemetery
DeRossett

McKinney, Thomas J. B.
LOCATION: McKinney Family Cemetery **RANK:** Private
COMPANY: L / District #13 **REGIMENT:** 35th Tennessee Infantry / White County Home Guard of Minute Men **BIRTH:** c. 1829
DEATH: Unknown **MARRIED:** Mekey Ann

Moore Cemetery (Walling)
Old Kentucky Road—In hay field 200 feet off east side of Old Kentucky Road, 0.6 miles north of junction, Hickory Nut Mountain Road.

Crane, Alexander
LOCATION: Moore Cemetery **RANK:** Not listed
COMPANY: District #5 **REGIMENT:** White County Home Guard of Minute Men **BIRTH:** c. 1810 **DEATH:** Unknown
MARRIED: Mary "Polly" Templeton

Unmarked Grave

Moore, John T.
LOCATION: Moore Cemetery **RANK:** Private **COMPANY:** A
REGIMENT: 22nd (Murray's) Battalion Tennessee Infantry
BIRTH: 02 June 1841 **DEATH:** 18 January 1916
MARRIED: Pheobe Hillis **PENSION:** #S11123 (8th Tennessee Cavalry) **PARENTS:** Alexander and Mary "Polly" (Templeton) Moore

~

Moore, Madison
LOCATION: Moore Cemetery **RANK:** Private **COMPANY:** F
REGIMENT: 37th Tennessee Infantry **BIRTH:** 22 October 1811
DEATH: 18 February 1865 **MARRIED:** Elizabeth Cole, c. 1833
PARENTS: Samuel Alexander and Nancy Mourning (Denton) Moore

~

Moore, Ransom P.
LOCATION: Moore Cemetery **RANK:** Private **COMPANY:** B
REGIMENT: 16th Tennessee Infantry **BIRTH:** 28 November 1837 **DEATH:** 31 December 1862 **OTHER:** Killed at the Battle of Murfreesboro, a.k.a. Stone's River in Murfreesboro, Tennessee **PARENTS:** Alexander and Mary "Polly" (Templeton) Moore

Moore Cove Cemetery
In pasture 600 feet east of Pettit Cove Road, 0.3 miles south of junction, Franks Ferry Road, 1.9 miles east of junction, Old Kentucky Road.

Moore, Edward Gleason
LOCATION: Moore Cove Cemetery **RANK:** Private **COMPANY:** I
REGIMENT: 13th (Gore's) Tennessee Cavalry **BIRTH:** 31 August 1836 **DEATH:** 19 August 1873 **PARENTS:** Indimeon Benjamin and Nancy (Templeton) Moore

~

Moore, Hugh Losson Carrick
LOCATION: Moore Cove Cemetery **RANK:** Private **COMPANY:** G
REGIMENT: 16th Tennessee Infantry **BIRTH:** 29 November 1831 **DEATH:** 25 March 1926 **MARRIED:** (1) Leanne Greer; (2) Nancy C. Cantrell **PENSION:** #S15811 **PARENTS:** Indimeon Benjamin and Nancy (Templeton) Moore

Ogden, Henry L.

LOCATION: Moore Cove Cemetery **RANK:** Private **COMPANY:** D
REGIMENT: 1st (Colm's) Battalion Tennessee Infantry
BIRTH: 24 November 1840 **DEATH:** 09 September 1902 **MARRIED:**
Lydia Templeton Moore **PENSION:** #W10396 **PARENTS:** George
and Esther (Smith) Ogden

Montgomery-England Cemetery (Walnut Grove)
North side of Walter Stone Road, 0.1 miles east of junction, Walnut Grove Road

Cloyd, John S.
LOCATION: Montgomery-England Cemetery **RANK:** Private
COMPANY: E **REGIMENT:** 25th Tennessee Infantry
BIRTH: 22 March 1843 **DEATH:** 14 October 1906 **PENSION:** #S230

Mt. Gilead
Mt. Gilead Methodist Church

Arnold, Francis
LOCATION: Mt. Gilead Cemetery **RANK:** Lieutenant **COMPANY:** C
/ District #1 **REGIMENT:** 28th (Consolidated) Tennessee
Infantry / White County Home Guard of Minute Men
BIRTH: 21 March 1824 **DEATH:** 06 April 1897 **MARRIED:** Martha
Ann Smith, 07 September 1843, White County, Tennessee

~

Brown, James P.
LOCATION: Mt. Gilead Cemetery **RANK:** Private **COMPANY:** D
REGIMENT: 1st (Colm's) Battalion Tennessee Infantry
BIRTH: 1838 **DEATH:** 1917 **MARRIED:** Mary R. Bryant, 03
February 1865, White County, Tennessee **PENSION:** #S12207

~

Carrick, John M.
LOCATION: Mt. Gilead Cemetery **RANK:** Private
COMPANY: District #1 **REGIMENT:** White County Home Guard of
Minute Men **BIRTH:** 09 May 1828 **DEATH:** 09 December 1908
MARRIED: Mary Mitchell, 08 May 1851, White County,
Tennessee **PARENTS:** John Addison and Emily Carrick

Dodson, William M.

LOCATION: Mt. Gilead Cemetery **RANK:** Private **COMPANY:** G
REGIMENT: 28th (Consolidated) Tennessee Infantry
BIRTH: 29 October 1828 **DEATH:** 21 June 1896
MARRIED: Martha Hollingsworth, 30 December 1852, Van Buren County, Tennessee

~

Eastland, Charles Simpson

LOCATION: Mt. Gilead Cemetery **RANK:** Private
COMPANY: District #13 **REGIMENT:** White County Home Guard of Minute Men **BIRTH:** 18 July 1829 **DEATH:** 21 December 1887 **MARRIED:** Sarah E. Broyles

~

Eastland, George W.

LOCATION: Mt. Gilead Cemetery **RANK:** Private
COMPANY: District #13 **REGIMENT:** White County Home Guard of Minute Men **BIRTH:** 09 August 1820
DEATH: 03 January 1888

~

Gist, John

LOCATION: Mt. Gilead Cemetery **RANK:** Private
COMPANY: C / G **REGIMENT:** 84th Tennessee Infantry / 28th (Consolidated) Tennessee Infantry **BIRTH:** 17 December 1832
DEATH: 21 April 1907 **MARRIED:** (1) Susan Jane Green, 11 July 1854, White County, Tennessee; (2) Amanda Mitchell, 07 December 1898, White County, Tennessee
PARENTS: John and Elizabeth Gist

~

Gist, Vance Carrick

LOCATION: Mt. Gilead Cemetery **RANK:** Private
COMPANY: D / District #3 **REGIMENT:** 13th (Gore's) Tennessee Cavalry / White County Home Guard of Minute Men
BIRTH: 04 March 1835 **DEATH:** 31 August 1895
MARRIED: Mary Jane Horton, 03 November 1859, White County, Tennessee **PENSION:** #W124

Gooch, William W.

LOCATION: Mt. Gilead Cemetery **RANK:** Corporal **COMPANY:** D **REGIMENT:** 8th (Dibrell's) Tennessee Cavalry **BIRTH:** 19 June 1844 **DEATH:** 02 January 1924 **MARRIED:** Melcena Gist, 17 December 1868, White County, Tennessee **PARENTS:** Joseph and Lavina W. (O'Connor) Gooch

~

Hensley, Eli Lawson

LOCATION: Mt. Gilead Cemetery **RANK:** Private **COMPANY:** G **REGIMENT:** 13th (Gore's) Tennessee Cavalry **BIRTH:** 1843 **DEATH:** 1915 **MARRIED:** Margaret E. Hurd **PENSION:** #W9136 **PARENTS:** Obadiah and Elizabeth Jane (Mason) Hensley

~

Hooser, William M.

LOCATION: Mt. Gilead Cemetery **RANK:** Private **COMPANY:** D **REGIMENT:** 8th (Dibrell's) Tennessee Cavalry **BIRTH:** 10 April 1842 **DEATH:** 16 February 1926 **MARRIED:** Mary "Polly"

~

Horton, John Damron

LOCATION: Mt. Gilead Cemetery **RANK:** Private **COMPANY:** I **REGIMENT:** 13th (Gore's) Tennessee Cavalry **BIRTH:** 07 March 1848 **DEATH:** 16 September 1915 **MARRIED:** Amanda Melvina Holland, 23 February 1868, White County, Tennessee **PARENTS:** Jeptha Vinum and Sarah Elizabeth (Damron) Horton

~

Hudgens, James P.

LOCATION: Mt. Gilead Cemetery **RANK:** Private **COMPANY:** D **REGIMENT:** 13th (Gore's) Tennessee Cavalry / 8th (Dibrell's) Tennessee Cavalary **BIRTH:** 1842 **DEATH:** 1923 **MARRIED:** (1) Melvina Herd, 19 November 1865, White County, Tennessee; (2) America C. Baker, 11 January 1891, White County, Tennessee **PENSIONS:** #S10037 and #W7982 **PARENTS:** Hampton and Elizabeth (Waller) Hudgens

James P. Hudgens

Jarvis, Sylvester
LOCATION: Mt. Gilead Cemetery **RANK:** Private **COMPANY:** D / District #8 **REGIMENT:** 13th (Gore's) Tennessee Cavalry / 8th (Dibrell's) Tennessee Cavalry / White County Home Guard of Minute Men **BIRTH:** 11 May 1839 **DEATH:** 07 June 1912 **MARRIED:** Maranda Simrell, 14 July 1858, White County, Tennessee **PENSION:** #S2245 **PARENTS:** Levi and Martha (Ragsdale) Jarvis

~

Jett, Archibald Overton
LOCATION: Mt. Gilead Cemetery **RANK:** Private **COMPANY:** Not listed **REGIMENT:** 8th (Dibrell's) Tennessee Cavalry **BIRTH:** 08 February 1827 **DEATH:** 06 October 1905 **MARRIED:** Eliza Mitchell **PENSION:** #W4896 **PARENTS:** John W. and Mary "Polly" (White) Jett

~

Jett, John W.
LOCATION: Mt. Gilead Cemetery **RANK:** Private **COMPANY:** K **REGIMENT:** 14th Tennessee Infantry **BIRTH:** 04 March 1817 **DEATH:** 08 August 1874 **PARENTS:** John W., Sr and Mary "Polly" (White) Jett

~

Jett, Thomas J.
LOCATION: Mt. Gilead Cemetery **RANK:** Private **COMPANY:** D **REGIMENT:** 13th (Gore's) Tennessee Cavalry **BIRTH:** 11 January 1834 **DEATH:** 07 February 1889 **MARRIED:** Elizabeth Turner, 07 October 1858, White County, Tennessee **PENSION:** #W3923

~

Johnson, J. O.
LOCATION: Mt. Gilead Cemetery **RANK:** Private **COMPANY:** Not listed **REGIMENT:** 22nd (Murray's) Battalion Tennessee Infantry **BIRTH:** 05 March 1834 **DEATH:** After 1915 **MARRIED:** Mellie **PENSION:** #S8361

Jones, Andrew Jackson
LOCATION: Mt. Gilead Cemetery **RANK:** Private
COMPANY: B **REGIMENT:** 20th Tennessee Infantry
BIRTH: 24 November 1847 **DEATH:** 26 July 1917
MARRIED: Nancy Pamelia Jarvis **PARENTS:** Monroe and Jane (Meredith) Jones

~

Jordan, Benjamin F.
LOCATION: Mt. Gilead Cemetery **RANK:** Private
COMPANY: A **REGIMENT:** Welcher's Battalion Cavalry
BIRTH: 22 February 1845 **DEATH:** 09 April 1915
MARRIED: Eliza Jane Owings, 16 January 1870, Roane County, Tennessee **PENSION:** #S14172

~

Keathley, Thomas Robinson
LOCATION: Mt. Gilead Cemetery **RANK:** Private **COMPANY:** G
REGIMENT: 28th (Consolidated) Tennessee Infantry
BIRTH: 03 March 1826 **DEATH:** 09 January 1899
MARRIED: Susan Almeda Smith, 07 December 1853, White County, Tennessee **PARENTS:** Jesse and Susannah (Webster) Keathley

~

Keathly, William H.
LOCATION: Mt. Gilead Cemetery **RANK:** Private **COMPANY:** D
REGIMENT: 13th (Gore's) Tennessee Cavalry **BIRTH:** 1837
DEATH: 1925 **MARRIED:** Sarah Webb, 12 February 1857, White County, Tennessee **PARENTS:** Samuel Henderson and Matilda (Holland) Keathly

~

Lowery, John A.
LOCATION: Mt. Gilead Cemetery **RANK:** Private **COMPANY:** K
REGIMENT: 16th Tennessee Infantry **BIRTH:** 26 August 1824
DEATH: 29 May 1902 **MARRIED:** Martha Jane Taylor, 08 January 1846, White County, Tennessee

Meek, John Sperry

LOCATION: Mt. Gilead Cemetery **RANK:** Sergeant **COMPANY:** A **REGIMENT:** 25th Tennessee Infantry **BIRTH:** 18 September 1837 **DEATH:** 25 March 1888 **MARRIED:** Sara Jane Dibrell, 26 July 1867, White County, Tennessee

~

Simrell, Eli Daniel

LOCATION: Mt. Gilead Cemetery **RANK:** Captain **COMPANY:** K / District #6 **REGIMENT:** 28th Tennessee Infantry / White County Home Guard of Minute Men **BIRTH:** 07 March 1834 **DEATH:** 14 February 1912 **MARRIED:** Adeline Wilson **PARENTS:** Daniel and Rachel (Hunter) Simrell

~

Watson, Elijah B.

LOCATION: Mt. Gilead Cemetery **RANK:** Private **COMPANY:** C **REGIMENT:** 25th Tennessee Infantry **BIRTH:** 07 April 1827 **DEATH:** 12 September 1902 **MARRIED:** Martha J. Rogers, 14 June 1861, White County, Tennessee **PARENTS:** David and Betsy Watson

~

Webb, Waymon P.

LOCATION: Mt. Gilead Cemetery **RANK:** Private **COMPANY:** D **REGIMENT:** 13th (Gore's) Tennessee Cavalry **BIRTH:** 1839 **DEATH:** 1909 **MARRIED:** Amanda Gist, 12 January 1864, White County, Tennessee **PENSION:** #S181 **PARENTS:** Washington and Sarah "Saley" (Holland) Webb

~

Woods, James Burrough

LOCATION: Mt. Gilead Cemetery **RANK:** Private **COMPANY:** D **REGIMENT:** 13th (Gore's) Tennessee Cavalry **BIRTH:** 07 June 1832 **DEATH:** 13 August 1913 **MARRIED:** Elizabeth R. Keathley

Mt. Pisgah Cemetery
Mt. Pisgah Methodist Church, Quebeck

Anderson, Tilford
LOCATION: Mt. Pisgah Cemetery **RANK:** Private **COMPANY:** C
REGIMENT: 35th Tennessee Infantry

~

Badger, Alphonso L.
LOCATION: Mt. Pisgah Cemetery **RANK:** Private **COMPANY:** K
REGIMENT: 28th Tennessee Infantry **BIRTH:** 01 April 1836
DEATH: 13 January 1864 **MARRIED:** Helen C.
PARENTS: Dr. Felix A. and Sarah C. (Susannah) Badger

~

Badger, Dr. Felix A.
LOCATION: Mt. Pisgah Cemetery **RANK:** Private
COMPANY: District #5 **REGIMENT:** White County Home Guard of Minute Men **BIRTH:** 23 December 1810 **DEATH:** 16 June 1870 **MARRIED:** Sarah C. Susanna, c. 1830 **OTHER:** Dentist

~

Cantrell, Starling William
LOCATION: Mt. Pisgah Cemetery **RANK:** Private **COMPANY:** C
REGIMENT: 16th Tennessee Infantry **BIRTH:** 22 February 1829
DEATH: 11 September 1913 **MARRIED:** Mary Crowder
PARENTS: William and Mary Cantrell

~

Chisam, James W.
LOCATION: Mt. Pisgah Cemetery **RANK:** Private **COMPANY:** A
REGIMENT: 22nd (Murray's) Battalion Tennessee Infantry
BIRTH: 03 December 1843 **DEATH:** 30 May 1928 **MARRIED:** Florence Duncan **PENSION:** #W9225

Unmarked Grave

Cruise, Hanabel
LOCATION: Mt. Pisgah Cemetery **RANK:** Private **COMPANY:** D
REGIMENT: 16th Tennessee Infantry **BIRTH:** 20 March 1840
DEATH: 26 July 1895 **MARRIED:** Martha Allen, 17 March 1871, White County, Tennessee **PARENTS:** Walter and Levina Cruise

~

Fisher, James
LOCATION: Mt. Pisgah Cemetery **RANK:** 1st Lieutenant
COMPANY: G / District #4 **REGIMENT:** 16th Tennessee Infantry / White County Home Guard of Minute Men
BIRTH: 29 July 1820 **DEATH:** 10 March 1907
MARRIED: (1) Susannah S. Hutson; (2) Mrs. Harriet Boyd, 03 January 1885, White County, Tennessee

~

Fisher, Madison L.
LOCATION: Mt. Pisgah Cemetery **RANK:** Private **COMPANY:** G
REGIMENT: 16th Tennessee Infantry **BIRTH:** 03 July 1837
DEATH: 03 July 1897 **MARRIED:** Emily C. Haston, 27 October 1867 **PENSION:** #W23

~

Hembree, Martin VanBuren
LOCATION: Mt. Pisgah Cemetery **RANK:** Private
COMPANY: Not listed **REGIMENT:** Savage's Regiment of the Southern Confederacy **BIRTH:** 06 August 1839
DEATH: 03 July 1905 **MARRIED:** Elizabeth McPeak
PENSIONS: #S3288 and #W6287 **PARENTS:** James J. and Mary (Knowles) Hembree

~

Hill, William B.
LOCATION: Mt. Pisgah Cemetery **RANK:** Sergeant
COMPANY: Not listed **REGIMENT:** Captain Baxter's Company, Tennessee Light Artillery **BIRTH:** 10 May 1825
DEATH: 02 March 1895 **PARENT:** Prudence M. Hill

Hutson, John F.
LOCATION: Mt. Pisgah Cemetery **RANK:** Corporal **COMPANY:** K **REGIMENT:** 28th Tennessee Infantry **BIRTH:** 17 July 1840 **DEATH:** 20 December 1862 **PARENTS:** Thomas E. and Permelia (Webb) Hutson

~

Hutson, Thomas E.
LOCATION: Mt. Pisgah Cemetery **RANK:** Chaplain **COMPANY:** K / District #5 **REGIMENT:** 28th Tennessee Infantry / White County Home Guard of Minute Men **BIRTH:** 01 May 1813 **DEATH:** 12 July 1877 **MARRIED:** Permelia Webb **PARENTS:** Matthias and Sarah (Knowles) Hutson

~

Jenkins, G. W.
LOCATION: Mt. Pisgah Cemetery **RANK:** Private **COMPANY:** I **REGIMENT:** 28th Tennessee Infantry **BIRTH:** 29 March 1844 **DEATH:** 21 February 1922 **MARRIED:** Nancy Jane Winstead, 04 September 1873, White County, Tennessee **PARENTS:** John W. and Louisa America (Wilson) Jenkins

~

Knowles, Jasper A.
LOCATION: Mt. Pisgah Cemetery **RANK:** Private **COMPANY:** K / H **REGIMENT:** 16th Tennessee Infantry **BIRTH:** 15 May 1839 **DEATH:** 17 June 1921 **MARRIED:** (1) Cynthia Denton, 02 December 1862; (2) Cynthia Webb, 30 December 1902 **PARENTS:** William and Diana K. (Swindell) Knowles

~

Moore, Samuel A., II
LOCATION: Mt. Pisgah Cemetery **RANK:** Sergeant **COMPANY:** G **REGIMENT:** 3rd (Forrest's) Tennessee Cavalry **BIRTH:** 24 December 1844 **DEATH:** 18 July 1921 **MARRIED:** Nancy Anderson

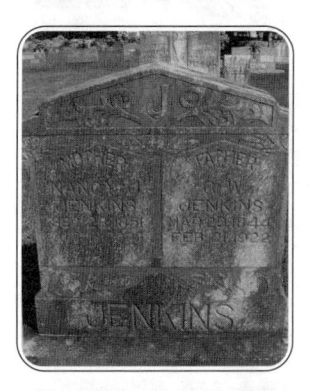

Rascoe, John R.
LOCATION: Mt. Pisgah Cemetery **RANK:** Private **COMPANY:** A / District #4 **REGIMENT:** 22nd (Murray's) Battalion Tennessee Infantry / White County Home Guard of Minute Men **BIRTH:** 14 October 1827 **DEATH:** 24 August 1898 **MARRIED:** Lucy F. Bates, 03 January 1859, Warren County, Tennessee **PARENTS:** John and Martha "Patsy" (Pleasant) Rascoe

~

Swindle, Cason
LOCATION: Mt. Pisgah Cemetery **RANK:** Private **COMPANY:** K **REGIMENT:** 28th Tennessee Infantry **BIRTH:** 27 December 1841 **DEATH:** 18 October 1861 **PARENTS:** Christerfer Columbus and Elizabeth "Eliza" (Webb) Swindle

~

Swindle, Christerfer Columbus
LOCATION: Mt. Pisgah Cemetery **RANK:** 2nd Lieutenant **COMPANY:** A **REGIMENT:** 35th Tennessee Infantry **BIRTH:** 03 January 1813 **DEATH:** 29 December 1886 **MARRIED:** Elizabeth "Eliza" Webb

~

Swindle, Jeremiah M.
LOCATION: Mt. Pisgah Cemetery **RANK:** Private **COMPANY:** K **REGIMENT:** 28th Tennessee Infantry **BIRTH:** 16 March 1838 **DEATH:** 10 February 1862 **PARENTS:** Christerfer Columbus and Elizabeth "Eliza" (Webb) Swindle

~

Templeton, Greenville H.
LOCATION: Mt. Pisgah Cemetery **RANK:** Private **COMPANY:** K / District #5 **REGIMENT:** 16th Tennessee Infantry / White County Home Guard of Minute Men **BIRTH:** 14 February 1828 **DEATH:** 11 September 1904 **MARRIED:** (1) Amanda S. Farris; (2) Margaret "Maggie" Denton **PENSION:** #W2372

Thompson, James Robertson
LOCATION: Mt. Pisgah Cemetery **RANK:** Private **COMPANY:** B **REGIMENT:** 16th Tennessee Infantry **BIRTH:** 29 August 1840 **DEATH:** 16 February 1918 **MARRIED:** Mary Caroline Chisam, 11 August 1874 **PENSIONS:** #S12425 and #W7039

~

Webb, James J.
LOCATION: Mt. Pisgah Cemetery **RANK:** Private **COMPANY:** K **REGIMENT:** 16th Tennessee Infantry **BIRTH:** c. 1842 **DEATH:** Unknown **PARENTS:** Elisha and Harriet Jane (Little) Webb

~

Webb, John M.
LOCATION: Mt. Pisgah Cemetery **RANK:** Private **COMPANY:** K **REGIMENT:** 16th Tennessee Infantry **BIRTH:** c. 1844 **DEATH:** Unknown **MARRIED:** Aurelia Knowles, 19 July 1860, White County, Tennessee **PARENTS:** Elisha and Harriet Jane (Little) Webb

~

Wilson, Jasper W.
LOCATION: Mt. Pisgah Cemetery **RANK:** 2nd Sergeant **COMPANY:** K **REGIMENT:** 16th Tennessee Infantry **BIRTH:** 28 August 1837 **DEATH:** 29 June 1912

~

Wright, Seth F.
LOCATION: Mt. Pisgah Cemetery **RANK:** Private **COMPANY:** G **REGIMENT:** 16th Tennessee Infantry **BIRTH:** 20 February 1822 **DEATH:** 22 November 1900 **PARENTS:** James, Jr., and Eleanor (Hutson) Wright

~

Wright, Wesley Deskin
LOCATION: Mt. Pisgah Cemetery **RANK:** Private **COMPANY:** G / D **REGIMENT:** 16th Tennessee Infantry / 8th (Dibrell's) Tennessee Cavalry **BIRTH:** 22 January 1837 **DEATH:** 28 May 1902 **MARRIED:** Nancy Caroline Fisher **PENSION:** #W2141 **PARENTS:** James, Jr., and Eleanor (Hutson) Wright

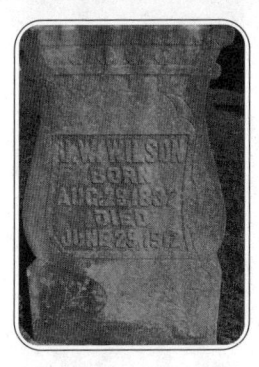

Nash Cemetery
Key Community

Cash, John
LOCATION: Nash Cemetery **RANK:** Private **COMPANY:** D
REGIMENT: 1st (Colm's) Battalion Tennessee Infantry
BIRTH: 02 February 1815 **DEATH:** 16 March 1896
MARRIED: Jane Gooch, 19 March 1840, White County, Tennessee

New Bon Air Cemetery
East side of Corolla Road, 0.4 miles from junction US 70 at Bon Air

Prater, Carrington
LOCATION: New Bon Air Cemetery **RANK:** Private **COMPANY:** A
REGIMENT: 22nd (Murray's) Battalion Tennessee Infantry
BIRTH: 08 October 1843 **DEATH:** 07 January 1902
MARRIED: (1) Sarah Jane Baker, 13 October 1860; (2) Ann White **PENSION:** #W7729 **PARENTS:** Joseph and Martha Prater

New Hope Cemetery
Cassville, New Hope Baptist Church

Anderson, Charles
LOCATION: New Hope Cemetery **RANK:** Private
COMPANY: District #11 **REGIMENT:** White County Home Guard of Minute Men **BIRTH:** 08 February 1818
DEATH: 25 January 1894 **MARRIED:** Caroline (Lowery) Baker, 19 January 1859, White County, Tennessee

~

Brady, Martin V.
LOCATION: New Hope Cemetery **RANK:** Private
COMPANY: A **REGIMENT:** 1st (Carter's) Tennessee Cavalry
BIRTH: 22 March 1840 **DEATH:** 09 February 1906
MARRIED: Mary **PENSION:** #S6239

Jones, Harmon Lafayette
LOCATION: New Hope Cemetery **RANK:** Private
COMPANY: D **REGIMENT:** 13th (Gore's) Tennessee Cavalry
BIRTH: 14 February 1837 **DEATH:** 29 May 1894
MARRIED: Lucy Malinda **PENSION:** #W1832

~

Jones, William W.
LOCATION: New Hope Cemetery **RANK:** Private
COMPANY: D **REGIMENT:** 13th (Gore's) Tennessee Cavalry
BIRTH: 16 February 1846 **DEATH:** 27 February 1869

~

Lewis, James M.
LOCATION: New Hope Cemetery **RANK:** Private
COMPANY: District #2 **REGIMENT:** White County Home Guard of Minute Men **BIRTH:** January 1804
DEATH: February 1894

Unmarked Grave

~

Martin, Abijah
LOCATION: New Hope Cemetery **RANK:** 1st Corporal
COMPANY: C **REGIMENT:** 1st (Colm's) Battalion Tennessee Infantry **BIRTH:** 08 April 1824 **DEATH:** 31 August 1880
MARRIED: Susan Gilbert, 08 April 1849

~

Montgomery, William M.
LOCATION: New Hope Cemetery **RANK:** Private **COMPANY:** D **REGIMENT:** 13th(Gore's) Tennessee Cavalry / 8th (Dibrell's) Tennessee Cavalry **BIRTH:** 06 November 1844 **DEATH:** 25 March 1935 **MARRIED:** Sarah E. Pirtle, 05 December 1878, White County, Tennessee **PENSION:** #S9684 and #W10865

~

Montgomery, Zackery
LOCATION: New Hope Cemetery **RANK:** Private **COMPANY:** D **REGIMENT:** 13th (Gore's) Tennessee Cavalry **BIRTH:** 25 March 1840 **DEATH:** 02 June 1902 **MARRIED:** Nancy Jane
PENSIONS: #S1065 and #W1003

Peek, James
LOCATION: New Hope Cemetery **RANK:** Private
COMPANY: F **REGIMENT:** 13th (Gore's) Tennessee Cavalry / 8th (Dibrell's) Tennessee Cavalry **BIRTH:** 25 June 1839
DEATH: 22 April 1913 **MARRIED:** Elizabeth
PENSION: #S12755

~

Russell, John D.
LOCATION: New Hope Cemetery **RANK:** Private
COMPANY: I **REGIMENT:** 17th Tennessee Infantry
BIRTH: 25 September 1833 **DEATH:** 07 March 1869
PARENTS: William, I, and Prazil P. Russell

~

Russell, Waman Mansfield
LOCATION: New Hope Cemetery **RANK:** Sergeant Major **COMPANY:** G **REGIMENT:** 28th Tennessee Infantry
BIRTH: 20 November 1828
DEATH: 08 October 1907
MARRIED: Nancy Y. Gracey, 18 February 1858, White County, Tennessee **PENSION:** #W3826

Waman Mansfield Russell

PARENTS: William, I, and Parazil P. Russell **UDC MEMBERS:** Anna Ruth Barnes, Sarah Looney Dodson, Carolyn Barnes Rankhorn

~

Russell, William Monroe
LOCATION: New Hope Cemetery **RANK:** Private **COMPANY:** E **REGIMENT:** 11th (Holman's) Tennessee Cavalry **BIRTH:** 26 February 1830 **DEATH:** 21 April 1863 **MARRIED:** Susan Bryant, 08 January 1852, White County, Tennesseel **PARENTS:** William, I, and Parazil P. Russell **UDC MEMBERS:** Anna Ruth Barnes, Sarah Looney Dodson, Carolyn Barnes Rankhorn

Norris Cemetery #2
Central View

Norris, Avery
LOCATION: Norris Cemetery #2 **RANK:** Private **COMPANY:** G **REGIMENT:** 16th Tennessee Infantry **BIRTH:** September 1832 **DEATH:** After 02 June 1900

Old Bon Air Cemetery
Bon Air Springs—South side of Old Bon Air Road, 1.2 miles from west junction, US 70 above Rock House, or 3.3 miles from east junction with US 70 at Bon Air.

Boles, George Randolph
LOCATION: Old Bon Air Cemetery **RANK:** Private **COMPANY:** B **REGIMENT:** 8th (Dibrell's) Tennessee Cavalry **BIRTH:** 17 September 1840 **DEATH:** 28 September 1925 **MARRIED:** Sarah Ann Poteet **PENSION:** #W8374 and #W8445 **PARENTS:** Robert and Jennie (Beason) Boles

~

Burden, Henery
LOCATION: Old Bon Air Cemetery **RANK:** Private **COMPANY:** E **REGIMENT:** 1st (Colm's) Battalion Tennessee Infantry **BIRTH:** 10 October 1825 **DEATH:** Between 1870 and 1880 **MARRIED:** Fannie White, 11 November 1845

~

DeRossett, John
LOCATION: Old Bon Air Cemetery **RANK:** Private **COMPANY:** A **REGIMENT:** 28th Tennessee Infantry **BIRTH:** c. 1816 **DEATH:** Unknown **PENSION:** #S6256 **PARENTS:** John and Elinder DeRossett

~

Dodson, Samuel
LOCATION: Old Bon Air Cemetery **RANK:** Private **COMPANY:** C **REGIMENT:** 25th Tennessee Infantry **BIRTH:** 04 June 1831 **DEATH:** 22 June 1908 **MARRIED:** Amanda Jane Prater, 30 August 1856

Unmarked Grave

Little, Hiram
LOCATION: Old Bon Air Cemetery **RANK:** Private **COMPANY:** K **REGIMENT:** 28th Tennessee Infantry **BIRTH:** 01 December 1822 **DEATH:** 06 December 1905 **MARRIED:** Sarah Cope, 12 October 1848

~

Marlow, William C., Sr.
LOCATION: Old Bon Air Cemetery **RANK:** Private **COMPANY:** K **REGIMENT:** 28th Tennessee Infantry **BIRTH:** 1831 **DEATH:** After 1880 **MARRIED:** (1) Elizabeth Ann Blankenship; (2) Nancy Hoof Dodson **PENSION:** #S398 and #W1984

Old Jericho Cemetery
Quebeck

Anderson, John D.
LOCATION: Old Jericho Cemetery **RANK:** Private **COMPANY:** C / District #4 **REGIMENT:** 25th Tennessee Infantry / White County Home Guard of Minute Men **BIRTH:** 06 December 1816 **DEATH:** 27 January 1863 **MARRIED:** Mary "Polly" Denton, 29 October 1840, White County, Tennessee **OTHER:** Although John D. Anderson is buried in Old Jericho Cemetery in an unmarked grave, a military marker was placed in the Jericho Church of Christ Cemetery next to his wife. **PARENTS:** Joseph and Nancy (Deweese) Anderson

~

Halterman, Spencer J.
LOCATION: Old Jericho Cemetery **RANK:** Private **COMPANY:** I **REGIMENT:** 13th (Gore's) Tennessee Cavalry **BIRTH:** 10 September 1845 **DEATH:** 05 March 1869 **MARRIED:** Nancy Anderson, 05 January 1867, White County, Tennessee

Old Philadelphia
Greenwood Southern Baptist Church—Doyle

Edwards, John B.
LOCATION: Old Philadelphia Cemetery **RANK:** Private **COMPANY:** G **REGIMENT:** 7th Tennessee Infantry **BIRTH:** 01 March 1827 **DEATH:** 24 May 1903

McWhirter, John Alexander
LOCATION: Old Philadelphia Cemetery **RANK:** Private
COMPANY: D **REGIMENT:** 16th Tennessee Infantry
BIRTH: 18 January 1842 **DEATH:** 22 September 1926
MARRIED: Eliza Ann Little, 11 March 1866, White County, Tennessee **PARENTS:** George Marlin and Sarah Elizabeth (Cunningham) McWhirter

~

Norris, Robert C.
LOCATION: Old Philadelphia Cemetery **RANK:** Private
COMPANY: C **REGIMENT:** 25th Tennessee Infantry
BIRTH: 15 April 1840 **DEATH:** 27 January 1918
MARRIED: Lucinda Lewis, 28 February 1868, White County, Tennessee

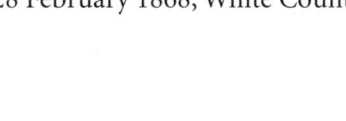

~

Norris, William Henderson
LOCATION: Old Philadelphia Cemetery **RANK:** Private
COMPANY: A **REGIMENT:** 22nd (Murray's) Battalion Tennessee Infantry **BIRTH:** 12 February 1838 **DEATH:** 17 January 1897
MARRIED: Mary C. McPherson, 25 March 1866, White County, Tennessee **PENSIONS:** #S396 and #W217
PARENTS: Avery and Mary Norris

Old Shady Grove—Shady Grove
On ridge in woods across creek, 800 feet bearing 034 degrees from abandoned frame community center building, north side C.B. Johnson Road, 0.2 miles east of junction, Old Kentucky Road (SR 136)

Arnold, Christopher Columbus
LOCATION: Old Shady Grove Cemetery **RANK:** Private
COMPANY: K **REGIMENT:** 28th Tennessee Infantry
BIRTH: 06 November 1837 **DEATH:** 10 May 1901
MARRIED: Susan Pirtle **PARENTS:** Samuel Dennis and Elizabeth (Glenn) Arnold

Glenn, Alexander
LOCATION: Old Shady Grove Cemetery **RANK:** Private
COMPANY: K **REGIMENT:** 16th Tennessee Infantry
BIRTH: 17 June 1843 **DEATH:** 02 March 1918 **PENSION:** #S3807
PARENTS: John Lewis and Jane (Womack) Glenn

~

Humphrey, David
LOCATION: Old Shady Grove Cemetery **RANK:** Private
COMPANY: B **REGIMENT:** 1st (Colm's) Battalion Tennessee Infantry **BIRTH:** 10 December 1844 **DEATH:** 01 March 1875
MARRIED: Nancy Swindle, 20 February 1871, White County, Tennessee **PARENTS:** John D. and Christine (Stubblefield) Humphrey

Old Sparta City Cemetery
S. Church Street, Sparta, Tennessee 38583

Argo, Elza Jones
LOCATION: Old Sparta City Cemetery **RANK:** Private
COMPANY: D **REGIMENT:** 35th Tennessee Infantry **BIRTH:** 09 August 1846 **DEATH:** 27 December 1901 **MARRIED:** Mary Jane Hoodenpyle, 19 October 1870, Warren County, Tennessee

~

Austin, Edward D.
LOCATION: Old Sparta City Cemetery **RANK:** Private
COMPANY: C / G / District #8 **REGIMENT:** 84th Tennessee Infantry / 28th (Consolidated) Tennessee Infantry / White County Home Guard of Minute Men **BIRTH:** 1845
DEATH: 1928 **MARRIED:** Laura B. Stoner, 16 September 1879, White County, Tennessee **PENSION:** #S2618 **PARENTS:** James M. and Mary (Anderson) Austin

~

Bradford, Thomas J.
LOCATION: Old Sparta City Cemetery **RANK:** Private
COMPANY: K **REGIMENT:** 16th Tennessee Infantry
BIRTH: 19 March 1836 **DEATH:** 27 July 1902 **PENSION:** #S4074

Clark, Wamon

LOCATION: Old Sparta City Cemetery **RANK:** Captain
COMPANY: G / District #1 **REGIMENT:** 28th (Consolidated) Tennessee Infantry / White County Home Guard of Minute Men **BIRTH:** 20 January 1822 **DEATH:** 14 February 1895
MARRIED: Elizabeth

~

Coleman, Ambrose Benton

LOCATION: Old Sparta City Cemetery **RANK:** Private
COMPANY: D **REGIMENT:** 1st (Colm's) Battalion Tennessee Infantry **BIRTH:** 08 August 1829 **DEATH:** 10 October 1898
MARRIED: Martha J. Oliver, 04 January 1870, White County, Tennessee

~

Colms, Stephen H.

LOCATION: Old Sparta City Cemetery **RANK:** Major
COMPANY: Field and Staff **REGIMENT:** 1st (Colm's) Battalion Tennessee Infantry **BIRTH:** 22 October 1815
DEATH: 18 December 1874 **MARRIED:** Harriet

~

Cummings, J. J.

LOCATION: Old Sparta City Cemetery **RANK:** Private
COMPANY: C **REGIMENT:** 8th Tennessee Infantry
BIRTH: 12 January 1818 **DEATH:** 06 February 1876
MARRIED: Sarah A.

~

Deweese, J. J.

LOCATION: Old Sparta City Cemetery **RANK:** Not listed
COMPANY: D **REGIMENT:** 8th (Dibrell's) Tennessee Cavalry
BIRTH: 17 July 1832 **DEATH:** 04 July 1876

Dibrell, George Gibbs

LOCATION: Old Sparta City Cemetery
RANK: Brigadier General **COMPANY:** Field and Staff
REGIMENT: 8th (Dibrell's) Tennessee Cavalry
BIRTH: 12 April 1822 **DEATH:** 09 May 1888 **MARRIED:** Mary Elizabeth Leftwich, 13 January 1842, White County, Tennessee **PARENTS:** Anthony and Millie (Carter) Dibrell **UDC MEMBER:** Carolyn Rollins Carr

George Gibbs Dibrell

George Gibbs Dibrell was born into a farming family in Sparta, White County, Tennessee. He managed to acquire a little more than the customary rural education. First, attending local common schools and then a year at East Tennessee University in Knoxville. Before he was eighteen years of age, he was elected clerk of the Bank of Tennessee at the Sparta branch. He held this office for six years. He left the bank and engaged in merchandising and farming. Dibrell was elected clerk of the county court and was three times re-elected, until he voluntarily retired in 1860. He continued his mercantile business and farming interest.

His family was predominantly Unionist in the growing national crisis. In February 1861, he was the Union candidate for the State convention, and was elected by a very large majority. He opposed secession, but always declared his adhesion to the South. The convention chose secession, but in the wake of the firing on Fort Sumter, Dibrell immediately sided with the majority.

In June, he assisted in raising and organizing the Twenty-fifth Regiment of Tennessee Infantry. On August 10, 1861, when the regiment officially organized, the men chose Dibrell as their lieutenant-colonel. He served with this regiment throughout most of his initial twelve-month enlistment.

Dibrell received authorization to raise a regiment of partisan rangers. He organized the twelve companies that would become the 13th Tennessee Calvary, which for most of the war would be more commonly known as the 8th Tennessee. Dibrell became colonel and soon reorganized in October as a regular cavalry regiment with ten companies. All Dibrell ever received from the War Department were six hundred sabers and four hundred old flintlock muskets. Thereafter, he armed his regiment by capturing weapons from the enemy.

The regiment went to Murfreesboro where it became part of Nathan B. Forrest's brigade, commencing an association that would continue for most of the war. Dibrell went with Forrest on the raid into west Tennessee, participating in the fight at Parker's Crossroads. Commanding a brigade, he played a prominent role in the defense of the important salt works during the Battle of Saltville and participated in many major campaigns throughout the war.

In March of 1864, Dibrell was ordered to north Georgia to join Johnston and the Army of Tennessee for the Atlanta Campaign. Following the fall of Atlanta, Dibrell and his brigade went with Wheeler on his raid into Tennessee. This brought the colonel and his men back to Sparta briefly where they rested for several days with their family and friends. Wheeler's raid was broken up and several of its commands were isolated, including Dibrell's. He finally rejoined Wheeler and helped in the unsuccessful resistance to Sherman's march from Atlanta to Savannah, Georgia.

On January 28, 1865, President Davis finally recognized Dibrell's long and good service with an appointment as brigadier general. The Senate confirmed it the same day and the appointment itself was backdated to July 26, 1864. Dibrell saw his last action on April 11, 1865, at Beulah, North Carolina.

He was ordered to report to President Jefferson Davis at Greensboro, North Carolina after the fall of Richmond. Dibrell and his regiment made the eighty-five mile march in two nights and a day, and escorted President Davis, guarding the trains carrying the archives of the Confederate War Department to Washington, Georgia, where they surrendered and were paroled May 9, 1865.

General Dibrell marched his men in a body back to White County, Tennessee. He found his home devastated, and his family almost suffering for the necessaries of life. He at once, with his son who had stood all the hardships of war with him, went to work on the farm, to try to build up his lost fortunes. Dibrell immediately became a community and state leader. He became the president of the Southwestern Railroad in 1869 and in 1870 he sat as a delegate in Tennessee's new constitutional convention. In 1874 he was elected to Congress and four times reelected, voluntarily retiring in 1884. After his congressional career, he gave his whole attention to his farm and in developing the Bon Air coal mine. He was a major player in the development of the coal mining industry in Middle Tennessee. Dibrell was a member of the Methodist Church for forty-four years; twice sent as a delegate to the conference of that church. When the veterans of his old brigade met in 1883 to form a "reunion brigade," General Dibrell became its commander. He took an active part in its meetings and affairs until his death at his home in Sparta, in 1888.

Dibrell, Joseph Anthony

Joseph Anthony Dibrell

LOCATION: Old Sparta City Cemetery **RANK:** 2nd Lieutenant **COMPANY:** A **REGIMENT:** 8th (Dibrell's) Tennessee Cavalry **BIRTH:** 17 November 1845 **DEATH:** 25 June 1913 **MARRIED:** Ritha Bruster, 11 December 1872, White County, Tennessee **PENSIONS:** #S13536 and #W5063 **PARENTS:** George Gibbs and Mary Elizabeth (Leftwich) Dibrell **UDC MEMBER:** Carolyn Rollins Carr

Dibrell, Montgomery C.

LOCATION: Old Sparta City Cemetery **RANK:** Adjutant / Quarter Master **COMPANY:** Field & Staff **REGIMENT:** 25th Tennessee Infantry **BIRTH:** 06 March 1813, Tennessee **DEATH:** 06 June 1881 **MARRIED:** Mary Ann Eastland, 01 September 1842, White County, Tennessee **PARENTS:** Anthony and Millie (Carter) Dibrell **UDC MEMBER:** Carolyn Rollins Carr

Unmarked Grave

Gracy, Wamon L.

LOCATION: Old Sparta City Cemetery **RANK:** Quartermaster Sergeant **COMPANY:** D **REGIMENT:** 1st (Colm's) Battalion Tennessee Infantry **BIRTH:** 26 February 1829 **DEATH:** 04 June 1887 **MARRIED:** Martha Hudgens, 22 December 1859, White County, Tennessee **PARENTS:** Hugh and Mary (Jones) Gracy

Leftwich, Jefferson

LOCATION: Old Spart City Cemetery **RANK:** Captain **COMPANY:** D **REGIMENT:** 8th (Dibrell's) Tennessee Cavalry **BIRTH:** 28 May 1836 **DEATH:** 09 October 1871 **MARRIED:** Louraine C. Lisk, 30 August 1854, White County, Tennessee **PARENTS:** Waman and Rebecca (Rowland) Leftwich **OTHER:** "On the morning of the 9th of August, 1863, our pickets, eight miles from our camp on the road to Spencer, were charged by Col. Minty's brigade of cavalry. The picket was Capt. Leftwich's Co. D. A running fight from there to camp, two miles above Sparta, was kept up. Capt. Leftwich, being on a fleet horse, would check the advance until overpowered, would then press on and urge his men out of the way. When the firing was heard as they came running at full speed through Sparta, at least two-thirds of our horses were loose in the fresh pasture just opened, and by the time we could get our horses the enemy was near us." (Story relayed by Gen. Dibrell, from *Legends and Stories of White County*)
UDC MEMBER: Carolyn Rollins Carr

Meek, Clark

LOCATION: Old Sparta City Cemetery **RANK:** Private **COMPANY:** D **REGIMENT:** 1st (Colm's) Battalion Tennessee Infantry **BIRTH:** 11 January 1842 **DEATH:** 28 December 1867 **PARENTS:** Charles and Nancy Meek

Pope, Thomas

LOCATION: Old Sparta City Cemetery **RANK:** Private **COMPANY:** D **REGIMENT:** 1st (Colm's) Battalion Tennessee Infantry **BIRTH:** 06 March 1826 **DEATH:** 05 May 1877

Rhea, John Simpson
LOCATION: Old Sparta City Cemetery **RANK:** Brevet 2nd Lieutenant **COMPANY:** H **REGIMENT:** 13th (Gore's) Tennessee Cavalry **BIRTH:** 15 December 1831 **DEATH:** 11 April 1882 **MARRIED:** Amanda Jane England, 23 December 1857, White County, Tennessee **PARENTS:** William P. and Mary Ann (Whitson) Rhea

John Simpson Rhea

~

Scott, James
LOCATION: Old Sparta City Cemetery **RANK:** Private **COMPANY:** A / District #1 **REGIMENT:** 25th Tennessee Infantry / White County Home Guard of Minute Men **BIRTH:** 24 March 1810 **DEATH:** 04 September 1881 **MARRIED:** Amanda Lowery **PARENTS:** Jonathan and Elizabeth (Millican) Scott

~

Scott, Jonathan
LOCATION: Old Sparta City Cemetery **RANK:** Private **COMPANY:** A **REGIMENT:** 25th Tennessee Infantry **BIRTH:** 08 October 1841 **DEATH:** 12 December 1864

~

Spurlock, George Jackson
LOCATION: Old Sparta City Cemetery **RANK:** 2nd Lieutenant **COMPANY:** 2A **REGIMENT:** 35th Tennessee Infantry **BIRTH:** 28 January 1841 **DEATH:** 01 February 1926 **MARRIED:** (1) Helen O. Richardson, 17 July 1870, DeKalb County, Tennessee; (2) Lucinda Smith, 30 May 1885, White County, Tennessee **PENSION:** #S6766

~

Williams, W. M.
LOCATION: Old Sparta City Cemetery **RANK:** Private **COMPANY:** L **REGIMENT:** 6th Alabama Infantry **BIRTH:** 1846 **DEATH:** 1912 **MARRIED:** Elizabeth Murray **PENSION:** #S5311

Young, Daniel W.
LOCATION: Old Sparta City Cemetery **RANK:** Private **COMPANY:** D **REGIMENT:** 13th (Gore's) Tennessee Cavalry **BIRTH:** 04 May 1842 **DEATH:** 04 December 1882 **MARRIED:** Mary Lowrey, 18 January, White County, Tennessee **PENSION:** #S5779 **PARENTS:** Austin C. and Lucetta (Clark) Young

Old Spring Hill Cemetery
On ridge beside pasture at end of dirt lane, 0.2 miles south off Monterey Highway (SR 84). Lane requires 4 wheel drive. Is 100 feet west of junction, Board Valley Road.

Brady, Edward
LOCATION: Old Spring Hill Cemetery **RANK:** Private **COMPANY:** D / H **REGIMENT:** 84th Tennessee Infantry / 28th (Consolidated) Tennessee Infantry **BIRTH:** 03 September 1837 **DEATH:** 18 April 1915 **MARRIED:** Catherine Officer **PENSION:** #S2268 **PARENTS:** Patrick and Mary (Morgan) Brady

Edward Brady

Carr, William M.
LOCATION: Old Spring Hill Cemetery **RANK:** Private **COMPANY:** D **REGIMENT:** 1st (Colm's) Battalion Tennessee Infantry **BIRTH:** January 1840 **DEATH:** 19 February 1906 **MARRIED:** Sarah H. **PENSION:** #S2068

Old Union Cemetery
River Hill, South side of Old Union Road at Paul Terry Road, 1 Mile SW of Junction E. Hickory Valley Road

Adair, Pleasant
LOCATION: Old Union Cemetery **REGIMENT:** Blacksmith, unassigned **BIRTH:** 1828 **DEATH:** Unknown **MARRIED:** Nancy J. Simmons **PENSION:** #S11806 **OTHER:** It is said that Pleasant Adair stayed up many nights shoeing horses for Confederate units who came through his area.

Pleasant Adair

Arnold, Colbird S.
LOCATION: Old Union Cemetery **RANK:** Private
COMPANY: District #2 **REGIMENT:** White County Home Guard of Minute Men **BIRTH:** 17 March 1834 **DEATH:** 08 May 1881

~

Austin, Thomas
LOCATION: Old Union Cemetery **RANK:** Private **COMPANY:** A **REGIMENT:** 28th Tennessee Infantry **BIRTH:** 18 February 1844 **DEATH:** 30 July 1931 **MARRIED:** Mary E. Miller, 29 August 1868, White County, Tennessee **PENSION:** #S11466 **PARENTS:** William Henry and Jinsey (Phifer) Austin

~

Bledsoe, R. H.
LOCATION: Old Union Cemetery **RANK:** Captain
COMPANY: F **REGIMENT:** 4th (Murray's) Tennessee Cavalry
BIRTH: 07 March 1828 **DEATH:** 20 March 1864

~

Brogden, John Alexander
LOCATION: Old Union Cemetery **RANK:** Private
COMPANY: D **REGIMENT:** 13th (Gore's) Tennessee Cavalry
BIRTH: 1828 **DEATH:** 07 June 1891 **MARRIED:** Stacy Mitchell, 22 September 1852, Van Buren County, Tennessee
PARENTS: Isaac S. and Amalie (Warren) Brogden

~

Dodson, Jesse
LOCATION: Old Union Cemetery **RANK:** Private **COMPANY:** C / District #9 **REGIMENT:** 84th Tennessee Infantry / Van Buren County Home Guard **BIRTH:** 02 February 1814, White County, Tennessee **DEATH:** 21 September 1873 **MARRIED:** (1) Jalie Shockley, 1837; (2) Mary Caroline Earls, 22 March 1855, White County, Tennessee **PARENTS:** Solomon and Margaret (Collins) Dodson

Unmarked Grave

~

Haston, William Carroll, Sr.
LOCATION: Old Union Cemetery **RANK:** Not listed
COMPANY: A **REGIMENT:** 4th (Murray's) Tennessee Cavalry
BIRTH: Unknown **DEATH:** Unknown **MARRIED:** Jane Denny

Unmarked Grave

Henderson, Henry C.

LOCATION: Old Union Cemetery
RANK: Personal Attendant (slave)
COMPANY: D **REGIMENT:** 14th North Carolina **BIRTH:** 1849, North Carolina **DEATH:** 14 September 1926 **MARRIED:** Miranda Shockley
PENSION: #C88

Henry Henderson was born on a plantation in Davidson County, North Carolina in 1849. He was the young slave of William F. Henderson. In 1862, Mr. Henderson (the plantation owner) enlisted in Co. D, 14th North Carolina Regiment and took 12 year-old Henry with him to serve as his cook and personal attendant. Henry served Colonel Henderson throughout the war, leaving the army at Salem, North Carolina in 1865. By this time, Henry was 16 years old and returned home to Davidson County. After eleven years, Henry left North Carolina in 1876 and migrated to Van Buren County, Tennessee. He later settled in the River Hill Community of Hickory Valley in White County. Henry married a local girl, Miranda Shockley and they had five children. Miranda Shockley Henderson died on 08 June 1897 and is buried in the Old Union Cemetery next to her husband. In the summer of 1921, Henry applied for a Tennessee Colored Confederate pension, which was approved on 09 October 1923. In order to qualify, an applicant had to be a Tennessee resident for three years if he served in a Tennessee command, or ten years if he served in a command from another state. They must have stayed with the army until the close of the war, unless they were legally relieved from service. An applicant must also have been indigent at the time of application. Henry had been a resident of Tennessee for forty-five years at the time of his pension application. At some point he was either in combat or wasn't far enough away from the actual fighting. It was stated in Henry's application that he was wounded during the war.

The descendants of Henry Henderson at the Confederate Gravemarking on 13 August 2006

Mrs. Ella Mae Price (left), granddaughter of Henry Henderson, with Pamela Wood, Captain Sally Tompkins #2123 UDC Member

Lawson, William

LOCATION: Old Union Cemetery **RANK:** Private **COMPANY:** A **REGIMENT:** 35th Tennessee Infantry **BIRTH:** 28 May 1840 **DEATH:** 20 May 1900 **MARRIED:** Elizabeth Dodson, 03 March 1875, Van Buren County, Tennessee **PARENTS:** Brazley and Mary Jane (Hodges) Lawson

Lewis, Bird
LOCATION: Old Union Cemetery **RANK:** Sergeant **COMPANY:** E
REGIMENT: 1st (Colms') Battalion Tennessee Infantry
BIRTH: 03 December 1820 **DEATH:** 07 November 1898
MARRIED: Martha D Bryan, 15 December 1843, White County, Tennessee **PARENTS:** William and Mary (Bray) Lewis

~

Mitchell, John Monroe
LOCATION: Old Union Cemetery **RANK:** Private **COMPANY:** I
REGIMENT: 13th (Gore's) Tennessee Cavalry / 8th (Dibrell's) Tennessee Cavalry **BIRTH:** 28 November 1844 **DEATH:** 19 December 1929 **PENSION:** #S12818 **PARENTS:** Joseph Gould and Susan (Parker) Mitchell

~

Passons, William D.
LOCATION: Old Union Cemetery **RANK:** Sergeant **COMPANY:** E
REGIMENT: 22nd (Murray's) Battalion, Tennessee Infantry
BIRTH: 28 November 1842 **DEATH:** 25 April 1913 **MARRIED:** Martha Jane (Wallace) Swafford, 04 November 1858, White County, Tennessee **PARENTS:** William J. T. and Celia (Grissom) Passons

~

Passons, William J. T.
LOCATION: Old Union Cemetery **RANK:** Private **COMPANY:** I
REGIMENT: 16th Tennessee Infantry **BIRTH:** 18 June 1822
DEATH: 02 February 1913 **MARRIED:** Celia Grissom, 27 January 1842, White County, Tennessee **PENSION:** #S12938 **PARENTS:** Major and Annie (Anderson) Passons

~

Poore, Samuel Claiborn
LOCATION: Old Union Cemetery
RANK: Private **COMPANY:** C **REGIMENT:** 13th (Gore's) Tennessee Cavalry
BIRTH: 18 December 1827, Tennessee
DEATH: 13 November 1910
MARRIED: Agnes Evaline Moore

Samuel Claiborn Poore

Wallace, Simon Doyle
LOCATION: Old Union Cemetery **RANK:** 2nd Lieutenant
COMPANY: C **REGIMENT:** 25th Tennessee Infantry
BIRTH: 21 October 1837 **DEATH:** 07 March 1903
MARRIED: Laura U. Stephens **PARENTS:** William and Mahala (Felton) Wallace

~

White, Simon D.
LOCATION: Old Union Cemetery **RANK:** Private **COMPANY:** E
REGIMENT: 1st (Colm's) Battalion, Tennessee Infantry
BIRTH: 26 May 1818 **DEATH:** 21 June 1888
MARRIED: (1) Delilah Wallace, 08 December 1845, White County, Tennessee; (2) Martha Evelyn Mays, 26 September 1853, White County, Tennessee **PARENT:** John White, Jr.

Old Zion Cemetery
Old Zion Cumberland Prebyterian Church, Old Zion

Baker, Dr. R. F.
LOCATION: Old Zion Cemetery **RANK:** Private **COMPANY:** A
REGIMENT: 13th (Gore's) Tennessee Cavalry
BIRTH: 15 June 1846 **DEATH:** 16 February 1916
MARRIED: Emily Lyda **PENSION:** #S14836

~

Boyd, B. F.
LOCATION: Old Zion Cemetery **RANK:** 1st Lieutenant
COMPANY: A **REGIMENT:** 4th (McLemore's) Tennessee Cavalry
BIRTH: 25 April 1822 **DEATH:** 29 April 1884
MARRIED: Louise Lyda, 24 July 1851, White County, Tennessee
PARENTS: John and Elizabeth (Leath) Boyd

~

Brock, Elmore
LOCATION: Old Zion Cemetery **RANK:** Private
COMPANY: I **REGIMENT:** 5th (McKenzie's) Tennessee Cavalry
BIRTH: 01 February 1829 **DEATH:** 11 November 1886

Broyles, John Summerfield

LOCATION: Old Zion Cemetery **RANK:** Private **COMPANY:** H
REGIMENT: 5th (McKenzie's) Tennessee Cavalry
BIRTH: 16 March 1833 **DEATH:** 12 January 1892
MARRIED: Mary Ann Crook, 18 January 1853, White County, Tennessee **PENSION:** #W2286 **PARENTS:** Mathias and Barbra (Letspeech) Broyles

Cass, James Moses

LOCATION: Old Zion Cemetery **RANK:** Private **COMPANY:** E **REGIMENT:** 25th Tennessee Infantry **BIRTH:** 04 October 1844 **DEATH:** After 1902
MARRIED: (1) Hester C. McConnell, 29 December 1869, White County, Tennessee; (2) Mary Daniels, 21 December 1901, White County, Tennessee
PENSION: #S16606

James Moses Cass

(1936 Obituary)
"Rites Held for Vet, James M. Cass

Funeral services for Mr. Cass, 91, Civil war veteran who fought with the Twenty-fifth regiment of Tennessee infantry under the late Gen. George G. Dibrell, were held yesterday at Old Zion church in Putnam county. Mr. Cass was wounded at the Battle of Murfreesboro. His regiment took part in the many engagements of the war between the states and he escorted President Jefferson Davis with all Confederate archives to Washington, Ga., where he surrendered to Union forces.

He was a native of North Carolina but spent most of his life in White county until his removal to the Eighth district of Putnam County eight years ago. He is survived by two daughters, Mrs. Nannie Lawson and Mrs. Fannie Cannon of Sparta; and four sons, Will and Beecher Cass, Cookeville, Finley, Sparta and J. Hershell, Charleston, S.C."

Note: The location of Old Zion Church, where he is buried is in White County, not Putnam County as the article states.

Cass, Louis W.

LOCATION: Old Zion Cemetery **RANK:** Private **COMPANY:** E
REGIMENT: 25th Tennessee Infantry **BIRTH:** 05 May 1846
DEATH: 26 January 1875 **MARRIED:** Nannie E. Crook, 17 December 1869, White County, Tennessee

Cloyd, James M.

LOCATION: Old Zion Cemetery **RANK:** Private
COMPANY: E **REGIMENT:** 25th Tennessee Infantry
BIRTH: 12 September 1840 **DEATH:** 08 August 1930
MARRIED: Nancy Ann Mills, 07 October 1869, White County, Tennessee **PENSION:** #S5217 **PARENTS:** Samuel G. and Catherine Cloyd

~

Cope, Marshall E.

LOCATION: Old Zion Cemetery **RANK:** Private **COMPANY:** K
REGIMENT: 16th Tennessee Infantry **BIRTH:** 09 April 1828
DEATH: 21 November 1879

~

Cope, William G. S.

LOCATION: Old Zion Cemetery **RANK:** Private **COMPANY:** K
REGIMENT: 28th Tennessee Infantry **BIRTH:** 07 November 1842
DEATH: 31 January 1862 **PARENTS:** John W. and Sarah A. Cope

~

Crook, Calvin Brown

LOCATION: Old Zion Cemetery **RANK:** 2nd Lieutenant
COMPANY: A / District #9 **REGIMENT:** 28th Tennessee Infantry / 28th (Consolidated) Tennessee Infantry / White County Home Guard of Minute Men **BIRTH:** 22 May 1831
DEATH: 11 November 1926 **MARRIED:** (1) Sarah Jane Kemmer, c. 1856 (Sarah Jane Kemmer is buried in Hill Cemetery, White County, Tennessee.); (2) Lucinda M. (Brester) Earl, 28 September 1873, White County, Tennessee

~

England, David S.

LOCATION: Old Zion Cemetery **RANK:** Private
COMPANY: I / District #8 **REGIMENT:** 13th (Gore's) Tennessee Cavalry / White County Home Guard of Minute Men
BIRTH: 22 April 1845 **DEATH:** 08 July 1927
PARENT: David England

Erwin, William L.

LOCATION: Old Zion Cemetery **RANK:** Private **COMPANY:** E
REGIMENT: 25th Tennessee Infantry **BIRTH:** 05 February 1841
DEATH: 01 September 1914 **MARRIED:** (1) Unity Caroline Taylor, 02 March 1866, White County, Tennessee; (2) Rebecca Jane **PENSION:** #W5655 **PARENTS:** John D. and Nancy Erwin

~

Fancher, James A. Polk

LOCATION: Old Zion Cemetery **RANK:** Private
COMPANY: K **REGIMENT:** 16th Tennessee Infantry
BIRTH: 26 February 1841 **DEATH:** 13 June 1912
MARRIED: (1) Jennie Landsen, 09 October 1867, White County Tennessee; (2) Lavina Trigg **PARENTS:** Thomas H. and Susanna (Officer) Fancher

~

Glenn, John Wilson

LOCATION: Old Zion Cemetery **RANK:** Sergeant **COMPANY:** A
REGIMENT: 22nd (Murray's) Battalion, Tennessee Infantry
BIRTH: 02 July 1833 **DEATH:** 23 February 1907
MARRIED: Margaret A.

~

Goodwin, Alexander M.

LOCATION: Old Zion Cemetery **RANK:** Private
COMPANY: District #8 **REGIMENT:** White County Home Guard of Minute Men **BIRTH:** 25 September 1818
DEATH: 27 March 1905 **MARRIED:** Martha Ann Jones, 12 January 1841, White County, Tennessee

~

Goodwin, James T.

LOCATION: Old Zion Cemetery **RANK:** Private
COMPANY: D **REGIMENT:** 13th (Gore's) Tennessee Cavalry
BIRTH: 07 November 1842 **DEATH:** 16 March 1905
PARENTS: Alexander and Martha Ann Goodwin

Goodwin, William (Billy)

LOCATION: Old Zion Cemetery **RANK:** Private **COMPANY:** E
REGIMENT: 25th Tennessee Infantry **BIRTH:** 17 April 1829
DEATH: 30 November 1916 **PENSION:** #S13903 and #S13391

~

Hennessee, Patric A.

LOCATION: Old Zion Cemetery **RANK:** Private / Musician
COMPANY: E **REGIMENT:** 25th Tennessee Infantry
BIRTH: 23 June 1838 **DEATH:** 07 June 1917 **MARRIED:** Loucinda Smith, 18 July 1865, White County, Tennessee **PENSION:** #S12779
PARENT: Mary Hennessee

~

Hennessee, William A.

LOCATION: Old Zion Cemetery **RANK:** Private **COMPANY:** E
REGIMENT: 25th Tennessee Infantry **BIRTH:** 28 July 1844
DEATH: 14 March 1867

~

Hickey, George

LOCATION: Old Zion Cemetery **RANK:** Private **COMPANY:** A
REGIMENT: 25th Tennessee Infantry **BIRTH:** 10 January 1828
DEATH: 12 April 1904 **MARRIED:** Margaret A. Lowery, 04 October 1865, White County, Tennessee **PARENT:** Elizabeth Hickey

~

Hudgens, Crockett

LOCATION: Old Zion Cemetery **RANK:** Private **COMPANY:** D
REGIMENT: 13th (Gore's) Tennessee Cavalry **BIRTH:** 28 June 1827
DEATH: 15 August 1900 **MARRIED:** Lucinda Fisk, 17 October 1850, White County, Tennessee **PARENT:** Mary Hudgens

~

Hughes, Samuel

LOCATION: Old Zion Cemetery **RANK:** Private **COMPANY:** F
REGIMENT: 22nd (Murray's) Battalion, Tennessee Infantry
BIRTH: 20 August 1837 **DEATH:** 28 February 1872
MARRIED: Caroline Metcalf, 27 March 1859, White County, Tennessee

Irwin, A. T. Davis
LOCATION: Old Zion Cemetery **RANK:** Private **COMPANY:** K
REGIMENT: 16th Tennessee Infantry **BIRTH:** 13 November 1839 **DEATH:** 17 June 1904 **MARRIED:** Amarilla Dempsey, 22 December 1874, White County, Tennessee
PENSIONS: #S5903 and #W4227

~

Jarvis, Alexander
LOCATION: Old Zion Cemetery **RANK:** Private **COMPANY:** D
REGIMENT: 13th (Gore's) Tennessee Cavalry **BIRTH:** 22 November 1836 **DEATH:** 17 May 1905 **MARRIED:** Susan Jane Franklin, 20 January 1858, White County, Tennessee
PARENTS: Levi and Martha (Ragsdale) Jarvis

~

Lowery, Mark
LOCATION: Old Zion Cemetery (Grave believed to be in the "Lowery" section of cemetery) **RANK:** Captain **COMPANY:** A
REGIMENT: 25th Tennessee Infantry **BIRTH:** 27 October 1842
DEATH: 10 January 1862 **PARENTS:** James and Jane Lowery

Unmarked Grave

~

Lowery, Thomas
LOCATION: Old Zion Cemetery **RANK:** 1st Sergeant
COMPANY: A **REGIMENT:** 25th Tennessee Infantry
BIRTH: 24 October 1833 **DEATH:** 17 November 1878
MARRIED: Margaret Lucretia Potts, 03 March 1869, White County, Tennessee **PARENTS:** James and Jane Lowery

~

Lowery, William
LOCATION: Old Zion Cemetery **RANK:** Captain **COMPANY:** K
REGIMENT: 16th Tennessee Infantry **BIRTH:** 12 July 1839
DEATH: 01 May 1918 **MARRIED:** Arachane T. Irwin, 27 December 1866, White County, Tennessee **PENSION:** #S11971

Lowrey, Hugh L. Sr.

LOCATION: Old Zion Cemetery **RANK:** Private **COMPANY:** A
REGIMENT: 25th Tennessee Infantry **BIRTH:** 29 July 1842
DEATH: 09 May 1909 **MARRIED:** Malinda Gracy, 19 December 1865, White County, Tennessee **PARENTS:** Burger and Salina Lowrey

~

Martin, Julius C.

LOCATION: Old Zion Cemetery **RANK:** Private **COMPANY:** B / H
REGIMENT: 1st (Colm's) Battalion Tennessee Infantry / 50th (Consolidated), Tennessee Infantry **BIRTH:** 02 March 1838
DEATH: 14 July 1915 **PENSION:** #W6021 **PARENT:** Green Martin

~

Meredith, Ed

LOCATION: Old Zion Cemetery **RANK:** Private **COMPANY:** D
REGIMENT: 8th (Dibrell's) Tennessee Cavalry / 13th (Gore's) Tennessee Cavalry **BIRTH:** 20 August 1830 **DEATH:** 17 November 1900 **MARRIED:** Elizabeth C. Wallace, 31 January 1861, White County, Tennessee **PENSION:** #S1571 and #W26

~

Meredith, J. W.

LOCATION: Old Zion Cemetery **RANK:** Private **COMPANY:** H / District #12 **REGIMENT:** 28th (Consolidated) Tennessee Infantry / White County Home Guard of Minute Men
BIRTH: 15 November 1833 **DEATH:** 27 July 1900
MARRIED: Mary E.

~

Robbins, A. Jordan

LOCATION: Old Zion Cemetery **RANK:** Private **COMPANY:** C
REGIMENT: 25th Tennessee Infantry **BIRTH:** 24 August 1841
DEATH: 26 January 1913 **MARRIED:** Susan Gracey, 06 October 1864, White County, Tennessee **PENSION:** #S13754
PARENTS: William and Susanna (Cope) Robbins

Simmes, Eli Parker

LOCATION: Old Zion Cemetery **RANK:** Captain **COMPANY:** K **REGIMENT:** 28th Tennessee Infantry / 28th (Consolidated) Tennessee Infantry **BIRTH:** 28 December 1829 **DEATH:** 05 September 1891 **PARENTS:** Eli and Rachel (Townsend) Simmes

~

Sims, Lawson C.

LOCATION: Old Zion Cemetery **RANK:** Private **COMPANY:** D **REGIMENT:** 13th (Gore's) Tennessee Cavalry / 8th (Dibrell's) Tennessee Cavalry **BIRTH:** 14 January 1837 **DEATH:** 01 March 1911 **MARRIED:** Isabella Crook, 01 September 1867, White County, Tennessee **PENSIONS:** #S5386 and #W3619 **PARENTS:** Andrew J. and Catharine (Lyda) Sims

~

Slatten, Berry

LOCATION: Old Zion Cemetery **RANK:** Private **COMPANY:** A / District #6 **REGIMENT:** 22nd (Murray's) Battalion, Tennessee Infantry / White County Home Guard of Minute Men **BIRTH:** 06 April 1824 **DEATH:** 31 March 1889 **MARRIED:** Nancy Ann Jones, 12 October 1853, White County, Tennessee

~

Smith, Richard G.

LOCATION: Old Zion Cemetery **RANK:** Private **COMPANY:** E **REGIMENT:** 25th Tennessee Infantry **BIRTH:** 31 November 1843 **DEATH:** 18 January 1923 **MARRIED:** Mary E. **PENSION:** #S10340

~

Steuart, Stephen W.

LOCATION: Old Zion Cemetery **RANK:** Brevet 2nd Lieutenant **COMPANY:** I **REGIMENT:** 17th Tennessee Infantry **BIRTH:** 28 May 1827 **DEATH:** 18 December 1905

Parks Cemetery
White's Cave Road, Lost Creek

Parks, John
LOCATION: Parks Cemetery **RANK:** Private **COMPANY:** A **REGIMENT:** 8th (Dibrell's) Tennessee Cavalry / 13th (Gore's) Tennessee Cavalry **BIRTH:** 06 November 1825, Ohio **DEATH:** 09 March 1916 **MARRIED:** Mary Myers **PENSION:** #S2678

John Parks

Peeled Chestnut Cemetery
Peeled Chestnut United Methodist Church

Cameron, Zachariah J.
LOCATION: Peeled Chestnut Cemetery **RANK:** Sergeant **COMPANY:** A **REGIMENT:** 1st (Colm's) Battalion Tennessee Infantry **BIRTH:** 20 September 1845 **DEATH:** Unknown **MARRIED:** Elizabeth A. Mitchell, 14 August 1877, White County, Tennessee **PENSION:** #S13620 **PARENTS:** James M. and Eliza (Jones) Cameron

~

Gracey, Hugh L.
LOCATION: Peeled Chestnut Cemetery **RANK:** Private **COMPANY:** K **REGIMENT:** 16th Tennessee Infantry **BIRTH:** 17 February 1827 **DEATH:** 19 August 1908 **MARRIED:** Anna Foster, 09 April 1844, White County, Tennessee **PARENTS:** William and Martha (Lewis) Gracey

~

Gracey, James B.
LOCATION: Peeled Chestnut Cemetery **RANK:** Private **COMPANY:** G **REGIMENT:** 51st Tennessee Infantry **BIRTH:** 03 August 1833 **DEATH:** 03 November 1911 **MARRIED:** Amanda Jones, 22 October 1858, White County, Tennessee

Hayes, John T. T.
LOCATION: Peeled Chestnut Cemetery **RANK:** Sergeant
COMPANY: C **REGIMENT:** 23rd Tennessee Infantry
BIRTH: 15 December 1840 **DEATH:** Unknown
MARRIED: Parzetta Jones, 16 December 1864, DeKalb County, Tennessee **PENSION:** #S12281

~

Johnson, Stephen W.
LOCATION: Peeled Chestnut Cemetery **RANK:** 2nd Lieutenant
COMPANY: K **REGIMENT:** 25th Tennessee Infantry
BIRTH: 12 March 1839 **DEATH:** 29 March 1902
MARRIED: Margaret R. Cope, 10 November 1859, White County, Tennessee

~

Jones, Zachariah
LOCATION: Peeled Chestnut Cemetery **RANK:** Private
COMPANY: H **REGIMENT:** 2nd Tennessee Infantry (Walker Legion) **BIRTH:** 12 February 1822 **DEATH:** Unknown
MARRIED: Mary Bennett

~

Knowles, John Fletcher
LOCATION: Peeled Chestnut Cemetery **RANK:** Sergeant
COMPANY: B **REGIMENT:** 1st (Colm's) Battalion Tennessee Infantry **BIRTH:** 1842 **DEATH:** 1930 **MARRIED:** (1) Mellie Gist; (2) Mary Ann Baker; (3) Donna Jane Terry; (4) Luttia Smith
PARENTS: James A. and Matilda (Webb) Knowles

~

Smith, Robert
LOCATION: Peeled Chestnut Cemetery **RANK:** Private
COMPANY: D **REGIMENT:** 13th (Gore's) / 8th (Dibrell's) Tennessee Cavalry **BIRTH:** 27 December 1840
DEATH: 06 March 1909 **MARRIED:** Lutetia "Ticia"
PENSION: #W3320

Pettit Family Graveyard
Pettit Cove

Pettit, Robert H.
LOCATION: Pettit Family Graveyard **RANK:** Private **COMPANY:** I **REGIMENT:** 13th (Gore's) Tennessee Cavalry **BIRTH:** 24 June 1843 **DEATH:** 23 April 1905 **MARRIED:** Cynthia Adeline Holder **PARENTS:** Lewis and Mary Elizabeth (Anderson) Pettit

Robert H. Pettit

~

Pettit, Thomas J.
LOCATION: Pettit Family Graveyard **RANK:** Private **COMPANY:** G **REGIMENT:** 16th Tennessee Infantry **BIRTH:** 15 December 1827 **DEATH:** 05 June 1895 **PARENTS:** Lewis and Mary Elizabeth (Anderson) Pettit

Pistole Cemetery
Pistole Road

Green, Riley
LOCATION: Pistole Cemetery **RANK:** Private **COMPANY:** A **REGIMENT:** 22nd (Murray's) Battalion Tennessee Infantry **BIRTH:** 17 September 1848 **DEATH:** 14 November 1935 **MARRIED:** Mary Jane Pistole **PENSION:** #S12955 **OTHER:** Pension says "2nd GA Scouts" **PARENTS:** William and Elizabeth Green

~

Pistole, Thomas
LOCATION: Pistole Cemetery **RANK:** 2nd Lieutenant **COMPANY:** E **REGIMENT:** 25th Tennessee Infantry **BIRTH:** 03 October 1841 **DEATH:** 18 October 1897 **MARRIED:** Susan Stone, 1860 **PARENTS:** Stephen C. and Mary Pistole **OTHER:** Was with General Lee at the courthouse in Appomottox, Virginia, 09 April 1865, at the time of surrender.

Plainview Cemetery
Monterey Highway (SR84)

Brown, Lawson C.
LOCATION: Plainview Cemetery; L.C.B.'s remains are buried in the Brown Family Cemetery in an unmarked grave. **RANK:** Private **COMPANY:** D / District #12 **REGIMENT:** 13th (Gore's) Tennessee Cavalry / White County Home Guard of Minute Men **BIRTH:** 10 March 1830 **DEATH:** 29 January 1907 **MARRIED:** (1) Amanda Jane Hudgens, 18 January 1855, White County, Tennessee; (2) Mary E. Dunn, 25 February 1878, White County, Tennessee **PARENTS:** John and Hannah (Broyles) Brown

Pleasant Hill Baptist Church Cemetery
Hickory Valley

Mabe, Samuel Nelson
LOCATION: Pleasant Hill Baptist Church Cemetery **RANK:** Private **COMPANY:** C **REGIMENT:** 63rd Tennessee Infantry **BIRTH:** 04 May 1829, Hawkins County, Tennessee **DEATH:** 14 August 1915 **MARRIED:** (1) Mariah Brown; (2) Letticia

Samuel Nelson Mabe

Moss, Amos Hugh
LOCATION: Pleasant Hill Baptist Church Cemetery **RANK:** Private **COMPANY:** B **REGIMENT:** 5th (McKenzie's) Tennessee Cavalry **BIRTH:** 1824 **DEATH:** 1909 **MARRIED:** Nancy Ann Collins, 25 May 1882, White County, Tennessee **PENSION:** #S2737

Williams, Madison
LOCATION: Pleasant Hill Baptist Church Cemetery **RANK:** Private **COMPANY:** E **REGIMENT:** 1st (Colm's) Battalion Tennessee Infantry **BIRTH:** 10 December 1826 **DEATH:** 22 September 1872 **MARRIED:** Sarah Young, 08 June 1848, White County, Tennessee

Unmarked Grave

Plum Creek Cemetery
Monterey Highway

Allison, Carter A.
LOCATION: Plum Creek Cemetery **RANK:** Quartermaster Sergeant **COMPANY:** D **REGIMENT:** 25th Tennessee Infantry **BIRTH:** 28 January 1828 **DEATH:** 09 August 1898 **MARRIED:** Margaret E. Selby, 09 June 1842

~

Beam, James A.
LOCATION: Plum Creek Cemetery **RANK:** Sergeant **COMPANY:** A **REGIMENT:** 28th Tennessee Infantry **BIRTH:** 07 December 1841 **DEATH:** 19 January 1922 **MARRIED:** Eliza Snodgrass, 14 January 1869, White County, Tennessee **PENSION:** #S12884

~

Bradley, Augustus Austin
LOCATION: Plum Creek Cemetery **RANK:** Private **COMPANY:** F **REGIMENT:** 13th (Gore's) Tennessee Cavalry **BIRTH:** 25 January 1832 **DEATH:** 04 October 1909 **MARRIED:** Mary E. Officer, 31 March 1859, White County, Tennessee **PARENTS:** Thomas Walton and Mary Elizabeth (Williams) Bradley

~

Bradley, John Phillip
LOCATION: Plum Creek Cemetery **RANK:** Private **COMPANY:** H **REGIMENT:** 13th (Gore's) Tennessee Cavalry **BIRTH:** 1800 **DEATH:** 1864 **MARRIED:** Nancy Johnson **OTHER:** Said to have been killed by Rufus Dowdy, US Army **PARENTS:** George Walton and Sarah Ann (Goodbread) Bradley

~

Carrick, George D.
LOCATION: Plum Creek Cemetery **RANK:** 1st Lieutenant **COMPANY:** D **REGIMENT:** 8th (Dibrell's) Tennessee Cavalry / 13th (Gore's) Tennessee Cavalry **BIRTH:** 25 January 1839 **DEATH:** After 1900 **MARRIED:** Martha G. Sims, 06 October 1868, White County, Tennessee

Unmarked Grave

Cox, William S.
LOCATION: Plum Creek Cemetery **RANK:** Private
COMPANY: White's Company **REGIMENT:** Sullivan County
Reserves **BIRTH:** 10 March 1841 **DEATH:** 13 March 1923
MARRIED: Mary Johnson, Sullivan County, Tennessee

~

Hickey, John B.
LOCATION: Plum Creek Cemetery **RANK:** Sergeant **COMPANY:** D
REGIMENT: 1st (Colm's) Battalion Tennessee Infantry
BIRTH: 21 February 1844, White County, Tennessee
DEATH: 03 May 1915 **MARRIED:** Mary Sims, 25 March 1866,
White County, Tennessee **PENSION:** #S12863 and #W5938
PARENTS: Cornelius and Eliza J. (Brown) Hickey

~

Johnson, Samuel
LOCATION: Plum Creek Cemetery **RANK:** Private **COMPANY:** D
REGIMENT: 8th (Dibrell's) Tennessee Cavalry / 13th (Gore's)
Tennessee Cavalry **BIRTH:** 18 March 1843
DEATH: 09 February 1929 **MARRIED:** Arminta Bradley, 14
March 1867, White County, Tennessee **PENSION:** #S13593
PARENTS: Thomas B. and Mary H. (England) Johnson

~

Miller, Luin
LOCATION: Plum Creek Cemetery **RANK:** Private
COMPANY: District #12 **REGIMENT:** White County Home
Guard of Minute Men **BIRTH:** 13 June 1813 **DEATH:** 05 April
1884 **MARRIED:** Margaret C. Officer, 09 November 1840,
White County, Tennessee

~

Officer, Alexander
LOCATION: Plum Creek Cemetery **RANK:** 1st Sergeant
COMPANY: B / District #11 **REGIMENT:** 25th Tennessee Infantry
/ White County Home Guard of Minute Men **BIRTH:** 24
January 1814 **DEATH:** 20 July 1883 **MARRIED:** (1) Lucinda
Bohannon, 28 April 1844, White County, Tennessee; (2)
Rebecca M. **PARENTS:** James and Nancy Officer

Officer, David S.
LOCATION: Plum Creek Cemetery **RANK:** Private **COMPANY:** A **REGIMENT:** 25th Tennessee Infantry **BIRTH:** 12 October 1839 **DEATH:** 17 February 1901 **MARRIED:** Mary Jane Little, 07 December 1865, White County, Tennessee **PENSION:** #W5397 **PARENTS:** Alexander and Lucinda (Bohannon) Officer

~

Officer, William P.
LOCATION: Plum Creek Cemetery **RANK:** Sergeant **COMPANY:** H **REGIMENT:** 8th (Dibrell's) Tennessee Cavalry / 13th (Gore's) Tennessee Cavalry **BIRTH:** 27 May 1838 **DEATH:** 13 October 1910 **MARRIED:** Emily **PENSION:** #S8209 **PARENTS:** James and Nancy Officer

~

Sims, Dr. James Glenn
LOCATION: Plum Creek Cemetery **RANK:** Private **COMPANY:** D **REGIMENT:** 8th (Dibrell's) Tennessee Cavalry **BIRTH:** 12 October 1847, White County, Tennessee **DEATH:** 19 October 1932 **MARRIED:** Fannie Metcalf, 20 November 1877, White County, Tennessee **PENSION:** #S16602 **PARENTS:** Oliver H. P. and Eliza Jane (Glenn) Sims

~

Sims, William E.
LOCATION: Plum Creek Cemetery **RANK:** Private **COMPANY:** D **REGIMENT:** 13th (Gore's) Tennessee Infantry / 8th (Dibrell's) Tennessee Cavalry **BIRTH:** 20 March 1846 **DEATH:** 27 February 1925 **MARRIED:** (1) Mary Jane Willhite, 24 December 1863, White County, Tennessee; (2) Nancy Metcalf, 26 September 1867, White County, Tennessee; (3) Josephine Snodgrass, 01 May 1884, White County, Tennessee **PENSION:** #S14426 **PARENTS:** Oliver H. P. and Eliza Jane (Glenn) Sims

~

Snodgrass, David
LOCATION: Plum Creek Cemetery **RANK:** Not listed **COMPANY:** D **REGIMENT:** 1st (Colm's) Battalion Tennessee Infantry

Unmarked Grave

Snodgrass, Joseph
LOCATION: Plum Creek Cemetery **RANK:** Private **COMPANY:** H **REGIMENT:** 13th (Gore's) Tennessee Cavalry **BIRTH:** 08 August 1834 **DEATH:** 24 May 1877 **MARRIED:** Mary Jane Horn **PENSION:** #W1418 **PARENTS:** Thomas and Margaret (Duff) Snodgrass

~

Snodgrass, LaFayette Duff
LOCATION: Plum Creek Cemetery **RANK:** Private **COMPANY:** D **REGIMENT:** 13th (Gore's) Tennessee Cavalry / 8th (Dibrell's) Tennessee Cavalary **BIRTH:** 1841 **DEATH:** 1920 **MARRIED:** Eliza J. Sims, 15 October 1868, White County, Tennessee **PENSIONS:** #S12861 and #W7525 **PARENTS:** Thomas and Margaret (Duff) Snodgrass

~

Stewart, James M.
LOCATION: Plum Creek Cemetery **RANK:** Private **COMPANY:** B **REGIMENT:** 1st (Colm's) Battalion Tennessee Infantry **BIRTH:** 19 May 1827 **DEATH:** 13 February 1908 **MARRIED:** Arreny McEwin, 13 March 1849, White County, Tennessee **PENSION:** #W1074

~

Townsend, Albert J.
LOCATION: Plum Creek Cemetery **RANK:** Private **COMPANY:** 2G **REGIMENT:** 24th Tennessee Infantry **BIRTH:** 24 July 1819 **DEATH:** 05 November 1891 **MARRIED:** Elizabeth Hill, 31 January 1839, White County, Tennessee

Pollard-Norris Cemetery
Center Point

Norris, William Alfred
LOCATION: Pollard-Norris Cemetery **RANK:** Private **COMPANY:** C **REGIMENT:** 25th Tennessee Infantry **BIRTH:** 1838 **DEATH:** September 1899 **MARRIED:** Elizabeth "Eliza" Threat **PARENTS:** John Francis and Priscilla (Davis) Norris

Pollard, Jr. Edward Varner

LOCATION: Pollard-Norris Cemetery **RANK:** Sergeant
COMPANY: K **REGIMENT:** 28th / 28th (Consolidated) Tennessee Infantry
BIRTH: March 1837, White County, Tennessee **DEATH:** 02 February 1893
MARRIED: Nancy Moore, 06 March 1866, White County, Tennessee
PARENTS: Edward Varner, Sr. and Thairsa "Thursy" (Pettus) Pollard

Preston Heights Cemetery
Quebeck

Davis, Sampson

LOCATION: Preston Heights Cemetery, buried next to Levi Richardson in an unmarked grave. **RANK:** Private **COMPANY:** E **REGIMENT:** 22nd (Murray's) Battalion Tennessee Infantry **BIRTH:** 31 May 1839
DEATH: 24 December 1914 **MARRIED:** Saraphine "Sally" Warner, 02 April 1857, Robertson County, Tennessee **PARENTS:** Reuben and Patsy Davis

Sparkman, Temple

LOCATION: Preston Heights Cemetery **RANK:** Private **COMPANY:** D
REGIMENT: 8th (Dibrell's) Tennessee Cavalry **BIRTH:** 11 July 1839 **DEATH:** 11 July 1926 **MARRIED:** (1) Lydia M. Witt; (2) Mary Ann Cooper, 27 January 1878, White County, Tennessee
PARENTS: Hardeman and Mary (Coffee) Sparkman **OTHER:** Living in Quebeck before and during the war were two friends: Mr. Temple Sparkman, who fought for the South, and Mr. Anderson, who joined the Northern ranks. Mr. Sparkman came home for a few days furlough and was taken by the Federals. He was to be hanged as a spy. The death noose had been placed around his neck when Mr. Anderson appeared on the scene. For a few seconds he stood aghast, but finally rushed forward and yelled, "Don't hang that man, he is not a bushwacker." Mr. Sparkman's life was spared on the word of his true friend.

Ray Cemetery
Hampton's Crossroads

Howard, William P.

LOCATION: Ray Cemetery **RANK:** Private **COMPANY:** E **REGIMENT:** 25th Tennessee Infantry **BIRTH:** 23 January 1831 **DEATH:** 01 December 1905
MARRIED: Mary S. Goodwin, 29 December 1849, White County, Tennessee

Ray, Mark
LOCATION: Ray Cemetery RANK: Private
COMPANY: B REGIMENT: 84th Tennessee Infantry
BIRTH: 1836 DEATH: 16 January 1913

Rice-Saylors Cemetery
Burgess Falls

Howell, Silas
LOCATION: Rice-Saylors Cemetery RANK: Private
COMPANY: B REGIMENT: 1st (Colm's) Battalion Tennessee Infantry BIRTH: c. 1822 DEATH: After 1880 MARRIED: Matilda C. Rice, 21 March 1843, White County, Tennessee

~

Rice, William
LOCATION: Rice-Saylors Cemetery RANK: Corporal
COMPANY: B REGIMENT: 25th Tennessee Infantry
BIRTH: 15 December 1843 DEATH: 09 April 1894

Roberts Cemetery
Center Point

Roberts, Jesse
LOCATION: Roberts Cemetery RANK: Private COMPANY: K
REGIMENT: 29th Tennessee Infantry BIRTH: 25 June 1823
DEATH: 20 May 1879 MARRIED: Winifred "Winnie" Brown, 02 December 1852, White County, Tennessee PARENTS: William and Sallie (Humphrey) Roberts

~

Roberts, William Franklin
LOCATION: Roberts Cemetery RANK: Corporal COMPANY: G
REGIMENT: 16th Tennessee Infantry BIRTH: 15 October 1848
DEATH: 27 April 1942 MARRIED: (1) Nancy Elizabeth Swindle, 15 October 1876, White County, Tennessee; (2) Minnerva Lucinda Swindle, 05 January 1882, White County, Tennessee
PARENTS: Jesse and Winifred "Winnie" (Brown) Roberts

Unmarked Grave

Rogers Cemetery
Hickory Valley

Rogers, George Washington
LOCATION: Rogers Cemetery **RANK:** Sergeant **COMPANY:** F **REGIMENT:** 2nd Ashby's Cavalry **BIRTH:** 07 December 1830 **DEATH:** 04 July 1862 **PARENTS:** Anderson S. and Delilah Jane (Bryant) Rogers

~

Rogers, James M.
LOCATION: Rogers Cemetery **RANK:** Not listed **COMPANY:** G **REGIMENT:** 35th Tennessee Infantry **BIRTH:** 09 December 1828 **DEATH:** 28 August 1863 **PARENTS:** Anderson S. and Delilah Jane (Bryant) Rogers

Saylors Cemetery
a.k.a. Macedonia Cemetery, Bunker Hill Road

Carlen, James "Jim"
LOCATION: Saylors Cemetery **RANK:** Private **COMPANY:** C **REGIMENT:** 16th Tennessee Infantry **BIRTH:** 1843 **DEATH:** 1863 **OTHER:** The tombstone was moved to Saylors Cemetery in June 2002 from the Jere Nash Farm. Remains still on farm.

~

Floyd, Robert Dowell
LOCATION: Saylors Cemetery **RANK:** Sergeant **COMPANY:** A **REGIMENT:** 7th Tennessee Infantry **BIRTH:** 16 March 1839 **DEATH:** 16 April 1913 **MARRIED:** Mary E. **PENSIONS:** #S11432 and #W4954

~

Hampton, Lawrence P.
LOCATION: Saylors Cemetery **RANK:** Private **COMPANY:** G **REGIMENT:** 12th Tennessee Infantry **BIRTH:** 27 December 1841 **DEATH:** 02 January 1863 **OTHER:** Tombstone reads "Fell in battle at Murfreesboro…" **PARENT:** George P. Hampton

Hitchcock, Benjamin

LOCATION: Saylors Cemetery **RANK:** Private **COMPANY:** B
REGIMENT: 1st (Colm's) Battalion Tennessee Infantry
BIRTH: 23 March 1847 **DEATH:** 15 March 1862
OTHER: Headstone was moved in 2002 from the Hitchcock Cemetery (Jere Nash Farm). Remains are still on the farm.

~

Hitchcock, William Luke

LOCATION: Saylors Cemetery
RANK: Private **COMPANY:** E
REGIMENT: 25th Tennessee Infantry **BIRTH:** 30 November 1822 **DEATH:** 04 April 1908
MARRIED: (1) Ruth Carland, 03 August 1844; (2) Elizabeth Carland, 03 May 1857

William Luke Hitchcock

~

Price, Shade

LOCATION: Saylors Cemetery **RANK:** Private
COMPANY: C **REGIMENT:** 8th (Dibrell's) Tennessee Cavalry
BIRTH: 05 September 1846 **DEATH:** 11 January 1915
MARRIED: Amanda Cash **PARENTS:** Dud and Ollie Price

~

Saylors, Abram

LOCATION: Saylors Cemetery **RANK:** Private **COMPANY:** A
REGIMENT: 22nd (Murray's) Battalion Tennessee Infantry
BIRTH: 01 August 1817 **DEATH:** 19 April 1880 **MARRIED:** Jane "Jincy" Price **PARENTS:** Leonard, Jr. and Amy (Gant) Saylors

~

Saylors, Burtis W.

LOCATION: Saylors Cemetery **RANK:** Private **COMPANY:** K
REGIMENT: 28th Tennessee Infantry **BIRTH:** 30 August 1842
DEATH: 10 January 1915 **MARRIED:** Harriet Southard
PARENTS: Abraham and Jane "Jincy" (Price) Saylors

Shores Cemetery
Corinth

Shores, William Mackie
LOCATION: Shores Cemetery RANK: 1st Lieutenant
COMPANY: L REGIMENT: 8th (Dibrell's) Tennessee Cavalry
BIRTH: c. 1813 DEATH: 1889

Scott Cemetery
O'Connor

Scott, Samuel
LOCATION: Scott Cemetery RANK: Private COMPANY: K
REGIMENT: 16th Tennessee Infantry BIRTH: 24 June 1822
DEATH: 22 February 1910

Simmerell / Simrell Cemetery
Frank's Ferry Road

Clark, Darius B.
LOCATION: Simmerell / Simrell Cemetery RANK: Private
COMPANY: D REGIMENT: 13th (Gore's) Tennessee Cavalry
BIRTH: 09 July 1842 DEATH: 02 May 1863 MARRIED: Maggie
Grissom PARENTS: Joseph W. and Elizabeth Clark

~

Clark, Joseph
LOCATION: Simmerell / Simrell Cemetery RANK: Private
COMPANY: A / H REGIMENT: 22nd (Murray's) Battalion
Tennessee Infantry BIRTH: 26 September 1825
DEATH: 01 October 1889 MARRIED: Keziah McGowen, 10
November 1844, White County, Tennessee

~

Clark, Phineas "Finn" B.
LOCATION: Simmerell / Simrell Cemetery RANK: Private
COMPANY: G REGIMENT: 16th Tennessee Infantry
BIRTH: 23 June 1839 DEATH: 22 December 1883
MARRIED: Sarah E. Wilson, 10 January 1864, White County,
Tennessee PARENTS: David and Ellender Clark

Parker, Joseph A.
LOCATION: Simmerell / Simrell Cemetery **RANK:** Private
COMPANY: D **REGIMENT:** 49th Tennessee Infantry
BIRTH: 18 November 1828 **DEATH:** 26 July 1893 **MARRIED:** Cecily Ann Clark, 11 October 1857, White County, Tennessee

Simril, Francis Vincent
LOCATION: Simmerell / Simrell Cemetery **RANK:** Corporal
COMPANY: K / C **REGIMENT:** 28th Tennessee Infantry / 28th (Consolidated) Tennessee Infantry **BIRTH:** 09 November 1841 **DEATH:** 17 September 1910 **MARRIED:** Nancy Jane Clark, 25 July 1866, White County, Tennessee **PARENTS:** Daniel and Rachel (Clark) Simril

Skurlock Cemetery
Onward

Earles, Pleasant G.
LOCATION: Skurlock Cemetery **RANK:** Private **COMPANY:** D
REGIMENT: 44th (Consolidated) Tennessee Infantry
BIRTH: 26 May 1818 **DEATH:** 1871 **MARRIED:** Elizabeth W. Baker, 23 January 1840, White County, Tennessee
PARENTS: Nathaniel and Rebecca (Hale) Earles

Earles, William T.
LOCATION: Skurlock Cemetery, probably in the Earles Family section of cemetery. **RANK:** Private **COMPANY:** C
REGIMENT: 25th Tennessee Infantry **BIRTH:** 14 May 1848
DEATH: 18 October 1914

Unmarked Grave

Haston, Samuel S.
LOCATION: Skurlock Cemetery **RANK:** Not listed **COMPANY:** M
REGIMENT: 1st (Colm's) Battalion Tennessee Infantry
BIRTH: 19 May 1844 **DEATH:** 01 November 1925
MARRIED: JoAnn (Earles) Simmons **PARENTS:** James W. and Jane (Shockley) Haston

Smith Cemetery
Unfenced, overgrown corner of pasture, Brock Cove

Smith, Daniel T.
LOCATION: Smith Cemetery **RANK:** 2nd Lieutenant
COMPANY: E **REGIMENT:** 8th (Dibrell's) Tennessee Cavalry
BIRTH: c. 1839 **DEATH:** After 1880 **MARRIED:** (1) Margaret E. Snodgrass, 27 December 1866, White County, Tennessee; (2) Margaret Bussell, 23 July 1895, White County, Tennessee
PENSION: #S8032

Snodgrass Cemetery #2
Blue Spring

Snodgrass, David Red
LOCATION: Snodgrass Cemetery #2 **RANK:** Private **COMPANY:** A
REGIMENT: 25th Tennessee Infantry **BIRTH:** 29 March 1843
DEATH: 07 March 1928 **PARENT:** Jackson Snodgrass

Southard Cemetery
Black Oak

Oliver, John F.
LOCATION: Southard Cemetery **RANK:** Sergeant
COMPANY: B **REGIMENT:** 1st (Colm's) Battalion Tennessee Infantry / 50th (Consolidated) Tennessee Infantry
BIRTH: 1837 **DEATH:** 1914 **MARRIED:** Amanda M. Hutson, 05 July 1860, White County, Tennessee **PENSION:** #S11868
PARENTS: Elexandria and Lucindy (Berks) Oliver

Southard, Dempsey Martin
LOCATION: Southard Cemetery **RANK:** Captain **COMPANY:** E
REGIMENT: 25th Tennessee Infantry **BIRTH:** c. 1820, North Carolina **DEATH:** After 1880 **MARRIED:** Eliza Lucinda McConnell, 23 February 1843

Southard, James Milus

LOCATION: Southard Cemetery **RANK:** 1st Lieutenant
COMPANY: E **REGIMENT:** 25th Tennessee Infantry
BIRTH: 17 September 1846 **DEATH:** 29 December 1870
MARRIED: Mary Ann McEwin, 04 February 1869, White County, Tennessee **PARENTS:** Dempsey Martin and Eliza Lucinda (McConnell) Southard **OTHER:** Milas Southard joined the Confederate army when nothing more than a boy. He was captured by bushwackers and on account of his age, was not killed, but punished in different ways for their amusement. He was placed in a railpen and whipped. For this, he made a vow to kill the leaders of this act. Soon after the war, Milas, and his brother, John, went to the mill. Two of the leaders Milas had vowed to kill were there. When Milas saw them he picked up a stick and raised it to strike one of the men. As he did so the other man shot Milas. John rushed forward, grabbed the man with the pistol and threw him into a big box. He then went to the side of his brother whom he found in a critical condition. Milas died in a few moments and his vow remained unfulfilled. (Taken from *Legends and Stories of White County, Tennessee*, Chapter 5.)

~

Stewart, James M.

LOCATION: Southard Cemetery **RANK:** Private
COMPANY: B **REGIMENT:** 1st (Colm's) Battalion Tennessee Infantry
BIRTH: 1828 **DEATH:** Unknown **MARRIED:** Irena, 13 March 1849, White County, Tennessee **PENSION:** #W1074

Unmarked Grave

Spring Hill Cemetery
Spring Hill Baptist Church of Christ

Humphrey, Rev. Sylvester E.

LOCATION: Spring Hill Cemetery **RANK:** Private **COMPANY:** K
REGIMENT: 16th Tennessee Infantry **BIRTH:** 10 October 1848
DEATH: 23 September 1929 **MARRIED:** Mary Jane Fisher, 18 August 1869, White County, Tennessee **PARENTS:** David Eastwood and Mahala (Knowles) Humphrey

Stringtown Cemetery
Eastland Road, Bon Air Mountain

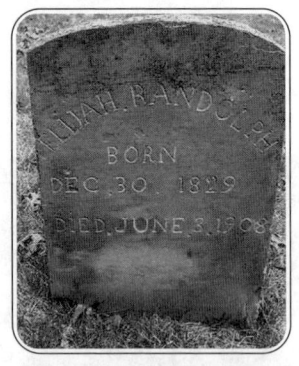

Randolph, Elijah
LOCATION: Stringtown Cemetery **RANK:** Private **COMPANY:** A **REGIMENT:** 25th Tennessee Infantry **BIRTH:** 30 December 1829 **DEATH:** 03 June 1908 **MARRIED:** Sarah Morris **PENSION:** #S4304 **PARENTS:** Reuben and Sally (Bumbalough) Randolph

Scarbrough, Alexander R.
LOCATION: Springtown Cemetery **RANK:** Sergeant **COMPANY:** I **REGIMENT:** 46th Tennessee Infantry **BIRTH:** 14 February 1834 **DEATH:** 03 August 1897 **MARRIED:** Martha Emeline Burgess **PARENTS:** William and Susanna (Bumbalough) Scarbrough

Welch, John Marion
LOCATION: Springtown Cemetery **RANK:** Private **COMPANY:** F **REGIMENT:** 25th Tennessee Infantry **BIRTH:** 15 June 1843 **DEATH:** 26 December 1917 **MARRIED:** (1) Nancy Bell Prater, 03 November 1875, White County, Tennessee; (2) Martha Patsy Frasier, 04 May 1881, White County, Tennessee **PARENTS:** Archibald and Stacy (McPaden) Welch

Swift Cemetery
Center Point

Swift, Rufus A.
LOCATION: Swift Cemetery **RANK:** Private **COMPANY:** A **REGIMENT:** 25th Tennessee Infantry **BIRTH:** 17 November 1827 **DEATH:** 09 August 1887 **MARRIED:** Nancy Jane Wilson, 16 June 1870, White County, Tennessee **PARENTS:** Elisha and Elizabeth Swift

Swift, Simon F.
LOCATION: Swift Cemetery **RANK:** Private **COMPANY:** A **REGIMENT:** 25th Tennessee Infantry **BIRTH:** 15 March 1835 **DEATH:** 11 March 1903 **MARRIED:** Martha Ann Wilson, 28 June 1880, White County, Tennessee **PARENTS:** Elisha and Elizabeth Swift

Unmarked Grave

Swindle Family Farm Cemetery
Center Point

Swindle, George Conrad
LOCATION: Swindle Family Farm Cemetery **RANK:** Private
COMPANY: Not listed **REGIMENT:** 38th Tennessee Infantry
BIRTH: 01 April 1837 **DEATH:** 14 March 1876 **MARRIED:** Manerva Clark, 12 January 1854, White County, Tennessee **PARENTS:** Cason and Winona Elizabeth Swindle

Unmarked Grave

Taylor Cemetery
East foot, Gum Spring Mountain in barnyard behind house; 200 feet south of Parker Road, .03 miles west of Sullivan Knowles Road junction, 1.7 miles north of Franks Ferry Road junction

Mitchell, Joseph B. (Jo B. Mitchell)
LOCATION: Taylor Cemetery **RANK:** Sergeant **COMPANY:** G / K
REGIMENT: 16th Tennessee Infantry **BIRTH:** 1839 **DEATH:** After 1864
PARENTS: Joseph Gould and Nancy (Taylor) Mitchell

Isaac Taylor Cemetery
Fancher's Mill on Taylor's Creek

Taylor, Thomas Edward
LOCATION: Isaac Taylor Cemetery **RANK:** 1st Lieutenant **COMPANY:** K
REGIMENT: 16th Tennessee Infantry **BIRTH:** 22 September 1829
DEATH: 17 June 1909 **MARRIED:** Harriet Louise McEwin, 30 October 1881, White County, Tennessee **PENSIONS:** #S4502 and #W4054
PARENTS: Isaac and Margaret Taylor

Templeton Cemetery
Mt. Pisgah

Templeton, Pleasant Carter
LOCATION: Templeton Cemetery **RANK:** 2nd Corporal **COMPANY:** K **REGIMENT:** 16th Tennessee Infantry **BIRTH:** 21 April 1844 **DEATH:** 30 December 1864 **MARRIED:** Not Married
PARENTS: William and Lydia Jane (Anderson) Templeton **OTHER:** Among the legends in the Templeton family is the story of Pleasant Carter Templeton, who was wounded at the Battle of Franklin. He lived 28 days near the battlefield before being transferred to Nashville where he died. Lydia Jane, his mother, was so distraught with the news of her baby son's death that she protested his burial. William, Pleasant's father, brought his son home in a metal casket, which would keep the body from further deterioration. His body was kept in an upstairs room in the family home for 28 years. It is said that Lydia Jane would at times sit in the room with her son's body. He was finally buried with his mother when she died.

Templeton, Thomas Jefferson
LOCATION: Templeton Cemetery RANK: Private COMPANY: K
REGIMENT: 16th Tennessee Infantry BIRTH: 14 February 1842
DEATH: 01 June 1924 MARRIED: (1) Tabbitha Holder; (2)
Miranda Evaline Holder, 06 March 1867, White County,
Tennessee PENSIONS: #S10081 and #W8216

Tollison Cemetery
Tollison Town

Baker, William L.
LOCATION: Tollison Cemetery
RANK: Private COMPANY: B
REGIMENT: 1st (Colm's)
Battalion Tennessee Infantry
BIRTH: 03 December 1839
DEATH: 15 September 1927
MARRIED: Margaret C. Bennett,
10 January 1866, White County,
Tennessee PENSION: #S2920
PARENTS: Jonathan and Minerva
(Cole) Baker

William L. Baker

~

Martin, James C.
LOCATION: Tollison Cemetery RANK: Not listed COMPANY: B
REGIMENT: 1st (Colm's) Battalion Tennessee Infantry
BIRTH: 01 May 1835 DEATH: 05 January 1897 MARRIED: Polly
PENSION: #S2150 PARENTS: Green and Rhoda (Elmore)
Martin

~

Tollison, James Robert
LOCATION: Tollison Cemetery
RANK: Private COMPANY: B
REGIMENT: 1st (Colm's)
Battalion Tennessee Infantry
BIRTH: 26 July 1834 DEATH: 14
April 1912 MARRIED: Nancy
Martin, 27 April 1861, White
County, Tennessee PARENTS:
Caliph and Allie (Cole) Tollison

James Robert Tollison

240 · Our Confederate Ancestors · White County

Tollison, Solomon

LOCATION: Tollison Cemetery **RANK:** Private **COMPANY:** H **REGIMENT:** 20th Tennessee Infantry **BIRTH:** 28 February 1828 **DEATH:** 24 December 1912 **MARRIED:** (1) Malinda Martin; (2) Nancy Revis **PENSION:** #S1929 **PARENTS:** Caliph and Allie (Cole) Tollison

Walling Church of Christ Cemetery
Walling

Hubbard, J. T.

LOCATION: Walling Church of Christ Cemetery **RANK:** Private **COMPANY:** I **REGIMENT:** 8th Tennessee Infantry **BIRTH:** 03 February 1838 **DEATH:** 26 June 1909

Walling-Randals Cemetery
Doyle

Green, Woodson P.

LOCATION: Walling-Randals Cemetery **RANK:** Private **COMPANY:** D **REGIMENT:** 1st (Colm's) Battalion Tennessee Infantry **BIRTH:** 01 December 1832 **DEATH:** 05 December 1863 **MARRIED:** Arethusa Randals, 30 September 1855, White County, Tennessee

Ward-Cashdollar Cemetery
Cashdollar Cove, near Shady Grove

Gleeson, Isaac Edward

LOCATION: Ward-Cashdollar Cemetery **RANK:** Private **COMPANY:** D **REGIMENT:** 13th (Gore's) Tennessee Cavalry **BIRTH:** 18 November 1846 **DEATH:** 1902 **MARRIED:** Edy (Eady) Elvira Ward, 22 November 1868, White County, Tennessee **PARENTS:** Edward and Malinda (Waller) Gleeson

Welch Family Cemetery
Scott's Gulf

Welch, Jasper
LOCATION: Welch Family Cemetery **RANK:** Private **COMPANY:** H **REGIMENT:** 38th Tennessee Infantry **BIRTH:** 29 August 1837 **DEATH:** 04 December 1913 **MARRIED:** Judith Caroline Yates **PARENTS:** Archibald and Stacy (McPaden) Welch

Wesley Chapel Cemetery
Wesley Chapel United Methodist Church

Griffin, Joseph
LOCATION: Wesley Chapel Cemetery **RANK:** Private **COMPANY:** I **REGIMENT:** 8th (Dibrell's) Tennessee Cavalry **BIRTH:** 04 May 1847 **DEATH:** 09 August 1921 **MARRIED:** Sarah Knowles, 23 July 1879, White County, Tennessee **PARENTS:** Samuel Jinck and Sarah (Dennis) Griffin

~

Holloway, Major B.
LOCATION: Wesley Chapel Cemetery **RANK:** Chief Musician **COMPANY:** Field and Staff **REGIMENT:** 26th Tennessee Infantry **BIRTH:** 12 June 1841 **DEATH:** 18 October 1882 **MARRIED:** Mary J.

~

Sullivan, James H.
LOCATION: Wesley Chapel Cemetery **RANK:** Private **COMPANY:** A **REGIMENT:** 50th (Consolidated) Tennessee Infantry **BIRTH:** 05 February 1832 **DEATH:** 29 October 1886 **MARRIED:** Mary Ann Taylor, 07 September 1870, White County, Tennessee

~

Terry, John Calhoun
LOCATION: Wesley Chapel Cemetery **RANK:** Private **COMPANY:** H **REGIMENT:** 23rd Tennessee Infantry **BIRTH:** 16 March 1843 **DEATH:** 01 March 1929 **MARRIED:** Martha Lou Erwin **PENSIONS:** #S12200 and #W9323

Wheeler Cemetery

On hill, north side of Doran Road, 0.3 miles east of north junction with (SR 84), Monterey Highway.

Austin, Nathanial (Nathan) Glenn
LOCATION: Wheeler Cemetery **RANK:** Private **COMPANY:** C / G **REGIMENT:** 84th Tennessee Infantry / 28th (Consolidated) Tennessee Infantry **BIRTH:** 10 September 1827 **DEATH:** 05 October 1888 **MARRIED:** Martha Jane Bryant, 21 January 1847, White County, Tennessee **PENSION:** #S1806

~

Copeland, Bailey Alred
LOCATION: Wheeler Cemetery **RANK:** Private **COMPANY:** D **REGIMENT:** 84th and 28th (Consolidated) Tennessee Infantry **BIRTH:** 13 June 1841, Overton County, Tennessee **DEATH:** 08 May 1928 **MARRIED:** Nellie Ellen Looper **PENSIONS:** #S13955 and #S16002 **PARENTS:** Phillip and Obedience (Cox) Copeland

~

Wheeler, Thomas
LOCATION: Wheeler Cemetery **RANK:** Private **COMPANY:** H **REGIMENT:** 8th (Dibrell's) Tennessee Cavalry / 13th (Gore's) Tennessee Cavalry **BIRTH:** 08 March 1828, Jackson County, Tennessee **DEATH:** 30 March 1913 **MARRIED:** Martha Ann Sliger, 28 October 1852, White County, Tennessee **PENSION:** #S2527 **PARENTS:** Jubilee and Lucinda (Brown) Wheeler

Thomas Wheeler

UDC MEMBERS: Sherrie Beth Broyles McCulley, Susan Broyles Harris

Wilhite Cemetery #2

Fountain Head

Bohannan, George W.
LOCATION: Wilhite Cemetery #2 **RANK:** Private **COMPANY:** E **REGIMENT:** 25th Tennessee Infantry **BIRTH:** 1833 **DEATH:** 05 February 1865

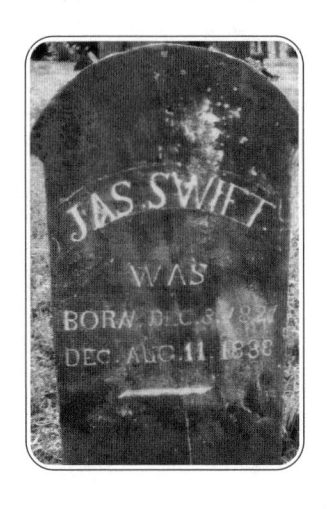

Wilhite, Elijah McCamel
LOCATION: Wilhite Cemetery #2 **RANK:** Private **COMPANY:** E **REGIMENT:** 13th (Gore's) Tennessee Cavalry **BIRTH:** 14 January 1832 **DEATH:** 14 September 1917 **MARRIED:** Rebecca Narcissa Anderson **PARENTS:** Solomon and Jeannette Rebecca (Sliger) Wilhite

~

Wilhite, Solomon Robinson
LOCATION: Wilhite Cemetery #2 **RANK:** Private **COMPANY:** H **REGIMENT:** 13th (Gore's) Tennessee Cavalry **BIRTH:** 10 March 1841 **DEATH:** 15 October 1872 **MARRIED:** Harriet E. Huddleston, 15 May 1862 **PARENTS:** Solomon and Jeannette Rebecca (Sliger) Wilhite

Wilhite Cemetery #4
Plainview

Wilhite, James
LOCATION: Wilhite Cemetery #4 **RANK:** Private **COMPANY:** H **REGIMENT:** 13th (Gore's) Tennessee Cavalry **BIRTH:** 01 January 1844 **DEATH:** 04 October 1934 **MARRIED:** Martha W. Hamilton **PARENTS:** Rhuben and Julia (Wisdom) Wilhite

James Wilhite

Wilson Memorial Cemetery
Lost Creek

Swift, James
LOCATION: Wilson Memorial Cemetery **RANK:** Private **COMPANY:** H **REGIMENT:** 13th (Gore's) Tennessee Cavalry **BIRTH:** 08 December 1821 **DEATH:** 11 August 1888

Wilson, William
LOCATION: Wilson Memorial Cemetery. **RANK:** 3rd Lieutenant **COMPANY:** E **REGIMENT:** 13th (Gore's) Tennessee Cavalry / 8th (Dibrell's) Tennessee Cavalry **BIRTH:** 22 March 1822 **DEATH:** 25 July 1872 **MARRIED:** (1) Sarah A. Green, 02 December 1845, White County, Tennessee; (2) Sarah Emily Cole, 06 April 1864, White County, Tennessee **PENSION:** #S5389 **PARENTS:** Thomas and Elizabeth (Gamble) Wilson

Witt Cemetery
Quebeck, Caney Fork Road

Witt, John W.
LOCATION: Witt Cemetery **RANK:** Private **COMPANY:** E **REGIMENT:** 5th (McKenzie's) Tennessee Cavalry **BIRTH:** 08 August 1840, Virginia **DEATH:** 03 July 1880 **MARRIED:** Mary Elizabeth Holder

Unmarked Grave

William Reed Sparkman Cemetery
Quebeck

Sparkman, William Reed
LOCATION: William Reed Sparkman Cemetery **RANK:** Private **COMPANY:** D **REGIMENT:** 13th (Gore's) Tennessee Cavalry **BIRTH:** 20 July 1835 **DEATH:** 16 August 1897 **MARRIED:** Margaret L. Holder, 23 December 1858, White County, Tennessee **PENSION:** #W4570

Unmarked Grave

Young Cemetery
Hensley Chapel, Gum Spring Mountain

Coakley, James A.
LOCATION: Young Cemetery **RANK:** Private **COMPANY:** B **REGIMENT:** 10th (Johnson's) Kentucky Cavalry **BIRTH:** 19 December 1838, Montgomery County, Tennessee **DEATH:** 15 May 1920 **MARRIED:** Louisa Baker, 08 January 1870, White County, Tennessee **PENSION:** #W7428

James A. Coakley

White County · Our Confederate Ancestors · 245

Unknown Burial Location
All unmarked graves

Farley, David
LOCATION: Unknown burial location **RANK:** Private
COMPANY: H **REGIMENT:** 13th (Gore's) Tennessee Cavalry
MARRIED: Elizabeth Willhite

Lewis, Jacob A.
LOCATION: Unknown burial location **RANK:** 2nd Lieutenant
COMPANY: E **REGIMENT:** 1st (Colm's) Battalion Tennessee Infantry **BIRTH:** c. 1832, Tennessee **DEATH:** Before 1900
MARRIED: Emily A. Clenny, 25 July 1854, White County, Tennessee

Lowery, John Wesley
LOCATION: Unknown burial location; possibly in old Bon Air Cemetery **RANK:** Private **COMPANY:** C **REGIMENT:** 16th Tennessee Infantry **BIRTH:** November 1822 **DEATH:** Between 1900–1908 **MARRIED:** Rose Ann Lance, 16 February 1850, White County, Tennessee **PENSION:** #S1816

Worley, James
LOCATION: Unknown burial location. Pension states he died in Bon Air, White County, Tennessee. He is believed to be buried in either Old Bon Air Cemetery or New Bon Air Cemetery. **RANK:** Private **COMPANY:** H **REGIMENT:** 52nd Georgia Infantry **BIRTH:** c. 1834, Rayborn County, Georgia **DEATH:** 07 January 1909 **MARRIED:** Arrie Malinda York **PENSIONS:** #S7324 and #W2283

OVERTON COUNTY

Bethlehem Methodist Church Cemetery

Rural Livingston, Overton County, Tennessee

Cullom, Sam

LOCATION: Bethlehem Methodist Church Cemetery
RANK: Private **COMPANY:** F **REGIMENT:** 8th Tennessee Infantry **BIRTH:** November 1831, Maryland
DEATH: After 1920, Overton County, Tennessee
MARRIED: Parmelia (Paralee)
OTHER: Farmer; School custodian (1910)

On 11 July 2004, more than 30 re-enactors from five Highland Brigade camps of the Sons of Confederate Veterans coordinated the solemn and historic memorial service at the Bethlehem Methodist Church in Overton County, Tennessee, to honor Private Sam Cullom of Company F, 8th Tennessee Infantry, CSA. Approximately 40 descendants of Sam Cullom including Dr. Althea Armstrong from Detroit, Michigan, Mrs. Juanita Page, Mrs. Joyce Gist, Mrs. Eileen Savage, and other family members attended the service. Sam Cullom went to war with the sons of Alvin Cullom, Jim and Ras Cullom, in Capt. Calvin E. Myers' company of Col. Alfred S. Fulton's Regiment, which went into service in 1861, the first company to leave Livingston, Tennessee. Sam performed faithful service throughout the entire War and was with this company when they surrendered at Greensboro, North Carolina. When Jim Cullom was killed at the Battle of Atlanta, it was Sam Cullom who buried him. On 12 July, 1921, three days after it was filed, Sam Cullom's application #58, for a Tennessee "Colored Man's Confederate Pension" was accepted.

Barbara Parsons and Dr. Althea Armstrong

Camp Ground Cemetery
Paran Methodist Church, Rickman

Cannon, Jasper Newton
LOCATION: Lot #361, A-E, Camp Ground Cemetery
RANK: Bugler **COMPANY:** E **REGIMENT:** 13th (Gore's) Tennessee Cavalry **BIRTH:** 26 May 1841 **DEATH:** 06 July 1924
PENSION: #S7584

Cash Cemetery
Livingston, Overton County, Tennessee

Cash, James M.
LOCATION: Cash Cemetery **RANK:** 1st Lieutenant
COMPANY: D **REGIMENT:** 4th (Murray's) Tennessee Cavalry
BIRTH: c. 1842, Tennessee **DEATH:** Before 1880
MARRIED: Lizzie T. (Lucy) Elizabeth Hart
PENSION: #W2067 **OTHER:** Lived in Georgia; Office clerk before the war; First joined the CSA in Georgia, then transferred to Tennessee; Member of the Immortal 600.

Daugherty Family Cemetery
Daugherty Street, Livingston, Overton County, Tennessee

Daugherty, Ferdinand H.
LOCATION: Daugherty Family Cemetery **RANK:** Lt. Colonel
COMPANY: D **REGIMENT:** 25th Tennessee Infantry / 13th (Gore's) Tennessee Cavalry **BIRTH:** 15 October 1823, Tennessee **DEATH:** 10 April 1895 **MARRIED:** (1) -- Snodgrass; (2) -- Cullum; (3) Laura Carr - 6 children **OTHER:** Lawyer; Postmaster; Overton County Registrar; Member of the Immortal 600

Massacre at Officer House

Compiled by Op Walker

UNION RECORDS
Headquarters, U. S. Forces
Sparta, Tennessee, March 28, 1864

Sir, I have the honor to make the following report of operations since my last report:

On the 11th instant, having heard of the enemy on Calfkiller, I sent out a scout of 80 men, under Captains Blackburn and Waters, in search of them. They met the enemy concentrated, numbering 150 men, 10 miles from this place, and after a stubborn and desperate resistance of 1 hour they succeeded in dispersing and running them into the mountains. The rebels lost 1 man killed and several wounded, the notorious Champ Ferguson being one of the latter. Our loss was 1 killed and 4 slightly wounded.

The next day I sent out a force of 200 men, but they were unable to find the enemy in any force. While out they succeeded in killing 7 Texas Rangers, men of the most daring and desperate character. Among these was Lieutenant Davis, the leader of the band. These men had been murdering and robbing Union citizens.

W. B. Stokes
Colonel Fifth Tennessee Volunteer Cavalry
Commanding Captain B. H. Polk
Assistant Adjutant-General
(Official report researched and provided by Grover Bennett)

~

The peaceful dawn of Saturday morning, March 12, 1864, was short-lived as 200 Federal troops quickly surrounded and invaded the home of William Alexander and Cynthia Holford Officer, located in the Sinking Cane Community of Overton County, Tennessee.

Mrs. Officer had risen early that morning and with the help of her 17-year-old daughter, Frances (Fannie) had prepared a good breakfast for their Confederate Army at home on leave that weekend.

Seeing the men in blue outside, young John Holford Officer, a 19-year-old Confederate private, jumped up from the table and ran into the kitchen where he climbed into the loft and hid. He was assisted by Abraham H. (Uncle Abe) Officer, a faithful and trusted slave of the Officers.

The six Confederate soldiers were powerless to do anything against such overwhelming odds and knew it was useless to go for their guns which were stacked in the hallway.

In just a short period of time the Federal troops burst into the house and proceeded to terrorize the family and guests.

Colonel William B. Stokes' men never quit until they had shot six unarmed Confederate soldiers in cold blood and inflicted a painful wound on William Alexander's wife.

Killed were 2nd Lieutenant Robert S. Davis, John P. York, Oliver Shipp, Samuel Garrett, William Slaughter and William Lipscomb.

Slaughter was a Texas Ranger, belonging to Company C, 1st Regiment of the Texas Rangers, while York, Shipp, Lt. Davis, and Garrett were members of the 8th Texas Cavalry. Lipscomb was in the 3rd Regiment, Alabama Cavalry.

All of the men were slain inside the home except for Lt. Davis. He was wounded and carried outside where they stood him up against the gatepost and shot him firing-squad style.

Johnny King, a young man from Manchester, Tennessee, was with the soldiers but he was not harmed. Uncle Abe told the Union troops that Johnny King was an orphan boy that was going from house to house.

Had not John Holdford Officer hid in the loft, he would have been killed also. Imagine the feeling he had when he heard Col. Stokes order his men to burn the house. John knew that if he came down from his hiding place and attempted to escape that he would meet the same fate as the other Confederate soldiers. On the other hand he knew if he remained in hiding and the house set on fire that he would be burned alive.

The Union soldiers started a fire at the corner of the house but William Alexander kicked it out before it could make any headway. The Yankees started the fire again and William Alexander kicked it out just as he did the first time. He was warned that if he kicked it out one more time that he would be shot. To this he replied: "Every time you try to burn my house I will surely put it out."

He then appealed to Col. Stokes and reminded him that his soldiers had already murdered six unarmed men and painfully wounded his wife while shooting at John Shipp. Alexander also told the men in blue that they had heaped upon him as much sorrow as any human being could endure. This seemed to touch what little human kindness that was left in them and Zeke Bass, one of Col. Stokes' men, told William Alexander that he would not be killed nor his house burned. Col. Stokes and his men then mounted their horses and rode away.

~

In 1922, Abraham H. (Uncle Abe) Officer gave a first hand report to the Tennessee Historical Committee:

My master came home once in awhile and during one of those visits there were six Confederate soldiers and a young man at his home. Their names were Lt. Bob Davis, Bill Slaughter, John Shipp, Sam Garrett, John York, Bill Lipscomb and John King. It just so happened that my master's son, Pvt. John Holford Officer, was at home on leave when the Feds rode up that morning. They never saw him though as I had fixed a place for him to hide.

When the Yanks shot at John Shipp he ran through the house and caught Mrs. Officer by the hand. One of the bullets was off mark and struck her in the shoulder, inflicting a painful wound from which she recovered.

Shipp was shot and killed inside the house as was Slaughter, Garrett, York and Lipscomb. When they shot Lt. Bob Davis I was within six feet of them. Bob was wounded and they carried him out of the house, stood him up against the gatepost and riddled his body much the same way a firing squad does.

Just before Lt. Davis was shot, he said, 'You ought not to do this. I have never done anything but my sworn duty.' He never flinched as the soldiers opened fire on him.

King, a young, boy-ish looking man from Manchester, was the only one to escape death. He hid in the corner of the house and I told the soldiers that he was an orphan boy going about from house to house.

Zeke Bass, one of Col. Stokes' men, told William Alexander that it was a shame that his wife got shot but at the same time 'it is a blessing in disguise to you because we were going to kill you and burn your house. I am going to spare your life so you can take care of your wife. You shan't be hurt.'

(Dillard, John Roy, *Standing Stone, Tennessee Monterey Early History*, 1989)

Uncle Abe collected the bodies of the fallen Confederates and laid them side-by-side in the front yard. Before loading them on a mule-drawn wagon for the trip to the burial site, he clipped off locks of hair from each man. These locks of hair were in the possession of Mrs. Sehon of Monterey as late as the 1960's. The fate of the locks of hair is unknown. The bodies were buried in a common grave in the Conely Cemetery, almost within site of the Officer house.

The original fence post against which Lt. Davis was stood before the firing squad killed him, may still be seen in the Overton County History Center. The bullet holes are still very visible.

Photos of the Officer Cemetery where the six murdered Confederates were buried by "Uncle Abe" Officer.

This is the actual gate post that Lt. Davis was tied to by Union men and shot execution style. It is in the Overton County History Center in Livingston, Tennessee.

The old home place of William Alexander Officer, which dates back over 150 years, is still standing in a remarkable state of preservation considering its age. This home was the scene of a bloody massacre on the morning of March 12, 1864, when six Confederate soldiers were shot within its walls by Federal troops. The gate post in the left foreground is the same one where they dragged a wounded Lt. Davis out of the house and stood him up before executing him. Paul Parrott is on the left, while Frank Officer stands near the gate.

Officer Cemetery

Rural Overton County, Tennessee

Davis, Robert S.
LOCATION: Officer Cemetery **RANK:** 2nd Lieutenant **COMPANY:** D (E) **REGIMENT:** 8th Texas Cavalry (Texas Rangers) **BIRTH:** 1838 **DEATH:** 12 March 1864

~

Garrett, Samuel
LOCATION: Officer Cemetery **RANK:** Private **COMPANY:** G (C) **REGIMENT:** 8th Texas Cavalry (Texas Rangers) **BIRTH:** Unknown **DEATH:** 12 March 1864

~

Lipscomb, William A.
LOCATION: Officer Cemetery **RANK:** Private **COMPANY:** C **REGIMENT:** 3rd Alabama Cavalry **BIRTH:** Unknown **DEATH:** 12 March 1864

254 · Our Confederate Ancestors · Overton County

Parrott, James Foster

LOCATION: Officer Cemetery **RANK:** 1st Sergeant
COMPANY: H **REGIMENT:** 28th Tennessee Infantry
BIRTH: 03 February 1830 **DEATH:** 06 May 1868
OTHER: Although Parrott was not one of those murdered at Officer House, he was murdered after the war.

In November 2002, Mr. Walter Herron, Jr., of Sparta, Tennessee, shared the story of his great-great grandfather, CSA Sergeant, James Forrester Parrot of the 28th Consolidated Infantry with the *Insider* newspaper. Several letters that James wrote home to his wife during the War were included in the series. The life of James Parrott was not an easy one and his death was just as tragic. While traveling through the Cumberland Mountain area, James contracted measles and his mother was forced to leave him with the Miller family where they had spent the night. She had intended to return for James, but she died on the trip and James was raised by the Miller family. James stayed in the Monterey area and married Mahala Ann Bowman.

On November 27, 1862, he enlisted at McMinnville in Company H of the 28th Tennessee Infantry, CSA. In his letter dated September 11, 1864, James said in part, "I have been touched with a bullet. God has been my shield and I hope He will be till the day I die. I want you to still ask God for his blessing and tell all of my Christian friends to remember me in their prayers."

Two years later on November 30, 1864, James was in the front ranks in the attack on Union positions in the battle of Franklin, Tennessee. He was shot in the lower right foot and his unit left him in a Confederate hospital while they went on to Nashville. The Union doctors amputated his foot and sent him to prison in Louisville. On June 16, 1865, he swore the oath, was paroled and returned home where he farmed in the Rock Springs area of Overton County.

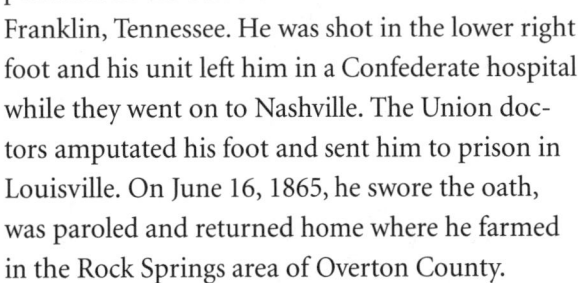

James made his own wooden leg and made it a habit to tie the wooden leg to the saddle of his horse as he rode. On May 6, 1868, the horse came home with the wooden leg attached to the saddle. The family went out looking for him and found his body where he had been gunned down. James Parrott was buried in the nearby Officer Cemetery where six Confederate soldiers who were murdered during the War were buried several years earlier. His wife never remarried and was buried beside him when she died in 1908.

~

Shipp, Oliver H.

LOCATION: Officer Cemetery **RANK:** Private **COMPANY:** S (D)
REGIMENT: 8th Texas Cavalry (Texas Rangers) **BIRTH:** 1842
DEATH: 12 March 1864

Slaughter, William M.
LOCATION: Officer Cemetery **RANK:** Private
COMPANY: C **REGIMENT:** 1st Texas Rangers (8th Texas Cavalry)
BIRTH: 1841 **DEATH:** 12 March 1864

~

York, John P.
LOCATION: Officer Cemetery **RANK:** Private
COMPANY: E **REGIMENT:** 8th Texas Cavalry
BIRTH: 1837
DEATH: 12 March 1864

Poplar Springs Cemetery
Overton County, Tennessee

Lawson, William Terry
LOCATION: Poplar Springs Cemetery **RANK:** Private
COMPANY: Not listed
REGIMENT: 8th (Dibrell's) Tennessee Cavalry
BIRTH: 19 September 1835, White County, Tennessee
DEATH: 25 February 1905
MARRIED: Susann (Susan Ann) Martin, 1860, Jackson County, Tennessee **UDC MEMBER:** Janet Lawson Trubee

William Terry Lawson

Shiloh Cemetery
Overton County, Tennessee

Buckner, Jacob
LOCATION: Shiloh Cemetery **RANK:** Private **COMPANY:** H
REGIMENT: 13th (Gore's) Tennessee Cavalry
BIRTH: 15 September 1844 **DEATH:** 04 May 1928
MARRIED: Leta Bowman, 1871, Putnam County, Tennessee
UDC MEMBER: Kimberly Ann Parker

Unmarked Grave

JACKSON COUNTY

Dodson's Branch Cemetery

Jackson County, Tennessee

Gentry, Martin B.
LOCATION: Dodson's Branch Cemetery
RANK: Private **COMPANY:** I **REGIMENT:** 25th Tennessee Infantry
BIRTH: 12 December 1818, Jackson County, Tennessee
DEATH: 10 June 1904 **MARRIED:** Mary "Polly Ann" Peek, 10 March 1846, Tennessee **UDC MEMBER:** Shirley Maberry Rodgers

John P. Mabury Cemetery

Jackson County, Tennessee

Mabury, John P.
LOCATION: John P. Mabury Cemetery **RANK:** Private
COMPANY: F **REGIMENT:** 16th Tennessee Infantry
BIRTH: 17 May 1842, Jackson County, Tennessee
DEATH: 02 July 1922 **MARRIED:** Margaret S. Matheny, 1862, Jackson County, Tennessee **UDC MEMBER:** Shirley Mabury Rodgers

Ace Anderson Cemetery

By Roaring River, Gainesboro, Jackson County, Tennessee

Anderson, Ace
LOCATION: Ace Anderson Cemetery **RANK:** Private
COMPANY: K **REGIMENT:** 13th (Gore's) Tennessee Cavalry
BIRTH: 1838, Jackson County, Tennessee
DEATH: 19 February 1903 **MARRIED:** Martha Hawkins
CHILDREN: Daughter, Fannie; Sons, Benjamin, John, and James A. Miles

Allen-Anderson Cemetery
Blackburn's Fork Road, Gainesboro, Tennessee

Allen, Jesse P.
LOCATION: Allen-Anderson Cemetery **RANK:** 2nd Lieutenant **COMPANY:** E **REGIMENT:** 13th (Gore's) Tennessee Cavalry **BIRTH:** c. 1840 **DEATH:** 24 May 1929 **MARRIED:** Mary Martha Anderson **PENSION:** #W9154

~

Anderson, Baily P.
LOCATION: Allen-Anderson Cemetery **RANK:** Private **COMPANY:** K **REGIMENT:** 13th (Gore's) / 8th (Dibrell's) Tennessee Cavalry **BIRTH:** 12 April 1837 **DEATH:** 19 October 1911 **MARRIED:** Elizabeth Hawkins **PENSION:** #S15289 **CHILDREN:** Daughters, Angeline, Juda, and Mary

~

Anderson, Miles Wesley
LOCATION: Allen-Anderson Cemetery **RANK:** Private **COMPANY:** G **REGIMENT:** 8th (Dibrell's) / 13th (Gore's) Tennessee Cavalry **BIRTH:** 10 July 1830 **DEATH:** 19 April 1892 **MARRIED:** Nancy Hawkins **CHILDREN:** William, Bailey, Asa, and Miles W., Manvera **PENSION:** #4968

Fox Chaffin Cemetery
Gainesboro, Jackson County, Tennessee

Chaffin, Fox C.
LOCATION: Fox Chaffin Cemetery **RANK:** Sergeant **COMPANY:** E **REGIMENT:** 28th Tennessee Infantry **BIRTH:** 05 February 1829 **DEATH:** 21 June 1902 **MARRIED:** Jane Fox **CHILDREN:** Sons, Authur, Jace, John, Abner, Ben, Lewis, Luther, and Nathan; Daughters, Daisy, Pruda, Nannie, Peggy, Mary, Martha, and Fanny.

Gainesboro City Cemetery
Gainesboro, Tennessee

Cox, Robert Alexander
LOCATION: Gainesboro City Cemetery **RANK:** Private / Musician **COMPANY:** K **REGIMENT:** 8th Tennessee Infantry **BIRTH:** 24 November 1832 **DEATH:** 18 June 1892 **MARRIED:** Nancy **CHILDREN:** Daugher, Clara Epperson

Maddux Cemetery
Gainesboro, Tennessee

Lee, Thomas Jefferson
LOCATION: Maddux Cemetery **RANK:** 1st Sergeant
COMPANY: K Regiment: 17th Tennessee Infantry
BIRTH: 17 October 1834 **DEATH:** 27 October 1923
MARRIED: Tennessee Stanton Parents: John and Sarah Harper Lee **CHILDREN:** Sally Rose, Oliver

Smith Cemetery
Holliman's Bend Road, Gainesboro, Tennessee

Dillard, Harvey H.
LOCATION: Smith Cemetery **RANK:** Captain **COMPANY:** K
REGIMENT: 16th Tennessee Infantry **BIRTH:** 1834
DEATH: 30 September 1904 **PARENTS:** Rev. John Leath and Candis T. (Baker) Dillard **OTHER:** Attorney

Captain Harvey H. Dillard formed the first Confederate company in Putnam County, Company K, 16th Tennessee Infantry, also known as the "Highlanders." During the Cheat Mountain campaign, the Confederates were required to wear a piece of white cloth tacked on the front of their hats so they would be able to identify their own men. Early one morning a group of riders approached Dillard's encampment. The guards were sure they were Union men and wanted to fire on them. Dillard ordered the guards to wait. As the riders came upon Dillard's group in the gray twilight, they could finally see the white patches on the hats of the riders. One of the riders was General Robert E. Lee, who, like Stonewall Jackson, could have been killed that evening by his own men. By his order to wait for better identification, Dillard very well may have saved the life of General Lee and his company. Dillard returned to Cookeville after the war to practice law and teach school. He never married and when in failing health he moved to the home of his sister, Frances, wife of Hugh B. Smith, near Granville, Tennessee where he died 30 September 1904. He was buried at the foot of his father's grave in the small family cemetery. (Story by Dale Welch, *Hilltop Express*)

~

Smith, Hugh B.
LOCATION: Smith Cemetery **RANK:** Private
COMPANY: G **REGIMENT:** 28th Tennessee Infantry
BIRTH: 06 December 1835 **DEATH:** 24 June 1897
MARRIED: Frances Dillard

WARREN COUNTY

Potter Cemetery
Warren County, Tennessee

Green, James M.
LOCATION: Potter Cemetery **RANK:** Private **COMPANY:** A **REGIMENT:** 35th Tennessee Infantry **BIRTH:** 02 March 1822, Warren County, Tennessee **DEATH:** 23 September 1900, Warren County, Tennessee **MARRIED:** (1) Elizabeth Nunn, 07 November 1839, Warren County, Tennessee; (2) Sarah Womack, 08 August 1846, Warren County, Tennessee; (3) Mary Angeline (Mullican) Hendrixson, 02 December 1884, Warren County, Tennessee **UDC MEMBER:** Ruby Yates Pruett

Riverside (City) Cemetery
McMinnville, Tennessee

Banks, Francis "Frank" M.
LOCATION: Riverside (City) Cemetery **RANK:** Private **COMPANY:** E **REGIMENT:** 45th Tennessee Infantry **BIRTH:** 13 July 1834 **DEATH:** 27 March 1864 **OTHER:** Banks was murdered by Union Colonel Stokes.

~

Biles, William H.
LOCATION: Riverside (City) Cemetery **RANK:** Sergeant **COMPANY:** I **REGIMENT:** 46th Tennessee Infantry **BIRTH:** 25 April 1845 **DEATH:** 16 April 1909 **MARRIED:** Bettie Johnston

~

Black, Thomas, Dr.
LOCATION: Riverside (City) Cemetery **RANK:** Hospital Steward **COMPANY:** C / Field & Staff **REGIMENT:** 16th Tennessee Infantry **BIRTH:** 13 June 1837 **DEATH:** 27 February 1904 **MARRIED:** Emma Jane Young, 13 February 1867

Cooksey, Enoch
LOCATION: Riverside (City) Cemetery
RANK: Private
COMPANY: H
REGIMENT: 16th Tennessee Infantry
BIRTH: 17 April 1842
DEATH: 15 November 1873

~

Drake, Uriah York, Sr.
LOCATION: Riverside (City) Cemetery **RANK:** Private
COMPANY: E **REGIMENT:** 22nd (Murray's) Battalion Tennessee Infantry **BIRTH:** 17 February 1837 **DEATH:** 05 March 1914
MARRIED: Lucy "Lucinda" Bright, 10 January 1856, Warren County, Tennessee **PENSION:** #W8854

~

Gribble, Samuel
LOCATION: Riverside (City) Cemetery **RANK:** Private
COMPANY: D **REGIMENT:** 16th Tennessee Infantry
BIRTH: 13 May 1829 **DEATH:** 30 June 1910
MARRIED: (1) Mary Jane Miller, 31 August 1848, Warren County, Tennessee; (2) Eliza Hutson; (3) Mollie Garrettson, 06 October 1872, Warren County, Tennessee

~

Harrison, John Samuel
LOCATION: Riverside (City) Cemetery **RANK:** Private
COMPANY: G **REGIMENT:** 7th Tennessee Infantry
BIRTH: 1831 **DEATH:** 1914 **MARRIED:** (1) Julia E. West, 28 December 1856, Warren County, Tennessee; (2) Jessie Miles Spurlock, 08 October 1907, Warren County, Tennessee
PENSION: #W11074

Morford, Henry C.
LOCATION: Riverside (City) Cemetery **RANK:** Not listed
COMPANY: H **REGIMENT:** 11th (Holman's) Tennessee Cavalry
BIRTH: 28 June 1845 **DEATH:** 10 November 1911
PENSION: #S14387

~

Morrow, Martin A.
LOCATION: Riverside (City) Cemetery
RANK: Private **COMPANY:** H **REGIMENT:** 11th (Holman's) Tennessee Cavalry **BIRTH:** 02 January 1828
DEATH: 07 May 1907 **MARRIED:** Ann Maria Garretson

~

Murray, Thomas B.
LOCATION: Riverside (City) Cemetery **RANK:** Major
COMPANY: Field & Staff **REGIMENT:** 22nd (Murray's) Battalion Tennessee Infantry **BIRTH:** 1829 **DEATH:** 1878
MARRIED: Mary Goodbar, 30 November 1852, Warren County, Tennessee

~

Ritchey, J. B., Dr.
LOCATION: Riverside (City) Cemetery
RANK: Adjutant Quarter Master **COMPANY:** Field & Staff
REGIMENT: 16th Tennessee Infantry
BIRTH: 02 December 1830 **DEATH:** 24 March 1909
MARRIED: Mira Smartt, 10 April 1867, Warren County, Tennessee

~

Rowan, Eldridge Stanwic
LOCATION: Riverside (City) Cemetery **RANK:** Private
COMPANY: C **REGIMENT:** 16th Tennessee Infantry
BIRTH: 1840 **DEATH:** 1907 **MARRIED:** Lucy Wood Lee, 16 May 1874, Warren County, Tennessee
PENSION: #S6652 and #W2579

Savage, John Houston

LOCATION: Riverside (City) Cemetery **RANK:** Colonel
COMPANY: Field & Staff **REGIMENT:** 16th Tennessee Infantry
BIRTH: 09 October 1815, McMinnville, Tennessee
DEATH: 05 April 1904 **PARENTS:** George and Elizabeth (Kenner) Savage **OTHER:** A Representative from Tennessee; attended the common schools; served as a private in the Seminole War; studied law; was admitted to the bar and commenced practice in Smithville, Tennessee; colonel of State militia; attorney general of the fourth Tennessee district 1841-1847; major of the Fourteenth United States Infantry during the Mexican War and subsequently promoted to lieutenant colonel; elected as a Democrat to the Thirty-first and Thirty-second Congresses (March 4, 1849-March 3, 1853); declined to be a candidate for reelection; elected to the Thirty-fourth and Thirty-fifth Congresses (March 04, 1855-March 03, 1859); colonel of the Sixteenth Regiment Tennessee Infantry, in the Confederate Army during the Civil War; member of the State house of representatives 1877-1879 and 1887-1891 and the State senate 1879-1881; died in McMinnville, Tennessee. (Taken from *The Biographical Directory of the United States Congress*); The Colonel John H. Savage #2227 United Daughters of the Confederacy meet in McMinnville, Tennessee.

Savage, Lucien Napoleon

LOCATION: Riverside (City) Cemetery **RANK:** Captain
COMPANY: A **REGIMENT:** 16th Tennessee Infantry
BIRTH: 25 April 1837 **DEATH:** 12 March 1863
PARENTS: George and Elizabeth (Kenner) Savage
OTHER: Died from wounds received at the Battle of Murfreesboro, Tennessee; Brother of Colonel John H. Savage

Smallman, M. D.

LOCATION: Riverside (City) Cemetery **RANK:** Adjutant
COMPANY: Field & Staff **REGIMENT:** 13th (Gore's) Tennessee Cavalry **BIRTH:** 08 May 1838 **DEATH:** 17 August 1928
MARRIED: (1) Cordelia A. Magness; (2) Lula Alice Leonard
PENSION: #S16069

Stubblefield, Hanibal L.

LOCATION: Riverside (City) Cemetery
RANK: Private COMPANY: B REGIMENT: 35th Tennessee Infantry BIRTH: 30 July 1839 DEATH: 11 November 1901
MARRIED: Sarah S. Smith, 12 May 1869,
Warren County, Tennessee

~

Tate, J. D.

LOCATION: Riverside (City) Cemetery
RANK: Private COMPANY: B REGIMENT: 35th Tennessee Infantry BIRTH: 21 May 1839 DEATH: 02 August 1902
MARRIED: Mary Jane McGregor, 03 January 1858,
Warren County, Tennessee

~

Walling, Jesse

LOCATION: Riverside (City) Cemetery
RANK: 1st Lieutenant
COMPANY: E REGIMENT: 16th Tennessee Infantry
BIRTH: 15 March 1841 DEATH: 11 March 1930
MARRIED: Belle Winton, 07 October 1863,
Warren County, Tennessee

~

Walling, Joseph D.

LOCATION: Riverside (City) Cemetery RANK: Private
COMPANY: I REGIMENT: 16th Tennessee Infantry
BIRTH: 11 June 1818 DEATH: 21 December 1883
MARRIED: Harriet LaBonnie Green, 22 November 1854,
Warren County, Tennessee

Willey, Addison Gardiner
LOCATION: Riverside (City) Cemetery
RANK: Private COMPANY: E
REGIMENT: 11th Battalion Cavalry
BIRTH: 30 March 1833
DEATH: 08 December 1884
MARRIED: Cloe M.

~

Womack, James J.
LOCATION: Riverside (City) Cemetery
RANK: Captain COMPANY: E
REGIMENT: 16th Tennessee Infantry
BIRTH: 07 July 1834 DEATH: 18 July 1922
MARRIED: (1) Tennie C. Amonett, 20 March 1862, Warren County, Tennessee; (2) Mary Ann Bass PENSION: #S3639

Webb's Cemetery
Smithville, Warren County

Bass, John W.
LOCATION: Webb's Cemetery RANK: Captain COMPANY: D
REGIMENT: 22nd (Murray's) Battalion Tennessee Infantry
BIRTH: 24 November 1824 DEATH: 16 February 1907
MARRIED: Rachel Turner, 15 March 1849, Warren County, Tennessee

~

Potter, Perry Green
LOCATION: Webb's Cemetery RANK: Sergeant
COMPANY: B REGIMENT: 22nd (Murray's) Battalion Tennessee Infantry BIRTH: 27 September 1842 DEATH: 16 March 1924
MARRIED: (1) Malvinia Webb; (2) Sue Fugitt

Vanhooser, John

LOCATION: Webb's Cemetery **RANK:** Sergeant
COMPANY: E **REGIMENT:** 16th Tennessee Infantry
BIRTH: 21 November 1837 **DEATH:** 24 November 1929
MARRIED: Melvina L. Williams, 19 January 1868, Warren County, Tennessee **PENSION:** #W9780

~

Webb, James M.

LOCATION: Webb's Cemetery **RANK:** Sergeant
COMPANY: E **REGIMENT:** 3rd (Forrest's) Tennessee Cavalry
BIRTH: 13 September 1819 **DEATH:** 1902
MARRIED: Mary Byars, 25 August 1842, Warren County, Tennessee

UDC MEMBER'S ANCESTORS

Members' Ancestors Buried in Other Locations

NAME	BURIAL LOCATION
Gladys Boyd Anderson	
John W. Boyd	UBL, Coffee Co., TN
Robert A. Boyd	UBL, (Monroe Co., TN)
Elijah Cagle	Big Creek Baptist Church, Monroe Co., TN
John Cagle, Jr.	UBL, (AL)
Lot Cagle	UBL, Red River Co., TX
Anderson Moses	Piney Grove Cemetery, Monroe Co., TN
Andrew Moses	Joshua Moses Cemetery, Monroe Co., TN
James Moses	Joshua Moses Cemetery, Monroe Co., TN
Samuel Moses	New Zion Baptist Cemetery, McMinn Co., TN
Michael McKinney	McKinney Family Cemetery, Fannin Co., GA
Anna Ruth Russell Barnes	
Monroe Russell	New Hope Cemetery, White Co., TN
Frances Ensor Benedict	
William Asbury Ensor	Jared Cemetery, Putnam Co., TN
Dorothea Beatrice Cowen Brodhag:	
George W. Cowen	McBroom Cemetery, Putnam Co., TN
Martha Sue Bell Broyles	
Nathan Bouldin	Long Cemetery, Van Buren Co., TN
William B. Cummings	Cummingsville Cemetery, Van Buren Co., TN
Alexander Grissome	Long Cemetery, Van Buren Co., TN
Elijah Grissom	Laurel Creek Cemetery, Van Buren Co., TN
Esau Grissom	Long Cemetery, Van Buren Co., TN
Samuel B. Grissom	Long Cemetery, Van Buren Co., TN
Thomas Grissom	UBL, Shiloh, TN
William T. Grissom	Noble, OK
Allen Carroll Johnson - UG	UBL, (Van Buren Co., TN)
Andrew Johnson - UG	UBL, (Van Buren Co., TN)
Esquire Johnson	Laurel Creek Cemetery, Van Buren Co., TN
Greenberry Johnson	Laurel Creek Cemetery, Van Buren Co., TN
Stokley D. Johnson	Greenwood Cemetery, White Co., TN
Peter Shockley	Battlefield, Perryville, KY - KIA
Phillip Shockley	Long Cemetery, Van Buren Co., TN
Thomas H. Shockley	UBL, (Tennessee)
William B. Shockley - UG	Big Fork Cemetery, Van Buren Co., TN
*Martha Louise Harding Burns**	
Fletcher Hamilton Cheatham	UBL, Tennessee
Carolyn Jeaneane Rollins Carr:	
George Gibbs Dibrell	Old Sparta City Cemetery, White Co., TN
Joseph A. Dibrell	Old Sparta City Cemetery, White Co., TN
Montgomery C. Dibrell - (UG)	Old Sparta City Cemetery, White Co., TN
Waman L. Dibrell	Bethlehem Cemetery, White Co., TN
Jefferson Leftwich - (UG)	Old Sparta City Cemetery, White Co., TN
Columbus McBride	Zollicoffer Park, Mill Springs Battlefield Cemetery, Somerset, KY
*Genevera Crowder Carter**	
Same ancestors as Sarah Lou Looney Dodson	

NAME	BURIAL LOCATION
Margaret Louise Haston Cordell	
John Johnson	Battlefield, Petersburg, VA - KIA
Samuel J. Johnson (Immortal 600)	Johnson Baptist Church, Putnam Co., TN
Solomon Johnson	Battlefield, Murfreesboro, TN - KIA

Cynthia Ann Harris Diminovich

Thomas W. Burt	Pearidge Cemetery, Grenada Co., GA

Sarah Lou Looney Dodson

Waman Mansfield Russell	New Hope, White Co., TN
William Monroe Russell	New Hope, White Co., TN
John Jacob Robinson	Dyer-Cash, White Co., TN

Ada Jewell Carter Fox

James McMann Carter	UBL, Jackson Co., TN

Elizabeth Anne Tyson Gentry

James Barnett Townsend	McNeil-Townsend Cemetery, Pike Co., AL

Donna Jo Randolph Hamilton

James M. Barnes	Mt. Olivet Cemetery, Nashville, TN
Jesse Barnes	Double Springs Cemetery, Putnam Co., TN
Lewis Thomas Barnes	UBL
Riley Barnes	UBL, Madison Co., AR
Thomas E. Barnes	UBL, Ash Flat, AR
John Hunter	UBL
Joseph Hyder	Old Hyder Cemetery, Putnam Co., TN
John Mills	UBL
William J. Mills	Mills Cemetery, White Co., TN
Killis J. Mills	Mills Cemetery, White Co., TN
Samuel Poteet KIA	Battlefield, Huntersville, WV -

Hattie Clarissa Hendrix Harris

Thomas Wesley Ford	Grassy Cove Cemetery, Cumberland Co., TN

NAME	BURIAL LOCATION
Aurelia Louise Hurlbert Hannon, Real Daughter:	
Francis Telesford Hurlbert	Eubank Family Cemetery, Jacksonville, FL
William N. Eubanks	Eubank Family Cemetery, Jacksonville, FL

Susan Raye Broyles Harris

Same ancestors as Martha Sue Bell Broyles, in addition to the following:

George G. Broyles	Broyles Family Cemetery, White Co., TN
William Lafayette Sliger	Phillips Cemetery, Putnam Co., TN
Jubilee W. Wheeler	Macomb Cemetery, Grayson Co., TX
Thomas Wheeler	Wheeler Cemetery, White Co., TN
William C. Wheeler	Wheeler Memorial Cemetery, Jackson Co., TN

Norma Lucille Hall Hay

Zachariah Hall	Oak Park Cemetery, Pulaski Co. KY

Bonnie Lamb Lee

John P. Huddleston	Salem Cemetery, Putnam Co., TN

Margaret Ann Lee Markum

John Dillard Smith - (UG)	Florence City Cemetery, Lauderdale Co., AL

*Lola Belle Brown McCormick**

Hiram A. Brown	Brown's Mill Cemetery, Putnam Co., TN
J. S. Holman	Stewart Cemetery, Putnam Co., TN

Sherrie Beth Broyles McCulley

Same ancestors as Martha Sue Bell Broyles and Susan Raye Broyles Harris

*Josephine Bell McDonald**

Same ancestors as Martha Sue Bell Broyles

276 · Our Confederate Ancestors · UDC Member's Ancestor

NAME	BURIAL LOCATION
Alma Faye Harris Monk	
Same ancestor as Cynthia Ann Harris Diminovich	
7Kimberly Ann Parker	
Jacob Buckner	Shiloh Cemetery, Overton Co., TN
Bettye Grace Keese Parrish	
Warren Franklin Hearn	Oak Woods Cemetery, Cook Co., IL
Ruby Clone Yates Pruett	
James M. Green	Potter Cemetery, Warren Co., TN
Barbara Jean Buchanan Parsons	
Benjamin S. Garrett	UBL, Richmond, VA
William Garrett	UBL, Richmond, VA
James F. Goodman	Sparks Cemetery, Sparks, GA
Robert H. Goodman - (UG)	Battlefield, Atlanta, GA - KIA
George W. Harris	UBL, Echols Co., GA
James Harris	UBL, Cook Co., GA
John W. Harris	Harris Family Cemetery, Odom, GA
John W. Powell	Fender Cemetery, Lanier Co., GA
William C. Powell	Fine Oak Cemetery, Lanier Co., GA
Benjamin Sirmans	Fender Cemetery, Clinch Co., GA
Harris Sirmons	UBL
John J. Sirmons - (UG)	Battlefield, Cold Harbor, VA - KIA
Jesse Smith	UBL, Clinch Co., GA
James M. Smith	UBL
George Washington Stephens	Fellowship Missionary Baptist, Cecil, GA
David Stone	UBL
John Raines Stone	UBL, Berrien Co., GA
Ferman Westberry	UBL
Rabon Westberry	UBL
*Thelma Ford Parsons**	
Elbert Henley Ford - (UG)	UBL
Elijah Jehu Ford	(Nashville, TN)
John Fletcher Ford	Grassy Cove Cemetery, Cumberland Co., TN
Thomas Wesley Ford	Grassy Cove Cemetery, Cumberland Co., TN

NAME	BURIAL LOCATION
*Shirley Rose Maberry Rodgers**	
Martin B. Gentry	Dodson's Branch Cemetery, Jackson Co., TN
John P. Maberry	John P. Mabury Cemetery, Jackson Co., TN
Joshua M. Maberry	Smith Cemetery, Putnam Co., TN
Josiah R. Maberry	UBL, Mississippi
George Mabery - (UG)	Battlefield, Reseca, GA
Janet McElhaney Randolph	
Columbus Luther McElhaney	Cleburne Memorial Cemetery, Cleburne, TX
Carolyn Jean Barnes Rankhorn	
Same ancestor as Anna Ruth Barnes in addition to:	
W. M. Russell	New Hope Cemetery, White Co., TN
Thomas M. T. Wall	UBL, DeKalb Co., TN
Elizabeth Hope Parsons Schubert	
George Washington Stephens	Fellowship Missionary Baptist, Cecil, GA
Deborah McDonald Spriggs	
Same ancestors as Martha Sue Bell Broyles	
Ruth Jean Watson Traughber	
Benjamin R. H. Watson - (UG)	Watson Family Cemetery, Putnam Co., TN
John Watson	Watson Family Cemetery, Putnam Co., TN
Janet Alice Lawson Trubee	
William Terry Lawson	Poplar Springs Cemetery, Overton Co, TN
Deborah Gay Powell Ward	
Clark Powell, Sr.	Lott Cemetery, Marion Co., MS
Kristie Gwen Hamilton Welch	
Same ancestors as Donna Jo Randolph Hamilton	

NAME	BURIAL LOCATION

Martha Elizabeth Summers Willis

Ridley Draper	Kuykendall Cemetery, Putnam Co., TN
Harvey Lewis Swift - (UG)	Old Flatt Creek Cemetery, Putnam Co., TN

Pamela Marie Mikulski Wood

Edwin Allen (UG)	Battlefield, Murfreesboro, TN - KIA
Isaac Allen	Pikey John Allen Cemetery, Cocke Co., TN
John J. Allen	Lillard Family Cemetery, Cocke Co., TN
John "Shortfinger" Allen - (UG)	UBL, Cocke Co., TN
Calvin Lillard	Lillard Family Cemetery, Cocke Co., TN
John Lillard	Lillard Family Cemetery, Cocke Co., TN
Mark Lillard	Mark Lillard Family Cemetery, Cocke Co., TN
Russell Lillard	Confederate Cemetery, Chattanooga, TN
William Lillard	Confederate Cemetery, Chattanooga, TN
Robert Large	Holders Grove Methodist, Cocke Co., TN
Edward Lowry - (UG)	UBL, Thoroughfare Gap, VA
Thomas J. Lowry	Old Methodist Church Cemetery, Surry Co., NC
William H. Lowry - (UG)	UBL, Vicksburg, MS
DeMarcus Suttenfield	UBL, VA
James Suttenfield	UBL, Rockingham, NC
John Webb - (UG)	UBL, Sevier Co., TN

UBL=Unknown burial location

* Member is deceased

Boyd, John W.
LOCATION: Unknown **RANK:** Private **COMPANY:** F **REGIMENT:** 35th Tennessee Infantry **BIRTH:** c. 1829, Monroe County, Tennessee **DEATH:** 18 April 1863, Tullahoma, Coffee County, Tennessee **MARRIED:** Flora Jane Cagle, 22 April 1852, Monroe County, Tennessee **OTHER:** Soldier died at camp near Tullahoma. **UDC MEMBER:** Gladys Boyd Anderson

Unknown Burial Location

Cagle, Elijah
LOCATION: Big Creek Baptist Church Cemetery, Monroe County, Tennessee **RANK:** Private **COMPANY:** G **REGIMENT:** 2nd (Ashby's) Tennessee Cavalry **BIRTH:** 02 November 1841, Monroe County, Tennessee **DEATH:** 29 August 1911, Monroe County, Tennessee **MARRIED:** Susan Sharp, 26 December 1889, Monroe County, Tennessee **UDC MEMBER:** Gladys Boyd Anderson

Moses, Anderson
LOCATION: Piney Grove Cemetery, East of Madisonville, Monroe County, Tennessee **RANK:** Private **COMPANY:** K **REGIMENT:** 31st Tennessee Infantry **BIRTH:** 20 May 1830, Tennessee **DEATH:** 06 August 1910, Monroe County, Tennessee **MARRIED:** Rutha Jane Hicks, 16 March 1859, Monroe County, Tennessee **UDC MEMBER:** Gladys Boyd Anderson

Anderson Moses

Moses, Samuel
LOCATION: New Zion Baptist Cemetery, Athens, McMinn County, Tennessee **REGIMENT:** Tennessee Militia for the 13th District, Monroe County, Tennessee **BIRTH:** c. 1819, Tennessee **DEATH:** 23 January 1892, McMinn County, Tennessee **MARRIED:** Susana McKinney, 11 March 1847, Monroe County, Tennessee **UDC MEMBER:** Gladys Boyd Anderson

Unknown Burial Location

Shockley, Peter
LOCATION: Unknown **RANK:** Private **COMPANY:** I
REGIMENT: 16th Tennessee Infantry **BIRTH:** 1836, Tennessee
DEATH: 03 November 1862, Perryville, Kentucky
MARRIED: Minerva Miller after 1860 (Tennessee)
UDC MEMBERS: Martha Sue Bell Broyles, Susan Broyles Harris, Sherrie Broyles McCulley, Josephine Bell McDonald, Deborah McDonald Spriggs

~

McBride, Charles Columbus
LOCATION: Mill Springs Battlefield Cemetery, Zollicoffer Park
RANK: Private **COMPANY:** A **REGIMENT:** 25th Tennessee Infantry **BIRTH:** c. 1841, White County, Tennessee
DEATH: 19 January 1862, Somerset, Kentucky
UDC MEMBER: Carolyn Rollins Carr

~

Unknown Burial Location

Johnson, John
LOCATION: Unknown, Battlefield, Petersburg, Virginia
RANK: Private **COMPANY:** K **REGIMENT:** 25th Tennessee Infantry **BIRTH:** c. 1843, Tennessee **DEATH:** 31 December 1862, Murfreesboro, Tennessee **OTHER:** Private Johnson was killed in the Battle of Petersburg in Virginia
UDC MEMBER: Margaret Haston Cordell

~

Unknown Burial Location

Johnson, Solomon
LOCATION: Unknown, Battlefield, Murfreesboro, Tennessee
RANK: Sergeant **COMPANY:** K **REGIMENT:** 25th Tennessee Infantry **BIRTH:** c. 1841, White County, Tennessee
DEATH: 31 December 1862, Murfreesboro, Tennessee
UDC MEMBER: Margaret Haston Cordell

~

Townsend, James Barnett
LOCATION: McNeill-Townsend Family Cemetery, China Grove, Pike County, Alabama **RANK:** Private **COMPANY:** K
REGIMENT: 2nd Alabama Cavalry **BIRTH:** 22 May 1835, Montgomery County, Alabama **DEATH:** 29 February 1904
MARRIED: Susan Frances **UDC MEMBER:** Elizabeth Tyson Gentry

Hurlbert, Francis "Frank" Telesford

LOCATION: Eubanks Cemetery, Jacksonville, Duval County, Florida
RANK: Private **COMPANY:** F **REGIMENT:** 3rd Florida Infantry
BIRTH: 05 January 1847 **DEATH:** 30 September 1923, Jacksonville, Florida **MARRIED:** Lillie Deborah Eubanks, 22 October 1890 (Florida) **UDC MEMBERS:** Aurelia Hurlbert Hannon and Alice Jean Harr

Francis "Frank" Telesford Hurlbert

Francis Telesford Hurlbert was the father of Aurelia Hannon, who was a charter member of Capt. Sally Tompkins #2123 and our only member to be the Real Daughter of a Confederate soldier. She was active in the chapter, having perfect attendance until the last year of her life and died at age 94. Her last chapter office was as Vice President, where she was in charge of the scholarship programs. Aurelia helped the chapter establish a scholarship at Tennessee Tech University in her honor and was involved in the first presentation. The story of her father's service was one of the sketches chosen to be included in the book, "Papa Was A Boy In Gray" by Mary W. Schaller, published in 2001. Aurelia said, "Captured at the Battle of Bentonville, he was wounded in one knee. As he was being carried to the hospital on a litter a Union officer stopped them and said he wanted to speak to the prisoner. The officer said, 'This is General William T. Sherman. I want to know how many men were in your unit.' Frank kept saying he didn't know and the General kept pushing him so he finally gave him a number, for which Sherman cursed him and called him a liar." Aurelia was buried in the Eubank Family cemetery in Jacksonville, Florida, near her parents and grandparents, including William N. Eubanks, her grandfather, who was also a Confederate soldier.

~

Eubanks, William N.

LOCATION: Eubanks Cemetery, Jacksonville, Florida
RANK: Private **COMPANY:** B **REGIMENT:** 2nd Florida Cavalry **BIRTH:** 08 March 1828 **DEATH:** 31 March 1902 **MARRIED:** Eliza L. Walker
UDC MEMBERS: Aurelia Hurlbert Hannon, Alice Jean Harr

Marker Photo Not Available

Hall, Zachariah
LOCATION: Oak Park Cemetery, Science Hill, Pulaski County, Kentucky **RANK:** Private **COMPANY:** G **REGIMENT:** 32nd Kentucky Infantry **BIRTH:** 12 January 1837, Kentucky **DEATH:** 29 March 1914 **MARRIED:** Nancy Hinds, 29 October 1856, Somerset, Kentucky **UDC MEMBER:** Norma Hall Hay

Barnes, James M.
LOCATION: Mt. Olivet Cemetery, Nashville, Davidson County, Tennessee **RANK:** Captain **COMPANY:** H **REGIMENT:** 13th (Gore's) Tennessee Cavalry **BIRTH:** 24 March 1830, White County, Tennessee **DEATH:** 02 September 1886, Nashville, Tennessee **MARRIED:** Sallie Jane Buck, 03 January 1861, Nashville, Tennessee **UDC MEMBERS:** Donna Randolph Hamilton and Kristie Hamilton Welch

James M. Barnes

Unknown Burial Location

Barnes, Riley
LOCATION: Unknown, Madison County, Arizona **RANK:** Private **COMPANY:** A **REGIMENT:** 1st Battalion 1st Indian Brigade **BIRTH:** 25 November 1822, White County, Tennessee **DEATH:** 11 November 19--, Madison County, Arkansas **MARRIED:** Elizabeth Jane Holland, c. 1866 (Arkansas) **UDC MEMBERS:** Donna Randolph Hamilton, Kristie Hamilton Welch

Riley Barnes

Poteet, Samuel

LOCATION: Unknown, probably buried on battlefield in Huntersville, West Virginia **RANK:** Private **COMPANY:** F **REGIMENT:** 8th Tennessee Infantry **BIRTH:** c. 1829, North Carolina **DEATH:** 25 August, 1861, Huntersville, West Virginia **OTHER:** Killed in battle at Huntersville, West Virginia **MARRIED:** Mary "Polly", c. 1846 (Tennessee) **UDC MEMBERS:** Donna Jo Randolph Hamilton, Kristie Gwen Hamilton Welch

Unknown Burial Location

Smith, John Dillard

LOCATION: Florence City Cemetery, Florence City Cemetery, Lauderdale County, Alabama **RANK:** 2nd Lieutenant **COMPANY:** K **REGIMENT:** 8th (Dibrell's) Tennessee Cavalry **BIRTH:** c. 1838, Jackson County, Tennessee **DEATH:** 05 April 1863, Florence, Alabama **MARRIED:** Margaret Swearingen, 14 September 1858, Jackson County, Tennessee **PENSION:** #W43 **UDC MEMBER:** Margaret Ann Lee Markum **OTHER:** Lieutenant Smith died of Typhoid Fever and is buried in an unmarked grave in the Florence City Cemetery in Alabama.

Unmarked Grave

Hearn, Warren F.

LOCATION: Oak Woods Cemetery, Chicago, Cook County, Illinois **RANK:** Private **COMPANY:** G **REGIMENT:** 17th Alabama Infantry **BIRTH:** 27 April 1840, Lauderdale County, Mississippi **DEATH:** 08 March 1865, Chicago, Cook County, Illinois **MARRIED:** Jane Nichols, 19 November, 1857, Marengo County, Alabama **UDC MEMBER:** Bettye Keese Parrish

Garrett, Benjamin S.

LOCATION: Unknown, Richmond, Virginia **RANK:** Private **COMPANY:** K **REGIMENT:** 29th Georgia Infantry **BIRTH:** c. 1835, Telfair County, Georgia **DEATH:** 09 November 1861, Richmond, Virginia **OTHER:** Died at Chimborazo Military Hospital in Richmond, the same day and place as his brother, William **UDC MEMBER:** Barbara Buchanan Parsons

Unknown Burial Location

Garrett, William

LOCATION: Unknown, Richmond, Virginia **RANK:** Private **COMPANY:** I **REGIMENT:** 17th Georgia Infantry **BIRTH:** c. 1835, Telfair County, Georgia **DEATH:** 09 November 1861 **OTHER:** Died at Chimborazo Hospital, Richmond, Virginia, the same day and place as his brother, Benjamin. **UDC MEMBER:** Barbara Buchanan Parsons

Goodman, James F.

LOCATION: Sparks Cemetery, Sparks, Georgia **BIRTH:** 13 May 1821, Wilkinson County, Georgia **DEATH:** 28 April 1905, Sparks, Georgia **MARRIED:** Lemanda Deans, 14 October 1849, Wilkinson County, Georgia **OTHER:** Judge Goodman was the first County School Commissioner of Berrien County, Georgia, and held that position for twenty-one years. He was a member of the Duncan Lodge #234 F & A M in Nashville, Georgia and held offices in the lodge for twenty-seven years. He was a member of the Nashville Baptist church. Throughout the War (1861–1868), and some years after the end of the War, he served as a Justice of the Inferior Court in Berrien County, Georgia. He also served as Justice of the Peace, 1157th district, 1873–1877. **UDC MEMBER:** Barbara Buchanan Parsons

Goodman, Robert H.

LOCATION: Unknown, Probably on battlefield, Atlanta, Georgia **RANK:** Private **COMPANY:** G **REGIMENT:** 29th Georgia Infantry **BIRTH:** c. 1831, Wilkinson County, Georgia **DEATH:** 22 July 1864, near Atlanta, Georgia **MARRIED:** Nancy Dean, 27 November 1849, Wilkinson County, Georgia **UDC MEMBER:** Barbara Buchanan Parsons

Harris, George W.

LOCATION: Old Union Baptist Church Cemetery (Burnt Cemetery), Lakeland, Georgia **RANK:** Private **COMPANY:** I **REGIMENT:** 4th (Clinch's) Georgia Cavalry **BIRTH:** c. 1821, Appling County, Georgia **DEATH:** c. 1894, Echols County, Georgia **MARRIED:** Julia Ann Westberry, c. 1841, Georgia - 10 children **UDC MEMBER:** Barbara Buchanan Parsons

Harris, James

LOCATION: Fellowship Baptist Church Cemetery, Cook County, Georgia
RANK: Private **COMPANY:** I
REGIMENT: 4th (Clinch's) Georgia Cavalry
BIRTH: 16 February 1844, Erwin County, Georgia
DEATH: 12 December 1928, Cook County, Georgia
MARRIED: Mary Alice Stone, c. 1865 - 8 children
UDC MEMBER: Barbara Buchanan Parsons

James Harris

Marker Photo Not Available

Harris, John W.

LOCATION: Harris Cemetery, 5 miles south of Odom, Georgia
BIRTH: 23 October 1816, Appling County, Georgia
DEATH: 25 March 1875, Odom, Georgia **MARRIED:** Martha Carter, c. 1839, Georgia **UDC MEMBER:** Barbara Buchanan Parsons **OTHER:** Justice of the Peace, 583rd District, Georgia 1859–1869

Marker Photo Not Available

Powell, John W.

LOCATION: Fender Cemetery **RANK:** Private / Sergeant
COMPANY: G / E **REGIMENT:** 29th Georgia Volunteer Infantry / 1st Battalion Georgia Infantry **BIRTH:** 12 November 1839, Jones County, Georgia **DEATH:** 18 April 1918, Lanier County, Georgia **MARRIED:** Matilda Sirmans, 08 April 1865, Clinch County, Georgia **UDC MEMBER:** Barbara Buchanan Parsons

John W. Powell in buggy with his wife, Matilda Sirmans

Powell, William C.

LOCATION: Fine Oak Cemetery, Lanier County, Georgia
RANK: Private **COMPANY:** G **REGIMENT:** 29th Georgia Infantry
BIRTH: 1840, Jones County, Georgia **DEATH:** 19 February 1906, Lanier County, Georgia **MARRIED:** Catherine Guthrie, June 1868, Berrien County, Georgia **UDC MEMBER:** Barbara Buchanan Parsons

Marker Photo Not Available

Sirmans, Benjamin

LOCATION: Fender Cemetery **BIRTH:** 06 February 1792, Effingham County, Georgia **DEATH:** 01 May 1863, Clinch County, Georgia **MARRIED:** Martha Johnson (daughter of David Johnson), July 1814, Emanuel County, Georgia - 11 children **PARENTS:** Josiah and Harty Sirmans (daughter of Thomas Hardeman (Hardyman)) **OTHER:** Benjamin Sirmans served as a Georgia State Representative from Lowndes County, State Senator from Clinch County, a Whig. He was a delegate to the State Whig Convention from Lowndes County. He was one of five commissioners to layout and organize Clinch County. He was one of two delegates from Clinch County to the State Secession Convention in January 1861. Sirmans was originally opposed to secession, but voted for it following the 1860 presidential election and the events following. **UDC MEMBER:** Barbara Buchanan Parsons

Sirmons, Harris

LOCATION: Unknown **RANK:** Private **COMPANY:** H **REGIMENT:** 4th (Clinch's) Georgia Cavalry **BIRTH:** c. 1847, Clinch County, Georgia **DEATH:** Unknown **MARRIED:** Lavina Johnson, c. 1869 **UDC MEMBER RELATIVE:** Barbara Buchanan Parsons

Sirmons, John J.

LOCATION: Unknown, Probably buried on battlefield—Battle of Cold Harbor, Virginia **RANK:** 1st Lieutenant **COMPANY:** G **REGIMENT:** 50th Georgia Infantry **BIRTH:** c. 1835, Lowndes County, Georgia **DEATH:** 03 June 1864, Cold Harbor, Virginia **MARRIED:** Catherine Amanda McLean, 1858, Clinch County, Georgia **UDC MEMBER:** Barbara Buchanan Parsons

Smith, James Madison

LOCATION: Unknown **RANK:** Private **COMPANY:** D **REGIMENT:** 26th Georgia Cavalry **BIRTH:** c. 1830, Ware County, Georgia **DEATH:** Unknown **MARRIED:** Winnifred Moore, c. 1855 **UDC MEMBER:** Barbara Buchanan Parsons

Smith, Jesse

LOCATION: Unknown, Clinch County, Georgia **RANK:** Private
COMPANY: I **REGIMENT:** 4th (Clinch's) Georgia Cavalry
BIRTH: 25 August 1820, Appling County, Georgia
DEATH: 1884, Clinch County, Georgia **MARRIED:** Nancy Tomlinson, 1842, Ware County, Georgia
UDC MEMBER: Barbara Buchanan Parsons

Unknown Burial Location

Stephens, George W.

LOCATION: Fellowship Missionary Baptist Church Cemetery, Outside Cecil, Georgia
RANK: Private **COMPANY:** I **REGIMENT:** 50th Georgia Infantry **BIRTH:** 08 January 1833, Cook County, Georgia **DEATH:** 20 February 1909, Cook County, Georgia **MARRIED:** Sophia Garrett, c. 1855, Telfair County, Georgia **OTHER:** A prisoner at Point Lookout, Maryland and Ft. Delaware. Captured at Gettysburg, Pennsylvania on 03 July 1863, exchanged 18 Feb. 1865. Received a bayonet wound in the foot during the battle.
UDC MEMBERS: Barbara Buchanan Parsons, Hope Parsons Schubert

Confederate Veterans - Hahira, Georgia - January 1, 1908			
Name	Birth	Name	Birth
1. W. A. Ham	2/3/1846	35. M. R. Lightsey	2/8/1843
2. J. W. Rouce	8/12/1843	36. A. Wethington	3/15/1842
3. H. C. Lang	7/13/1839	37. H. M. Zeigler	6/15/1844
4. E. J. Williams	10/21/1842	38. Blu Sirmans	11/15/1839
5. J. A. Mobley	6/29/1839	39. J. A. Lawson	7/10/1836
6. M. M. Howard	12/19/1848	40. J. J. Parrish	9/11/1834
7. J. H. Tilman	1842	41. R. W. Roan	6/18/1846
8. Hardy Christian	8/31/1838	42. A. T. Tadlock	3/27/1835
9. Jno. L. Right	12/20/1844	43. R. W. Starling	5/3/1831
10. J. P. Powers	1840	44. W. M. Lawson	9/7/1834
11. M. C. Futch	8/20/1835	45. W. E. Stephens	12/15/1849
12. C. H. Shaw	6/8/1842	46. H. W. Powell	3/3/1847
13. S. B. Dampier	11/18/1835	47. J. F. Barfield	7/7/1838
14. T. A. Judge	11/22/1843	48. W. W. Rutherford	10/18/1825
15. J. W. Taylor	10/25/1833	49. J. J. Hutchinson	10/1/1843
16. B. J. Sirmans	2/24/1847	50. G. C. Hodges	10/13/1846
17. S. W. Register	8/5/1939	51. T. E. Swilley	9/22/????
18. A. Cowart	12/29/1843	52. J. I. Martin	9/21/1844
19. J. T. Courson	3/22/1848	53. E. J. Shanks	3/2/1840
20. J. M. Patterson	5/27/1840	54. H. L. Smith	12/28/1841
21. Elbert Mathis	10/4/1836	55. G. W. Stephens	1/8/1833
22. M. A. Tolar	12/8/1832	56. T. A. Roberts	7/6/1844
23. J. H. King	11/3/1839	57. T. L. Wiseman	6/4/1838
24. G. W. Robinson	5/1/1833	58. W. W. Wilkerson	6/10/1830
25. W. M. Watson	1840	59. H. B. Lawson	8/15/1844
26. Jessie Moore	6/12/1839	60. I. J. Weldon	8/28/1844
27. N. J. Money	3/28/1845	61. H. M. Cannon	7/12/1846
28. A. Dixon	5/10/1847	62. L. F. Lawson	1/29/1844
29. W. J. Lamb	4/20/1837	63. G. W. Coppage	3/29/1835
30. Troy Thomas	1/11/1833	64. Jno. A. Folsome	7/14/1834
31. W. W. Joyce	5/3/1832	65. Dave Clanton	5/10/1846
32. W. H. Green	4/13/1834	66. J. M. Hall	1/8/1849
33. W. H. Dent	10/12/1844	67. S. L. Hill	8/13/1837
34. James W. Parrish	3/2/1847	72. L. W. Mobley	3/4/1842

Stone, David

LOCATION: Unknown, Homerville, Georgia **RANK:** Private
COMPANY: Not listed **REGIMENT:** 4th (Clinch's) Georgia Cavalry **BIRTH:** c. 1838, Georgia **DEATH:** c. 1899
MARRIED: Elizabeth Harris, c. 1865
UDC MEMBER: Barbara Buchanan Parsons

Unknown Burial Location

Stone, John Raines

LOCATION: Flat Creek Missionary Baptist Church Cemetery, Berrien County, Georgia **RANK:** Private **COMPANY:** K **REGIMENT:** 26th Georgia Volunteers Infantry **BIRTH:** 04 July 1837, Clinch County, Georgia **DEATH:** 19 March 1916, Berrien County, Georgia **MARRIED:** (1) Mary Ann Harris, c. 1865 - 7 children; (2) Dicy Ruth Woodard - 3 children **UDC MEMBER:** Barbara Buchanan Parsons

Westberry, Ferman

LOCATION: Unknown **RANK:** Private **COMPANY:** E **REGIMENT:** 4th (Clinch's) Georgia Cavalry **BIRTH:** c. 1826, Liberty County, Georgia **DEATH:** Unknown **MARRIED:** Lucy Harris, c. 1844 (Georgia) - 12 children **UDC MEMBER:** Barbara Buchanan Parsons

Westberry, Rabon

LOCATION: Unknown **RANK:** Private **COMPANY:** Not listed **REGIMENT:** 47th Georgia Infantry **BIRTH:** c. 1821, Appling County, Georgia **DEATH:** Unknown **MARRIED:** (1) Saleta Ann "Leacy" Strickland, c. 1840 (Georgia) - 12 children; (2) Caroline Strickland - 1 child **UDC MEMBER:** Barbara Buchanan Parsons

McElhaney, Columbus L.

LOCATION: Cleburne Memorial Cemetery, Block 47, Lot 12, Space 12, Cleburne, Texas **RANK:** Private **COMPANY:** A **REGIMENT:** 45th Tennessee Infantry **BIRTH:** 09 July 1844, Marshall County, Tennessee **DEATH:** 28 June 1925, Gordon, Palo Pinto County, Texas **MARRIED:** Nancy MacLin McCory, 27 July 1868, Marshall County, Tennessee **UDC MEMBER:** Janet McElhaney Randolph

Maberry, George

LOCATION: Unknown, Battlefield, Reseca, Georgia **RANK:** Private **COMPANY:** K **REGIMENT:** 28th (Consolidated) Tennessee Infantry **BIRTH:** 17 May 1836, Tennessee **DEATH:** Unknown. Killed in battle at Reseca, Georgia. **UDC MEMBER:** Shirley Maberry Rodgers

Powell, Clark, Sr.

LOCATION: Lot Cemetery, Marion County, Mississippi
RANK: Private **COMPANY:** B/D **REGIMENT:** 17th Battalion, Mississippi Cavalry **BIRTH:** 15 April 1845, Mississippi
DEATH: 25 July 1888, Marion County, Mississippi **MARRIED:** Rose Anna Pittman, 03 December 1868, Marion County, Mississippi **UDC MEMBER:** Deborah Gay Powell Ward

~

Allen, Edwin

LOCATION: Lydia McNabb Family Cemetery, on land owned by Col. M. M. Bullard of Newport, Rural Cosby, Cocke County, Tennessee **RANK:** Captain
COMPANY: C **REGIMENT:** 26th Tennessee Infantry **BIRTH:** 09 October 1818, Cocke County, Tennessee **DEATH:** 31 December 1862, Murfreesboro, Rutherford County, Tennessee **MARRIED:** Lydia Vinson, 10 August 1842, Cosby Cocke County, Tennessee **OTHER:** Captain Allen was killed in action at the battle of Murfreesboro when making the charge across the "Cedar thicket" near Stone's River. Captain Allen was hastily buried near the battlefield. His grave has never been located, though several attempts have been made. A memorial marker stands in the Lydia McNabb Cemetery in Cocke County, Tennessee, for Captain Allen and his son, Lewis Allen. The inscription reads "Fell at Murfreesboro, Tenn., in defense of the South."
UDC MEMBER: Pamela Mikulski Wood

Letter written to Lydia Allen from her husband, Captain Edwin Allen

Camp near Bowling Green, Kentucky
December 31st, 1861

My Dear wife it is now the last hour of the last day of 1861 I am acting officer of the day have just been the guard rounds of Sentinels on post and returned to my Shanty and found the water bucket dry and our cook being gone over to town to take a little new year it became necessary for me to go down the steep bluffy banks of Barren river for water and if Jim Rice had not Piloted me down and back I am not certain I should have made the trip but I am up with my water the rest of my mess is in bed and I am before my little fire and candle with my camp stool across my knees for a writing desk many soldiers are concentrating at this point and much has been said of late about an expected fight withe [sic] the forces at Green River and McCook but to all appearance the right is nearer than it was two months ago   still however it may come off almost any day for if we are ordered to advance it will not take long to reach them and if they advance on us they have only forty five miles to travel and in fact our advance port and theirs are almost together and our pickets and theirs have already had some Skirmmishing and a few killed on boath [sic] sides. Captain James M. Bottles of Washington County, Tenn will start home in the morning   I tried to get a furlough for Lewis to go along and fetch you hear [sic] to me but it failed   Cat Bottles has a sevier [sic] rising on his right arm or he would not get to go   he is going to bring his wife here and also Lieut. Gaba's wife   now your only chance to come here is to meet him at Morristown on the 16th sixteenth of January and if any thing occurs that he is about to fail at that day he will notify you and set a new day by letter from Washington county   Spring to eat what little clover I have on hand and be sure to sell all the poor calvs [sic] on the place and ask Thos McNabb in particular to watch my upland field and not allow sheep to spoil it   tell Tom. & Nanc howdy for me   I think of them often till [sic] Bro. John the same and that I was shocked and mortified almost perhaps as much as himself whin [sic] I heard of Hendersons Death and that I have taken the strictest care of Wilson in his sickness and have the Satisfaction to know him almost entirely out of danger   Several others of my company are complaining some, I think none verry [sic] serious except perhaps Hiram Rains and Edward Kenyon   Chamberlain Mantooth has had a long and sevier [sic] spell is not a little on the mend   it makes my heart bleed when one of my boys dies, although at times for dicipline [sic] sake I am obliged to speak harshly to them yet I love them all, tell all the kin howdy and that I hope at least to be permitted to see them again

Well I believe I have not much more to write   this leaves Lewis and myself boath [sic] well and I hope it may reach you at least well enough to come see us.   we cant [sic] come to you now without disgracing ourself which we would die sooner than do. Show this letter to any of our friends who may have a desire to see it and if you see any of my brother Soldiers who is defending my home whills [sic] I am on the frontiers bid them god speed in the name of our comon [sic] glorious country that we are all willing to die for in necessary to maintain its rites [sic]   the camps are now still as death   I have had other dutys [sic] & business to transact   until it is now 3. o clock on new years morning January the 1st 1862 and I must finish my letter and take a little repose.

Yours Edwin Allen

Allen, Isaac

LOCATION: "Pikey" John Allen Cemetery, Rural Cosby, Cocke County, Tennessee **BIRTH:** 04 June 1817, Cocke County, Tennessee **DEATH:** 16 July 1895, Rural Cosby, Cocke County, Tennessee **MARRIED:** Mary Weaver, Cocke County, Tennessee **OTHER:** Provided Material Aid to the South
UDC MEMBER: Pamela Mikulski Wood

Allen, John J.

LOCATION: Lillard Family Cemetery, Rural Cosby, Cocke County, Tennessee **RANK:** Private **COMPANY:** C **REGIMENT:** 26th Tennessee Infantry **BIRTH:** 23 November 1828, Cosby, Cocke County, Tennessee **DEATH:** 23 November 1909, Cosby, Cocke County, Tennessee **MARRIED:** Elizabeth Wood, Cocke County, Tennessee **UDC MEMBER:** Pamela Mikulski Wood

~

Large, Robert

LOCATION: Holders Grove Methodist Church Cemetery, Cocke County, Tennessee **BIRTH:** 21 February 1811, Sevier County, Tennessee **DEATH:** 02 January 1880, Cocke County, Tennessee **MARRIED:** Virginia Jane McMahan, c. 1831, Sevier County, Tennessee **OTHER:** Provided Material Aid to the South **UDC MEMBER:** Pamela Mikulski Wood

~

Lillard, Calvin A.

LOCATION: Lillard Family Cemetery, Rural Cosby, Cocke County, Tennessee **RANK:** Private **COMPANY:** C **REGIMENT:** 26th Tennessee Infantry **BIRTH:** 28 February 1845, Cosby Creek, Cocke County, Tennessee **DEATH:** 30 March 1900, Cosby, Cocke County, Tennessee **MARRIED:** Letitcia "Neppie" Seal, December 1869, Tennessee **UDC MEMBER:** Pamela Mikulski Wood

~

Lillard, John

LOCATION: Lillard Family Cemetery, Rural Cosby, Cocke County, Tennessee **BIRTH:** 20 August 1819, Cosby Creek, Cocke County, Tennessee **DEATH:** 08 May 1875, Cosby Creek, Cocke County, Tennessee **MARRIED:** Nancy Allen (Cosby), Cocke County, Tennessee **OTHER:** Provided Material Aid to the South **UDC MEMBER:** Pamela Mikulski Wood

Lillard, Russell

LOCATION: Chattanooga Confederate Cemetery, Chattanooga, Hamilton County, Tennessee **RANK:** Private **COMPANY:** C **REGIMENT:** 26th Tennessee Infantry **BIRTH:** c. 1829, Cosby, Cocke County, Tennessee **DEATH:** 13 March 1863, Chattanooga, Hamilton County, Tennessee **MARRIED:** Elizabeth Clevenger, Cocke County, Tennessee **OTHER:** Plaque in cemetery states these were Confederate soldiers who died of wounds received at the battle of Murfreesboro near Stone's River. Actual burial location in the cemetery is unknown. **UDC MEMBER:** Pamela Mikulski Wood

Lillard, William

LOCATION: Chattanooga Confederate Cemetery, Chattanooga, Hamilton County, Tennessee **RANK:** Private **COMPANY:** C **REGIMENT:** 26th Tennessee Infantry **BIRTH:** c. 1824, Cosby, Cocke County, Tennessee **DEATH:** 08 April 1863, Chattanooga, Hamilton County, Tennessee **MARRIED:** Nancy Clevenger,, c. 1856, Cocke County, Tennessee **OTHER:** Plaque in cemetery states these were Confederate soldiers who died of wounds received at battle of Murfreesboro, near Stone's River. Mass grave of Confederate soldiers located near plaque. Actual burial location in cemetery unknown. **UDC MEMBER:** Pamela Mikulski Wood

Unmarked Grave

Lowry, Edward

LOCATION: Unknown, Thoroughfare Gap, Virginia **RANK:** Private **COMPANY:** F **REGIMENT:** 21st North Carolina Infantry **BIRTH:** 06 August 1846, Stokes County, North Carolina **DEATH:** 06 September 1861, Thoroughfare Gap, Virginia **MARRIED:** Mariah Clouse, 31 October 1850, Surry County, North Carolina **OTHER:** Died in camp of Typhoid Fever **UDC MEMBER:** Pamela Mikulski Wood

Edward Lowry

Lowry, Thomas J.

LOCATION: Old Methodist Church Cemetery, Mt. Airy, Surry County, North Carolina (Off South Main Street)
BIRTH: 18 December 1818, Surry/Stokes County, North Carolina **DEATH:** 08 February 1881, Mt. Airy, Surry County, North Carolina **MARRIED:** Mary Midkiff, 07 January 1840, North Carolina **OTHER:** Provided Material Aid to the South; Blacksmith **UDC MEMBER:** Pamela Mikulski Wood

Lowry, William H.

LOCATION: Unknown, Near Vicksburg, Mississippi
RANK: Private **COMPANY:** D **REGIMENT:** 62nd Mounted Tennessee Infantry **BIRTH:** c. 1842, Surry County, North Carolina **DEATH:** 09 February 1863, Vicksburg, Mississippi **OTHER:** Probably not buried in a cemetery; Participated in the Battle of Chickasaw Bayou and Chickasaw Bluffs; Died shortly afterwards, possibly from wounds received in battle **UDC MEMBER:** Pamela Mikulski Wood

Unmarked Grave

THE IMMORTAL 600

The Immortal 600 Medal

Produced c. 1900 for surviving members of the Immortal 600

Bar

1861–65 SURVIVOR OF IMMORTAL 600

Second Bar

CONFEDERATE PRISONERS OF WAR

Circular

1864–65

42 DAYS UNDER FIRE

ON MORRIS ISLAND, S.C.

65 DAYS ON

ROTTEN CORN MEAL

AND PICKLE RATIONS

HILTON HEAD AND

FT. PULASKI

ON PRISON SHIP

CRESCENT

18 DAYS

1920 Reunion of the 8th Tennessee Cavalry (photo courtesy of Sons of Confederate Veterans)

Note that this soldier at the White County, Tennessee 1920 Reunion is wearing both his Confederate military cross and the badge of the Immortal 600.

The Immortal 600
A Short History

When the Federal government learned of the deprivation of Union prisoners at Andersonville prison, they determined that some kind of retribution should be taken on the Confederate prisoners. No consideration was given to the fact that Federal government itself had caused the problems at Andersonville by refusing to continue prisoner exchanges. The Union prisoners at Andersonville began to overrun the facility. It was unable to care for such numbers of people.

The civilians in the South were themselves suffering from lack of food, clothing, and any medical facilities. The local people as well as the prison guards and staff at Andersonville were not faring much better than the Union prisoners. In Northern prisons Confederate captives were already being denied food, clothing, blankets, and medicine although all of those items were readily available to the general population in the North. At Rock Island Union Prison the local people tried to provide the Confederate prisoners food and blankets when they were freezing to death, but they were turned away by the prison authorities.

Six hundred Confederate officer-prisoners at Fort Delaware Union prison were chosen to be transferred to Hilton Head, South Carolina, which was occupied by the Union. In August, 1864, these men began their journey to be placed in an open one and a half acre pen under Federal guns. They travelled on the paddlewheel ship, "Crescent City," packed like sardines, and kept there until the stockade was completed. The Union forces hoped that the Confederates would be killed as their troops fired upon Morris Island, at the mouth of the Charleston Harbor. Under the protection of God, none of the prisoners were killed by Confederate shelling, and all cannon balls landing near them were duds.

After 45 days in the open, under fire of their own comrades' guns, the weakened prisoners were moved to Fort Pulaski, Georgia. They were crowded into damp cells at the Fort. Thirteen men died at this facility. To relieve overcrowding, 197 men were shipped back to Hilton Head. For 42 days the prisoners were fed "retaliation rations" consisting of 10 ounces of moldy cornmeal ground in 1861, and soured onion pickles as their only meals. Five men who had been shipped back to Hilton Head died at that facility.

The remaining survivors were returned to Fort Delaware in March 1865, where an additional 25 Confederate prisoners died and were buried on the Jersey Shore. The men were so emaciated from their ordeal that the Federal authorities kept them several weeks after the end of the war to get them recovered enough to begin their long trips to their homes. Six men with ties to Tennessee died and are buried on the Jersey Shore, one died at Morris Island, one at Charleston Harbor, and one at Fort Pulaski.

The Immortal 600 became famous throughout the South for their adherence to principle, all but eighteen of them refusing to take the "Nasty Oath" under such adverse conditions.

Joseph Hastings, Civil War Captain, was used as a human shield by the Yankees. Buried at New Hope, Capt. Hastings is #12 on this photo of the Immortal 600. (1) J. Ogden Murray, (2, 3, 4) Unknown; (5) J. L. Hempstead; (6) B. D. Merchant; (7) Henry Howe Cook; (8) Erasmas Lee Bell; (9) Robertson Cruseo Bryan (10) unknown (11) George Knox Cracraft (12) Joseph Hastings (13) Capt. D. C. Cuapos (14) R. H. Miller (15) William Epps (16) Z. H. Loudermilk (17) Capt. W. J. Matthews (18) Maj. Lamar Fontaine (19) Capt. Jacob Fickerson (20) Rev. George Eaves. Cook, Bryan and Hastings all have Tennessee ties to the Immortal 600. (photo from Confederate Veteran magazine)

The Finns Point Confederate monument of Pea Patch in New Jersey was erected by the U.S. Government in 1910. It is an 85-foot tall obelisk of concrete and granite. Around the base of the monument the plaque's display the names of 2,436 Confederates who died at Fort Delaware during the War. There were six of the Immortal 600 with ties to Tennessee who died at Fort Delaware. Photos of their names from the monument are included in this book.

Men of the Immortal 600 with ties to Tennessee

Born in Tennessee, enlisted in Tennessee, or buried in Tennessee

States noted (KY, VA, AR, AL) when listed in another state

RANK	NAME	COUNTY/STATE	DISPOSITION AFTER WAR
2LT	ADAMS, William H.	Tipton County, TN	lived in Tipton Co., TN
2LT	ALBRIGHT, George Nicholas	North Carolina	d. 1918 Stanton, Haywood Co., TN
2LT	ALDERSON, Willam H.	Maury Co., TN	Buried on Jersey Shore
2LT	ALLEN, William Edwin	Cocke Co., TN	d. 17 July 19098, Bristol, TN
2LT	ARNOLD, Bonaparte	White Co., TN	Arnold Cemetery Shady Grove White Co., TN
2LT	ARRANTS, John Granville Sharp	Sullivan Co., TN	Bu. Fresno, CA
CPT	AUSTIN, John B.	(KY) Danielsville	Dickson Co., TN
1LT	BAXTER, John B.	(AR) Wilson Co., TN	Brinkley, AR
1LT	BENSON, Peru Hardy	(AR) Elkton, Giles Co., TN	Citizens Cemetery Clerendon, Donley Co., TX
1LT	BODDIE, Elijah	Gallatin, Sumner Co., TN	Buried on Jersey Shore
CPT	BOYD, James W.	Jackson, Madison Co., TN	Went to Washington, D.C.
2LT	BRADLEY, Thomas Edward	Dixon Springs, Smith Co., TN	Gallatin Cemetery, Sumner Co., TN
2LT	BRYAN, Robertson Crusoe	Virginia	Bu. East Hill Cemetery, Bristol, VA/TN
CPT	BURKE, John H.	Tazewell, Claiborne Co., TN	Clairborne Co., TN
2LT	BURNETT, John Anderson	(VA) Union Depot, Sullivan Co., TN	Pleasant Grove Cem., Sullivan Co., TN

300 · Our Confederate Ancestors · The Immortal 600

Rank	Name	Origin	Fate/Burial
1LT	CALLAHAN, William P.	Lawrenceburg, Lawrence Co., TN	Died at Morris Island
2LT	CAMERON, William Newton	Sparta, White Co., TN	Coleman Cem., Coleman, TX
CPT	CAMPBELL, Gilbert R.	Summitville, Coffee Co., TN	Manchester, Coffee Co., TN
2LT	CAMPBELL, Watson C.	Double Springs Putnam Co., TN	National Cemetery, Beaufort, SC
CPT	CARSON, Leroy P.	McMinnville, Warren Co., TN	Buried Jersey Shore
1LT	CASH, James M.	Livingston Overton Co., TN	Charleston Harbor Paroled
CPT	CHISHOLM, John N.	(AL) Nashville	Buried on Jersey Shore
CPT	COFFEE, Holland T.	Mississippi	Resident Columbia, Maruy Co., TN (80)
2LT	COOK, Henry Howe	Franklin, Williamson Co., TN	d. 2 November 1921, Franklin, TN
2LT	COVINGTON, Cameron D.	Lebanon, Wilson Co., TN	Lebanon, TN, 1900
CPT	CRAFT, William Henry	Nashville Davidson Co., TN	d. 6 April 1882, Nashville, TN
LTC	DAUGHTERY, Ferdinand H.	Livingston, Overton Co., TN	Daughterty Street Cemetery, Livingston, TN
1LT	DOUGLASS, Merry A.	Gallatin, Sumner Co, TN	Stayed at Hilton Head, SC (65)
1LT	DUNLAP, Hugh Pendleton	(KY) Paris, Henry Co., TN	d. 26 February 1918, Dover, TN
2LT	EASLEY, William B. W.	Vernon, Hickman Co., TN	Lived there in 1870
2LT	ELLIOTT, Galen R.	KY; Joined in Overton Co., TN	Returned to Clinton Co., KY
2LT	ELZEY, Andrew Jackson	Berlin, Marshall Co., TN	Lauderdale Co., TN 1880
2LT	EVANS, William C.D.	(AR) B. TN Arkansas in 1860	Sprindale, Washington Co., AR 1880
2LT	EWING, Z. Whitefield "Zeke"	Lewisburg, Marshall Co., TN	Maplewood Cemetery, Pulaski, TN
1LT	FLEMING, Henry Clay	Spencer, Van Buren Co., TN	New Pine Creek Cemetery, Oregon
2LT	FULCHER, James T.	Virginia	In Knoxville, Knox Co., TN (80)
COL	FULKERSON, Abram	Join / Rogersville, Hawkins Co., TN	East Hill Cemetery, Bristol, VA (1902)
1LT	GOODLOE, Thomas J.	Estell Springs, Franklin Co., TN	d. 27 February 1865, Ft. Pulaski
1LT	HALLIBURTON, William	(MO) Humphreys, Benton Co., TN	Steeleville, Crawford Co., MO (1900)
2LT	HASTINGS, Joseph H.	Shelbyville, Bedford Co., TN	New Hope Church Cemetery, Bedford Co., TN
2LT	HAYNES, Robert B.	(KY) B. TN; Raised in MS	Res. Denton Co., TX
2LT	HENDERSON, John H.	Sweetwater, Monroe Co., TN	Res. Monroe Co., TN (65)
2LT	HENRY, John M.	Hartsville, Sumner Co., TN	Bransford, Trousdale Co., (1910)
1LT	HIXSON, Madison	(AR) B. Bledsoe Co., TN	May Cemetery Shoal Creek, Logan Co., AR
2LT	HOOBERRY, John W.	Nashville, TN	Nashville, TN, 1870
1LT	HUNTER, Philander D.	Nashville, TN	Gen. Hospital, Richmond, 1865
1LT	HUTCHISON, Charles L.	Knoxville, Knox Co, TN	Hamilton Co., TN (1880)
2LT	IRVINE, Joseph A.	Columbia, Maury Co., TN	Rose Hill Cemetery, Maury Co., TN 1890
2LT	IRWIN, Thomas	Nashville, 1860	Nashville, 1880
CPT	ISRAEL, Abner B.	(AR) B. TN	Walnut Ridge, Lawrence Co., AR
CPT	JAMES, William N.	New Middleton, Smith Co., TN	Farm Cemetery, Hickman, Smith Co., TN
1LT	JENKINS, John D.	Clarksville, Montgomery Co., TN	Teague, Freestone Co., TX (1914)
CPT	JOHNSON, H. L. W.	B. TN / Okolona, TN	Paroled Charleston, SC 1864
CPT	JOHNSON, Samuel Joseph	Cookeville, Putnam Co.	Johnson Family Cemetery, Putnam Co., TN
CPT	JONES, James McG.	(AR) B. TN, Carroll Co., AR	Eureka Springs, Carroll Co., AR (80)
2LT	KING, John Stanton	Virginia	Cole Spring Cemetery, Sullivan Co., TN
1LT	KIRKMAN, Alexander Jackson	(AL) B. AL, D. W., D.C. (?)	Buried Boliver, TN with sister
2LT	KNOX, William C.	Statesville, Wison Co., TN	Buried Jersey Shore
1LT	LAUDERDALE, John F.	Cleveland, Bradley Co., TN	Ford Hill Cemetery, Cleveland, TN
1LT	LEDFORD, Jesse A.	Livingston, Overton Co., TN	Buried on Jersey Shore
2LT	LEWIS, James B.	Tazewell, Clairborne Co., TN	Clairborne Co., TN (1865)
CPT	LYTLE, James K. Polk	Rober, Bedford Co., TN	Bedford Co., TN (1865)
CPT	McCALLUM, James R.	Knoxville, Knox Co., TN	Old Gray Cemetery, Knoxville, TN
1LT	MORGAN, Algernon Sidney	Sparta, White Co., TN	Bethlehem Cemetery, White Co., TN
CPT	NICKS, John H.	Centerville, Hickman Co., TN	d. 11 May 1909, Hickman Co., TN
CAP	PERKINS, Thomas Fear, Jr.	Franklin, Williamson Co., TN	d. 15 January 1898, Williamson Co., TN
CPT	POLK, James H.	Franklin / joined at Columbia, TN	Fort Worth, TX (1923)

This list was compiled using the book "The Biographical Roster of the Immortal 600" by Mauriel Joslyn, 1992.

Unknown Grave

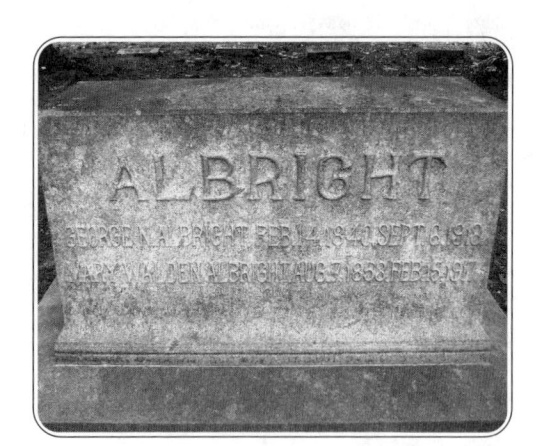

Adams, William H.
CEMETERY: Unknown **LOCATION:** Unknown **RANK:** 2nd Lieutenant **COMPANY:** K **REGIMENT:** 51st Tennessee Infantry **BIRTH:** Unknown **DEATH:** Unknown **OTHER:** Captured at Ringgold, Georgia; After the War, lived in Tipton County, Tennessee

~

Albright, George Nicholas
CEMETERY: Stanton Cemetery **LOCATION:** Haywood County, Stanton, Tennessee Located just off the south side of Covington Road, not far west of the Stanton Methodist Church. **RANK:** 2nd Lieutenant **COMPANY:** F **REGIMENT:** 6th North Carolina Infantry **BIRTH:** 14 February 1840, North Carolina **DEATH:** 06 September 1918 at Stanton, Haywood County, Tennessee **MARRIED:** (1) Barbara E. Thompson; had 5 children: Charlie, James, Stella, Jennie, and Barbara; (2) Mary Walden (b. 07 August 1853, d. 15 February 1917); had 3 sons: W. Baxter (b. 11 December 1879, d. 10 January 1905), Fenton, and George Albright **OTHER:** Captured at Rappahannock Station, Virginia; Prisoner at Johnson's Island; Settled in Fayette County after the War; Moved to Stanton in the 1890s and was a merchant there; Also a lumber dealer and cotton farmer

~

Alderson, William H.
CEMETERY: Buried on Jersey Shore **LOCATION:** Ft. Delaware Union Prison, New Jersey **RANK:** 2nd Lieutenant **COMPANY:** E **REGIMENT:** 2nd Battalion (Biffle's) Tennessee Cavalry / "The Maury County Braves" **BIRTH:** c. 1844, Maury County, Tennessee **DEATH:** 30 March 1865 of erysipelas (bacterial infection of the skin) **OTHER:** Captured at Columbia, Tennessee

~

Allen, William Edwin
CEMETERY: East Hill Cemetery **LOCATION:** State Street, Bristol, Tennessee / Virginia **RANK:** 2nd Lieutenant **COMPANY:** I **REGIMENT:** 60th Tennessee Mounted Infantry **BIRTH:** 27 February 1829, Cocke County, Tennessee **DEATH:** 14 July 1908, Bristol, Tennessee **MARRIED:** Mary Carter Dawson - 8 children **OTHER:** Captured at Big Black, Mississippi; Salesman/grocer

Arnold, Bonaparate

CEMETERY: Arnold Cemetery **LOCATION:** Shady Grove, White County, Tennessee **RANK:** 2nd Lieutenant **COMPANY:** C **REGIMENT:** 28th Tennessee Infantry **BIRTH:** 21 September 1835, White County, Tennessee **DEATH:** 30 March 1918 **MARRIED:** (1) Martha Ann Denton - 2 children; (2) Malissa Camilla Thweatt **OTHER:** Captured at Flint River, Alabama; Farmer

~

Arrants, John Granville Sharp

CEMETERY: West Cemetery **LOCATION:** Selma, Fresno County, California **RANK:** 2nd Lieutenant **COMPANY:** K **REGIMENT:** 3rd (Lillard's) Mounted Infantry **BIRTH:** 09 September 1838, Sullivan County, Tennessee **DEATH:** 23 October 1914 **MARRIED:** (1) Mary Alice Gray - 3 children. (2) Mary A. Freeland **OTHER:** Captured at Petersburg; Merchant; Bank president

West Cemetery entrance

~

Austin, John B.

CEMETERY: Unknown **LOCATION:** Unknown **RANK:** Captain **COMPANY:** F **REGIMENT:** 2nd (Duke's) Kentucky Cavalry **BIRTH:** c. 1822, Tennessee **DEATH:** died after 1880 **MARRIED:** Fredonia - 3 children: James B., Williamson, Samuel D. **OTHER:** Captured at Dickson County, Tennessee; Farmer

Unknown Grave

~

Baxter, John Bell

CEMETERY: Oaklawn Cemetery **LOCATION:** Brinkley, Arkansas **RANK:** 1st Lieutenant **COMPANY:** F **REGIMENT:** 23rd Arkansas Infantry **BIRTH:** 26 May 1839, Wilson County Tennessee **DEATH:** 13 December 1891 **MARRIED:** Josephine Pickens **OTHER:** Surrendered at Port Hudson; merchant; farmer; lawyer; Arkansas State Legislature, 1882-1886; Mayor of Brinkley, Arkansas; a Mason

Benson, Peru Hardy

CEMETERY: Citizens Cemetery **LOCATION:** Clarendon, Donley County, Texas **RANK:** 1st Lieutenant **COMPANY:** I **REGIMENT:** 23rd Arkansas Infantry **BIRTH:** 23 September 1829, Elkton, Giles County, Tennessee **DEATH:** 14 October 1906, Hall County, Texas **MARRIED:** (1) Nancy Delina McCracken - 5 children; (2) Helen R. James **OTHER:** Wounded at Corinth, Mississippi; Surrendered at Port Hudson; a Mason; Farmer.

Boddie, Elijah

CEMETERY: Buried on Jersey Shore **LOCATION:** Ft. Delaware Union Prison, New Jersey **RANK:** 1st Lieutenant **COMPANY:** C **REGIMENT:** 7th Tennessee Infantry **BIRTH:** c. 1843, Sumner County, Tennessee **DEATH:** 18 March 1865 **OTHER:** Captured at Wilderness. Died of acute diarrhea in hospital at Ft. Delaware.

Boyd, James W.

CEMETERY: Unknown **LOCATION:** Unknown **RANK:** Captain **COMPANY:** F **REGIMENT:** 6th Tennessee Infantry **BIRTH:** c. 1822, Kentucky **DEATH:** Unknown **MARRIED:** Caroline - 6 children **OTHER:** Captured in Corinth, Mississippi; 1860 lived in Jackson, Madison County, Tennessee; Took the oath 21 October 1864 at Morris Island, was taken out of the stockade, and sent to Washington, D.C.

Bradley, Thomas Edward

CEMETERY: Gallatin City Cemetery **LOCATION:** Cemetery Street, Gallatin, Sumner County, Tennessee **RANK:** 2nd Lieutenant **COMPANY:** A **REGIMENT:** 23rd (Martin's) Tennessee Infantry **BIRTH:** 08 April 1842, Sumner County, Tennessee **DEATH:** 28 March 1921 **MARRIED:** Mary Rankin **PENSION:** #S12738, Tennessee

Bryan, Robertson Crusoe
CEMETERY: East Hill Cemetery **LOCATION:** Bristol VA / TN
RANK: 2nd Lieutenant **COMPANY:** F **REGIMENT:** "Holston Forester's" 48th Virginia Infantry **BIRTH:** 24 August 1842
DEATH: 11 February 1912 **MARRIED:** Caroline M. Hunter - 3 children **PENSION:** #S12232; #W4744, Tennessee
OTHER: Had Typhoid fever; Captured at Spottsylvania Courthouse, Virginia; Saloon keeper and tobacco factory worker.

~

Burke, John H.
CEMETERY: Unknown **LOCATION:** Unknown **RANK:** Captain
COMPANY: B **REGIMENT:** 2nd (Ashby's) Tennessee Cavalry
BIRTH: c. 1824, Tennessee **DEATH:** Unknown
MARRIED: Eliza **OTHER:** Resident of Tazewell, Claiborne County, Tennessee

Unknown Grave

~

Burnett, John Anderson
CEMETERY: Pleasant Grove **LOCATION:** Pleasant Grove Road, Bluff City, Sullivan County, Tennessee **RANK:** 2nd Lieutenant
COMPANY: E **REGIMENT:** 50th Virginia Infantry
BIRTH: 10 June 1840, Union Depot, Sullivan County, Tennessee
DEATH: 29 August 1920, Bluff City, Tennessee
MARRIED: Ellen R. Miller - 11 children **PENSION:** #S5599, Tennessee
OTHER: Captured at Spottsylvania Courthouse, Virginia; Farmer

~

Callahan, William P.
CEMETERY: On Morris Island, South Carolina
LOCATION: (All) unmarked. Confederate solders were left where they died. Union dead were removed to the National Cemetery.
RANK: 1st Lieutenant **COMPANY:** B **REGIMENT:** 25th Tennessee Cavalry
BIRTH: c. 1832, Tennessee **DEATH:** Died of chronic diarrhea, 27 September 1864, Morris Island, South Carolina
MARRIED: Ellen Jane - 3 children

Unknown Grave

> Saturday, September 24, 1864—*Battery kept up a fire all night. Slept sound notwithstanding. Awoke quite late. Had dreams of home last night. O! if they were only true.*
>
> —Capt. Junius Hempstead, 25th Virginia Infantry

Morris Island, South Carolina

The men had been lucky so far. Under fire for three weeks, none had been killed. Guards had been killed on the parapet, and outside the stockade. Many Union soldiers were wounded and some killed at Batteries Wagner and Gregg. Shells had fallen among the prisoners, sending geysers of sand in the air, raining down on men standing nearby. Strangely enough those of the 600 in the most obvious place for execution had escaped even a scratch from falling shell fragments. They were convinced only Divine Providence had saved them.

Finally death found the first of their number, but it was not from a random shell, or a hasty sentry that First Lieutenant William P. Callahan died. It was from starvation. His death was unfeelingly reported by his captors.

*Letter, Capt. Thomas Appleton,
54th Mass. Inf. to Lt. Colonel W. T. Bennett,
Provost Marshall General,
September 30, 1864*

I have the honor to report the death of 1st Lt. W. P. Callahan, 25th Tennessee Cavalry (Prisoner of War) who died of chronic diarrhea at the Post Field Hospital at Morris Island, S. C., September 27, 1864. He was buried at Morris Island and a head board with his name was placed at the head of his grave.

~

Cameron, William Newton

CEMETERY: Coleman City Cemetery **LOCATION:** Coleman, Texas **RANK:** 2nd Lieutenant **COMPANY:** A **REGIMENT:** 25th Tennessee Infantry **BIRTH:** 13 October 1841, near Sparta, White County, Tennessee **DEATH:** 04 August 1922, at son's home in Victoria, British Columbia, Canada **MARRIED:** (1) Mary Louisa Officer - 3 children; (2) Martha Capps **OTHER:** Took oath 04 March 1865 at Hilton Head, South Carolina; A tanner and farmer; Organized the 1st National Bank of Sparta, Tennessee; Moved to Coleman, Texas and organized Coleman National Bank; Bank president until 1912.

Major General Patrick Cleburne gave the following report of (Color Sergeant) Cameron's actions at the Battle of Stone's River: *He advanced in front of his regiment so far that when it fell back he was captured. He tore the colors from the staff, concealed them upon his person, and made his escape from Bowling Green (KY), bringing with him the flag of the 25th TN Regt.* He was promoted to 2nd Lieutenant.

Campbell, Gilbert R.

CEMETERY: Manchester City Cemetery
LOCATION: Manchester, Coffee County, Tennessee
RANK: Captain **COMPANY:** Major General Wheeler's Scouts **REGIMENT:** Col. Nathan Carter's Independent Cavalry Company (Scouts) Provisional Army, Confederate States (PACS)
BIRTH: 19 September 1830, Virginia
DEATH: 22 February 1919, Manchester, Coffee County, Tennessee **MARRIED:** (1) Elizabeth P. Spurlock - 7 children; (2) Josephine **OTHER:** Farmer

~

Campbell, Watson C.

CEMETERY: Beaufort National Cemetery **LOCATION:** Beaufort, South Carolina **RANK:** 2nd Lieutenant **COMPANY:** E **REGIMENT:** 25th Tennessee Infantry **BIRTH:** c. 1839, Tennessee
DEATH: 18 February 1865 in Hilton Head, South Carolina hospitol of chronic diarrhea **MARRIED:** Unmarried
OTHER: Farmer

~

Carson, Leroy P.

CEMETERY: Buried on Jersey Shore **LOCATION:** Ft. Delaware Union Prison, New Jersey **RANK:** Captain **COMPANY:** D **REGIMENT:** 2nd Tennessee Infantry (formerly Company F, 35th Tennessee Infantry) **BIRTH:** c. 1820, Tennessee
DEATH: 18 May 1865, Ft. Delaware Union Prison
MARRIED: Elizabeth - 7 children **OTHER:** Noted at death at Ft. Delaware, "No effects"; Farmer

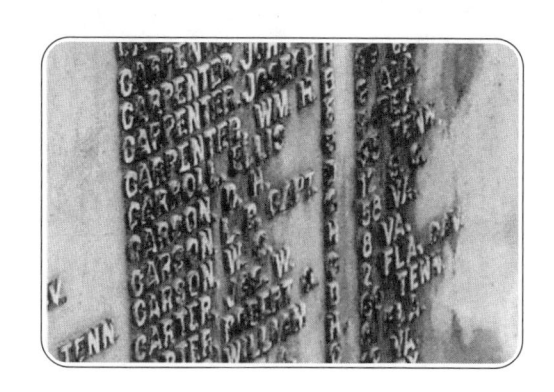

~

Cash, James M.

CEMETERY: Cash Cemetery **LOCATION:** Overton County, Livingston, Tennessee **RANK:** 1st Lieutenant **COMPANY:** D **REGIMENT:** 4th (Murray's) Tennessee Cavalry **BIRTH:** c. 1842, Tennessee **DEATH:** before 1880 **MARRIED:** Lizzie E. T. (Lucy) Hart **PENSION:** #W2067, Overton County **OTHER:** Office clerk; "Memorial Marker," gravesite unknown

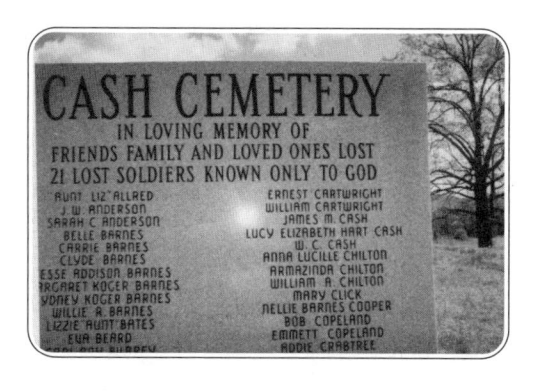

Chisholm, John N.

CEMETERY: Buried on Jersey Shore **LOCATION:** Ft. Delaware Union Prison, New Jersey **RANK:** Captain **COMPANY:** I **REGIMENT:** 9th Alabama Infantry **BIRTH:** c. 1835, Nashville, Tennessee **DEATH:** 16 March 1965, Ft. Delaware Union Prison **MARRIED:** unmarried **OTHER:** Mechanic; Captured at Gettysburg, Pennsylvania; Allowed another officer to be exchanged in his place; Died of chronic dysentery

Coffee, Holland T.

CEMETERY: Unknown **LOCATION:** Unknown **RANK:** Captain **COMPANY:** A **REGIMENT:** 48th Mississippi Infantry **BIRTH:** c. 1839, Mississippi **DEATH:** Unknown **MARRIED:** Julia - 2 children **OTHER:** Plumber; Resided in Columbia, Maury County, Tennessee after the war (1880)

Unknown Grave

Cook, Henry Howe

CEMETERY: Mt. Hope Cemetery **LOCATION:** Mt. Hope Street, Franklin, Tennessee **RANK:** Brevet 2nd Lieutenant (Battlefield promotion) **COMPANY:** D / I **REGIMENT:** "Williamson Grays" 1st (Maney's) Tennessee Infantry / 44th (Reed & McEwen's) Tennessee Infantry **BIRTH:** 23 November 1843, Franklin, Williamson County, Tennessee **DEATH:** 02 November 1921, Franklin, Tennessee **MARRIED:** Frances Marshall - 1 child **OTHER:** Attended Franklin College; Promoted to Captain on the field at Chickamauga for conspicuous bravery; Wounded on shoulder and head at Battle of Murfreesboro; Lawyer; Judge; Chancellor of Davidson and Williamson Counties.

Henry Howe Cook
Photo reprinted by permission from "Immortal Captives" by Mauriel Joslyn

Covington, Cameron D.

CEMETERY: Unknown **LOCATION:** Unknown **RANK:** 2nd Lieutenant **COMPANY:** B **REGIMENT:** 45th Tennessee Infantry **BIRTH:** c. October 1837, Tennessee **DEATH:** Unknown **OTHER:** Had smallpox while in prison; Took oath 04 March 1865 at Hilton Head, South Carolina; Farmer in Lebanon, Wilson County, Tennessee; Widower (1900).

Unknown Grave

Craft, William Henry

CEMETERY: Nashville City Cemetery **LOCATION:** Section 11.2, I.D. # 110172-1001, 4th Avenue South, Nashville, Tennessee **RANK:** Captain **COMPANY:** B / A **REGIMENT:** 1st Battalion (McNairy's) Tennessee Cavalry / 15th Tennessee Infantry **BIRTH:** 19 April 1828 **DEATH:** 06 April 1882, Nashville, Tennessee **MARRIED:** Mary - 1 child **OTHER:** Watchman; Raised Cavalry Company because he was wounded in the ankle. He wrote President Jefferson Davis for permission to raise this company; After War he worked as a Detective Policeman, tinner, employee at City Work House; Also served in the Mexican War and may have known President Davis; Took oath 04 March 1865 at Hilton Head, South Carolina.

Daugherty, Ferdinand H.

CEMETERY: Daugherty Family Cemetery **LOCATION:** Daugherty Street, Livingston, Overton County, Tennessee **RANK:** Lieutenant Colonel **COMPANY:** D **REGIMENT:** 25th Tennessee Infantry / Also, 13th (Dibrell's) Cavalry **BIRTH:** 15 October 1823, Tennessee **DEATH:** 10 April 1895 **MARRIED:** (1) -- Snodgrass; (2) -- Cullum; (3) Laura Carr - 6 children **OTHER:** Lawyer, postmaster, Overton County registrar.

Douglass, Merry A.

CEMETERY: Unknown **LOCATION:** Unknown **RANK:** 1st Lieutenant **COMPANY:** H **REGIMENT:** 44th (Consolidated) Tennessee Infantry **BIRTH:** Unknown **DEATH:** Unknown **OTHER:** Resident of Gallatin, Sumner County, Tennessee; Captured at Petersburg, Virginia 17 June 1864; Took oath 04 March 1865 at Hilton Head, South Carolina.

Unknown Grave

Dunlap, Hugh Pendleton

CEMETERY: Paris City Cemetery **LOCATION:** End of North Ruff Street, 3 blocks east of the court square, Paris, Tennessee **RANK:** Major **COMPANY:** H (F and S) / F **REGIMENT:** 10th (Johnson's) Kentucky Cavalry / 5th Tennessee Infantry / 154th Infantry **BIRTH:** 10 September 1843, Paris, Henry County, Tennessee **DEATH:** 26 February 1918, Dover, Tennessee **MARRIED:** Sarah Atkins - 6 children **OTHER:** Captured at Cheshire, Ohio; Member of Morgan's Raid;

From *Confederate Veteran* magazine, Vol. XXVIL, March 1919, page 106:

Maj. Hugh Dunlap

The committee composed of W. D. Payne, Commander, S. A. Miller, Adjutant, P. P. Pullen, and W. P. Erwin, of Joe Kendall Camp, U. C. V., Paris, Tenn., prepared resolutions in honor of Maj. Hugh Dunlap, from which the following is taken: "Major Dunlap was born in Paris, Tenn., in the year 1843. He enlisted in the 5th Tennessee Regiment as sergeant, and was then tansferred to the 154th Regiment, then to the 10th Kentucky Cavalry as lieutenant, commanding Company H in Morgan's raid in Ohio. He was captured at Cheshire, Ohio, in 1863 and confined in prison at Johnson's Island, from which he was taken with six hundred other officers and place on an island in Charleston Harbor and exposed to the fire of the Federal fleet and the Confederate batteries. He was later taken back to Chicago and kept several months after the close of the war before being released. Comrade Dunlap was true in all that it takes to make a valiant soldier. He died at Dover, Tenn., but was taken to Paris for burial. Joe Kendall Camp thus loses one of its best members."

Easley, William B. W.

CEMETERY: Petty Cemetery (Old Easley Cemetery) **LOCATION:** on Highway 48, near bridge over Piney River, about 10 miles off Highway 100. Cemetery was originally known as the Rose Cemetery and also the old Easley Cemetery in Hickman County, Tennessee.
RANK: 2nd Lieutenant **COMPANY:** G / B **REGIMENT:** 48th (Voorhies') Tennessee Infantry / 42nd Tennessee Infantry **BIRTH:** 01 October 1838, Tennessee **DEATH:** 26 October 1870 **MARRIED:** Emily L. Petty (b. 25 November 1843, d. 25 May 1882), daughter of Hardy and Susan Petty **OTHER:** Farmer; Resident of Vernon, Hickman County, Tennessee (1870)

Unknown Grave

Elliott, Galen R.
CEMETERY: Unknown **LOCATION:** Unknown **RANK:** 2nd Lieutenant **COMPANY:** F **REGIMENT:** (Murray's) 4th Tennessee Cavalry; Reorganized as Company I, (Baxter Smith's) 8th Tennessee Cavalry **BIRTH:** c. 1840 **DEATH:** Unknown
OTHER: Lived at Clinton County, Kentucky after war.

Elzey, Andrew Jackson
CEMETERY: Indian Creek Cemetery
LOCATION: Tipton County, Tennessee **RANK:** 2nd Lieutenant
COMPANY: H **REGIMENT:** 17th Tennessee Infantry
BIRTH: 12 April 1837, Marshall County, Tennessee
DEATH: 28 January 1900, Holly Grove Community, Tipton County, Tennessee **MARRIED:** Mary Tennessee Caldwell - 8 children **PENSION:** #W5313, Tipton County, Tennessee
OTHER: Farmer

Evans, William C. D.
CEMETERY: Unknown **LOCATION:** Unknown
RANK: 2nd Lieutenant **COMPANY:** E **REGIMENT:** 17th (Griffith's) Arkansas Infantry **BIRTH:** c. 1842, Tennessee
DEATH: Unknown **MARRIED:** Lee Anne - 6 children
OTHER: Teacher; Lived at Springdale, Washington County, Arkansas (1880)

Ewing, Zewingle " Zeile" Whitefield
CEMETERY: Maplewood Cemetery **LOCATION:** South Sam Davis Avenue, Pulaski, Giles County, Tennessee **RANK:** 2nd Lieutenant **COMPANY:** H **REGIMENT:** 17th Tennessee Infantry **BIRTH:** 14 August 1843, Lewisburg, Marshall County, Tennessee **DEATH:** 09 August 1909
MARRIED: (1) Harriet "Hattie" P. Jones - 1 daughter, Marietta; (2) Kate Bradley - 1 child, Rebecka **PARENTS:** Lile A. and Rebekah A. Ewing
PENSION: #W10741, Williamson County, Tennessee **OTHER:** Attended Maryville College, Law School at University of Virginia; Lawyer; Tennessee State Senator; Speaker of the Tennessee Senate, 1887-1889; First President of Pulaski, Giles County, Tennessee School Board; President, National People's Bank; At Chickamauga He learned all senior officers had been killed in his unit and he returned to field duty from being assigned to Provost Guard at Bushrod Johnson's Brigade; Elected to Roll of Honor.

Fleming, Henry Clay
CEMETERY: New Pine Creek **LOCATION:** Lake County, Oregon **RANK:** 1st Lieutenant **COMPANY:** K **REGIMENT:** 25th Tennessee Infantry **BIRTH:** 15 July 1842, Van Buren County, Tennessee **DEATH:** 29 September 1930 **MARRIED:** Winifred Marshbanks - 8 children **OTHER:** Teacher; school superintendent; farmer

~

Fulcher, James T.
CEMETERY: Old Gray Cemetery **LOCATION:** Knoxville, Knox County, Tennessee **RANK:** 2nd Lieutenant **COMPANY:** H **REGIMENT:** "Kings Mountain Rifles" 37th Virginia Infantry **BIRTH:** c. 1843, Virginia **DEATH:** c. 1891 **MARRIED:** Anna M. - 6 children **OTHER:** Lawyer

~

Fulkerson, Abram
CEMETERY: East Hill Cemetery **LOCATION:** Bristol, Tennessee/Virginia **RANK:** Colonel **COMPANY:** K **REGIMENT:** 19th Tennessee Infantry; Later, with 63rd Tennessee Infantry **BIRTH:** 13 May 1834, near Bristol, Virginia **DEATH:** 17 December 1902, from the effects of a stroke **MARRIED:** Selina Johnson of Clarksville, Tennessee - 1 son **CHILDREN:** Son, S. V. Fulkerson; Sisters living at the time of his death, Mrs. B. F. Hurt of Abingdon, Virginia, and Mrs. Harriet Armstrong of Rogersville, Tennessee. **RELATIVES:** Parents were Scotch-Irish; Abram Fulkerson was named for his father who was a Captain in the War of 1812; Mother was Margaret Vance; Brothers: Samuel B. Fulkerson, Colonel of 37th Virginia Infantry, Isaac Fulkerson, Captain of 8th Texas Cavalry, and Frank Fulkerson; All three of his brothers served in the Mexican War and left him in charge of the family farm. **OTHER:** Graduated 1857, from VMI (Virginia Military Institute); A student of Professor T. J. "Stonewall" Jackson; Taught school at Palmyra, Virginia, and then Rogersville, Tennessee, when the Civil War began; In 1862, he was granted a furlough to Clarksville to marry, and married just in time to escape the Federals who were pouring into Clarksville. He took his bride home and returned to his post; In Hawkins County, he raised the first volunteer company, took it to Knoxville and joined the 19th Tennessee Regiment, CSA of which he was elected major; With the 19th he fought in the battles of Wild Cat and Shiloh. At Shiloh his horse was shot under him and he was severely wounded in the thigh. After recovering he assisted in organizing the 63rd Tennessee Regiment and was made its 1st lieutenant colonel; 12 Feb 1864, President Jefferson Davis made him colonel of the 63rd. He led it at Chickamauga where he was again wounded in the left arm; His regiment was then attached to Longstreet's Corps. He took part in the battles of Drewry's Bluff, and the affairs at Walthall's Junction, Swift Creek,

Abram Fulkerson

Abram Fulkerson
Photo reprinted by permission from "Immortal Captives" by Mauriel Joslyn

Bermuda Hundred, and Petersburg. During the fight at Petersburg he was wounded and captured, 17 June 1864, and imprisoned at Fort Delaware; Sent to Morris Island with the 600, and to Fort Pulaski and placed on "starvation rations"; He was returned to Fort Delaware until discharged from prison on 25 July 1866, more than 3 months after the surrender; 1866, began to practice law with York & Fulkerson and continued until 6 March 1900 when he suffered a stroke in his office; Served ten years in the Virginia Legislature; Three terms in the House; One term in the Senate; Member of the 47th U.S. Congress; Citizen of Bristol.

Inscribed on his memorial marker:

IN MEMORY OF ABRAM FULKERSON 1834–1902
SOLDIER, LAWYER, LEGISLATOR
A GRADUATE OF THE VA MILITARY INSTITUTE CLASS OF
1857, AND A PUPIL OF THOMAS J. JACKSON
AFTERWARDS KNOWN AS STONEWALL. MAJOR OF THE
19TH & COLONEL OF THE 63RD TENNESSEE REGIMENTS
OF INFANTRY CSA 1861–1865.
SERVED 10 YEARS AS DELEGATE & SENATOR IN THE
LEGISLATURE OF VA FROM WASHINGTON CO
& AS A MEMBER OF THE 47TH CONGRESS OF
THE US FROM THE 9TH VA DISTRICT.
HE WAS HONEST COURAGEOUS & PATRIOTIC.
ERECTED BY HIS WIDOW & SON 1902

Goodloe, Thomas J.

CEMETERY: Unmarked **LOCATION:** Fort Pulaski, GA **RANK:** 1st Lieutenant **COMPANY:** D **REGIMENT:** 44th Tennessee Infantry **BIRTH:** c. 1828, Virginia **DEATH:** 27 February 1865 of chronic diarrhea, Fort Pulaski, GA **MARRIED:** -- , 2 children **OTHER:** Lived in Estell Springs, Franklin County, Tennessee; Farmer.

From *Immortal Captives* by Mauriel Josylen: At Fort Pulaski there is no mention of the "Six Hundred" and the ordeal they endured here. The spirits of those who died never left, for their cemetery outside the fort walls is unmarked. Headboards were made by their fellow prisoners but they were not allowed to be erected. Thirteen lie beside a paved lot, where cars and buses callously disturb their rest, their presence unsuspected, in the salt marshes of Georgia.

Unfortunately there are no markers on the Confederate grave sites. As many as thirteen Confederate prisoners died while at Fort Pulaski. Crude wooden headboards were erected by fellow Confederate prisoners. The wooden headboards, however, quickly deteriorated and gradually disappeared. The Army closed Fort Pulaski in 1880. Afterwards, the fort endured more than fifty years of neglect and decay until it was added to the National Park Service in 1933. There was no evidence of Confederate burials when the National Park Service took over.

An archaelogical investigation was conducted in 1999, in an effort to locate the Confederate burials. As many as 37 grave sites were located. However, since the area was so badley disturbed, and since many Federal internments were later relocated (and later burials subsequently buried within the site), nothing definitely is known about any of the sites.

According to archival records Lt. Goodlow is buried outside Fort Pulaski. But due to the impermanent method of marking these graves, and due to decades of neglect, loss and movement, there will probably never be any way of locating any individual grave site.

—Mike Ryan, Chief Ranger, Fort Pulaski National Monument

Halliburton, William

CEMETERY: Confederate Cemetery **LOCATION:** Confederate Memorial State Historic Site, Higginsville, Missouri
RANK: 1st Lieutenant **COMPANY:** State Guards
REGIMENT: 7th Missouri Cavalry, later was with Company B, Freeman's Regiment, Missouri Cavalry **BIRTH:** 15 September 1823, Humphreys (now Benton County), Tennessee
DEATH: 1906 at Missouri Confederate Soldiers Home
MARRIED: (1) Roxana Wilson - 2 children; (2) Lucy Anderson - 3 children; (3) Louisa **OTHER:** Hardware salesman; Sent by General Sterling Price to raise troops; Took oath 4 March 1865 at Hilton Head, South Carolina.; Deputy sheriff; Deputy collector; Probate judge.

Hastings, Joseph Hezekiah

CEMETERY: Hastings Camp Ground or New Hope Cemetery
LOCATION: New Hope Road, Shelbyville, Tennessee
RANK: Brevet 2nd Lieutenant
COMPANY: A **REGIMENT:** 17th Tennessee Infantry **BIRTH:** 01 February 1836, Tennessee
DEATH: 25 September 1925

Joseph Hezekiah Hastings

MARRIED: 23 October 1868 to Mary Latinia Crunk (b. 26 August, 1846, d. 27 January 1920). Five children: John, Jerome, Tiny, and twin boys, Samuel Porter and Lowe (b. 07 October 1878). **PENSION:** #S1214, Tennessee
PARENTS: John M. Hastings (b. 26 January 1801, North Carolina–d. 05 February 1863) **OTHER:** Farmer and carpenter; Wounded at Chickamauga, Georgia.

~

Haynes, Robert Bell

CEMETERY: Community Cemetery **LOCATION:** Pilot Point, Texas **RANK:** 2nd Lieutenant **COMPANY:** A
REGIMENT: Gand's Squadron, Texas Cavalry; Unit became Company A, 7th Kentucky Cavalry. **BIRTH:** 27 November 1832, Tennessee **DEATH:** 04 October 1899, Denton County, Texas **MARRIED:** Seigneora Drake (b. 20 October 1831, d. 6 August 1900) in Mississippi - 2 sons **PENSION:** #04578, Texas **OTHER:** Stock herder; Mason.

~

Henderson, John H.

CEMETERY: Unknown **LOCATION:** Unknown **RANK:** 2nd Lieutenant **COMPANY:** K **REGIMENT:** 39th Tennessee Infantry
BIRTH: c. 1844, Tennessee **DEATH:** Unknown
OTHER: Lived in Sweetwater, Monroe County, Tennessee

Unknown Grave

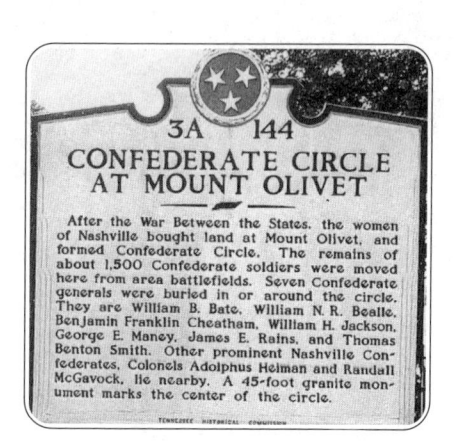

Henry, John Mitchell

CEMETERY: Hartsville Cemetery **LOCATION:** Cemetery Road, which branches east from Highway 141 South, south section of the town of Hartsville, Tennessee **RANK:** 2nd Lieutenant **COMPANY:** H **REGIMENT:** 44th (Consolidated) Tennessee Infantry **BIRTH:** 09 February 1837, Tennessee **DEATH:** 15 May 1919 **MARRIED:** Mary A. - 6 children **PARENTS:** John H. Henry of Virginia and Elizabeth Mitchell of Kentucky **OTHER:** Severely wounded in side at Murfreesboro, Tennessee; Resident of Bransford, Trousdale County, Tennessee; Built Willow Grove Methodist Church with Reuben Brown Harris.

~

Hixson, Madison

CEMETERY: May Cemetery **LOCATION:** Near Shoal Creek, Arkansas **RANK:** 1st Lieutenant **COMPANY:** B **REGIMENT:** 16th Arkansas **BIRTH:** 25 December 1843, Bledsoe County, Tennessee **DEATH:** 27 April 1904, Logan County, Arkansas **MARRIED:** Delilah Ann Sadler - 3 children **OTHER:** Wounded twice; Had smallpox in Union prison; Farmer and store clerk, general merchandise business; Served in Arkansas State Legislature, 1874-1875.

~

Hooberry, John W.

CEMETERY: Mt. Olivet Cemetery **LOCATION:** 1101 Lebanon Pike, Nashville, Tennessee; Section 14, Lot S. Pt. #140, in the P.L. - H.C. & Lug Stump family plot. **RANK:** 2nd Lieutenant **COMPANY:** I **REGIMENT:** 55th (McKoin's) Tennessee / 44th (Consolidated) Tennessee Infantry **BIRTH:** c. 1841, Tennessee **DEATH:** 1874; reinterred 11 April 1907 **MARRIED:** 15 November 1860 to Martha Cassandra Stump (b. 09 December 1839, d. 28 October 1916) **PENSION:** #W4284, Tennessee **OTHER:** Farmer; Enlisted 30 December 1861, as a private with Company I, 55th Tennessee Regiment; On the muster roll of Company I, 44th Consolidated Tennessee Infantry (formed in part of Company I, 55th Tennessee Infantry), dated 31 December 1864, he is reported as 2nd Lieutenant "captured at Petersburg, Virginia on 17 June 1864."; Prisoner of war records show him captured 17 June 1864, at Petersburg, Virginia, and paroled 15 December 1864, at Charleston Harbor, South Carolina; Surrendered 11 May 1865, Augusta, Georgia; Released 3 June 1865, after taking the oath of allegiance.

"April 18, 1913—My Dear Sir: Your letter of the 15th received this morning. I remember very well Lieutenant Hooberry, who came to my Father's house late in the war, just after he had been exchanged.…When Hooberry came to my Father's house at Society Hill he could hardly stand and was put to bed at once, a very sick man. Our Doctor thought his chances of recovery were very poor. My mother and sisters nursed him carefully and gave him such nourishment as he could bear and after a long time he began to improve in strength. The war ended while he was at my Father's house and he was very anxious to get back to Tennessee. After a while, although still quite feeble, he determined to set out on his long journey. As I remember it, my Father sent him to my house at Hartsville and I sent him on further west, but how far I do not now remember. We heard of his safe arrival at his home after a long and tedious journey, and my sister Mary, then a girl of seventeen, corresponded with him from time to time for several years. I did not know Lieutenant Hooberry was dead until I received your letter, but my sister Mary and myself can testify that during the period referred to he was a loyal and devoted Officer of the Confederate States Army and that he was kept out of the service because of his extreme illness.…"

—*Excerpt from letter written by Major James Lide Coker, 6th South Carolina Infantry, C.S.A. of Hartsville, South Carolina to Mr. W. B. Paul, 206 Union Street, Nashville, Tennessee.*

Hunter, Philander D.

CEMETERY: Unknown **LOCATION:** Unknown **RANK:** 1st Lieutenant **COMPANY:** Artillery **REGIMENT:** Ordinance Officer to General J. W. Frazier **BIRTH:** c. 1830, Tennessee **DEATH:** Unknown **OTHER:** Clerk; Resident of Nashville, Davidson County, Tennessee; Had pneumonia, dropsy, and ascites; Last record a statement from Gen Hosp #9 Richmond, 24 March 1865.

Unknown Grave

Hutchinson, Charles L.

CEMETERY: Unknown **LOCATION:** Unknown **RANK:** 1st Lieutenant **COMPANY:** H **REGIMENT:** 63rd Tennessee Infantry **BIRTH:** 1837, Tennessee (service record gives age as 27 in 1864) **DEATH:** Unknown **MARRIED:** Adelia - 4 children **OTHER:** Captured at Petersburg, Virginia on 17 June 1864; Resident of Hamilton County, Tennessee (1880); Farmer.

Unknown Grave

Irvine, Joseph A.

CEMETERY: Rose Hill Cemetery **LOCATION:** Maury County, Tennessee **RANK:** 2nd Lieutenant **COMPANY:** A **REGIMENT:** 9th (Gantt's) Battalion Tennessee Cavalry **BIRTH:** 25 September 1841, Tennessee **DEATH:** 12 April 1890, Sylva, North Carolina **MARRIED:** Mary Davis Cross **OTHER:** In the timber business; Deputy Sheriff; Iron Cross at grave.

~

Irwin, Thomas

CEMETERY: (Mt.) Calvary Cemetery **LOCATION:** Section 5, Lot 48, 1001 Lebanon Road, Nashville, Tennessee **RANK:** 2nd Lieutenant **COMPANY:** G **REGIMENT:** 11th Tennessee Infantry **BIRTH:** 14 March 1836, County Longford, Ireland **DEATH:** 09 December 1894 **MARRIED:** 08 September 1866 to Ellen O'Conner (b. 15 December 1846, County Kerry, Ireland, d. 24 December 1914) - 5 children **PENSION:** #W49 **OTHER:** Printer; Enlisted 10 May 1861 as a private with Company G, 11th Regiment, Tennessee Infanty; Elected to 2nd Lieutenant of same company 1 May 1862; Wounded (gunshot wound to left back) and captured at Missionary Ridge 25 November 1863; Released 12 June 1865 after taking the oath of allegiance; Resident of Nashville, Davidson County, Tennessee (1880); In 1894, listed address as "Corner of 1st and Josephine", occupation as "Merchant", and cause of death, "pistol shot wound"; Others in Irwin family plot: Ellen Irwin, John M. Irwin (b. 19 May 1869– d. 24 December 1899), and Annie Irwin (02 July 1880–05 September 1881).

~

Israel, Abner B.

CEMETERY: Unknown **LOCATION:** Unknown **RANK:** Captain **COMPANY:** G **REGIMENT:** 1st Arkansas Battalion Infantry **BIRTH:** c. 1835, Tennessee **DEATH:** In Arkansas; date Unknown. **MARRIED:** Anna - 7 children **OTHER:** Resident of Walnut Ridge, Lawrence County, Arkansas; Postmaster.

James, William N.

CEMETERY: Family Farm (James Cemetery) **LOCATION:** Hickman, Tennessee **RANK:** Captain **COMPANY:** C **REGIMENT:** 44th (Consolidated) Tennessee Infantry **BIRTH:** c. 1836, Tennessee **DEATH:** 31 January 1907 **MARRIED:** Eliza - 9 children **OTHER:** Resident of Smith County, Tennessee

William N. James
Photo reprinted by permission
from "Immortal Captives" by Mauriel Joslyn

Jenkins, John D.

CEMETERY: Pecan Grove Cemetery **LOCATION:** McKinney, Texas **RANK:** 1st Lieutenant **COMPANY:** K **REGIMENT:** 14th Tennessee Infantry **BIRTH:** 16 February 1838, Clarksville, Montgomery County, Tennessee **DEATH:** 11 June 1919, Collin County, Texas **MARRIED:** Mary E.; Children: William G., John H., Wallace, Roy, and Mattie. **PENSION:** #01230, applied 1899, Italy City, Ellis County, Texas **OTHER:** Spy for General Stonewall Jackson, August 1862.

Johnson, H. L. W.

CEMETERY: Unknown **LOCATION:** Unknown **RANK:** Captain **COMPANY:** C **REGIMENT:** 12th Arkansas Infantry **BIRTH:** c. 1833, Tennessee **DEATH:** Unknown **OTHER:** Music teacher; Gunshot wound in left leg; Amputated leg, 28 August 1864, at U.S. Hospital at Beaufort, South Carolina; Sent him to two more prisons after amputation; Last record, paroled 15 December 1864 at Charleston Harbor, South Carolina.

Unknown Grave

Johnson, Samuel Joseph

CEMETERY: Johnson Family Cemetery **LOCATION:** Mill Creek, Putnam County, Tennessee **RANK:** Captain **COMPANY:** K **REGIMENT:** 25th Tennessee Infantry **BIRTH:** 09 June 1839, White County, Tennessee **DEATH:** 12 January 1900 **MARRIED:** Fannie Officer - 8 children **OTHER:** Merchant, farmer, mill and lumber business.

Samuel Joseph Johnson

The Immortal 600 • Our Confederate Ancestors • 319

Unknown Grave

Jones, James McG.
CEMETERY: Unknown **LOCATION:** Unknown **RANK:** Captain
COMPANY: Not listed **REGIMENT:** (Cocke's) Arkansas Infantry
BIRTH: c. 1841, Tennessee **DEATH:** Unknown **OTHER:** Resident of Eureka Springs, Carroll County, Arkansas, 1880.

~

King, John Stanton
CEMETERY: Cold Springs Presbyterian Church Cemetery
LOCATION: Holston Valley, across Virginia line, Sullivan County, Tennessee **RANK:** 2nd Lieutenant
COMPANY: B **REGIMENT:** "Virginia Moutain Boys" 37th Virginia Infantry **BIRTH:** 02 April 1830, Virginia
DEATH: 30 March 1911 **MARRIED:** Mary Gray - 9 children
OTHER: Farmer

~

Kirkman, Alexander Jackson
CEMETERY: Polk Cemetery **LOCATION:** Buried next to his sister, Mary Kirkman (Mrs. Paul Jones), in Boliver, Tennessee
RANK: 1st Lieutenant / Captain **COMPANY:** D
REGIMENT: 4th Battalion Alabama Cavalry (Served in General John H. Morgan's Cavalry) **BIRTH:** December 1842, Florence, Lauderdale County, Alabama **DEATH:** 11 May 1909, Garfield Hospital, Washington, D.C. of heart trouble
MARRIED: bachelor of 63 years **RELATIVES:** Sister: Mary Kirkman (Mrs. Paul Jones) d. 1890; Brothers: Hugh Kirkman of Birmingham, Alabama, and Samuel Kirkman of Florence, Alabama **OTHER:** Merchant; Attended Georgetown University in Washington, D.C. and Heidelburg University in Germany in 1859; When he heard Alabama joined the CSA he came home from Germany and ran the blockade at Charleston; Taken prisoner and sent to Fort Delaware; After the war, he was editor of "The Coahomian" in Mississippi; During the 1878 Yellow Fever epidemic he organized the Howard Society, a relief association; Left Tunica County, Mississippi in 1893 for Washington, D.C.; He was Chief of Division at the U.S. Treasury under the Cleveland administration; Under the Harrison administration he was transferred to a clerkship in the Pension Office.

Alexander Jackson Kirkman
Photo reprinted by permission from "Immortal Captives" by Mauriel Joslyn

Knox, William C.

CEMETERY: Ft. Delaware Union Prison
LOCATION: Buried on Jersey Shore, New Jersey
RANK: 2nd Lieutenant **COMPANY:** D **REGIMENT:** 8th (Baxter Smith's) Tennessee Cavalry **BIRTH:** c. 1826, Tennessee
DEATH: 12 April 1865 **MARRIED:** Elizabeth - 1 daughter
OTHER: Merchant; Note at death "$5 in personal effects".

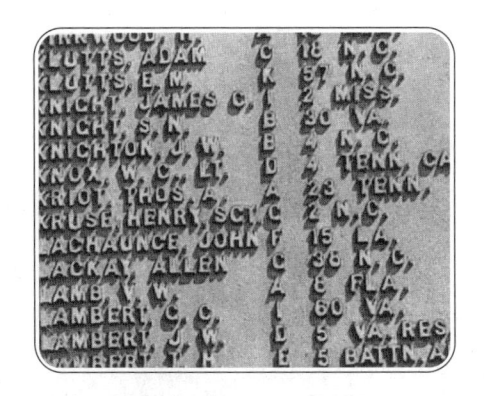

Lauderdale, John F.

CEMETERY: Fort Hill Cemetery **LOCATION:** Cleveland, Tennessee **RANK:** 1st Lieutenant
COMPANY: A **REGIMENT:** 5th Battalion Tennessee Cavalry; Became 2nd (Ashby's) Tennessee Cavalry
BIRTH: c. 1837, Tennessee **DEATH:** Unknown
MARRIED: Lou T. - 6 children **OTHER:** Farmer; no tombstone; Marker for 270 Unknown Confederate soldiers buried in Fort Hill Cemetery.

Ledford, Jesse A.

CEMETERY: Ft. Delaware Union Prison **LOCATION:** Buried on the Jersey Shore, New Jersey **RANK:** 1st Lieutenant
COMPANY: H **REGIMENT:** 25th Tennessee Infantry
BIRTH: c. 1829, Tennessee **DEATH:** 01 May 1865 of acute dysentery **OTHER:** Captured at Petersburg, Virginia

Lewis, James B.

CEMETERY: Unknown **LOCATION:** Unknown **RANK:** 2nd Lieutenant **COMPANY:** F **REGIMENT:** 1st (Carter's) Tennessee Cavalry **BIRTH:** c. 1832, Tazewell, Tennessee **DEATH:** Unknown
OTHER: Residence in Clairborne County, Tennessee.

Unknown Grave

Lytle, James Knox Polk

CEMETERY: Taylor Cemetery
LOCATION: Near Unionville in Bedford County, Tennessee, at Taylor's Cross Roads **RANK:** Captain
COMPANY: F **REGIMENT:** 23rd Tennessee Infantry **BIRTH:** 25 February 1838, Tennessee
DEATH: 18 July 1879 **MARRIED:** Mary A. E. Taylor (1848–1886)
CHILDREN: (1) Flora Lytle (1870–1950), married Hugh McLean Elmore (1864–1907); (2) Dr. William Abel Lytle (1872–1907); (3) Addie Lytle (1876–1956); (4) Mary Lockie Lytle (1879–1956); (5) James "Jimmy" Lee Lytle, married Jean Usery, lived in Texas.
PARENTS: Abel (Able) Lytle (1804–1841) and Millie Ann Hale (1814–1903) **OTHER:** Placed on Roll of Honor at Chickamauga, Georgia; Farm laborer.

James Knox Polk Lytle

~

McCallum, James Rogers

CEMETERY: Old Gray Cemetery **LOCATION:** Knoxville, Knox County, Tennessee **RANK:** Captain
COMPANY: D **REGIMENT:** 63rd Tennessee Infantry
BIRTH: 25 January 1839, Knox County, Tennessee
DEATH: 24 June 1905 **MARRIED:** Lurinda Hardin - 7 children
PENSION: #W3008, Tennessee **OTHER:** Building contractor; President of Jones Brick Company.

~

Morgan, Sydney Algernon

CEMETERY: Bethlehem Church of Christ Cemetery
LOCATION: Behind church on Bethlehem Road, White County, Tennessee **RANK:** 1st Lieutenant **COMPANY:** A
REGIMENT: 25th Infantry Tennessee **BIRTH:** 27 December 1834, Tennessee **DEATH:** 03 April 1902, White County, Tennessee **MARRIED:** Vina **PENSION:** #W2501, Tennessee
OTHER: Farmer; Captured at Murfreesboro, Tennessee; Exchanged and returned to unit; Captured at Battle of Petersburg, Virginia on 17 June 1864; Residence in White County, Tennessee; Note: Grave marker says "Algie S. Morgan" or "Sydney Algernon Morgan". Confederate Record says S. A. Morgan and Sydney Morgan.

322 · Our Confederate Ancestors · The Immortal 600

Nicks, John H.

CEMETERY: Nicks Cemetery on Bill Nicks Farm
LOCATION: Double headstone with wife; About 3 miles from Centerville, Tennessee on Gray's Bend Road **RANK:** Captain
COMPANY: D **REGIMENT:** 9th (Gantt's) Battalion Tennessee Cavalry **BIRTH:** 05 April 1826, Centerville, Tennessee
DEATH: 11 May 1909 **MARRIED:** Susanna Elizabeth Easley (b. 10 January 1827) - 2 sons **PENSION:** #W5735, Tennessee
RELATIVE: Great grandfather of Paul Rochelle
OTHER: Farmer; an Elder in The Church of Christ

Marker Photo Not Available

Perkins, Thomas Fearn, Jr.

CEMETERY: Mt. Hope Cemetery
LOCATION: Mt. Hope Street, Franklin, Tennessee **RANK:** Captain **COMPANY:** Perkins' Company I **REGIMENT:** Douglas' Battalion, Partisin Rangers; Later the 11th (Homan's) Tennessee Cavalry
BIRTH: 06 December 1842, Williamson County, Tennessee
DEATH: 15 January 1893
MARRIED: Louise Henrietta Cochrane, charter member of Franklin Chapter #14, UDC, organized October 1895.
OTHER: Graduate of Western Military Institute, Nashville, Tennessee; Farmer; Williamson County Court Clerk; Clerk and Master Chancery Court; Senator, Tennessee General Assembly, 1881–1883; Master Mason; Royal Arch Mason; Knights Templar; Brigadier General and Tennessee President of Association of Confederate Soldiers.

Thomas Fearn Jr.
Photo reprinted by permission from "Immortal Captives" by Mauriel Joslyn

Thomas Fearn Perkins, Jr. Stained glass window, St. Paul's Episcopal Church, Franklin, Tennessee. Inscribed "To the Greater Glory of God and in loving memory of Captain Thomas Fearn Perkins 1842–1893"

James Hilliard Polk
Photo reprinted by permission from
"Immortal Captives" by Mauriel Joslyn

Polk, James Hilliard

CEMETERY: Greenwood Cemetery **LOCATION:** Ft. Worth, Texas **RANK:** Captain **COMPANY:** E **REGIMENT:** 6th (Wheeler's) Tennessee Cavalry **BIRTH:** 08 January 1842, near Franklin, Williamson County, Tennessee **DEATH:** 27 November 1926, Fort Worth, Terrant County, Texas **MARRIED:** Mary De Moville Harding of Nashville, Tennessee (b. 18 October 1858, d. 26 June 1943) - 2 children **PENSION:** #A51430, Texas **OTHER:** Captured while scouting for General Nathan Bedford Forrest.

324 • Our Confederate Ancestors • The Immortal 600

REFERENCES & INDEX

References

Ancestry. Com-census & military records

Bedford Co, Tennessee Family History Book
Biographical Roster of the Immortal 600
Bolivar Tennessee *Bulletin*

Cemeteries of Trousdale County, Tennessee
Census records of all counties & states 1840-1930
City of Tipton, Tennessee
Confederate Veterans Magazine
Crossville Chronicle
Cumberland County Tennessee Cemetery Records
Cumberland County Tennessee Confederate Pension Records
Cumberland County Tennessee Reference Department Microfilm Services

Descendants of Confederate Veterans (Special thanks for contributed information & photos)

FindAGrave.com
Ft. Delaware Society
Ft. Pulaski Internet site

Hickman County Tennessee Cemetery Records
History of Haywood County, Tennessee
History of Rover & the 10th District of Bedford County, Tennessee
History of Van Buren County, Tennessee

Immortal Captives

McEvoy Funeral Home Records Paris, Tennessee
Members of Tennessee Division, United Daughters of the Confederacy
The Military Annals of Tennessee

Nashville City Cemetery Association
National Park Service website "Civil War Soldiers Roster"

Papa Was a Boy in Gray
Pictorial History of Putnam County, Tennessee
Pioneers of Wiregrass Georgia
Putnam County Tennessee Library, Tennessee Room
Rosters from various Confederate Regiments

Siftings from Putnam County, Tennessee
Stray Leaves from Putnam County, Tennessee History
Sumner County Tennessee Cemetery Records

Tennessee Civil War Veterans Questionnaires
Tennessee State Library & Archives (Special thanks to the staff at TSLA)
Tennesseans in the Civil War, Volumes I & II

Valor in Gray
Van Buren County, Tennessee Cemetery Book
Van Buren County, Tennessee Confederate Pension Records

Warren County, Tennessee Confederate Pension Records
Warren County, Tennessee Marriage Book
White County, Tennessee Archives (Special thanks to Geraldine (Elrod) Pollard for assistance)
White County, Tennessee Cemetery Books Vol I, II & III
White County, Tennessee Confederate Pension Records
White County, Tennessee Heritage Book

This is a listing only of materials used for our research. You may contact us for any specific title, author, or other information on each reference.

Index

A

Acuff, Jasper Sylvester 121
Adair, Pleasant 210
Adams, R. Thomas 18
Adams, William H. 300, 302
Agee, I. N. 18
Albright, George Nicholas 300, 302
Alcorn, Richard A. 57
Alderson, William H. 302
Allen, Edwin 289
Allen, Isaac 290
Allen, Jesse P. 260
Allen, John J. 291
Allen, William Edwin 300, 302
Allison, Carter A. 226
Allison, John H. 54
Allison, Robert Donald 54
Amonett, Francis Marion 25
Anderson, Ace 259
Anderson, Baily P. 260
Anderson, Charles 198
Anderson, John D. 202
Anderson, Miles Wesley 260
Anderson, Riley W. 73
Anderson, Thomas J. 138
Anderson, Thomas M. 139
Anderson, Tilford 193
Anderson, William Pleasant 139
Andrews, Alvin N. 3
Argo, Elza Jones 204
Arnold, Bonaparate 303
Arnold, Bonaparte 138, 300
Arnold, Christopher Columbus 203
Arnold, Colbird S. 211
Arnold, Francis 187
Arrants, John Granville Sharp 300, 303
Atnip, John 179
Austin, Edward D. 204
Austin, John Jr. 138
Austin, John B. 300, 303
Austin, Nathanial (Nathan) Glenn 243
Austin, Thomas 211
Austin, William H. 167
Anderson, William T. 171

B

Badger, Alphonso L. 193
Badger, Dr. Felix A. 193
Bagwell, Drury H. 3
Baker, Goodwin 140
Baker, Jordan Jabes 101
Baker, Matthew (Mathew) 6
Baker, Dr. R. F. 214
Baker, Richard D. 171
Baker, Samuel 18
Baker, William L. 240
Bandy, Thomas E. 8
Banks, Francis "Frank" M. 265
Barnes, James M. 282
Barnes, Jesse 44
Barnes, Riley 282
Barnes, William H. 26
Bartlett, Joseph D. 25
Bartlett, Nathan 75
Bass, John W. 270
Baxter, John Bell 303
Bazell, John 3
Beam, James A. 226
Beasley, Hiriam H. 25
Benson, Peru Hardy 300, 304
Bibee, Thomas 3
Biles, William H. 265
Billingsley, Cyrus 119
Black, George W. 136
Black, Thomas, Dr. 265
Blankenship, Gilford G. 93
Bledsoe, R. H. 211
Blevins, A. C. 3
Boddie, Elijah 300, 304
Bohanon, John 26
Bohannan, George W. 243
Bohannon, James E. 27
Bohannon, Thomas 27
Bohannon, William 27
Boles, George Randolph 201
Bolin, John V. 3
Bouldin, Nathan 107
Bowen, Henry Porter 58
Bowington, John B. 58
Boyd, B. F. 214
Boyd, James Alexander 28
Boyd, James W. 300, 304
Boyd, John 94, 279
Boyd, John W. 279
Boyd, William M. 94
Bradford, Charlie 28
Bradford, Thomas J. 204
Bradley, Augustus Austin 226
Bradley, Charles H. 144
Bradley, John Phillip 226
Bradley, Thomas D. 148
Bradley, Thomas Edward 300, 304
Brady, Edward 210
Brady, Martin V. 198
Brady, Samuel H. 3
Brady, Samuel Houston 4
Bray, William R. 48
Brewer, George L. 3
Bristow, George G. 3
Brock, Allen 96
Brock, John 115
Brock, Elmore 214
Brogden, J. S. 67
Brogden, John Alexander 211
Bronson, Robert L. 172
Broom, Joel 184
Brown, Hiram A. 30
Brown, Jackson Van Buren, Rev. 15
Brown, James P. 187
Brown, L. B. 18
Brown, Lawson C. 225
Brown, Samuel 172
Brown, Stephen W. 29
Brown, Franklin 3
Brown, W. A. 60
Brown, Wamon 161
Brown, William H. 3
Brown, William 3
Brown, Willie (William) 4
Broyles, George G. 148
Broyles, John Summerfield 215
Broyles, O. G. M. 3
Broyles, Onslow G. 172
Bryan, Robertson Crusoe 300, 305
Bryant, A. B. 33
Bruce, O. P. 140
Buck, Enoch J. 31
Buck, Isaac N. 65
Buck, Jesse H. 65
Buckner, Jacob 256
Bullock, Frank M. 45
Burden, Henery 201
Burgess, Charles L. 48
Burnett, James 67
Burgess, James C. 150
Burgess, James M. 65
Burgess, William S. 151
Burke, John H. 300, 305
Burnett, John Anderson 300, 305
Burton, Frank 32
Bush, Frances Asbury 87
Butler, William L. 73
Butram, William 3
Byrne, George D. 83

C

Cagle, Elijah 279
Callahan, William P. 301, 305
Cameron, Zachariah J. 222
Cameron, William Newton 301, 306
Camp, Miles Newton 140
Campbell, Gilbert R. 301, 307
Campbell, Isaac S. 32

Our Confederate Ancestors · 329

Campbell, Watson C. 301, 307
Cannon, Jasper Newton 250
Cantrell, Starling William 193
Carlen, James "Jim" 232
Carlen, William B. 56
Carmichael, Hance 163
Carmichael, Solomon 163
Carmichael, Thomas 163
Carmichael, William L. 164
Carr, Elijah W. 34
Carr, Zebidee C. 73
Carr, William M. 210
Carrick, George D. 226
Carrick, John M. 187
Carroll, S. L. 176
Carson, Leroy P. 301, 307
Carter, Meredith "Bud" 178
Carter, Peter 113
Caruthers, Benjamin F. 61
Cash, Carroll 175
Cash, James M. 250, 301, 307
Cash, John 198
Cash, William M. Simpson 149
Cass, James Milas 61
Cass, James Moses 215
Cass, Louis W. 215
Chaffin, Fox C. 260
Chastain, John 18
Chapin, Hiram Foster 34
Chapin, William P. 34
Chisam, James R. 180
Chisam, James W. 193
Chisholm, John N. 301, 308
Chisam, Overton Deweese 153
Chisam, William M. 153
Claghorn, Wyatt 64
Clark, Byrd 118
Clark, Carroll Henderson 121
Clark, Darius B. 234
Clark, I. P. 63
Clark, James P. 178
Clark, John E. 121
Clark, Joseph 234
Clark, Phineas "Finn" B. 234
Clark, Wamon 205
Clenny, James T. 107
Clenny, William H. 167
Clouse, Thomas J. 33
Cloyd, James M. 216
Cloyd, John S. 187
Coakley, James A. 245
Coatney, Samuel Frank 151
Cobb, William P. 164
Coffee, Holland T. 301, 308

Coffman, David B. 151
Cole, Walter Wilkins 136
Cole, William A. 75
Coleman, Ambrose Benton 205
Coleman, B. F. 60
Colms, Stephen H. 205
Cook, Henry Howe 301, 308
Cooksey, Enoch 266
Cooley, John Franklin 5
Cooper, Gabreil M. 29
Cooper, Levi P. 149
Cooper, Nathan C. 42
Cooper, William Kennedy 42
Cope, Harrison H. 184
Cope, James Madison 179
Cope, Marshall E. 216
Cope, William G. S. 216
Copeland, Bailey Alred 243
Copeland, James E. 34
Copeland, Soloman Addison 18
Covington, Cameron D. 301, 309
Cowen, George W. 58
Cox, David 7
Cox, Hardy (Hardie) 9
Cox, Nathan M. 28
Cox, Robert Alexander 260
Cox, William S. 227
Craft, William Henry 301, 309
Crain, Oliver Cleveland 94
Crane, Alexander 185
Crook, Calvin Brown 216
Crook, David C. 3
Crowder, John A. 156
Cruise, Hanabel 194
Crutcher, Joseph W. 34
Cullom, Sam 249
Cumby, Jimmie 176
Cummings, Gabriel Marion 97
Cummings, J. J. 205
Cummings, Joseph D. 92
Cummings, Joseph Denney 97
Cummings, William Burrell 97
Cunningham, Lane 156
Curtis, James H. 35

D

Dalton, James Isom 166
Daniel, George D. 87
Daniel, William N. 63
Daniels, Emery 146
Daugherty, Ferdinand H. 250, 309

Davis, A. G. 42
Davis, Absolom 157
Davis, Columbus J. 82
Davis, Darius 158
Davis, George W. 165
Davis, Henry Polk 35
Davis, Henry "Tinker" 121
Davis, James 158
Davis, Nelson Clay 157
Davis, Robert 135, 158, 254
Davis, Robert S. 254
Davis, Sampson 230
Davis, Tillmon 157
Deck, John V. 83
Denny, James Preston 116
Denny, Nathan Austin 92
Denton, Elijah W. 181
Denton, Erasmus R. 181
Denton, Holland 28
DeRossett, John 201
DeRossett, Elijah J. 3
DeRossett, Elias (Elijah) 3, 8
Deweese, J. J. 205
Dibrell, George Gibbs 206
Dibrell, Joseph Anthony 207
Dibrell, Montgomery C. 207
Dibrell, Wayman Leftwich 140
Dickson, Zachariah 3
Dillard, Harvey H. 261
Dillon, Carter 113
Ditty, Alexander H. 35
Dixon, Daniel H. 18
Dodson, Jesse 211
Dodson, Noah, Jr. 116
Dodson, Samuel 201
Dodson, Simpson 99
Dodson, William M. 188
Douglass, Merry A. 301, 309
Dowell, George R. 75
Dowell, Joseph L. 75
Dowell, Matisson N. 76
Drake, Eligha 117
Drake, Uriah York, Sr. 266
Draper, Ridley 54
Dunlap, Hugh Pendleton 301, 310
Dyer, James P. 26
Dyer, Logan R. 87
Dyer, William L. 159

E

Eanes, Joseph Cloud 181
Earles, Pleasant G. 235
Earles, William T. 235
Eastland, Charles Simpson 188
Easley, William B. W. 301, 310
Early, Robert 35
Eastland, George W. 188
Edwards, John B. 202
Eldridge, John David 160
Eldridge, John F. 15
Elliott, Galen R. 301, 311
Elmore, Alfred B. 6
Elmore, Alford 3, 6
Elmore, Daniel 3
Elrod, Andrew J. 64
Elrod, Anthony J. 160
Elrod, Giles 30, 160
Elrod, John E. 35
Elrod, William 53
Elzey, Andrew Jackson 301, 311
England, Aaron W. 161
England, David S. 216
England, Enos 161
England, George Dallas 172
England, Wesley 138
Ensor, William A. 52
Erwin, William L. 217
Eubanks, William N. 281
Evans, John D. 46
Evans, William C. D. 301, 311
Ewing, Zewingle " Zeile" Whitefield 311

F

Fancher, James A. Polk 217
Farley, David 86, 246
Farley, Jesse 46
Farley, John 67
Farley, Howard 159
Farley, Simpson M. 149
Farmer, Thomas 139
Farris, John 56
Farris, Thomas 82
Ferguson, Benjamin T. 81
Ferguson, Champ 164
Fisher, Alford T. 162
Fisher, Ambrose "Ambers" Thomas 178
Fisher, George Washington 162
Fisher, James 73, 194
Fisher, James Harvey 73

Fisher, Madison L. 194
Fisk, Andrew Jackson 163
Fisk, Marion 163
Fleming, Henry Clay 301, 312
Fletcher, J. C. 47
Floyd, Robert Dowell 232
Floyd, William T. 148
Ford, Andrew J. 24
Franks, Spencer Holder 167
Freeze, Joseph C. 36
Frost, White 8
Frost, John F. 3
Ford, Abraham 68
Ford, John Fletcher 11
Ford, Christopher A. 3
Ford, Christopher Archibald 10
Ford, Thomas W. 3, 68
Ford, Thomas Wesley 11
Ford, Dr. John 3, 11
Ford, Elijah J. 3
Ford, Elijah Jehu 10
Ford, Elbert H. 3
Ford, Elbert Henley 10
Freiley, J. M. 122
Fulkerson, Abram 301, 312

G

Gabbert, Joel C. 36
Galloway, James S. 181
Gamble, William S. 172
Garrett, Benjamin S. 283
Garrett, Samuel 254
Garrett, William 252, 284
Gentry, George W. 82
Gentry, Martin B. 43, 259
Gibson, Calvin G. 7
Gibson, James C. 3
Gibson, Joseph H. 3
Gilliam, W. S. 76
Gillihan, Uriah R. 87
Gilliland, Robert 184
Gillentine, Harrison C 98
Gillentine, John 98
Gipson, Joseph 31
Gist, John 9, 188
Gist, John 9, 188
Gist, Vance Carrick 188
Glass, Alexander 18
Gleeson, Isaac Edward 241
Glenn, Alexander 204
Glenn, John Wilson 217
Goddard, James C. 136

Goddard, Robert A. 136
Godsey, Jerry P. 3
Gooch, Talamachus C. 159
Gooch, William W. 189
Gooch, William Alexander 159
Goodloe, Thomas J. 301, 313
Goodman, James F. 284
Goodman, Robert H. 284
Goodwin, Alexander M. 217
Goodwin, James T. 217
Goodwin, John W. 166
Goodwin, William (Billy) 218
Gracey, Crockett D. 65
Gracey, Hugh L. 222
Gracey, James B. 222
Gracy, Wamon L. 208
Graham, Christopher Columbus 8
Graham, John F. 3
Graham, Jessee W. S. 3
Graham, William 18
Grayham, John T. 145
Green, A. J. 141
Green, Harrison T. 141
Green, Henry G. 166
Green, James M. 265
Green, Joseph A. 146
Green, Lewis L. 185
Green, Riley 224
Green, William E. 141
Green, Woodson P. 241
Greer, Elijah W. 3
Greer, Henry Clay 3
Greer, Wothington S. 3
Gribble, Samuel 266
Grider, William 78
Griffin, Joseph 242
Grissom, Alexander 107
Grissom, Elijah 103
Grissom, Elisha 101
Grissom, Esau 107
Grissom, James C. 108
Grissom, John R. 108
Grissom, Samuel Burton 108
Grissom, Toliver 108
Grissom, William Buck 109
Groves, George W. 98
Gully, Alfred J. 99

H

Hale, Andrew J. 3
Hale, James 109
Hale, John H. 147
Halfacre, Andrew 47
Hall, John T. 84
Hall, Zachariah 282
Halliburton, William 301, 314
Halteman, John S. 181
Halterman, Spencer J. 202
Hamby, Albert N. 3, 17
Hamby, Gilbert N. 3
Hamby, Reuben M. 3
Hamby, William A. 3
Hamby, William Anderson 7
Hamilton, Hiram H. 43
Hampton, Lawrence P. 232
Harris, Benjamin 3
Harris, Benjamin, Jr. 3
Harris, George W. 284
Harris, James 285
Harris, John W. 285
Harris, Lorenzo D. 3
Harris, Lorenzo Dow 13
Harris, Thomas F. 172
Harris, W. H. H. 18
Harris, William 3
Harris, William L. 3
Harrison, John Samuel 266
Hastings, Joseph Hezekiah 315
Haston, E. Cyrus 109
Haston, Isaac T. 100
Haston, J. W., Sr. 141
Haston, John Taylor 122
Haston, Montgomery Greenfield 92
Haston, Richmond T. 109
Haston, Samuel S. 235
Haston, Wiley B. 122
Haston, William C. 100
Haston, William Carroll, Sr. 211
Hatfield, William G. 175
Hawkins, John D. 156
Hayes, John T. T. 223
Hayes, W. C., Dr. 141
Haynes, Robert Bell 315
Head, John A. 100
Head, Richard J. 117
Head, Thomas Anthony 78
Head, W. H. 114
Hearn, Warren F. 283
Hedgecoth, Hugh L. 3
Hedgecoth, John 3
Hedgecoth, William J. 3

Hembree, Martin VanBuren 194
Henderson, Henry C. 212
Henderson, John H. 301, 315
Hennessee, Patric A. 218
Hennessee, Scott Patrick 18
Hennessee, William A. 218
Henry, George W. 68
Henry, Jacob 36
Henry, James J. 3
Henry, Jasper 51
Henry, John Mitchell 316
Hensley, Eli Lawson 189
Herd, James Vance 177
Hickey, Cornelius 171
Hickey, George 218
Hickey, John B. 227
Hill, Arthur L. 3
Hill, Isaac A. 33
Hill, James Anderson 142
Hill, John 47
Hill, Richard 173
Hill, Thomas 3
Hill, William B. 194
Hill, William Ransom 142
Hillis, Archibald M. 100
Hillis, Esquire 101
Hillis, Isaac Jr. 123
Hillis, James 94, 109, 123
Hillis, James H. 94
Hillis, James K. 109
Hillis, Lawson H. 95
Hillis, Robert 101-102
Hillis, Robert Oliver 101
Hillis, Roswell 124
Hillis, William Robisson 118
Hillis, Woodson P. 114
Hinch, Thomas H. 3
Hitchcock, Benjamin 233
Hitchcock, John 110
Hitchcock, William Luke 233
Hixson, Madison 301, 316
Hodges, Jasper 102
Holder, John D. 176
Holder, John Simpson 182
Hollingsworth, John 102
Hollingsworth, William M. 167
Holloway, Major B. 242
Holloway, S. (Samuel) H., Jr. 12
Holman, James Spencer 78
Hooberry, John W. 301, 316
Hooser, William M. 189
Horn, J. R. 51
Horn, Sherard 18
Horn, Sherod 84

Our Confederate Ancestors · 331

Horton, John Damron 189
Horton, Newton M. 167
Howard, Allen 48
Howard, James 175
Howard, Sampson J. 86
Howard W. S. 68
Howard, William P. 230
Howell, John 161
Howell, Rev. Lewis 177
Howell, Silas 231
Hubbard, J. T. 241
Huddleston, Alvin C. 66
Huddleston, Byrum F. 50
Huddleston, David D. 66
Huddleston, John P. 66
Huddleston, William Jasper 50
Hudgens, Crockett 218
Hudgens, James 177, 189
Hudgens, James P. 189
Hudgens, Joseph 86
Huges, J. B. 18
Hughes, H. I. 48
Hughes, J. D. 87
Hughes, Samuel 218
Humphrey, Benjamin B. 183
Humphrey, David 204
Humphrey, Rev. Sylvester E. 237
Hunter, James W. 162
Hunter, Philander D. 301, 317
Hurlbert, Francis "Frank" Telesforo 281
Hutchens, Lawson H. 179
Hutchings, Francis Marion 178
Hutchinson, Charles L. 317
Hutson, Isaiah Asbury 178
Hutson, John F. 195
Hutson, Thomas E. 195
Hyder, Jacob Simon 49
Hyder, Jasper Sevier 17
Hyder, Jesse E. 49
Hyder, Joseph Nelson 49
Hyder, Pleasant Milton 49

I

Irwin, A. T. Davis 219
Irwin, Thomas 301, 318
Irvine, Joseph A. 301, 318
Isom, Elizirah 63
Israel, Abner B. 301, 318

J

Jackson, James 68
Jackson, John W. 69
Jackson, Levi 69
Jared, Archibald S. 50
Jared, Brice B. 48
Jared, Charles Brasford 53
Jared, John 50, 175
Jared, John Madison 175
Jared, Josiah 53
Jared, William Cleveland 51
Jared, William J. 36
Jarvis, Alexander 219
Jarvis, James Alexander 16
Jarvis, Sylvester 190
Jeffers, George W. 3
Jeffers, Claiborne 3
Jenkins, G. W. 195
Jenkins, John D. 301, 319
Jervis, John 3
Jett, Archibald Overton 190
Jett, John W. 190
Jett, Thomas J. 190
Johnson, Francis Marion 103
Johnson, Greenberry 104
Johnson, H. L. W. 301, 319
Johnson, J. O. 190
Johnson, John 117, 280
Johnson, John Manus 117
Johnson, Samuel 51, 227, 301, 319
Johnson, Samuel J. 51
Johnson, Samuel Joseph 301, 319
Johnson, Solomon 280
Johnson, Squire 104
Johnson, Stephen W. 223
Johnson, Stokely D. 168
Johnson, Wesley J. 184
Johnson, William Rye 104
Jones, Andrew Jackson 191
Jones, B. F. M. 18
Jones, David 122
Jones, Harmon Lafayette 199
Jones, James McG. 301, 320
Jones, Robert (Robin) 95
Jones, William W. 199
Jones, Zachariah 223
Jordan, Benjamin F. 191
Judd, Andrew J. 61
Judd, Ben 25
Judd, George W. 53
Judd, John 53

K

Keathley, Thomas Robinson 191
Keathly, William H. 191
Kell, George Easterly 105
King, Hiram Houston 139
King, John Stanton 301, 320
King, Joseph C. 72
Kinnaird, Alexander 31
Kirby, Laban 114
Kirby, Thomas J. 155
Kirkman, Alexander Jackson 301, 320
Knight, James C. 80
Knowles, Jasper A. 195
Knowles, John Fletcher 223
Knowles, John Monroe 183
Knox, Daniel C. 3
Knox, David C. 13
Knox, S. A. (Arch) 9, 18
Knox, William C. 301, 321
Kuykendall, Newton C. 54

L

Lack, Benjamin 179
Large, Robert 291
Lansden, Dr. Hugh H. 168
Lauderdale, John F. 301, 321
Lawson, William 212, 256
Lawson, William Terry 256
Lay, Zaccharyer A. 157
Ledford, Jesse A. 301, 321
Lee, James P. 55
Lee, John M. 55
Lee, James H. 55
Lee, Thomas Jefferson 261
Lee, Zebulon P. 37
Leftwich, Jefferson 208
Lewis, Bird 213
Lewis, Byrd A. 171
Lewis, Jacob A. 246
Lewis, James B. 301, 321
Lewis, James M. 134, 199
Lewis, John P. 155
Lewis, Martin V. 37
Lewis, William I. 183
Lewis, William P. 56
Lillard, Calvin A. 291
Lillard, John 291
Lillard, Russell 292
Lillard, William 292
Linder, George W. 6
Lipscomb, William A. 254
Little, Harmon 173
Little, Hiram 202
Lively, Francis M. 3
Lively, Rufus R. 3
Loden, Benjamin 18
Loden, James 3, 14
Loden, N. H. 18
Loden, Pleasant 3, 18
Loden, Reuben 3, 18
Loden, W. M. 15
Loden, William 3
Loden, Reuben 3, 18
Loden, James 3, 14
Loden, John F. 3
Loftis, Bailey P. 43
Long, William H. 63
Lowe, Leonard John 37
Lowery, John A. 191
Lowery, John Wesley 246
Lowery, Mark 219
Lowery, Simpson 142
Lowery, Thomas 219
Lowery, William 219
Lowrey, Hugh L. Sr. 220
Lowry, Edward 292
Lowry, Thomas J. 293
Lowry, William H. 293
Lytle, James Knox Polk 322

M

Mabe, David 154
Mabe, Samuel Nelson 225
Mabery, Joshua M. 74
Maberry, George 288
Mabury, John P. 259
Maddux, William C. 57
Madewell, Charles, Jr. 92
Manier, Allen Howes 5
Marlow, James 57
Marlow, William C., Sr. 202
Martin, Abijah 199
Martin, Absolam 93
Martin, Daniel 155
Martin, Hiram L. 43
Martin, James C. 240
Martin, James I. 93
Martin, Jesse 185
Martin, Julius C. 220
Martin, William Carroll 110
Mason, Elyhu (Eli) 151
Matheny, M. S. 84
Matheny, Thomas R. 79

Mathis, Stephen H. 3
Matlock, William H. 173
Matthews, James W. 12
Maxwell, C. W. 47
Maxwell, David Mock 56
Maxwell, David W. 57
McBride, Charles Columbus 280
McBride, Danal 95
McBride, Nathan Mathew 95
McBride, William B. 168
McCallum, James Rogers 322
McClain, Lemuel Rux 32
McCormick, Samuel 106
McCormick, James M. "Mack" 110
McCoy, John L. 105
McDaniel, Thomas F. 74
McDonald, Andrew 58
McDowell, Lucien Lafayette 152
McElhaney, Columbus L. 288
McElroy, Andrew J. 114
McKinley, James Donald 37
McKinney, Thomas J. B. 185
McManus, Samuel V. 173
McWhirter, John Alexander 203
Medley, Alen 116
Meek, Clark 208
Meek, John Sperry 192
Meredith, Ed 220
Meredith, J. W. 220
Merritt, Larkin 74
Messenger, Samuel M. 59
Miller, Luin 227
Minton, William Carroll 58
Mitchell, James H. 62
Mitchell, John Monroe 213
Mitchell, Joseph B. 241
Mitchell, Martin 145
Monday, Malchi 3
Monday, John 3
Montgomery, Robert 59
Montgomery, William M. 199
Montgomery, Zackery 199
Moody, Robert F. 55
Moore, Edward Gleason 186
Moore, George M. 88
Moore, George W. 182
Moore, Hugh Losson Carrick 186
Moore, James 142
Moore, James M. 142
Moore, John T. 186
Moore, Madison 186
Moore, Ransom P. 186
Moore, Reverand William Patrick 105

Moore, Samuel A., II 195
Moore, William 3, 37
Moore, William H. 3
Moores, W. T. 182
Morford, Henry C. 267
Morgan, Algernon Sidney 142, 301
Morgan, George H. 38
Morgan, Isaac Clinton 97
Morgan, Sydney Algernon 322
Morgan, William C. 38
Morris, William R. 152
Morrow, Alexander 6
Morrow, Isham E. 3
Morrow, Martin A. 267
Morrow, Thomas S. 3
Morton, William J. 3
Moses, Anderson 279
Moses, Samuel 279
Moss, Amos Hugh 225
Murray, Thomas B. 267
Myatt, John C. 14
Myatt, Eldridge 16

N

Nash, Newton H. 60
Neal, B. J. 78
Neal, John 69
Neal, W. R. 69
Neese, H. H. 38
Nicholas, Henry M. 66
Nickles, James M. 56
Nicks, John H. 301, 323
Norris, Avery 201
Norris, David M. 60
Norris, Robert C. 203
Norris, William Alfred 229
Norris, William Henderson 203

O

Oakes, George W. 3
Oakes, Lewis S. 3-4
Odell, James L. 168
Officer, Alexander 227
Officer, David S. 228
Officer, John H. 52
Officer, William P. 228
Ogden, George W. 162
Ogden, Henry L. 187
Oliver, John F. 236

Osborn, Henry 146
Owen, Milton M. 74

P

Page, Dr. Titus 105
Palk, Adam Littleton 44
Parker, Reverand Arthur L. 110
Parker, Rev. C. A. 175
Parker, Joseph A. 235
Parker, William B. 110
Parkins, Levi J. 38
Parkinson, Odicia Denton 79
Parkison, Richard F. 38
Parks, John 222
Parrott, James Foster 255
Parson, W. F. 18
Passons, Andrew Jackson 111
Passons, Edward Thockmorton 111
Passons, James 111
Passons, Tilford A. 111
Passons, William D. 213
Passons, William J. T. 213
Patton, John A. 3
Patton, Robert 3
Payne, William R. 95
Peek, James 200
Peek, Martin 82
Peek, Robert 66
Perkins, Thomas Fearn, Jr. 323
Petrified Confederate Soldier 19
Pettit, Robert H. 224
Pettit, Thomas J. 224
Phifer, Forrester 136
Phifer, J. W. 137
Phifer, James M. 137
Phifer, Joseph 30
Phifer, William H. 30
Phillips, T. W. 88
Phrasier, John A. 54
Pieland, R. H. 39
Pippin, A. C. 85
Pippin, Andrew 59
Pippin, Richard F. 44
Pippin, Simeon 59
Pistole, James H. 27
Pistole, Thomas 224
Plumlee, Finis E. 120
Polk, James Hilliard 324
Pollard, Jr. Edward Varner 230
Pollard, James 7
Poore, Samuel Claiborn 213

Pope, Thomas 208
Poteet, Samuel 283
Potter, Perry Green 270
Powell, Clark, Sr. 289
Powell, John W. 285
Powell, William C. 285
Prater, Carrington 198
Price, Elijah W. 137
Price, George W. 137
Price, Shade 233
Proffitt, George C. 26

Q

Qualls, Francis R. 31
Quarles, John S. 39
Quarles, Joseph L. 173
Quarles, Stephen D. 62
Quarles, William Braxton 62
Quillen, Elijah 180

R

Ragland, William H. 39
Ramsey, William Jason 155
Randolph, Elijah 238
Randolph, Jesse V. 82
Rascoe, John R. 196
Rash, William A. 39
Ray, George W. 71
Ray, William L. 83
Reagan, Alvin Alexander 40
Reagan, Isaac D. 40
Reagor, Samuel 116
Rector, Isaac E. 32
Ragan, D. R. 5
Rains, James M. 3, 16
Rains, James Mat 16
Ray, Mark 231
Ray, William 83
Rayburn, John M. 44
Reace, John A. 24
Rector, Jackson Burnett 156
Rector, William J. 29
Rector, William J., Jr. 29
Reed, Andrew J. 3
Renfro, George 3
Renfro, John A. 14
Revis, James T. 3
Rhea, John Simpson 209
Rice, William 231
Rices, William J. 3

Richards, D. R. 143
Richardson, R. 174
Richardson, William Crockett 182
Riddle, Joseph J. 84
Ritchey, J. B., Dr. 267
Rives, Thomas M. 182
Robbins, A. Jordan 220
Roberson, Charles 69
Roberson, Pleasant Prior 63
Roberts, F. M. 96
Roberts, Jesse 231
Roberts, Nathan A. 45
Roberts, William Franklin 231
Robertson, R. 165
Robinson, John H. 147
Robinson, John Jacob 159
Robinson, Preston 70
Robirds, John Wesley 96
Rodgers, Benjamin F. 64
Rogers, George Washington 232
Rogers, James M. 232
Rogers, James W. 177
Romines, Isaac 71
Rowan, Eldridge Stanwic 267
Rush, William B. 3, 12
Russell, John D. 200
Russell, Thomas 106
Russell, Waman Mansfield 200
Russell, William Monroe 200
Rutledge, James M. 96

S

Sanderson, James M. 168
Savage, John Houston 268
Savage, Lucien Napoleon 268
Savage, Starling John 118
Saylors, Abram 233
Saylors, Burtis W. 233
Scarbrough, Alexander R. 238
Scarbrough, James 33
Scarlett, Thomas N. 45
Scoggins, William M. 169
Scott, Elijah 160
Scott, James 209
Scott, Jonathan 209
Scott, Samuel 3, 234
Sehon, John F. 84
Seitz, Logan 119
Selby, James 147
Shaw, Joseph 40
Sherrel, John J. 46

Sherrell, Adam 14
Sherrill, Andrew (Andy) 13
Sherrill, Samuel S. 3
Sherrill, Thomas 3
Shipp, Oliver H. 255
Shockley, Hickman 117
Shockley, Louis D. 112
Shockley, Peter 280
Shockley, Phillip 112
Shockley, William Burrell 92
Shores, William Mackie 234
Shugart, Thomas Coats 176
Simmes, Eli Parker 221
Simmons, Andrew Jackson 169
Simmons, Benjamin Lewis 99
Simons, George Washington 106
Simpson, William Martin 143
Simrell, Eli Daniel 192
Simril, Francis Vincent 235
Sims, Henry W. 174
Sims, Dr. James Glenn 228
Sims, Lawson C. 221
Sims, William E. 228
Sims, William Glenn 174
Sirmans, Benjamin 286
Sirmons, Harris 286
Sirmons, John J. 286
Slatten, Berry 221
Slatten, Martin Van Buren 183
Slatten, Samuel D. 180
Slatton, William Edward 114
Slaughter, Samuel G. 40
Slaughter, William M. 256
Sliger, Adam, Sr. 180
Sliger, Christopher III 180
Sliger, Elias 72
Sliger, John W. 72
Sliger, Samuel 24
Sliger, Thomas L. 72
Smallman, M. D. 268
Smith, Hugh B. 262
Smith, William Gooch 174
Sliger, William L. 62
Smith, Abner C. 52
Smith, Alexander 4
Smith, Benjamin David 170
Smith, Daniel T. 236
Smith, Henry P. 143
Smith, Hugh B. 261
Smith, James Madison 286
Smith, Jesse 287
Smith, John Dillard 283
Smith, Matthew S. 75
Smith, Richard G. 221

Smith, Robert 223
Smith, Thomas G. 40
Smith, Walton W. 88
Smith, William F. 3
Smith, George W. 3, 15
Smotherman, James H. 60
Snodgrass, David 228, 236
Snodgrass, David Red 236
Snodgrass, Joseph 229
Snodgrass, LaFayette Duff 229
Southard, Dempsey Martin 236
Southard, James Milus 237
Sparkman, George W. 120
Sparkman, James 115
Sparkman, John B. 120
Sparkman, John R. 120
Sparkman, Solomon Clay 115
Sparkman, Temple 230
Sparkman, Thomas Bryant 169
Sparkman, W. B. 102
Sparkman, William Reed 245
Sparks, Nicholas 18
Sparks, Solomon 70
Speakman, William 41
Spurlock, George Jackson 209
Staley, Elmore Douglass 41
Stamps, Edmond 79
Stamps, James J. 41
Stanton, Sidney Smith 88
Steakley, Wiley Jr. 169
Steakley, William L. 115
Steelmon, John M. 12
Stephens, George W. 287
Stephens, Monroe 3
Stephens, John 3
Steuart, Stephen W. 221
Stewart, Dempsy 149
Stewart, James "Jim" Daniel 149
Stewart, James M. 229, 237
Stewart, Samuel Levi 150
Stewart, Thomas W. 137
Stipes, Alf C. 98
Stipes, George W. 120
Stone, David 287
Stone, James 176
Stone, John Raines 288
Stroud, Rezi Jarvis 143
Stubblefield, Hanibal L. 269
Sullivan, James H. 242
Suttles, Jesse 52
Swack, Andrew Jackson 145
Swallows, I. J. 85
Swift, Harvey L. 61
Swift, James 244

Swift, Rufus A. 238
Swift, Simon F. 238
Swindell, John Rasco 143
Swindle, Cason 196
Swindle, Christerfer Columbus 196
Swindle, George Conrad 239
Swindle, Jeremiah M. 196

T

Tabor, John 17
Tabor, Wheeler Reece 30
Tallent, Isel 81
Tallent, Samuel 153
Tate, J. D. 269
Taylor, Alexander 3
Taylor, Ervin C. 3
Taylor, Henry C. 41
Taylor, Hosea 144
Taylor, James W. 73
Taylor, John 3
Taylor, Martin Kittsworth 170
Taylor, Richardson 3
Taylor, Thomas Edward 239
Tabor, John 17
Templeton, Greenville H. 196
Templeton, Pleasant Carter 239
Templeton, Thomas Jefferson 240
Terry, Elijah W. 76
Terry, Hugh R. 79
Terry, John 76, 242
Terry, John Calhoun 242
Terry, Roland 76
Terry, W. C. 77
Terry, W. J. 77
Terry, William A. 76
Thompson, Esquire L. 74
Thompson, James A. "Jack" 3
Thompson, James F. 83
Thompson, James Robertson 197
Thompson, John 3
Thompson, Newton J. 77
Thompson, Thomas C. 77
Thompson, William H. 3, 61
Tinch, A. G. 71
Tollett, William W. 3
Tollison, James Robert 240
Tollison, Solomon 241
Tosh, Daniel Alexander 106
Townsend, Albert J. 229
Townsend, James Barnett 280
Treadway, Henry H. 150

Treadway, John 150
Turner, James K. "Jack" 3
Turner, D. C. 18
Turner, David C. 3
Turner, William 155
Tyree, Robert J. 86

U

Unknowns 18, 19, 154, 246

V

Vandever, George A. 3
Vandever, James C. 3, 150
Vandever, Eli N. 3
Vanhooser, John 271

W

Walker, Abraham Washington 70
Walker, James M. 145
Walker, James S. 3
Walker, Jefferson J. 112
Walker, John A. 153
Walker, John W. 150
Walker, Joseph 99, 122
Walker, Joseph Hardy 122
Walker, John M. B. 3
Walker, William H. 27
Wallace, John Calvin 171

Wallace, Simon Doyle 18, 214
Wallace, William C. 17
Walling, Jesse 269
Walling, Joseph D. 269
Ward, Henry B. 170
Wasson, Pleasant M. 80
Watson Benjamin 80
Watson, Elijah B. 192
Watson, Henry Thomas 46
Watson, J. R. 41
Watson, John Saul 81
Watts, John W. 81
Weaver, Benjamin 147
Weaver, Jephthath 152
Weaver, William 145, 147
Weaver, William J. 145
Webb, Isaac N. 31
Webb, James J. 197
Webb, James M. 271
Webb, John M. 197
Webb, Waymon P. 192
Webster, Daniel Stewart 170
Webster, John C. 154
Welch, Alexander 70
Welch, James Thomas 70
Welch, Jasper 242
Welch, John Marion 238
West, Alexander Washington 80
West, Granville F. 45
Westberry, Ferman 288
Westberry, Rabon 288
Wheeler, Burdin 123
Wheeler, Thomas 243
Whitaker, John H. 71
Whitaker, Ligard J. 85

White, Simon D. 214
Whiteaker, James M. 71
Whitehead, James Madison 85
Whitley, John H. 93
Whitson, Jeremiah M. 67
Witt, John W. 245
Whittaker, J. J. 85
Whittenburg, Issac 123
Wiggins, Tillman 59
Wilhite, Elijah McCamel 244
Wilhite, Solomon Robinson 244
Wilhite, James 244
Willhite, Haliard 146
Willhite, Steven 152
Willey, Addison Gardiner 270
Williams, Henry 148
Williams, James T. 152
Williams, Jesse 86
Williams, John H. 42
Williams, Madison 225
Williams, W. M. 209
Williams, William W. 52
Williamson, Amos K. 24
Wilson, Hartwell G. 158
Wilson, Jasper W. 197
Wilson, William 245
Wiser, James M. 64
Webb, James C. 3
Welch, James A. 77
West, Wilson 83
Womack, James J. 270
Womack, James Knowles P. 170
Wood, Errage "Er" 115
Woody, Alexander 3
Woody, Preston Alexander 18

Woody, Harrison 3, 18
Woods, James Burrough 192
Worley, James 246
Worthington, James 112
Worthington, Samuel 113
Worthingon, William 113
Wright, Seth F. 197
Wright, Wesley Deskin 197

Y

Yates, Larkin 124
Yates, Samuel 144
York, Harmon 113
York, John P. 256
York, Uriah 96
Young, Charles Coker 174
Young, D. H. 144
Young, Daniel W. 210
Young, James S. 144